RAND McNALLY

Historical Atlas of the World

Table of Contents

Introduction

Information about the past is compiled, stored, and made accessible in a variety of ways. One of these ways is historical maps. Historical maps provide a chronology of important events and show the impact these events had on the places where they occurred. Historical maps support and extend information from primary historical resources such as letters, treaties, and census data. Historical maps are summaries of past events presented in graphic form.

The maps in the Rand McNally *Historical Atlas of the World* portray the rich panoply of the world's history from preliterate times to the present. They show how cultures and civilizations were linked and how they interacted. These maps make it clear that history is not static. Rather, it is about change and movement across time. The maps in this atlas show change by presenting the dynamics of expansion, cooperation, and conflict.

Benefits of Using the Rand McNally *Historical Atlas of the World*

Events gain fuller meaning.
Knowing where events took place gives them fuller meaning and often explains causes and effects. For example, the map showing Russia's expansion in Europe clearly illustrates a major territorial goal of the czars was to access warm water ports that would connect their realm to the world's seas and oceans.

Connections among events are clarified.
Through the visual power of historical maps, the links between and among events become clearer. The maps showing diffusion of languages and religions are good illustrations of this, as is the map of Native Americans that details the rise and fall of indigenous peoples of North and South America.

Similarities and differences become apparent.
The maps in this historical atlas provide the opportunity to compare and contrast places over time. The maps of Africa in the 10th and 15th centuries present time capsules of human migrations. They also act as an inventory of the continent's resources in two specific time frames.

The influence of sense of place is conveyed.
Maps in this atlas can convey a people's sense of place at a particular time in history. The map of Europe's Age of Discovery is a good illustration. The cartographer has deliberately centered the continent so the map's projection reflects the extent and ambition of Europe's exploration at the end of the Renaissance.

Trends emerge.
Another benefit of using this historical atlas is that trends emerge. Maps of the westward expansion of the United States show how the nation was settled, what technologies were used, who was displaced, and in what sequence. In another example, the map of the Mogul Empire in India under Aurangzeb reveals how a dynasty can become powerfully established in little more than a century.

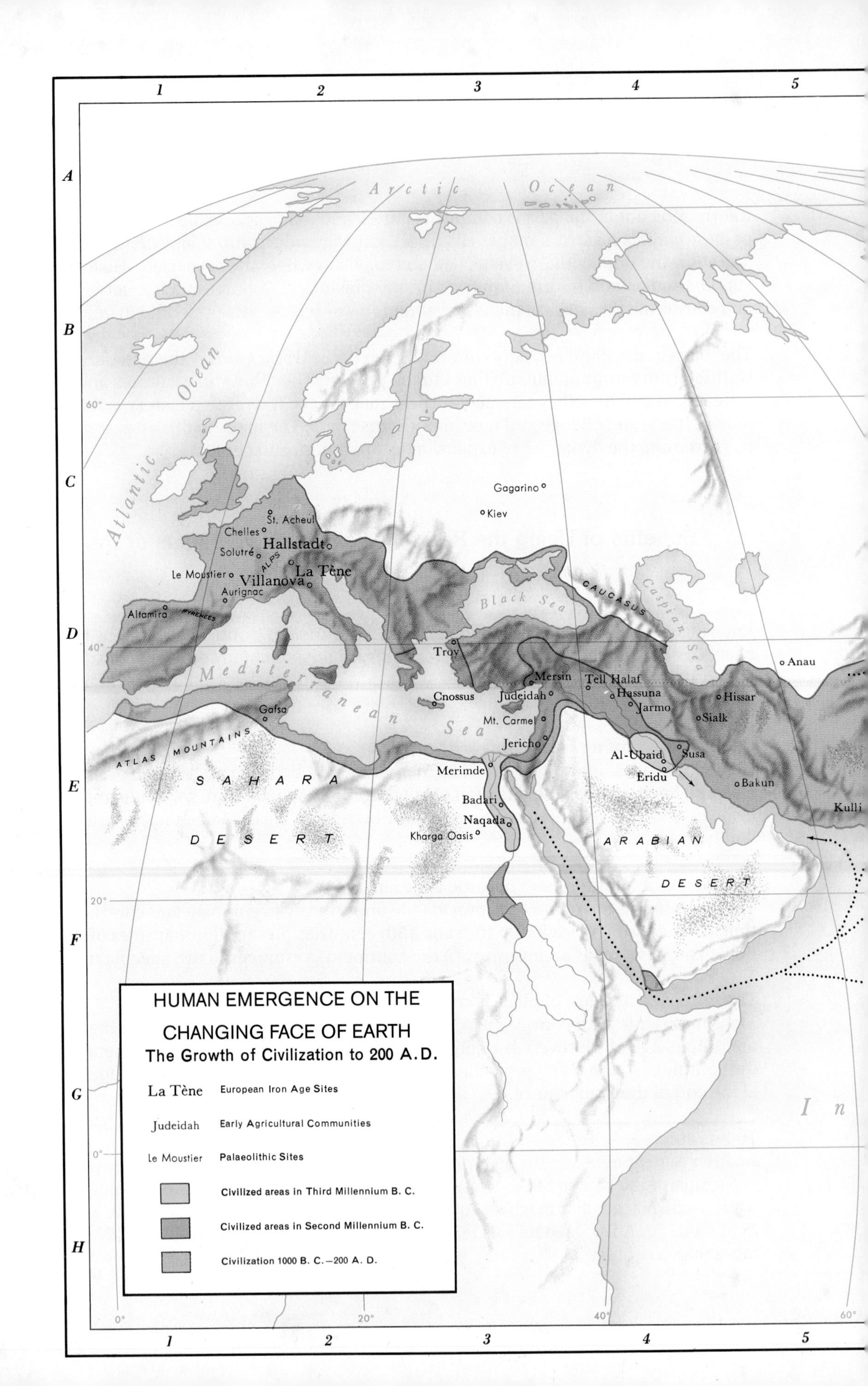
HUMAN EMERGENCE ON THE
CHANGING FACE OF EARTH
The Growth of Civilization to 200 A.D.
La Tène European Iron Age Sites
Judeidah Early Agricultural Communities
Le Moustier Palaeolithic Sites
Civilized areas in Third Millennium B. C.
Civilized areas in Second Millennium B. C.
Civilization 1000 B. C.—200 A. D.
Arctic Ocean
Atlantic Ocean
Black Sea
Caspian Sea
Mediterranean Sea
CAUCASUS
ALPS
PYRENEES
ATLAS MOUNTAINS
SAHARA DESERT
ARABIAN DESERT
Gagarino
Kiev
St. Acheul
Chelles
Hallstadt
Solutré
La Tène
Le Moustier
Villanova
Aurignac
Altamira
Troy
Mersin
Tell Halaf
Hassuna
Jarmo
Judeidah
Cnossus
Gafsa
Mt. Carmel
Jericho
Merimde
Al-Ubaid
Susa
Eridu
Badari
Naqada
Kharga Oasis
Anau
Hissar
Sialk
Bakun
Kulli
In
60°
40°
20°
0°
1
2
3
4
5
A
B
C
D
E
F
G
H

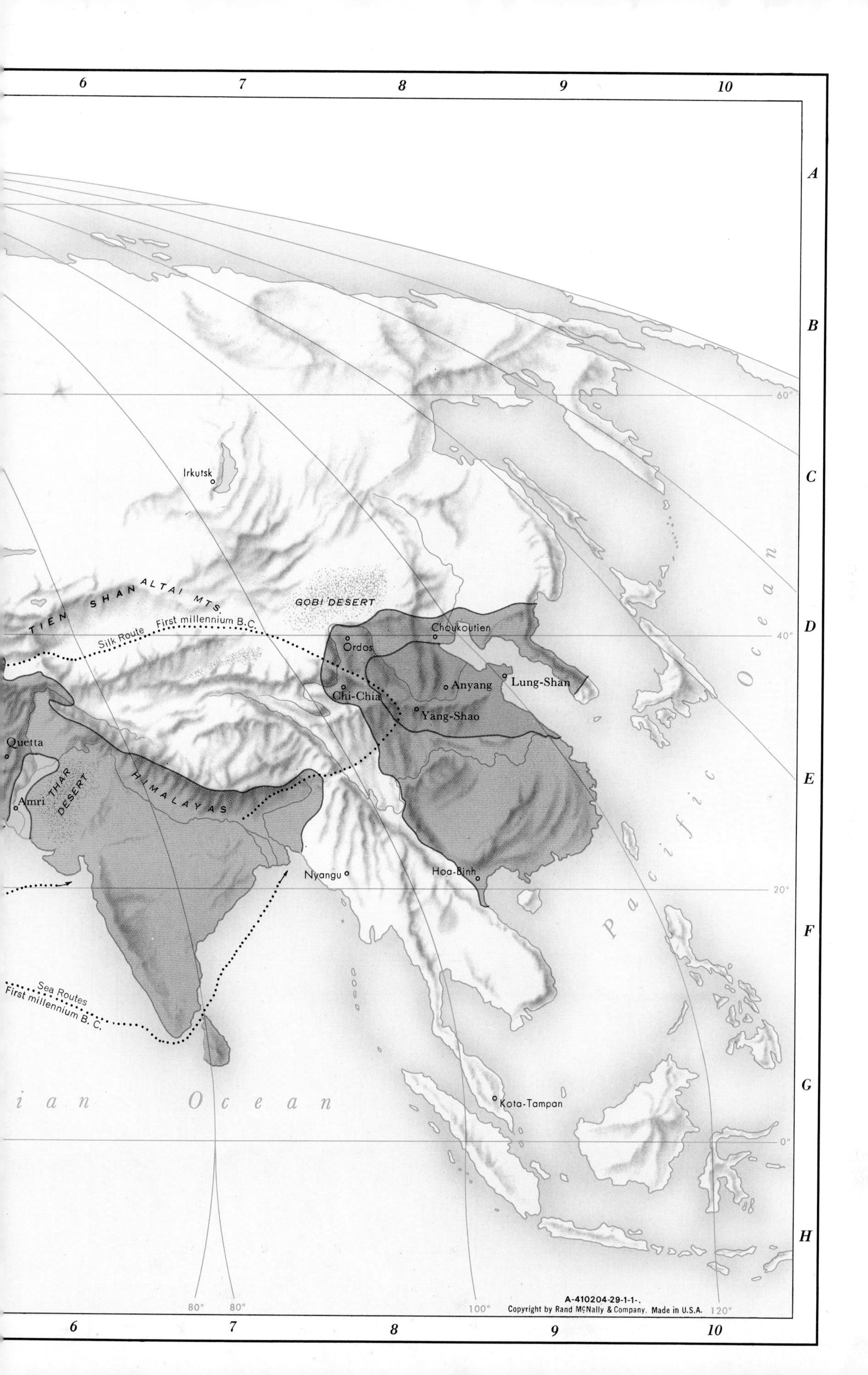
Irkutsk
TIEN SHAN
ALTAI MTS.
GOBI DESERT
Silk Route First millennium B.C.
Choukoutien
Ordos
Anyang
Lung-Shan
Chi-Chia
Yang-Shao
Quetta
Amri
THAR DESERT
HIMALAYAS
Nyangu
Hoa-Binh
Sea Routes
First millennium B.C.
Kota-Tampan
Pacific Ocean
ian Ocean
60°
40°
20°
0°
80°
100°
120°
A-410204-29-1-1-.
Copyright by Rand McNally & Company. Made in U.S.A.

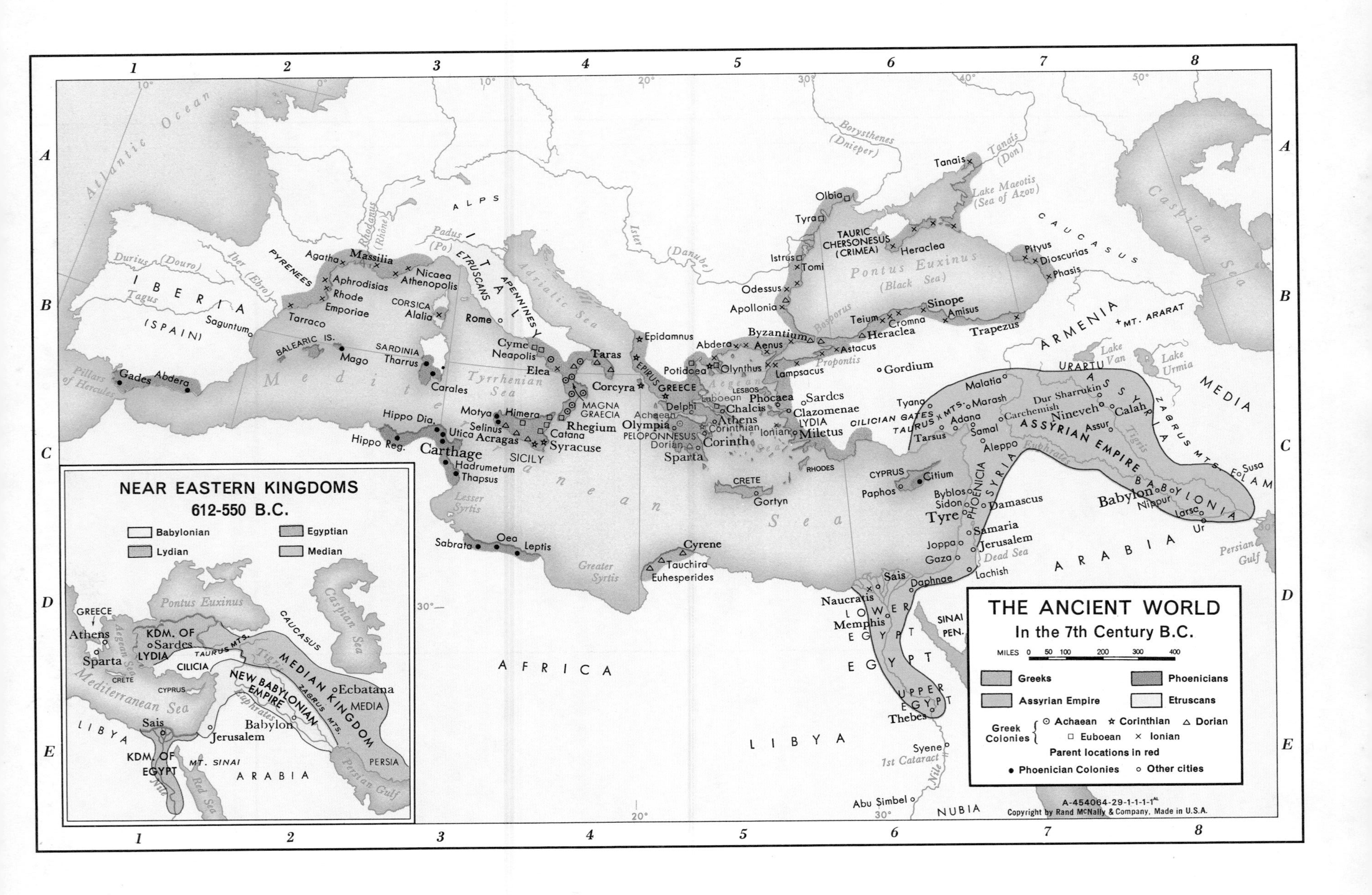

THE ANCIENT WORLD
In the 7th Century B.C.
MILES 0 50 100 200 300 400
Greeks
Phoenicians
Assyrian Empire
Etruscans
Greek Colonies
Achaean
Corinthian
Dorian
Euboean
Ionian
Parent locations in red
Phoenician Colonies
Other cities
A-454064-29-1-1-1
Copyright by Rand McNally & Company, Made in U.S.A.
NEAR EASTERN KINGDOMS
612-550 B.C.
Babylonian
Egyptian
Lydian
Median
GREECE
Athens
Sparta
KDM. OF LYDIA
Sardes
CILICIA
TAURUS MTS.
CAUCASUS
MEDIAN KINGDOM
Ecbatana
MEDIA
NEW BABYLONIAN EMPIRE
ZAGRUS MTS.
Babylon
Jerusalem
PERSIA
CYPRUS
CRETE
Mediterranean Sea
Caspian Sea
Pontus Euxinus
Persian Gulf
Red Sea
LIBYA
Sais
KDM. OF EGYPT
MT. SINAI
ARABIA
Atlantic Ocean
IBERIA
(SPAIN)
Gades
Abdera
Saguntum
Tarraco
PYRENEES
Agatha
Massilia
Nicaea
Athenopolis
Aphrodisias
Rhode
Emporiae
CORSICA
Alalia
SARDINIA
Tharrus
Carales
BALEARIC IS.
Mago
ALPS
ETRUSCANS
ITALY
APENNINES
Rome
Cyme
Neapolis
Elea
Taras
Tyrrhenian Sea
Adriatic Sea
MAGNA GRAECIA
Rhegium
Catana
Syracuse
SICILY
Motya
Himera
Selinus
Acragas
Carthage
Utica
Hippo Dia.
Hippo Reg.
Hadrumetum
Thapsus
Lesser Syrtis
Sabrata
Oea
Leptis
Greater Syrtis
Mediterranean Sea
AFRICA
LIBYA
Cyrene
Tauchira
Euhesperides
Epidamnus
EPIRUS
Corcyra
GREECE
Delphi
Olympia
PELOPONNESUS
Sparta
Corinth
Athens
Chalcis
Euboean
Potidaea
Olynthus
Abdera
Aenus
Byzantium
Lampsacus
Astacus
Propontis
LESBOS
Phocaea
Sardes
Clazomenae
LYDIA
Miletus
Ionian
RHODES
CRETE
Gortyn
Odessus
Apollonia
Istrus
Tomi
Tyra
Olbia
TAURIC CHERSONESUS (CRIMEA)
Heraclea
Pontus Euxinus (Black Sea)
Sinope
Amisus
Cromna
Teium
Trapezus
Tanais
Lake Maeotis (Sea of Azov)
Borysthenes (Dnieper)
Ister (Danube)
Gordium
CAUCASUS
Pityus
Dioscurias
Phasis
ARMENIA
MT. ARARAT
URARTU
Lake Van
Lake Urmia
MEDIA
Caspian Sea
CILICIAN GATES
TAURUS MTS.
Tyana
Tarsus
Adana
Marash
Malatia
Samal
Carchemish
Aleppo
Dur Sharrukin
Nineveh
Calah
Assur
ASSYRIAN EMPIRE
ZAGRUS MTS.
ELAM
Susa
BABYLONIA
Babylon
Nippur
Larsa
Ur
ARABIA
Persian Gulf
CYPRUS
Citium
Paphos
PHOENICIA
Byblos
Sidon
Tyre
SYRIA
Damascus
Samaria
Jerusalem
Dead Sea
Joppa
Gaza
Lachish
Daphnae
Sais
Naucratis
LOWER EGYPT
Memphis
SINAI PEN.
UPPER EGYPT
Thebes
Syene
1st Cataract
Abu Simbel
NUBIA

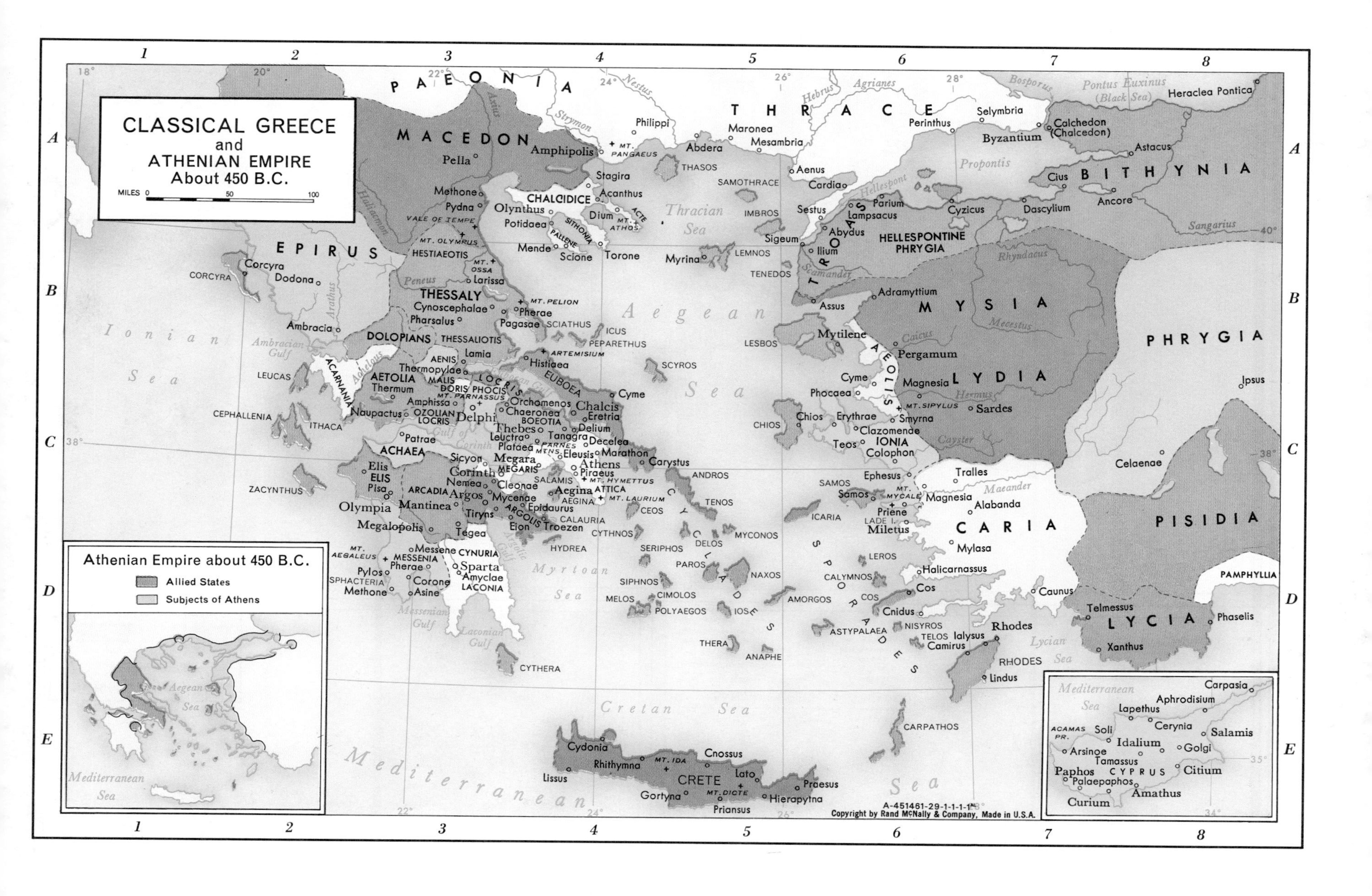

CLASSICAL GREECE
and
ATHENIAN EMPIRE
About 450 B.C.
MILES 0 50 100
Athenian Empire about 450 B.C.
Allied States
Subjects of Athens
PAEONIA
MACEDON
THRACE
BITHYNIA
EPIRUS
THESSALY
CHALCIDICE
HELLESPONTINE PHRYGIA
TROAS
MYSIA
PHRYGIA
LYDIA
AEOLIS
IONIA
CARIA
PISIDIA
LYCIA
PAMPHYLIA
DOLOPIANS
THESSALIOTIS
HESTIAEOTIS
AETOLIA
ACARNANIA
AENIS
MALIS
DORIS
PHOCIS
LOCRIS
OZOLIAN LOCRIS
BOEOTIA
EUBOEA
ATTICA
MEGARIS
ACHAEA
ELIS
ARCADIA
ARGOLIS
MESSENIA
CYNURIA
LACONIA
CYCLADES
SPORADES
CRETE
CYPRUS
Pella
Methone
Pydna
Amphipolis
Philippi
Abdera
Maronea
Mesambria
Aenus
Cardia
Perinthus
Selymbria
Byzantium
Calchedon (Chalcedon)
Astacus
Heraclea Pontica
Cius
Dascylium
Ancore
Cyzicus
Parium
Lampsacus
Abydus
Sestus
Sigeum
Ilium
Assus
Adramyttium
Pergamum
Mytilene
Cyme
Phocaea
Magnesia
Sardes
Smyrna
Clazomenae
Erythrae
Chios
Teos
Colophon
Ephesus
Samos
Priene
Miletus
Magnesia
Tralles
Alabanda
Mylasa
Halicarnassus
Cnidus
Caunus
Ialysus
Camirus
Rhodes
Lindus
Telmessus
Xanthus
Phaselis
Celaenae
Ipsus
Stagira
Acanthus
Olynthus
Potidaea
Mende
Scione
Torone
Dium
Corcyra
Dodona
Ambracia
Larissa
Cynoscephalae
Pherae
Pharsalus
Pagasae
Lamia
Thermopylae
Histiaea
Thermum
Amphissa
Naupactus
Delphi
Orchomenos
Chaeronea
Thebes
Leuctra
Plataea
Tanagra
Chalcis
Eretria
Delium
Decelea
Marathon
Eleusis
Athens
Piraeus
Carystus
Cyme
Patrae
Sicyon
Megara
Corinth
Nemea
Cleonae
Argos
Mycenae
Tiryns
Epidaurus
Aegina
Troezen
Eion
Tegea
Mantinea
Olympia
Elis
Pisa
Megalopolis
Messene
Pherae
Pylos
Methone
Corone
Asine
Sparta
Amyclae
Cydonia
Rhithymna
Lissus
Cnossus
Gortyna
Lato
Priansus
Hierapytna
Praesus
Myrina
Mediterranean Sea
Ionian Sea
Aegean Sea
Thracian Sea
Myrtoan Sea
Cretan Sea
Lycian Sea
Propontis
Hellespont
Bosporus
Pontus Euxinus (Black Sea)
Ambracian Gulf
Gulf of Corinth
Saronic Gulf
Argolic Gulf
Laconian Gulf
Messenian Gulf
Carpasia
Aphrodisium
Lapethus
Cerynia
Soli
Salamis
Idalium
Golgi
Arsinoe
Tamassus
Paphos
Palaepaphos
Citium
Curium
Amathus
A-451461-29-1-1-1
Copyright by Rand McNally & Company, Made in U.S.A.

ANCIENT PERSIA 549 B.C. – 651 A.D.

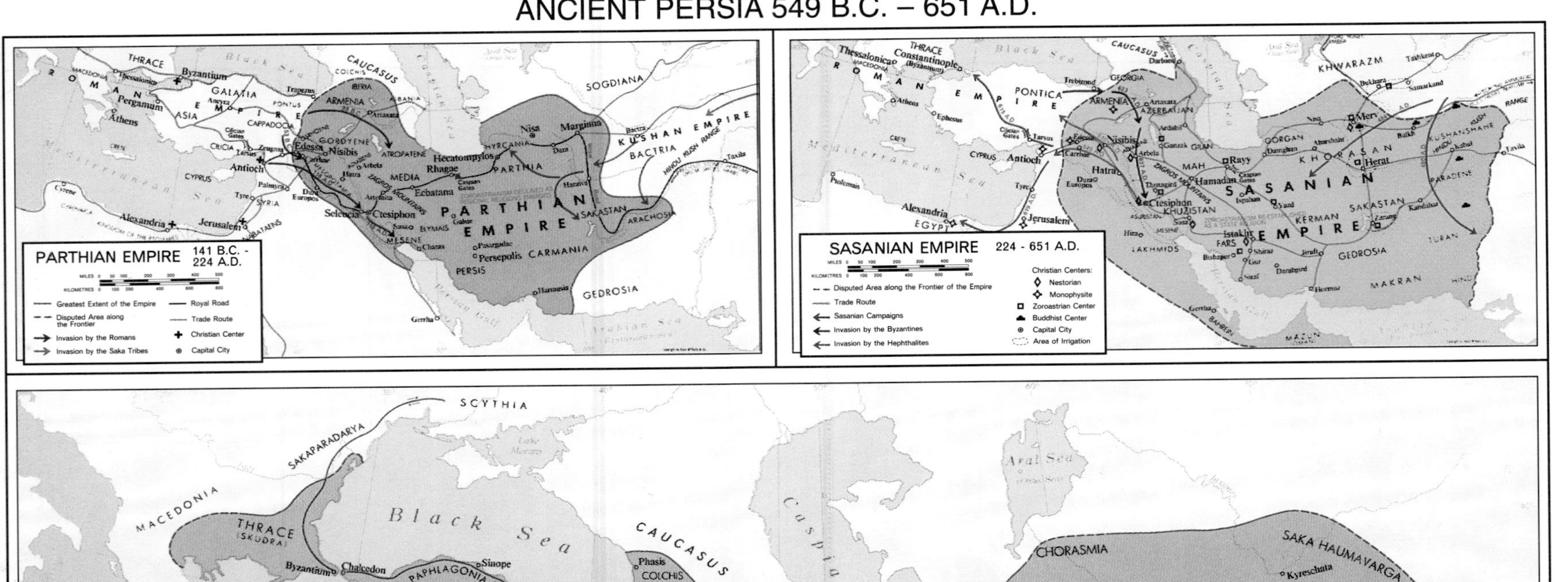

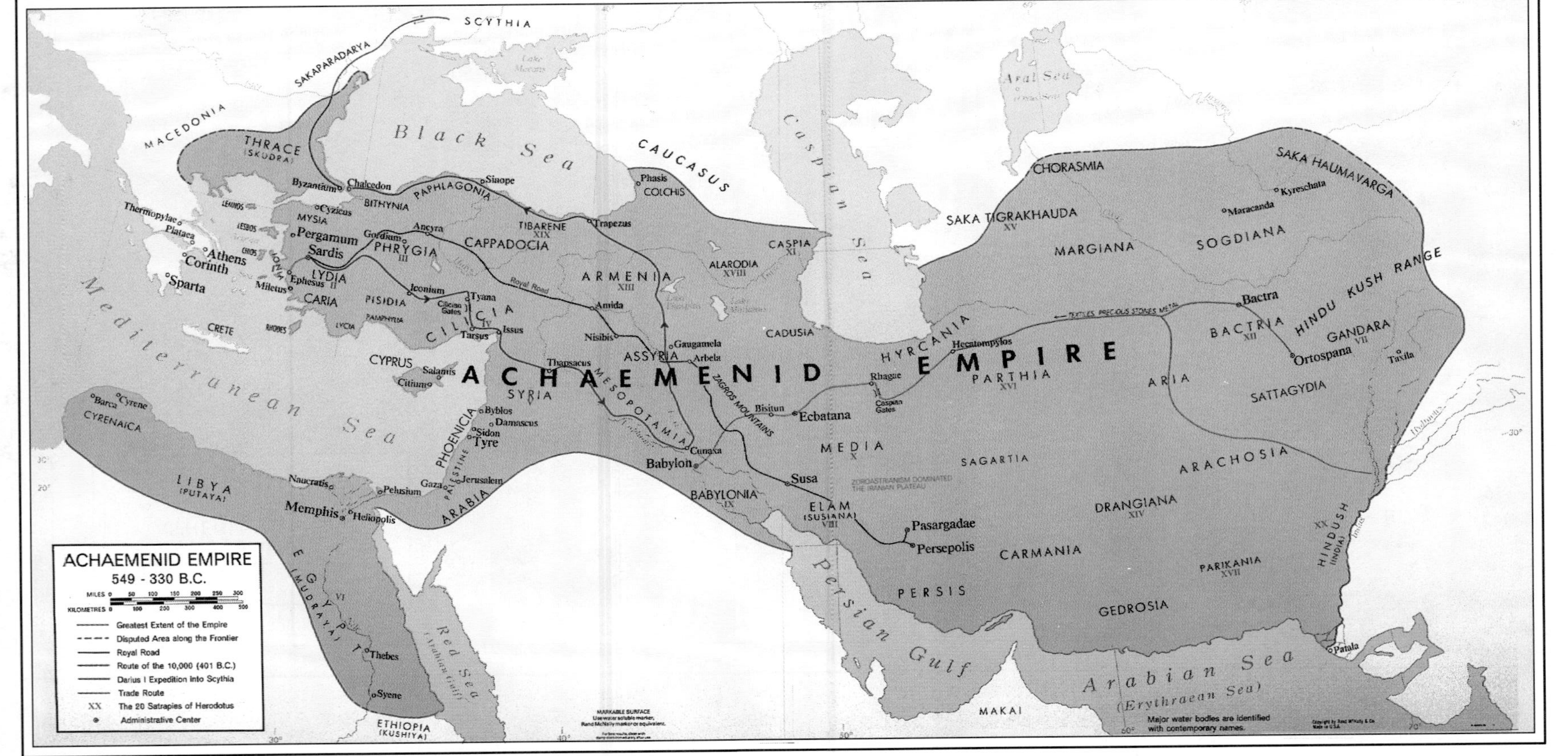

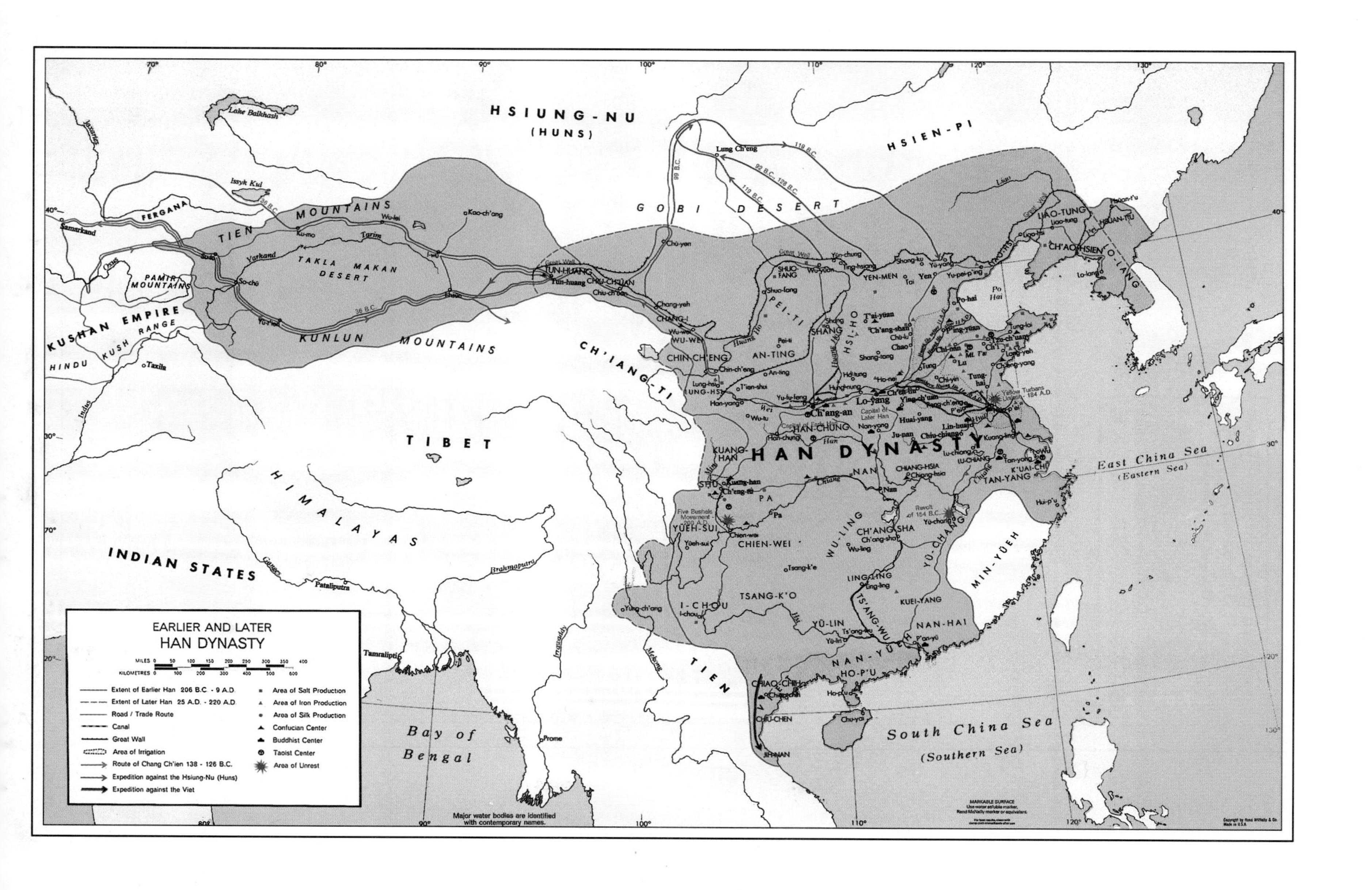
EARLIER AND LATER
HAN DYNASTY
MILES 0 50 100 150 200 250 300 350 400
KILOMETRES 0 100 200 300 400 500 600
Extent of Earlier Han 206 B.C. - 9 A.D.
Extent of Later Han 25 A.D. - 220 A.D.
Road / Trade Route
Canal
Great Wall
Area of Irrigation
Route of Chang Ch'ien 138 - 126 B.C.
Expedition against the Hsiung-Nu (Huns)
Expedition against the Viet
Area of Salt Production
Area of Iron Production
Area of Silk Production
Confucian Center
Buddhist Center
Taoist Center
Area of Unrest
HSIUNG-NU
(HUNS)
HSIEN-PI
GOBI DESERT
TIEN MOUNTAINS
TAKLA MAKAN DESERT
KUNLUN MOUNTAINS
PAMIR MOUNTAINS
KUSHAN EMPIRE
HINDU KUSH RANGE
CH'IANG-TI
TIBET
HIMALAYAS
INDIAN STATES
HAN DYNASTY
MIN-YÜEH
TIEN
East China Sea
(Eastern Sea)
South China Sea
(Southern Sea)
Bay of Bengal
Po Hai
Lake Balkhash
Issyk Kul
Jaxartes
Oxus
Indus
Ganges
Brahmaputra
Irrawaddy
Mekong
Samarkand
Fergana
Kashgar
Yarkand
So-chü
Yü-t'ien
Ku-mo
Wu-lei
Tarim
Kao-ch'ang
Taxila
Pataliputra
Tamralipti
Prome
TUN-HUANG
Tun-huang
CHIU-CH'ÜAN
Chiu-ch'üan
Chang-yeh
CHANG-I
WU-WEI
Chü-yen
Lung Ch'eng
119 B.C.
99 B.C.
92 B.C., 128 B.C.
36 B.C.
CHIN-CH'ENG
Chin-ch'eng
AN-TING
PEI-TI
SHUO FANG
Shuo-fang
Yün-chung
Ting-hsiang
YEN-MEN
Shang-ku
Yü-yang
Yen
Yu-pei-p'ing
LIAO-HSI
LIAO-TUNG
Liao-tung
HSÜAN-TU
CH'AO-HSIEN
LO-LANG
Lo-lang
Po-hai
Great Wall
Liao
T'ai-yüan
Ch'ang-shan
Chao
Shang-tang
Ho-nei
Ho-tung
Hung-nung
HSI-HO
SHANG
Shang
Pei-ti
Huang Ho
Wei
An-ting
T'ien-shui
LUNG-HSI
Lung-hsi
Han-yang
Yu-fu-feng
Ch'ang-an
Lo-yang
Capital of Later Han
Ying-ch'uan
HAN-CHUNG
Han-chung
Nan-yang
Huai-yang
Ju-nan
Chiu-chiang
Lin-huai
Kuang-ling
Tung
Tung-lai
Ch'i
Chi-nan
Lu
Ch'eng-yang
Lang-yeh
Yellow Turbans Uprising 184 A.D.
Tan-yang
K'UAI-CHI
TAN-YANG
LU-CHIANG
Lu-chiang
KUANG-HAN
SHU
Kuang-han
Ch'eng-tu
PA
Pa
Five Bushels Movement 200 A.D.
YÜEH-SUI
Yüeh-sui
CHIEN-WEI
Chien-wei
NAN
Nan
Han
Chiang
CHIANG-HSIA
Chiang-hsia
Revolt of 154 B.C.
Yü-chang
YÜ-CHANG
CH'ANG SHA
Ch'ang-sha
WU-LING
Wu-ling
Tsang-k'e
TSANG-K'O
LING-LING
Ling-ling
KUEI-YANG
TS'ANG-WU
Ts'ang-wu
YÜ-LIN
Yü-lin
NAN-HAI
P'an-yü
NAN-YÜEH
HO-P'U
Ho-p'u
Chu-yai
CHIAO-CHIH
CHIU-CHEN
JIH-NAN
I-CHOU
I-chou
Yung-ch'ang
Hsi
Hui-p'u
Major water bodies are identified with contemporary names.
MARKABLE SURFACE
Copyright by Rand McNally & Co.
Made in U.S.A.

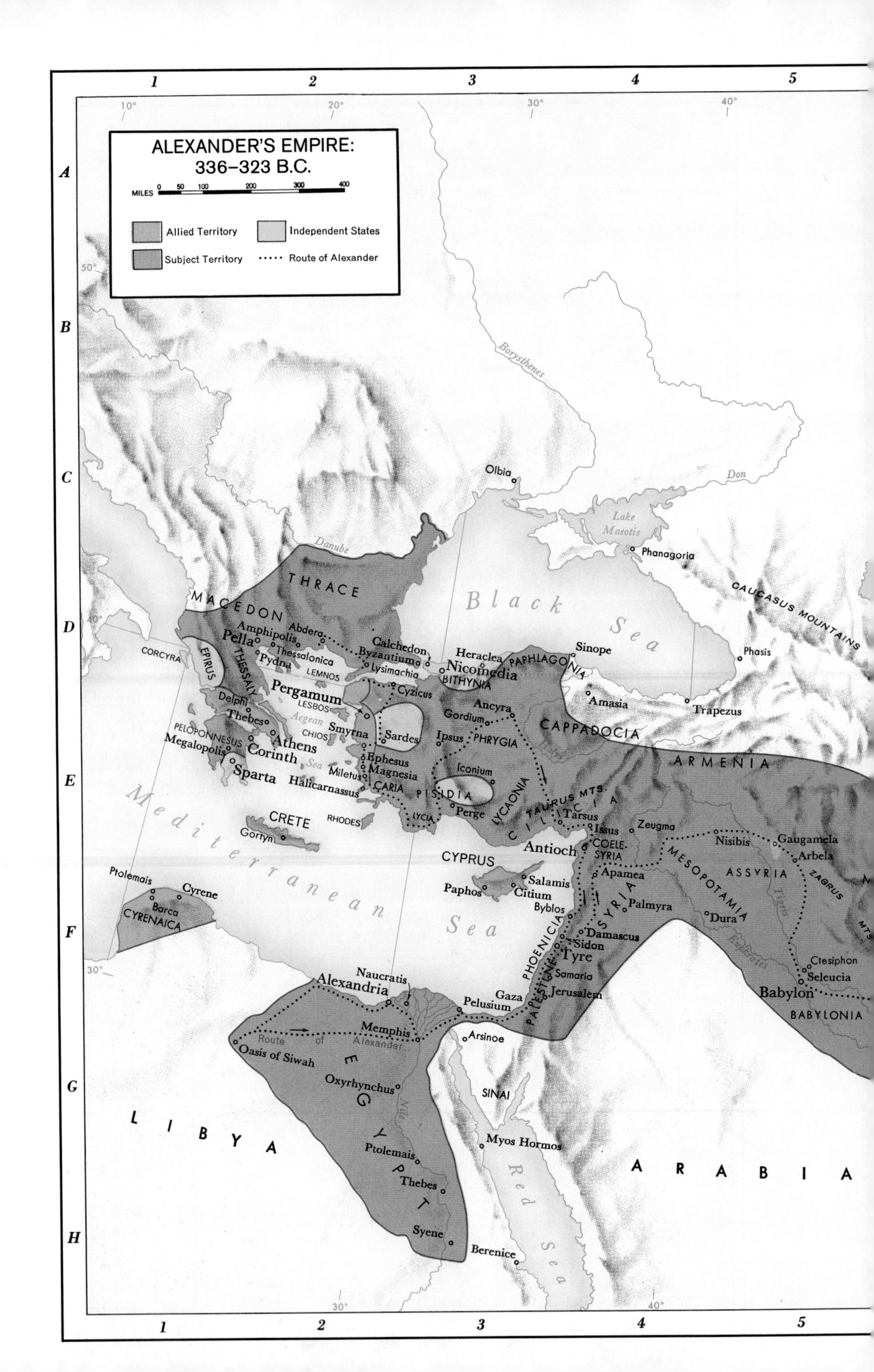
ALEXANDER'S EMPIRE:
336–323 B.C.
MILES 0 50 100 200 300 400
Allied Territory
Independent States
Subject Territory
Route of Alexander
THRACE
MACEDON
Black Sea
Mediterranean Sea
Pella
Amphipolis
Abdera
Thessalonica
Pydna
EPIRUS
THESSALY
CORCYRA
Byzantium
Calchedon
Lysimachia
LEMNOS
Pergamum
LESBOS
Cyzicus
Delphi
Thebes
Aegean Sea
CHIOS
Smyrna
Sardes
Athens
Corinth
PELOPONNESUS
Megalopolis
Sparta
Ephesus
Magnesia
Miletus
Halicarnassus
CARIA
CRETE
Gortyn
RHODES
LYCIA
PISIDIA
Perge
Iconium
LYCAONIA
Ipsus
PHRYGIA
Gordium
Ancyra
Heraclea
Nicomedia
BITHYNIA
PAPHLAGONIA
Sinope
Amasia
CAPPADOCIA
Trapezus
Phasis
CAUCASUS MOUNTAINS
ARMENIA
TAURUS MTS.
CILICIA
Tarsus
Issus
Zeugma
Antioch
COELE-SYRIA
Apamea
SYRIA
Palmyra
Damascus
Sidon
Tyre
PHOENICIA
PALESTINE
Samaria
Jerusalem
Gaza
Pelusium
Byblos
CYPRUS
Salamis
Citium
Paphos
MESOPOTAMIA
ASSYRIA
Nisibis
Gaugamela
Arbela
ZAGROS
Dura
Tigris
Euphrates
Ctesiphon
Seleucia
Babylon
BABYLONIA
Olbia
Borysthenes
Don
Lake Maeotis
Phanagoria
Danube
Ptolemais
Cyrene
Barca
CYRENAICA
Naucratis
Alexandria
Memphis
Route of Alexander
Oasis of Siwah
EGYPT
Oxyrhynchus
Nile
Ptolemais
Thebes
Syene
Arsinoe
SINAI
Myos Hormos
Red Sea
Berenice
LIBYA
ARABIA
10°
20°
30°
40°
50°
1 2 3 4 5
A B C D E F G H

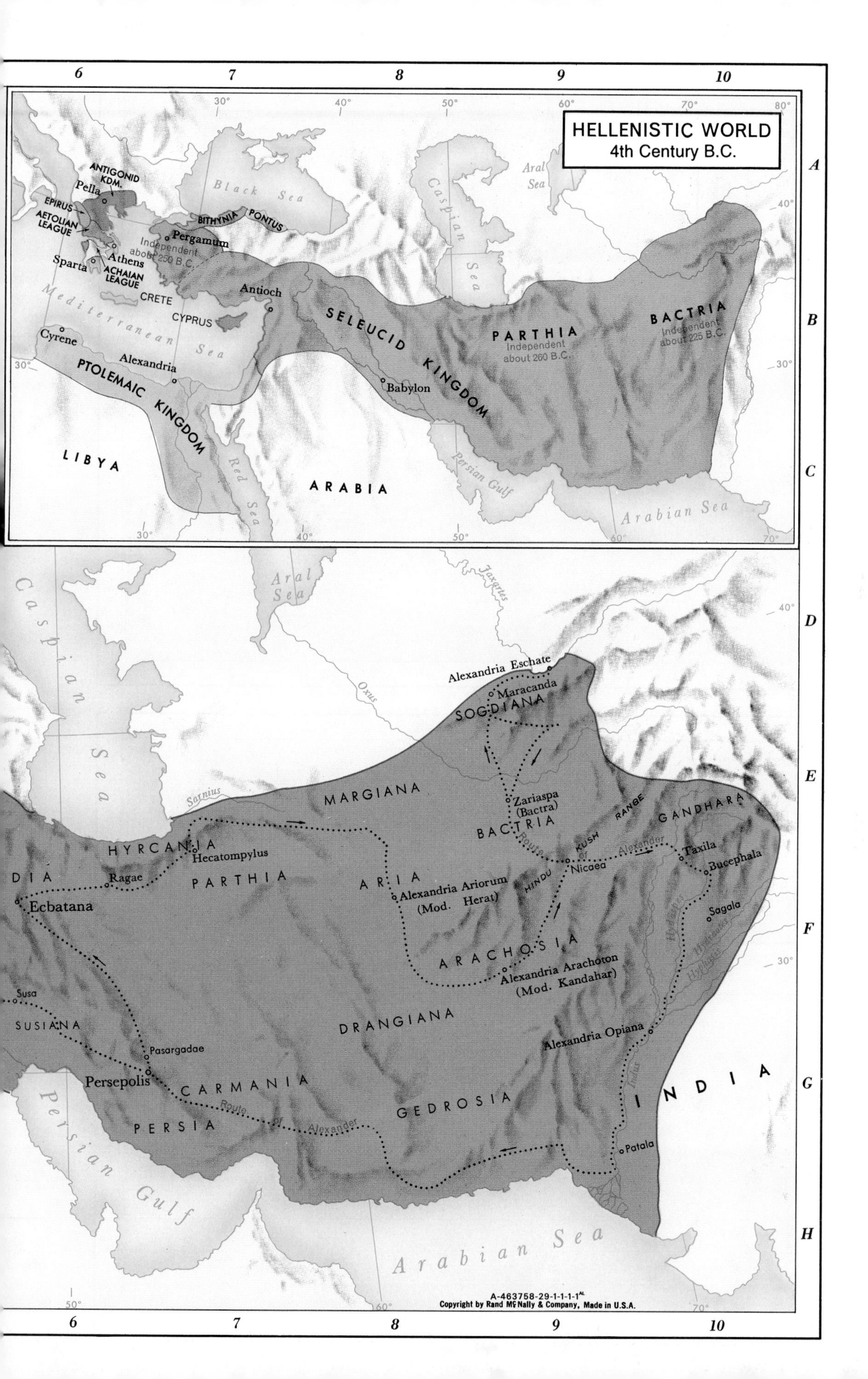

HELLENISTIC WORLD
4th Century B.C.
ANTIGONID KDM.
Pella
EPIRUS
AETOLIAN LEAGUE
Black Sea
BITHYNIA
PONTUS
Pergamum
Independent about 250 B.C.
Athens
Sparta
ACHAIAN LEAGUE
CRETE
Antioch
CYPRUS
Mediterranean Sea
Cyrene
Alexandria
PTOLEMAIC KINGDOM
LIBYA
Red Sea
ARABIA
SELEUCID KINGDOM
Babylon
Caspian Sea
Aral Sea
PARTHIA
Independent about 260 B.C.
BACTRIA
Independent about 225 B.C.
Persian Gulf
Arabian Sea
Jaxartes
Oxus
Alexandria Eschate
Maracanda
SOGDIANA
MARGIANA
Sarnius
Zariaspa (Bactra)
BACTRIA
HINDU KUSH RANGE
GANDHARA
Route of Alexander
Taxila
Nicaea
Bucephala
HYRCANIA
Hecatompylus
Ragae
PARTHIA
ARIA
Alexandria Ariorum (Mod. Herat)
Ecbatana
Sagala
Hydaspes
Hyphasis
ARACHOSIA
Alexandria Arachoton (Mod. Kandahar)
Susa
SUSIANA
DRANGIANA
Alexandria Opiana
Pasargadae
Persepolis
CARMANIA
Indus
INDIA
PERSIA
GEDROSIA
Patala
A-463758-29-1-1-1
Copyright by Rand McNally & Company, Made in U.S.A.

INDIA 250 B.C. AND 400 A.D.

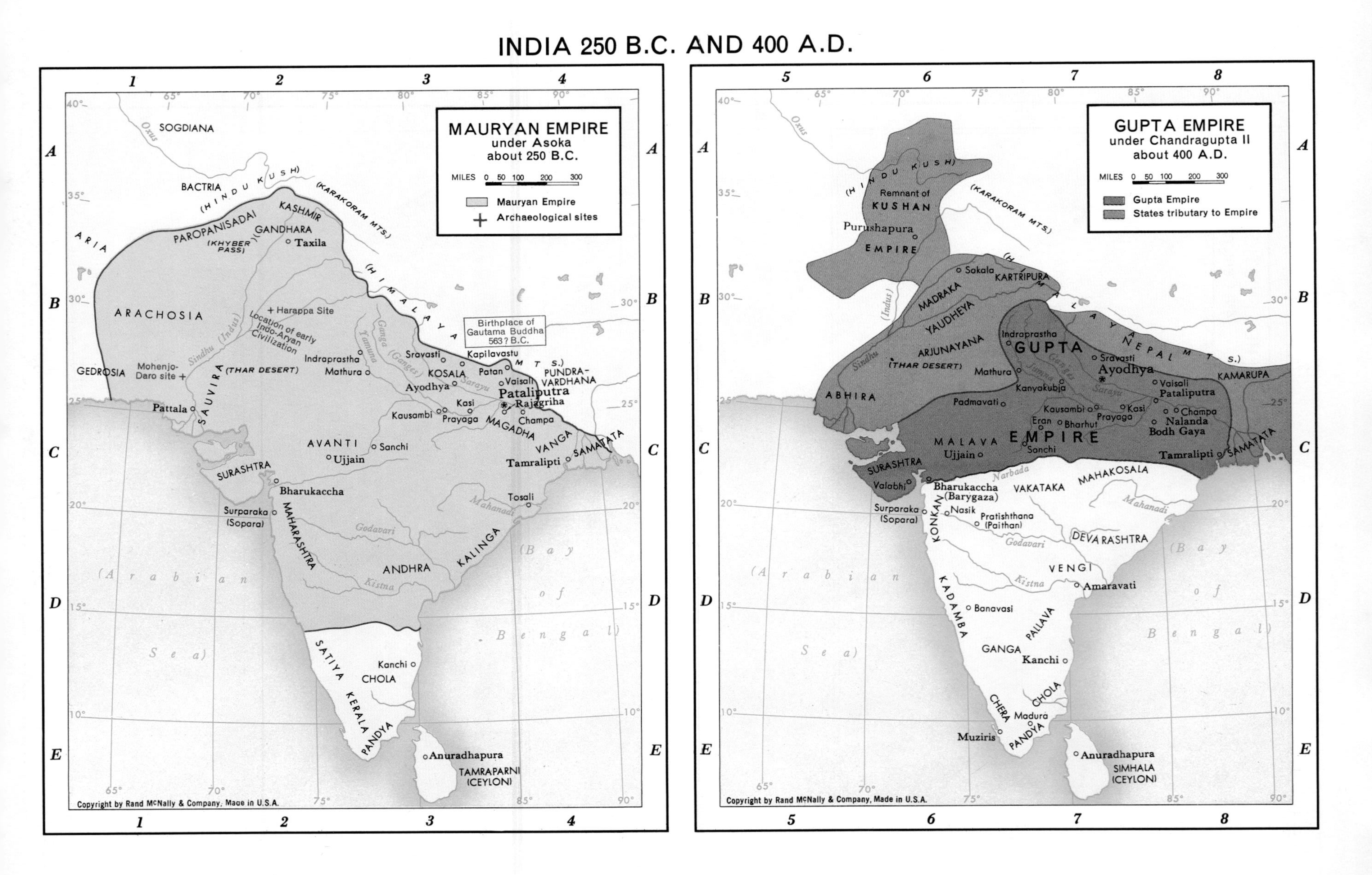

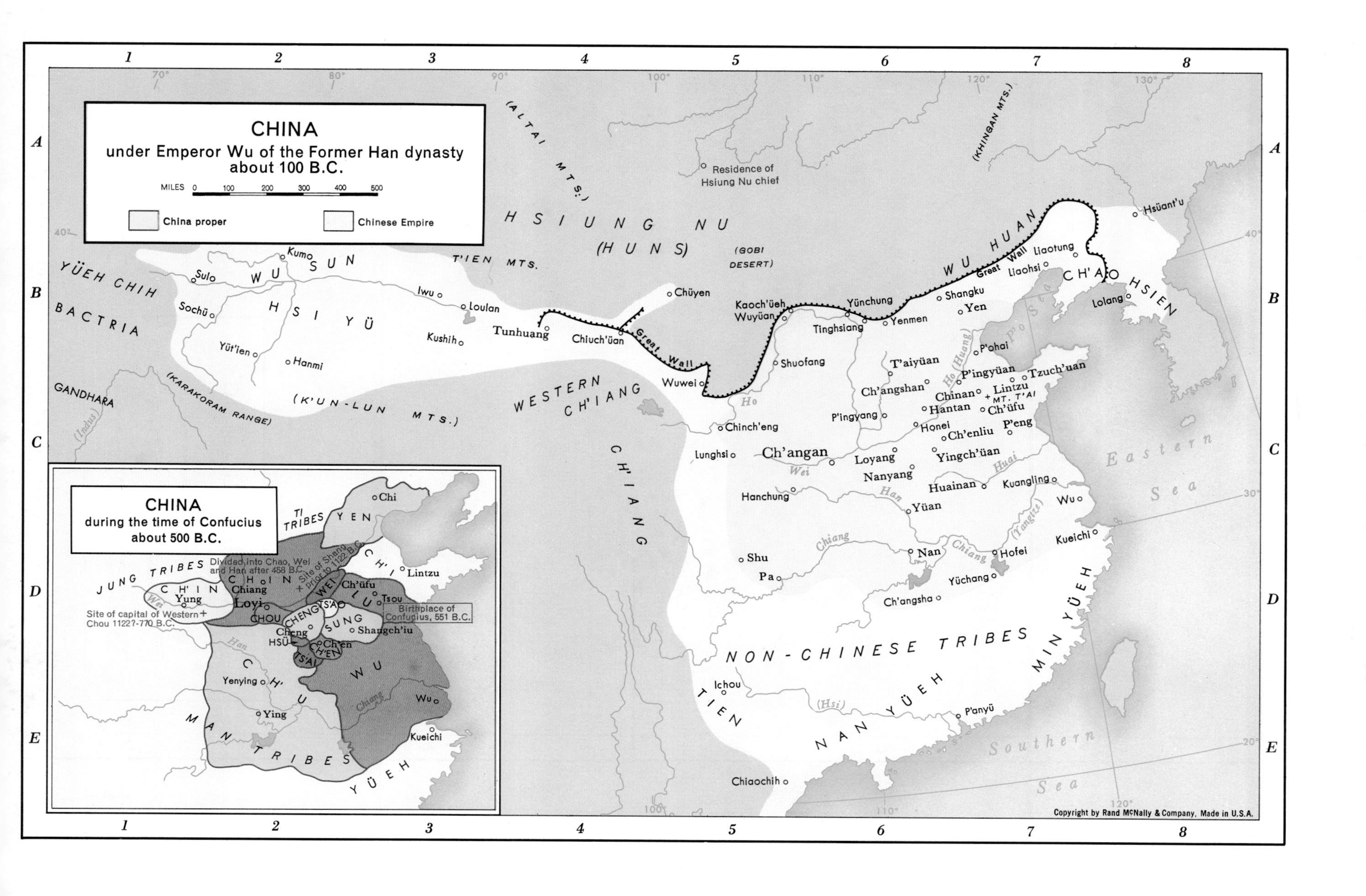

CHINA
under Emperor Wu of the Former Han dynasty
about 100 B.C.
MILES 0 100 200 300 400 500
China proper
Chinese Empire
HSIUNG NU
(HUNS)
(GOBI DESERT)
(ALTAI MTS.)
(KHINGAN MTS.)
Residence of Hsiung Nu chief
T'IEN MTS.
YÜEH CHIH
BACTRIA
GANDHARA
(Indus)
(KARAKORAM RANGE)
(K'UN-LUN MTS.)
WU SUN
HSI YÜ
Kumo
Sulo
Sochü
Yüt'ien
Hanmi
Iwu
Loulan
Kushih
Tunhuang
Chiuch'üan
Great Wall
Chüyen
Wuwei
WESTERN CH'IANG
CH'IANG
Kaoch'üeh
Wuyüan
Yünchung
Tinghsiang
Yenmen
Shuofang
Ho
Chinch'eng
Lunghsi
Ch'angan
Wei
Hanchung
Shu
Pa
T'aiyüan
Ch'angshan
P'ingyang
Loyang
Nanyang
Han
Yüan
Chiang
Nan
Ch'angsha
Ho (Huang)
P'ohai
P'ingyüan
Chinan
Lintzu
MT. T'AI
Tzuch'uan
Hantan
Ch'üfu
Honei
Ch'enliu
P'eng
Yingch'üan
Huai
Huainan
Kuangling
Wu
(Yangtze)
Hofei
Yüchang
Kueichi
WU HUAN
Shangku
Yen
Liaohsi
Liaotung
CH'AO HSIEN
Lolang
Hsüant'u
P'o Sea
Eastern Sea
NON-CHINESE TRIBES
MIN YÜEH
NAN YÜEH
TIEN
Ichou
(Hsi)
P'anyü
Chiaochih
Southern Sea
CHINA
during the time of Confucius
about 500 B.C.
JUNG TRIBES
TI TRIBES
YEN
Chi
CH'I
Lintzu
CH'IN
Yung
Wei
Site of capital of Western Chou 1122?-770 B.C.
CHIN
Divided into Chao, Wei and Han after 458 B.C.
Chiang
Site of Shang prior to 1122 B.C.
Loyi
CHOU
WEI
Ch'üfu
LU
Tsou
Birthplace of Confucius, 551 B.C.
TS'AO
CHENG
SUNG
Shangch'iu
Cheng
HSÜ
Ch'en
CH'EN
TS'AI
WU
Wu
Kueichi
CH'U
Yenying
Ying
Han
Chiang
MAN TRIBES
YÜEH
Copyright by Rand McNally & Company, Made in U.S.A.

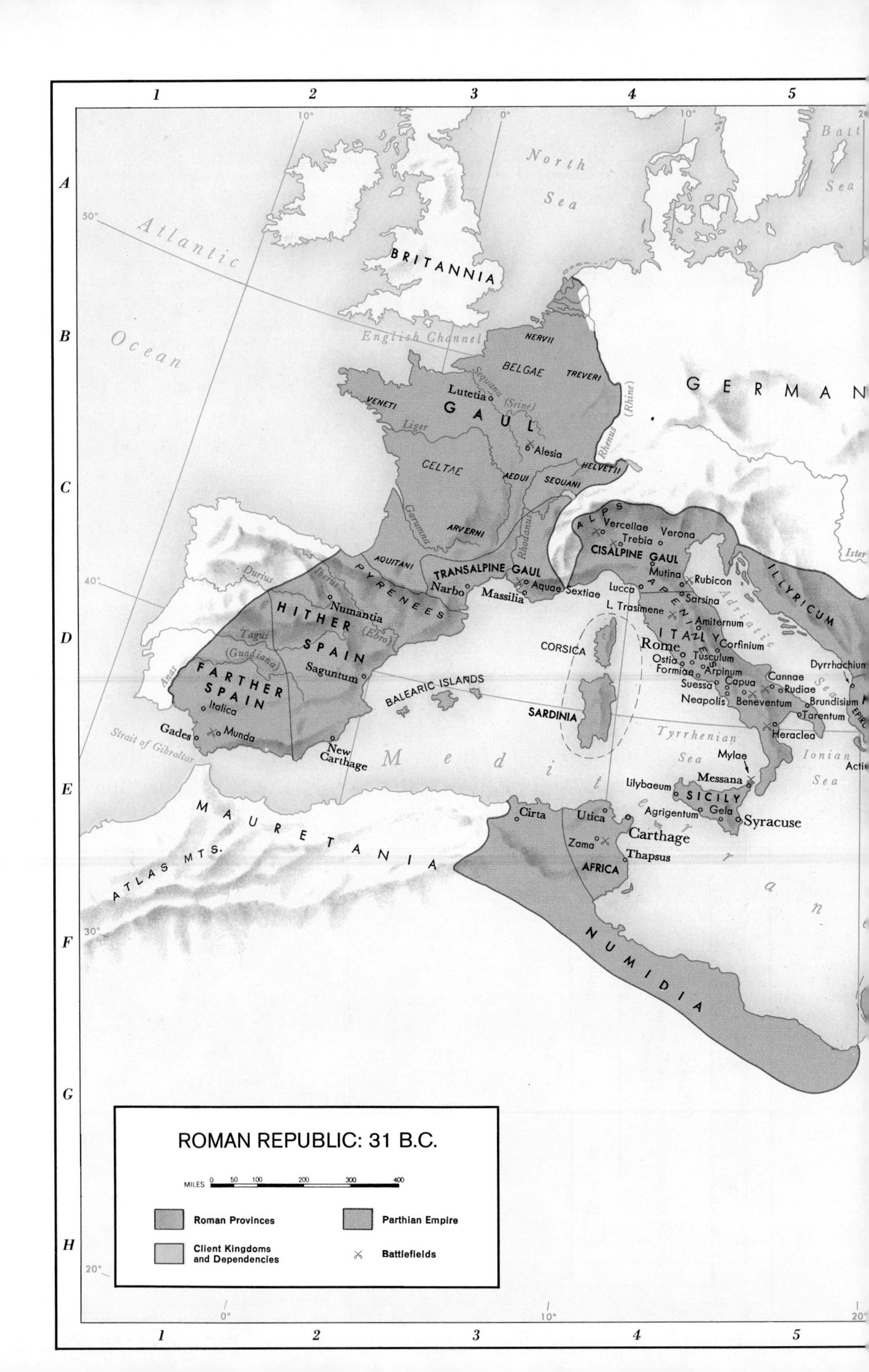
ROMAN REPUBLIC: 31 B.C.
MILES 0 50 100 200 300 400
Roman Provinces
Parthian Empire
Client Kingdoms and Dependencies
Battlefields
Atlantic Ocean
North Sea
Baltic Sea
BRITANNIA
English Channel
NERVII
BELGAE
TREVERI
GERMAN
Lutetia
Sequana (Seine)
VENETI
GAUL
Liger
Alesia
Rhenus (Rhine)
CELTAE
AEDUI
SEQUANI
HELVETII
Garumna
ARVERNI
ALPS
Vercellae
Trebia
Verona
CISALPINE GAUL
AQUITANI
TRANSALPINE GAUL
Rhodanus
Durius
Iberus
PYRENEES
Narbo
Massilia
Aquae Sextiae
Mutina
Rubicon
Lucca
Sarsina
L. Trasimene
ILLYRICUM
Adriatic
Istar
HITHER SPAIN
Numantia
(Ebro)
Tagus
(Guadiana)
Anas
FARTHER SPAIN
Saguntum
Italica
Gades
Munda
Strait of Gibraltar
New Carthage
BALEARIC ISLANDS
CORSICA
SARDINIA
APENNINES
ITALY
Amiternum
Corfinium
Rome
Tusculum
Ostia
Formiae
Arpinum
Suessa
Capua
Neapolis
Beneventum
Cannae
Rudiae
Brundisium
Tarentum
Dyrrhachium
EPIRUS
Heraclea
Tyrrhenian Sea
Ionian Sea
Mylae
Messana
Lilybaeum
SICILY
Agrigentum
Gela
Syracuse
Mediterranean
MAURETANIA
ATLAS MTS.
Cirta
Utica
Carthage
Zama
Thapsus
AFRICA
NUMIDIA
1 2 3 4 5
A B C D E F G H
10° 0° 10° 20°
50° 40° 30° 20°

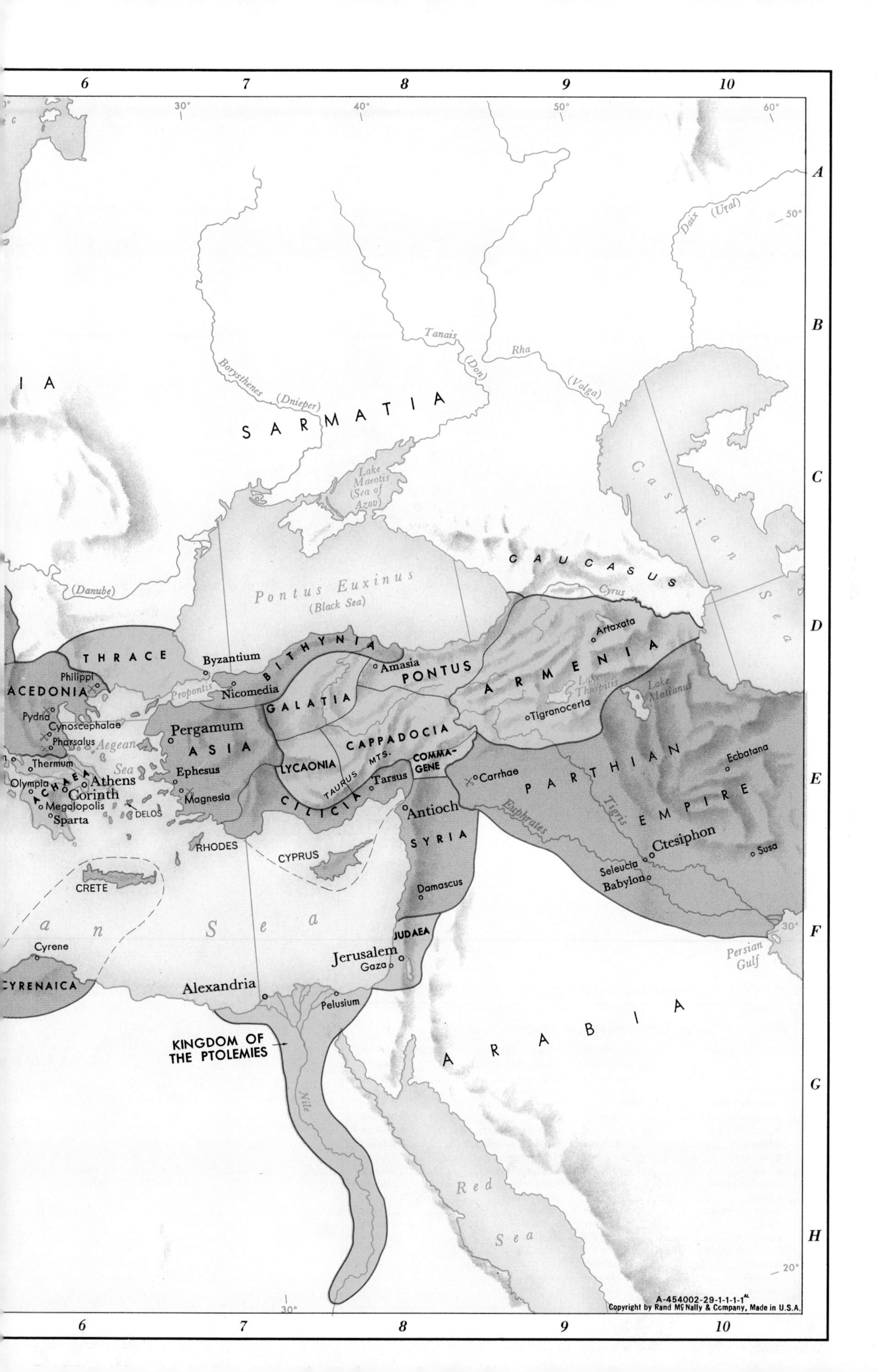
6
7
8
9
10
A
B
C
D
E
F
G
H
SARMATIA
Borysthenes (Dnieper)
Tanais (Don)
Rha (Volga)
Daix (Ural)
Lake Maeotis (Sea of Azov)
Caspian Sea
CAUCASUS
Cyrus
Pontus Euxinus (Black Sea)
(Danube)
THRACE
Byzantium
BITHYNIA
Nicomedia
Propontis
Amasia
PONTUS
ARMENIA
Artaxata
Lake Thospitis
Lake Matianus
Tigranocerta
GALATIA
CAPPADOCIA
LYCAONIA
TAURUS MTS.
COMMAGENE
Tarsus
CILICIA
MACEDONIA
Philippi
Pydna
Cynoscephalae
Pharsalus
Aegean Sea
Thermum
Olympia
ACHAEA
Athens
Corinth
Megalopolis
Sparta
DELOS
Pergamum
ASIA
Ephesus
Magnesia
RHODES
CYPRUS
CRETE
Carrhae
PARTHIAN EMPIRE
Ecbatana
Euphrates
Tigris
Ctesiphon
Seleucia
Babylon
Susa
Antioch
SYRIA
Damascus
JUDAEA
Jerusalem
Gaza
Persian Gulf
Cyrene
CYRENAICA
Alexandria
Pelusium
KINGDOM OF THE PTOLEMIES
Nile
ARABIA
Red Sea
A-454002-29-1-1-1-1
Copyright by Rand McNally & Company, Made in U.S.A.

Roman City Names and Modern Equivalents

ROMAN NAME	MODERN NAME	ROMAN NAME	MODERN NAME
Ancyra	Ankara	Londinium	London
Aquincum	Budapest	Lugdunum	Lyon
Arelate	Arles	Lugdunum Batavorum	Leiden
Augusta Treverorum	Trier, Treves	Lutetia	Paris
Augusta Vindelicorum	Augsburg	Malaca	Malaga
Augustodunum	Autun	Massilia	Marseille
Bononia	Bologna	Mazaca Caesarea	Kayseri
Burdigala	Bordeaux	Mediolanum	Milan
Caesar Augusta	Saragossa	Moguntiacum	Mainz
Camulodunum	Colchester	Nemausus	Nimes
Carales	Cagliari	Olisipo	Lisbon
Colonia Agrippina	Cologne	Patavium	Padua
Deva	Chester	Salmantica	Salamanca
Eburacum	York	Thessalonica	Salonika
Emerita Augusta	Merida	Toletum	Toledo
Gades	Cadiz	Tolosa	Toulouse
Hispalis	Seville	Valentia	Valencia
Lindum	Lincoln	Vindobona	Vienna

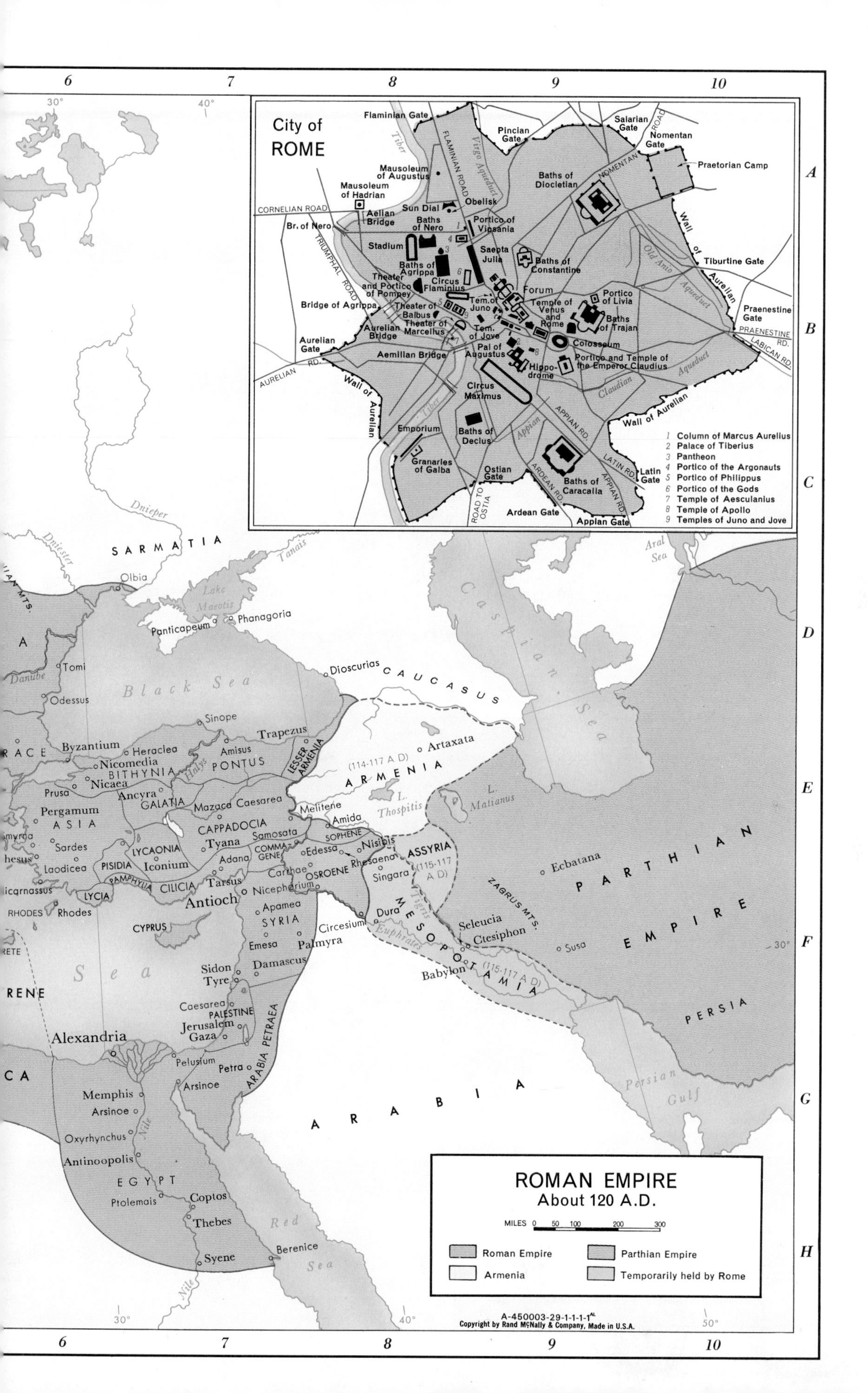
ROMAN EMPIRE
About 120 A.D.
MILES 0 50 100 200 300
Roman Empire
Parthian Empire
Armenia
Temporarily held by Rome
City of ROME
Flaminian Gate
Pincian Gate
Salarian Gate
Nomentan Gate
Praetorian Camp
Mausoleum of Augustus
Mausoleum of Hadrian
CORNELIAN ROAD
FLAMINIAN ROAD
Virgo Aqueduct
NOMENTAN ROAD
Baths of Diocletian
Sun Dial
Obelisk
Aelian Bridge
Br. of Nero
Baths of Nero
Portico of Vipsania
Stadium
Saepta Julia
Baths of Constantine
Baths of Agrippa
Theater and Portico of Pompey
Circus Flaminius
TRIUMPHAL ROAD
Wall of Aurelian
Tiburtine Gate
Old Anio
Aqueduct
Bridge of Agrippa
Theater of Balbus
Theater of Marcellus
Tem. of Juno
Tem. of Jove
Forum
Temple of Venus and Rome
Portico of Livia
Baths of Trajan
Praenestine Gate
PRAENESTINE RD.
LABICAN RD.
Aurelian Gate
Aurelian Bridge
Aemilian Bridge
Pal of Augustus
Colosseum
Portico and Temple of the Emperor Claudius
Hippodrome
AURELIAN RD.
Circus Maximus
Claudian
Tiber
Emporium
Granaries of Galba
Baths of Decius
Appian
APPIAN RD.
LATIN RD.
Latin Gate
Ostian Gate
ARDEAN RD.
Baths of Caracalla
ROAD TO OSTIA
Ardean Gate
Appian Gate
1 Column of Marcus Aurelius
2 Palace of Tiberius
3 Pantheon
4 Portico of the Argonauts
5 Portico of Philippus
6 Portico of the Gods
7 Temple of Aesculanius
8 Temple of Apollo
9 Temples of Juno and Jove
SARMATIA
Dnieper
Dniester
Tanais
Olbia
Lake Maeotis
Panticapeum
Phanagoria
Aral Sea
Caspian Sea
Danube
Tomi
Odessus
Black Sea
Dioscurias
CAUCASUS
Sinope
Trapezus
Byzantium
Heraclea
Amisus
PONTUS
LESSER ARMENIA
Artaxata
(114-117 A.D.)
ARMENIA
Nicomedia
BITHYNIA
Halys
Nicaea
Prusa
Ancyra
GALATIA
Mazaca Caesarea
L. Thospitis
L. Matianus
Pergamum
ASIA
Melitene
Amida
CAPPADOCIA
Samosata
SOPHENE
Sardes
LYCAONIA
Tyana
COMMAGENE
Edessa
Nisibis
ASSYRIA
(115-117 A.D.)
Laodicea
PISIDIA
Iconium
Adana
Carrhae
Rhesaena
OSROENE
Singara
Ecbatana
PAMPHYLIA
CILICIA
Tarsus
Nicephorium
LYCIA
RHODES
Rhodes
Antioch
Apamea
SYRIA
MESOPOTAMIA
Tigris
ZAGRUS MTS.
PARTHIAN EMPIRE
CYPRUS
Circesium
Dura
Seleucia
Ctesiphon
Emesa
Palmyra
Euphrates
Susa
Sidon
Tyre
Damascus
Babylon
(115-117 A.D.)
Sea
Caesarea
PALESTINE
Jerusalem
Gaza
ARABIA PETRAEA
PERSIA
Alexandria
Pelusium
Petra
Arsinoe
Persian Gulf
ARABIA
Memphis
Arsinoe
Oxyrhynchus
Nile
Antinoopolis
EGYPT
Ptolemais
Coptos
Thebes
Red Sea
Berenice
Syene
30°
40°
50°
6
7
8
9
10
A
B
C
D
E
F
G
H
A-450003-29-1-1-1-1
Copyright by Rand McNally & Company, Made in U.S.A.

Routes of the Barbarians
Huns
Visigoths
Vandals
Franks
Lombards
Ostrogoths
Burgundians
Anglo-Saxons
375 —date people passed through region
200-375—stop in region
507 —final occupation of region
SCANDIA
PICTS
SCOTIA
DIOCESE OF BRITAIN
DIOCESE OF GAUL
DIOCESE OF SPAIN
DIOCESE ITALY
DIOCESE OF ROME
DIOCESE OF AFRICA
Atlantic Ocean
North Sea
Bay of Biscay
Mediterranean
Tyrrhenian Sea
ALPS
PYRENEES
CORSICA
SARDINIA
BALEARIC ISLANDS
York
Chester
Lincoln
Caerleon
St. Albans
Colchester
London
Tournay
Cologne
Cambray
Soissons
Rouen
Treves
Reims
Mainz
Paris
Chalons
Metz
Orleans
Tours
Poitiers
Autun
Bordeaux
Lyon
Salzburg
Milan
Pavia
Aquileia
Genoa
Toulouse
Arles
Narbonne
Pamplona
Braga
Saragossa
Lisbon
Toledo
Barcelona
Tarragona
Tortosa
Merida
Valencia
Seville
Cadiz
Cartagena
Ceuta
Bologna
Ravenna
Pisa
Ancona
Spoleto
Rome
Naples
Taranto
Palermo
Reggio
Syracuse
Hippo Regius
Carthage
Tripoli
FRANKS
BURGUNDIANS
VANDALS
VISIGOTHS
OSTROGOTHS
ANGLO-SAXONS
HUNS
Rhine
Weser
Elbe
Oder
Danube
Drave
Save
Seine
Loire
Garonne
Rhone
Duero
Ebro
Tagus
Guadiana
Guadalquivir
547
367-550
C. 450
C. 500
C. 449
358
486
507
451
452
443
415
412-507
409-429
568
489
410
455
429

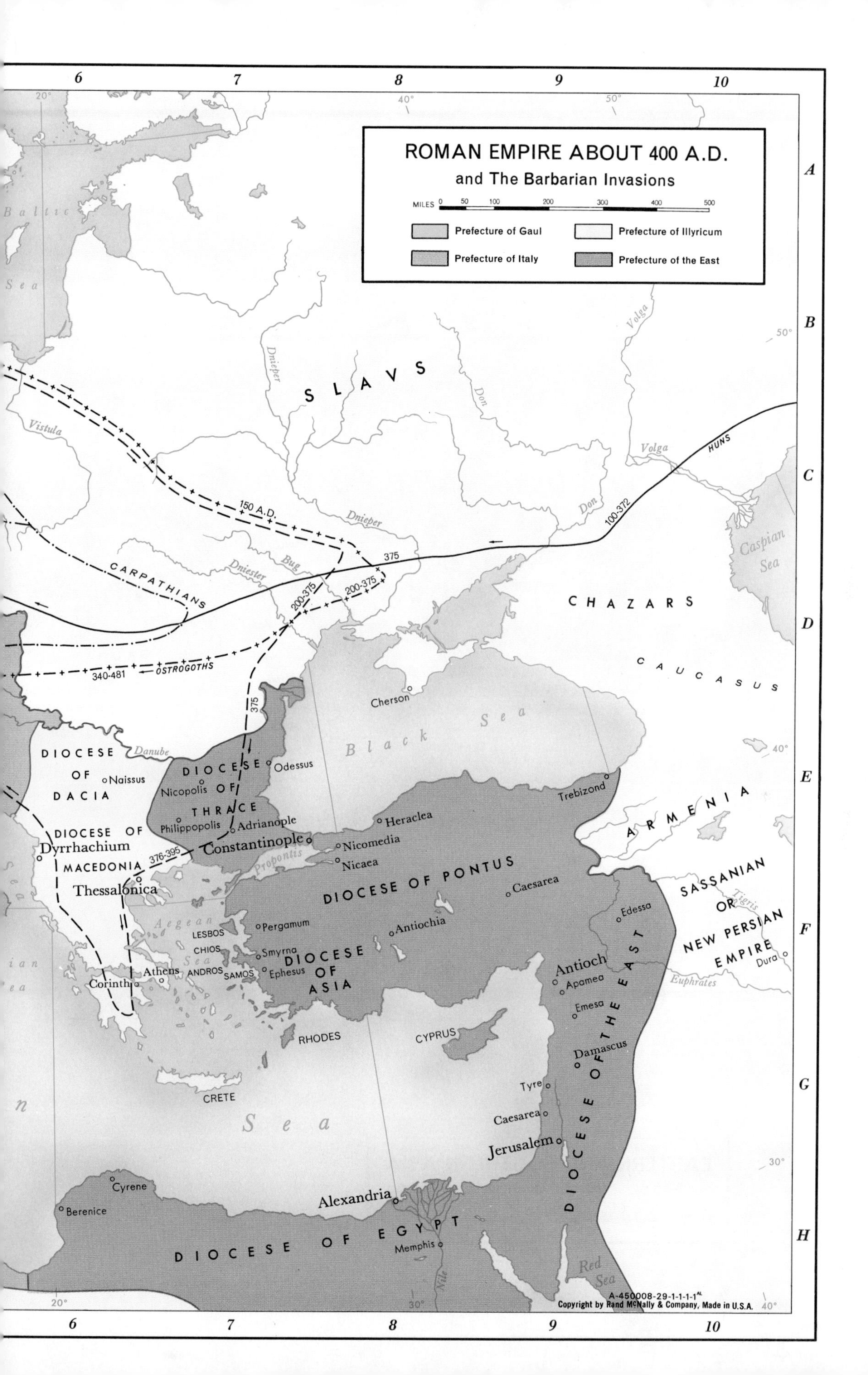
ROMAN EMPIRE ABOUT 400 A.D.
and The Barbarian Invasions
MILES 0 50 100 200 300 400 500
Prefecture of Gaul
Prefecture of Illyricum
Prefecture of Italy
Prefecture of the East
SLAVS
CHAZARS
CAUCASUS
ARMENIA
SASSANIAN OR NEW PERSIAN EMPIRE
HUNS
100-372
375
150 A.D.
200-375
340-481
OSTROGOTHS
376-395
CARPATHIANS
DIOCESE OF DACIA
DIOCESE OF THRACE
DIOCESE OF MACEDONIA
DIOCESE OF PONTUS
DIOCESE OF ASIA
DIOCESE OF THE EAST
DIOCESE OF EGYPT
Black Sea
Caspian Sea
Aegean Sea
Propontis
Red Sea
Baltic Sea
Vistula
Dnieper
Don
Volga
Dniester
Bug
Danube
Tigris
Euphrates
Nile
Cherson
Odessus
Naissus
Nicopolis
Philippopolis
Adrianople
Constantinople
Dyrrhachium
Thessalonica
Heraclea
Nicomedia
Nicaea
Trebizond
Caesarea
Edessa
Pergamum
Antiochia
Smyrna
Ephesus
Athens
Corinth
LESBOS
CHIOS
ANDROS
SAMOS
RHODES
CYPRUS
CRETE
Antioch
Apamea
Emesa
Damascus
Tyre
Caesarea
Jerusalem
Alexandria
Memphis
Cyrene
Berenice
Dura
A-450008-29-1-1-1
Copyright by Rand McNally & Company, Made in U.S.A.

EASTERN AND SOUTHERN ASIA
About 750 A.D.
MILES 0 100 200 400 600 800
1
2
3
4
5
A
B
C
D
E
F
G
H
40°
50°
60°
70°
80°
90°
30°
20°
10°
0°
Titlis
Caspian Sea
Tigris
Kath
Sayhun
Jayhun (Oxus)
ABBASID CALIPHATE
Umayyad Caliphate until 750
Abbassid Caliphate thereafter
Baghdad
Hamadan
Ray
Isfahan
Merv
Herat
Zarani
Bokhara
SOGDIANA
Samarkand
Balkh
TOKHARISTAN
Kabul
Ghazni
Talas
Decisive Battle 751
KARLUKS
(WESTERN TURKS)
Chinese control lost after 754
Peit'ing
FERGHANA
TIEN MTS.
Yenchi
Anhsi
(Kucha)
Ch'iasha
(Kashgar)
FOUR GARRISONS
Lost to Tibetans after 790
Yüt'ien
(Khotan)
BALTISTAN
Gilgit
KASHMIR
Purushapura
Chinese garrison 747-751
Tibetan conquest 751
TIB
NEPAL
(HIMALAYA MTS.)
Indus
Thanesar
Indraprastha
Ganges
Jumna
GURJARA
Kanauj
Prayaga
Pataliputra
GAUDA
(PALAS)
Nalanda
KAM
Anandapura
VALABHI
(MAITRAKAS)
Ujjain
Broach
Nerbudda
Tamralipti
RASHTRAKUTAS
Rise in power from about 750
By 9th Cent. dominated India from Gurjara and Kanauj to Kanchi
Ajanta
Nasik
CHALUKYAS
Power declining by 750
Manyakheta
(Malkhed)
Godavari
Vatapi
KALINGA
Amaravati
PALLAVAS
Power greatly diminished by 750
Kanchi
Mamallapuram
CHOLAS
Madura
PANDYAS
Anuradhapura
SIMHALA
Green Se
A-469015-29-1-1-1
Copyright by Rand McNally & Company, Made in U.S.A.

6
7
8
9
10
A
B
C
D
E
F
G
H
Uighur Capital
Orkhon
UIGHURS (EASTERN TURKS)
(GOBI DESERT)
KHITANS
Capital
P'O HAI
Liaotung
SILLA
Hanchow
Capital
Capital from 794
Heian
Nara
Capital from 710-784
JAPAN
Great Wall
Huang
Tunhuang
LUNGYU
T'UYÜHUNS
Shan
KUANNEI
T'aiyüan
HOTUNG
HOPEI
Weichow
Yün
HONAN
Loyang
TUCHI
Pien
Sung
Grand Canal
Yangchow
Eastern Sea
CHINGCHI
Ch'angan
SHANNAN HSI
SHANNAN TUNG
HUAINAN
Hsüan
Soochow
Yüeh
Hangchow
Chiangling
Yangtze
CHINA
Ch'engtu
CHIENNAN
CH'IENCHUNG
CHIANGNAN HSI
CHIANGNAN TUNG
Ch'üanchow
Lhasa
Brahmaputra
Tali
NAN CHAO (T'AI)
LINGNAN
Kwangchow
Hsi
Southern Sea
Halin
PYU
ANNAM
Chiaochow
(HAINAN)
UPPER (LAND) CHENLA
MONS
Srikshetra
Thaton
CHAMPA
Amaravati
Mekong
LOWER (MARITIME) CHENLA
DVARAVATI
KAUTHARA
Virapura
PANDURANGA
TAMBRALINGA
LANGKASUKA
KEDAH
(SUMATRA)
(BORNEO)
Malayu
BANKA
SRIVIJAYA
Srivijaya
(JAVA)
SAILENDRAS
TARUMA
Borobodur Built 772?
MATARAM
The Srivijayan Empire, perhaps under a Sailendran ruler, probably included more of Sumatra and Java and even portions of the Malay peninsula and Borneo by the end of the 8th Century

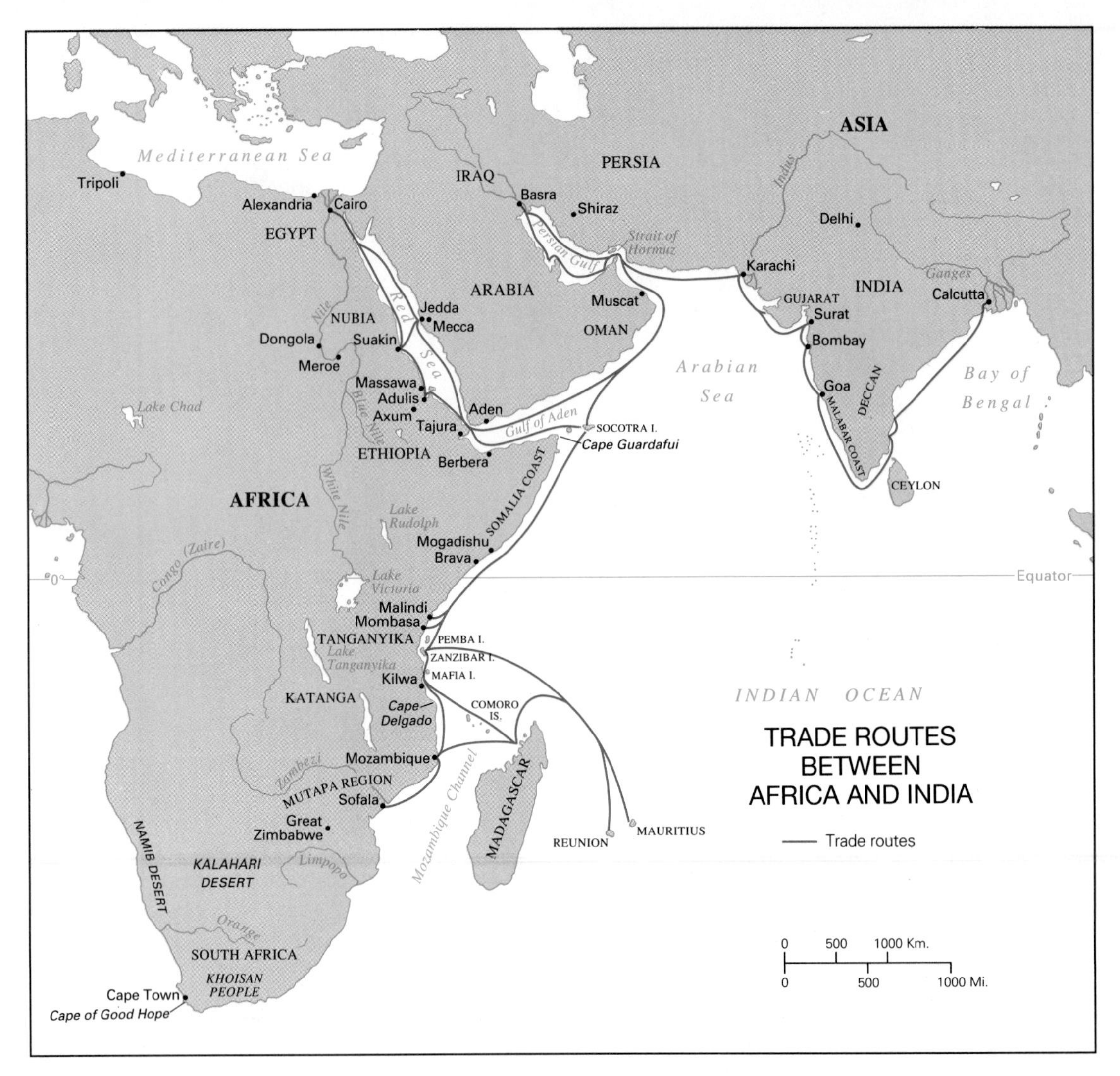
TRADE ROUTES
BETWEEN
AFRICA AND INDIA
Trade routes
ASIA
PERSIA
IRAQ
ARABIA
OMAN
INDIA
AFRICA
EGYPT
NUBIA
ETHIOPIA
TANGANYIKA
KATANGA
MUTAPA REGION
SOUTH AFRICA
KHOISAN PEOPLE
KALAHARI DESERT
NAMIB DESERT
MADAGASCAR
Mediterranean Sea
Red Sea
Persian Gulf
Strait of Hormuz
Gulf of Aden
Arabian Sea
Bay of Bengal
INDIAN OCEAN
Mozambique Channel
Tripoli
Alexandria
Cairo
Basra
Shiraz
Delhi
Karachi
Muscat
Jedda
Mecca
Dongola
Suakin
Meroe
Massawa
Adulis
Axum
Aden
Tajura
Berbera
SOCOTRA I.
Cape Guardafui
SOMALIA COAST
Mogadishu
Brava
Malindi
Mombasa
PEMBA I.
ZANZIBAR I.
MAFIA I.
Kilwa
Cape Delgado
COMORO IS.
Mozambique
Sofala
Great Zimbabwe
REUNION
MAURITIUS
Cape Town
Cape of Good Hope
GUJARAT
Surat
Bombay
Goa
DECCAN
MALABAR COAST
Calcutta
CEYLON
Indus
Ganges
Nile
Blue Nile
White Nile
Lake Chad
Lake Rudolph
Lake Victoria
Lake Tanganyika
Congo (Zaire)
Zambezi
Limpopo
Orange
Equator
0°
0 500 1000 Km.
0 500 1000 Mi.

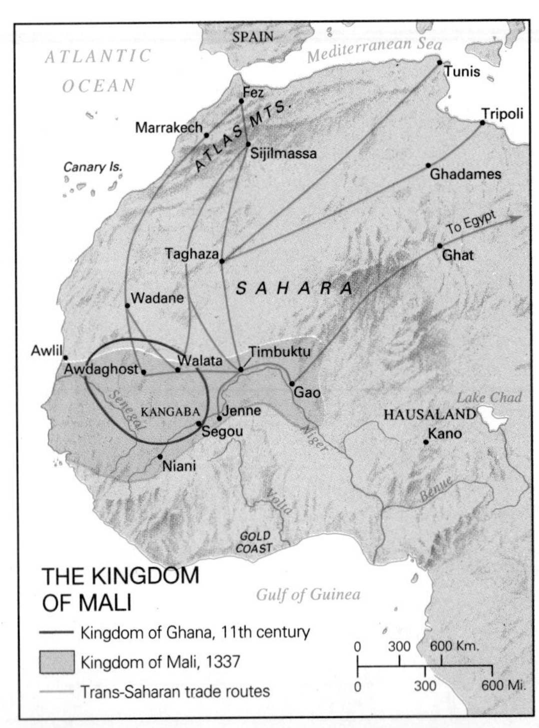
THE KINGDOM OF MALI
Kingdom of Ghana, 11th century
Kingdom of Mali, 1337
Trans-Saharan trade routes
SPAIN
ATLANTIC OCEAN
Mediterranean Sea
Tunis
Tripoli
Fez
Marrakech
ATLAS MTS.
Sijilmassa
Canary Is.
Ghadames
To Egypt
Ghat
Taghaza
SAHARA
Wadane
Awlil
Awdaghost
Walata
Timbuktu
Gao
KANGABA
Senegal
Jenne
Segou
Niani
Niger
Lake Chad
HAUSALAND
Kano
Benue
Volta
GOLD COAST
Gulf of Guinea
0 300 600 Km.
0 300 600 Mi.

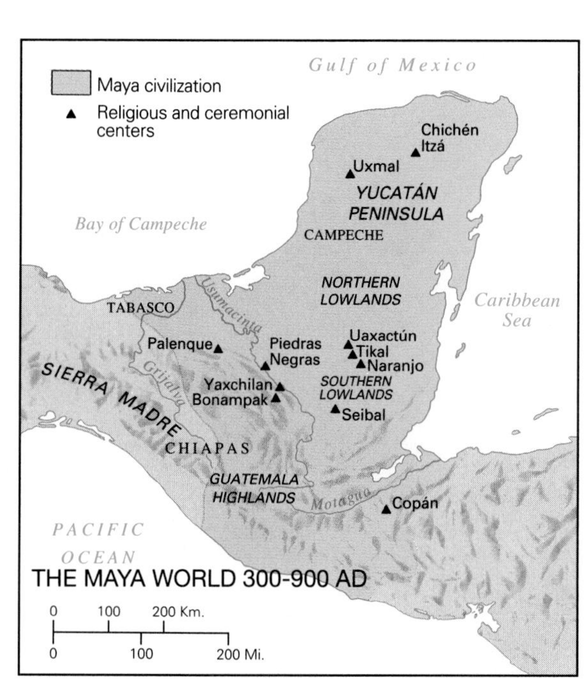
THE MAYA WORLD 300-900 AD
Maya civilization
Religious and ceremonial centers
Gulf of Mexico
Bay of Campeche
Caribbean Sea
PACIFIC OCEAN
Chichén Itzá
Uxmal
YUCATÁN PENINSULA
CAMPECHE
NORTHERN LOWLANDS
TABASCO
Usumacinta
Palenque
Piedras Negras
Uaxactún
Tikal
Naranjo
Grijalva
SIERRA MADRE
Yaxchilan
Bonampak
SOUTHERN LOWLANDS
Seibal
CHIAPAS
GUATEMALA HIGHLANDS
Motagua
Copán
0 100 200 Km.
0 100 200 Mi.

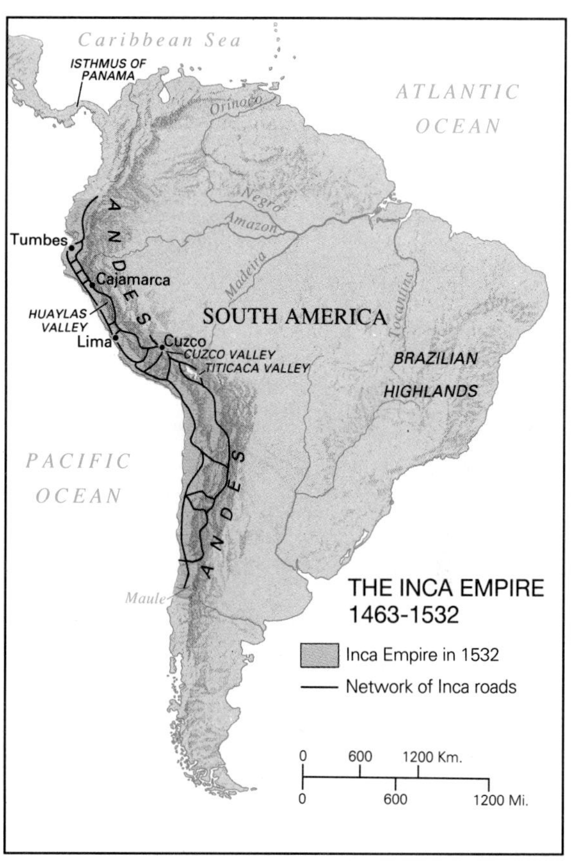
THE INCA EMPIRE 1463-1532
Inca Empire in 1532
Network of Inca roads
Caribbean Sea
ISTHMUS OF PANAMA
ATLANTIC OCEAN
Orinoco
Negro
Amazon
Madeira
Tocantins
ANDES
Tumbes
Cajamarca
HUAYLAS VALLEY
Lima
SOUTH AMERICA
Cuzco
CUZCO VALLEY
TITICACA VALLEY
BRAZILIAN HIGHLANDS
PACIFIC OCEAN
Maule
0 600 1200 Km.
0 600 1200 Mi.

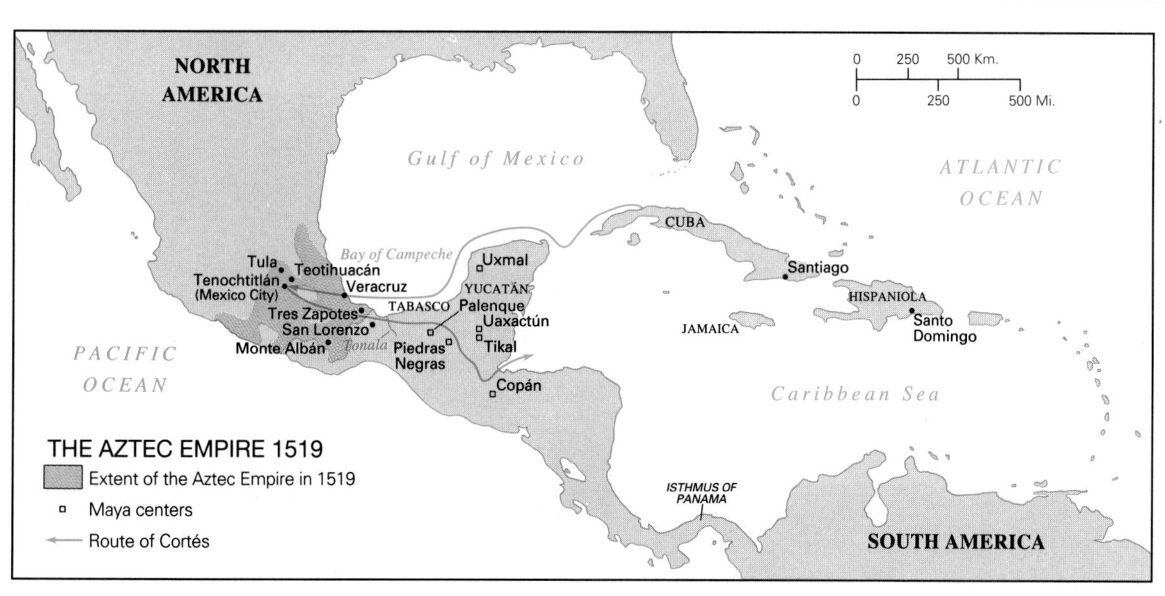
THE AZTEC EMPIRE 1519
Extent of the Aztec Empire in 1519
Maya centers
Route of Cortés
NORTH AMERICA
Gulf of Mexico
ATLANTIC OCEAN
CUBA
Bay of Campeche
Tula
Teotihuacán
Tenochtitlán (Mexico City)
Veracruz
Uxmal
YUCATÁN
TABASCO
Palenque
Tres Zapotes
San Lorenzo
Uaxactún
Monte Albán
Tonala
Piedras Negras
Tikal
Copán
Santiago
HISPANIOLA
Santo Domingo
JAMAICA
Caribbean Sea
PACIFIC OCEAN
ISTHMUS OF PANAMA
SOUTH AMERICA
0 250 500 Km.
0 250 500 Mi.

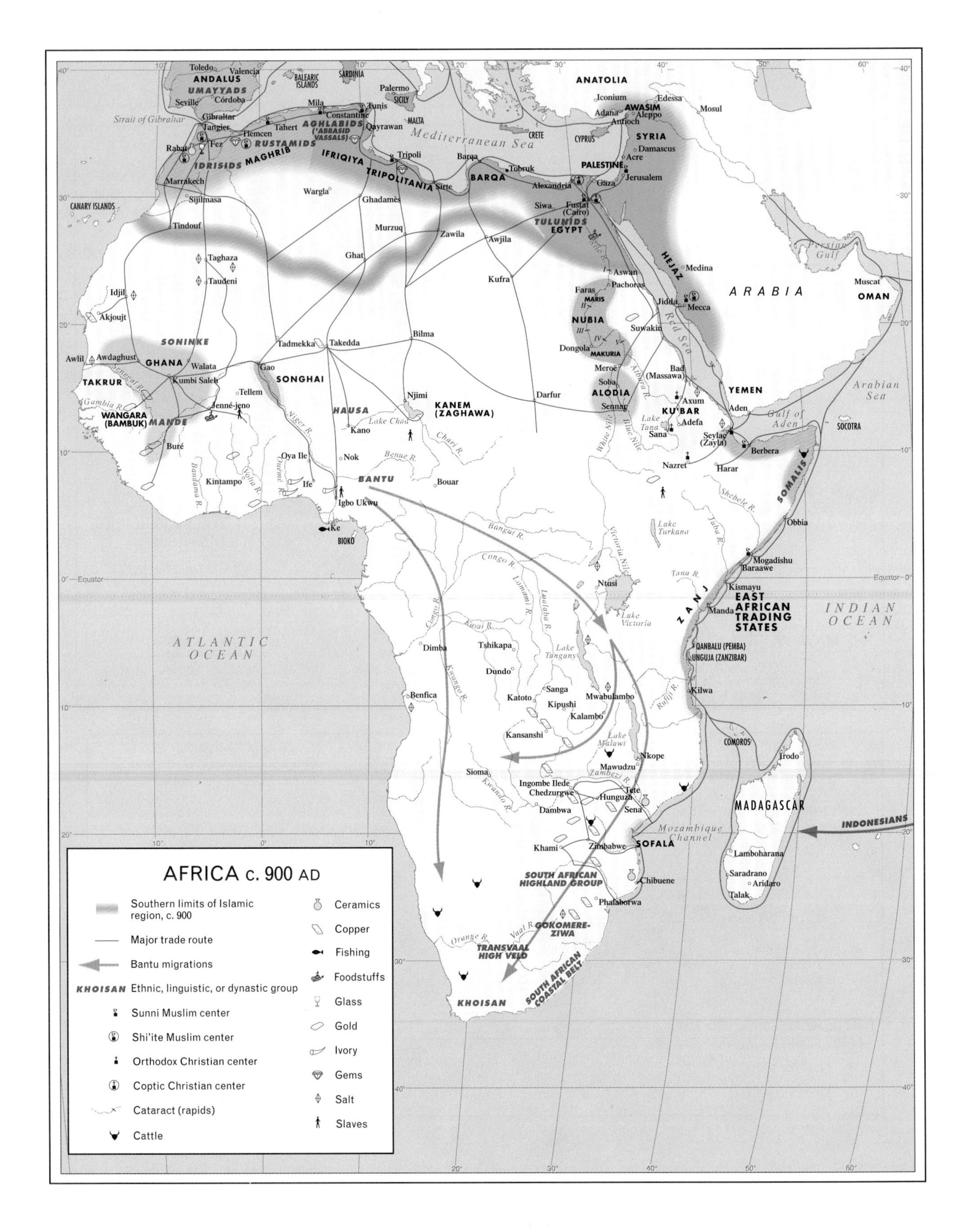

AFRICA c. 900 AD
Southern limits of Islamic region, c. 900
Major trade route
Bantu migrations
KHOISAN Ethnic, linguistic, or dynastic group
Sunni Muslim center
Shi'ite Muslim center
Orthodox Christian center
Coptic Christian center
Cataract (rapids)
Cattle
Ceramics
Copper
Fishing
Foodstuffs
Glass
Gold
Ivory
Gems
Salt
Slaves
ANDALUS
UMAYYADS
ANATOLIA
AWASIM
SYRIA
PALESTINE
Mediterranean Sea
AGHLABIDS ('ABBASID VASSALS)
RUSTAMIDS
IDRISIDS
MAGHRIB
IFRIQIYA
TRIPOLITANIA
BARQA
TULUNIDS
EGYPT
HEJAZ
ARABIA
OMAN
YEMEN
NUBIA
MAKURIA
ALODIA
KU'BAR
SONINKE
GHANA
TAKRUR
WANGARA (BAMBUK)
MANDE
SONGHAI
HAUSA
KANEM (ZAGHAWA)
BANTU
SOMALIS
ZANJ
EAST AFRICAN TRADING STATES
MADAGASCAR
INDONESIANS
SOFALA
SOUTH AFRICAN HIGHLAND GROUP
GOKOMERE-ZIWA
TRANSVAAL HIGH VELD
SOUTH AFRICAN COASTAL BELT
KHOISAN
ATLANTIC OCEAN
INDIAN OCEAN
Arabian Sea
Persian Gulf
Red Sea
Gulf of Aden
Mozambique Channel
Strait of Gibraltar
Equator

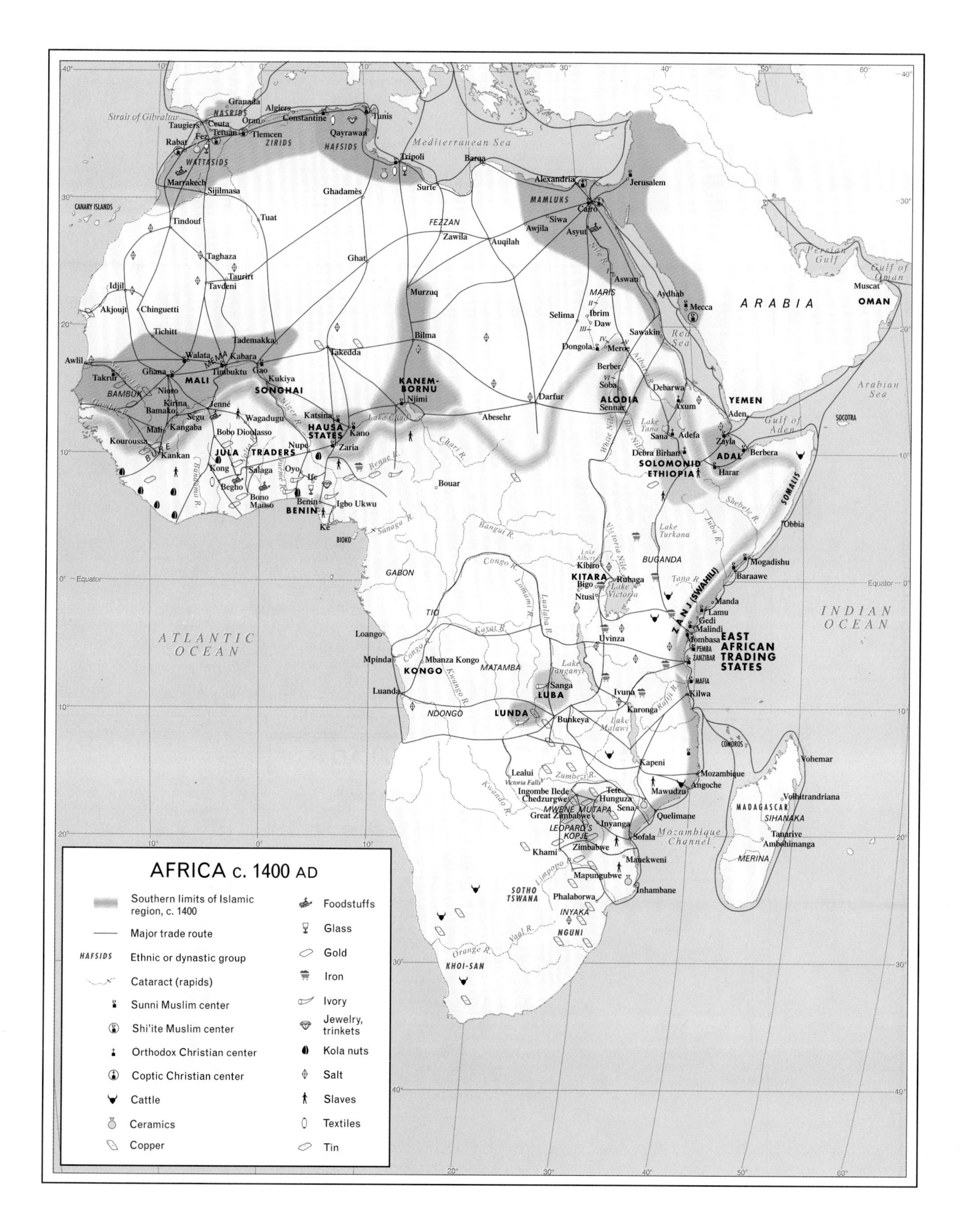
AFRICA c. 1400 AD
Southern limits of Islamic region, c. 1400
Major trade route
HAFSIDS Ethnic or dynastic group
Cataract (rapids)
Sunni Muslim center
Shi'ite Muslim center
Orthodox Christian center
Coptic Christian center
Cattle
Ceramics
Copper
Foodstuffs
Glass
Gold
Iron
Ivory
Jewelry, trinkets
Kola nuts
Salt
Slaves
Textiles
Tin
ATLANTIC OCEAN
INDIAN OCEAN
Mediterranean Sea
ARABIA
OMAN
YEMEN
MALI
SONGHAI
KANEM-BORNU
HAUSA STATES
JULA TRADERS
BENIN
MAMLUKS
HAFSIDS
ZIRIDS
NASRIDS
WATTASIDS
ALODIA
SOLOMONID ETHIOPIA
ADAL
SOMALIS
KITARA
BUGANDA
ZANJ (SWAHILI)
EAST AFRICAN TRADING STATES
KONGO
LUBA
LUNDA
MWENE MUTAPA
SOTHO TSWANA
NGUNI
KHOI-SAN
MADAGASCAR
MERINA
Cairo
Alexandria
Tripoli
Tunis
Timbuktu
Gao
Mecca
Kilwa
Mogadishu
Great Zimbabwe
Sofala
Mombasa
Malindi
Zanzibar

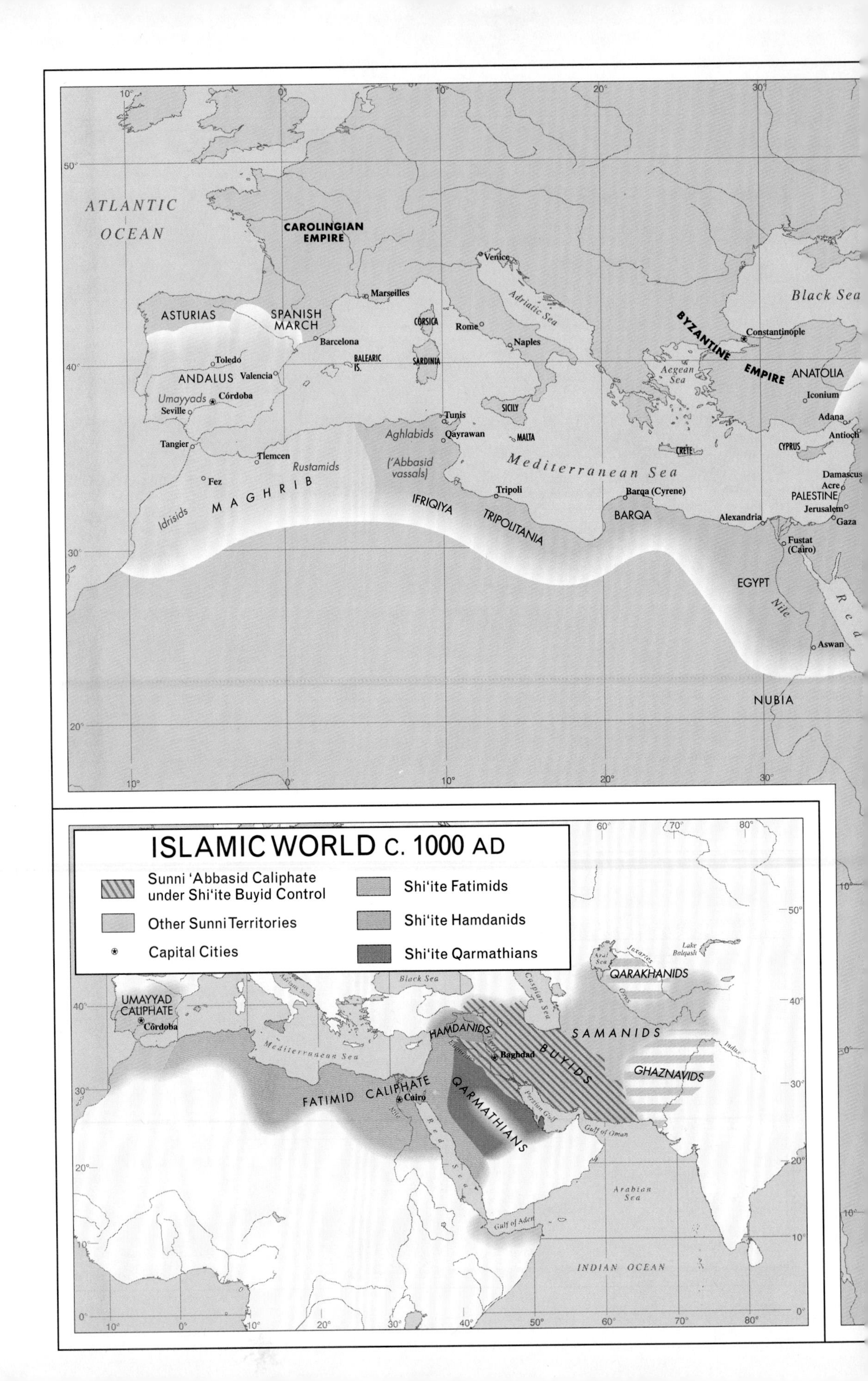
ATLANTIC OCEAN
CAROLINGIAN EMPIRE
Venice
Marseilles
Black Sea
ASTURIAS
SPANISH MARCH
Barcelona
CORSICA
Rome
Adriatic Sea
Naples
BYZANTINE EMPIRE
Constantinople
Toledo
ANDALUS
Valencia
BALEARIC IS.
SARDINIA
Aegean Sea
ANATOLIA
Umayyads
Córdoba
Seville
Iconium
Tunis
SICILY
Adana
Antioch
Aghlabids
Qayrawan
MALTA
Tangier
Tlemcen
CRETE
CYPRUS
Rustamids
('Abbasid vassals)
Mediterranean Sea
Damascus
Acre
Fez
Tripoli
Barqa (Cyrene)
PALESTINE
Jerusalem
Idrisids
MAGHRIB
IFRIQIYA
TRIPOLITANIA
BARQA
Alexandria
Gaza
Fustat (Cairo)
EGYPT
Nile
Aswan
NUBIA
ISLAMIC WORLD c. 1000 AD
Sunni 'Abbasid Caliphate under Shi'ite Buyid Control
Shi'ite Fatimids
Other Sunni Territories
Shi'ite Hamdanids
Capital Cities
Shi'ite Qarmathians
Black Sea
Aral Sea
Lake Balqash
QARAKHANIDS
UMAYYAD CALIPHATE
Córdoba
HAMDANIDS
SAMANIDS
Baghdad
BUYIDS
Mediterranean Sea
GHAZNAVIDS
FATIMID CALIPHATE
Cairo
QARMATHIANS
Persian Gulf
Gulf of Oman
Arabian Sea
Gulf of Aden
INDIAN OCEAN

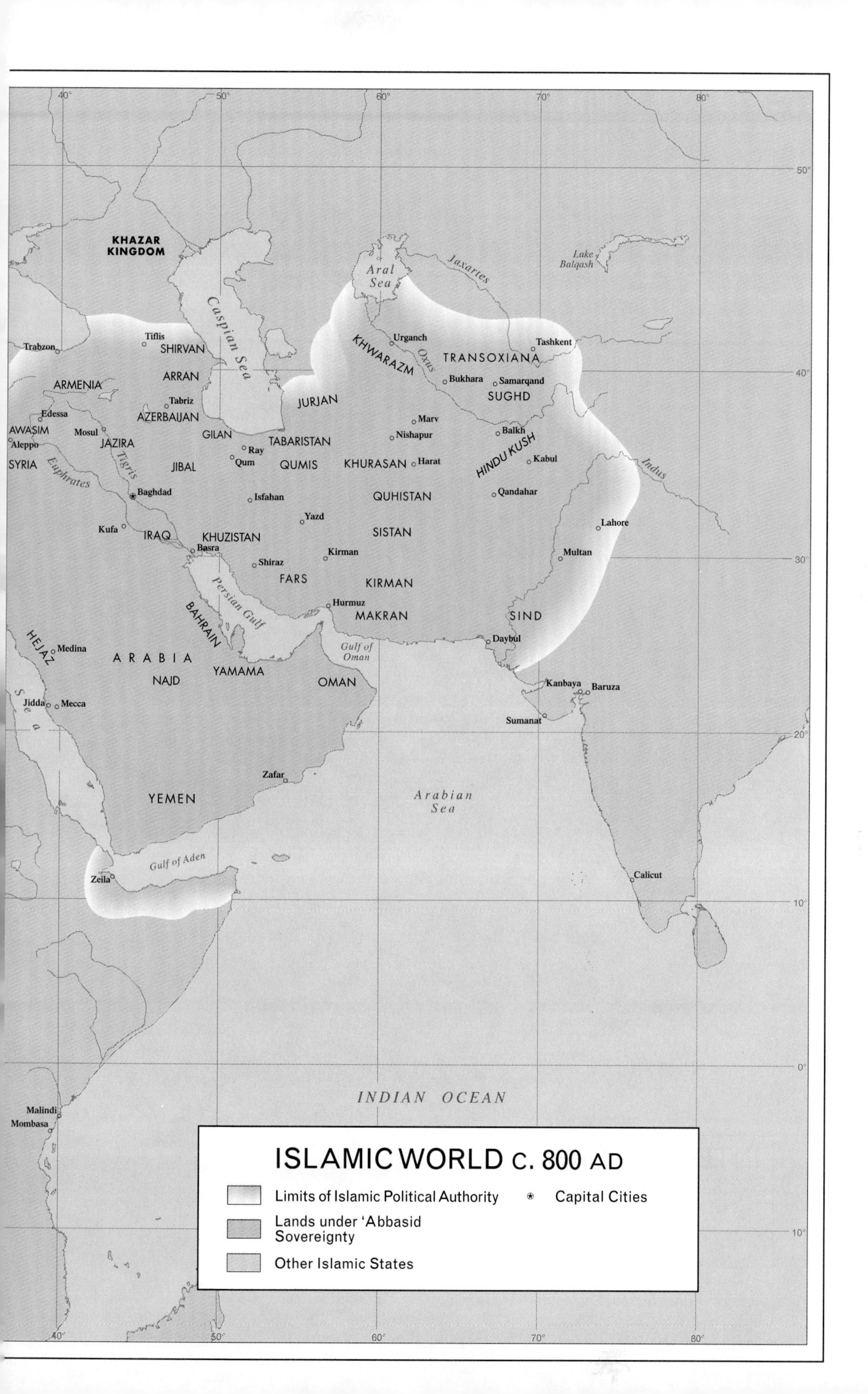

ISLAMIC WORLD C. 800 AD
Limits of Islamic Political Authority
Capital Cities
Lands under 'Abbasid Sovereignty
Other Islamic States
KHAZAR KINGDOM
Caspian Sea
Aral Sea
Jaxartes
Lake Balqash
Oxus
Indus
Tiflis
Trabzon
SHIRVAN
ARRAN
ARMENIA
Tabriz
AZERBAIJAN
Edessa
AWASIM
Aleppo
Mosul
JAZIRA
SYRIA
Euphrates
Tigris
GILAN
Ray
Qum
JIBAL
Baghdad
Kufa
IRAQ
Basra
KHUZISTAN
Isfahan
Shiraz
FARS
Persian Gulf
BAHRAIN
JURJAN
TABARISTAN
QUMIS
Urganch
KHWARAZM
TRANSOXIANA
Tashkent
Bukhara
Samarqand
SUGHD
Marv
Nishapur
KHURASAN
Harat
Balkh
HINDU KUSH
Kabul
Qandahar
QUHISTAN
Yazd
SISTAN
Kirman
KIRMAN
Hurmuz
MAKRAN
SIND
Daybul
Lahore
Multan
Gulf of Oman
HEJAZ
Medina
ARABIA
NAJD
YAMAMA
OMAN
Jidda
Mecca
Sea
Kanbaya
Baruza
Sumanat
Zafar
YEMEN
Arabian Sea
Gulf of Aden
Zeila
Calicut
INDIAN OCEAN
Malindi
Mombasa

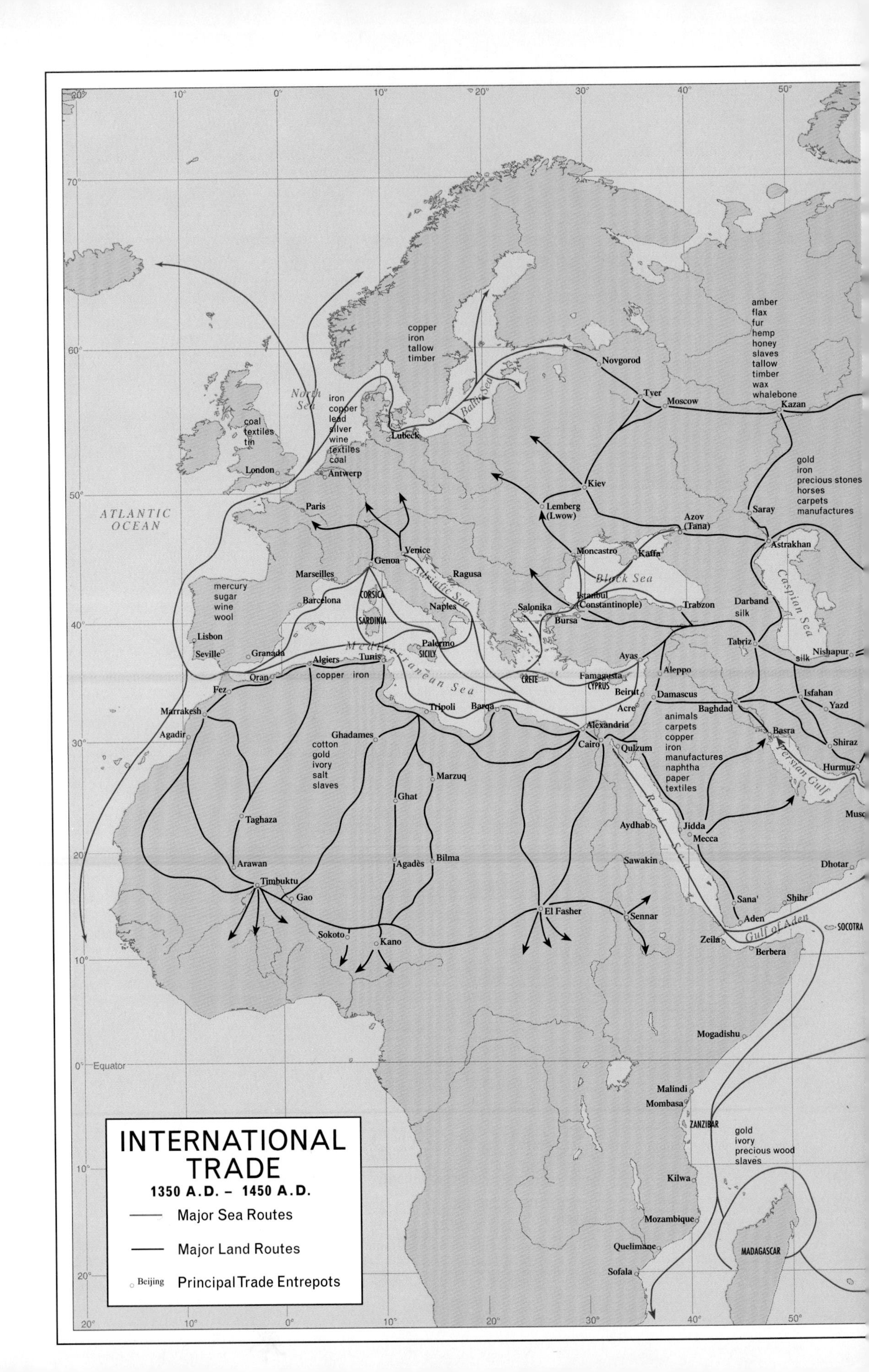
INTERNATIONAL TRADE
1350 A.D. – 1450 A.D.
Major Sea Routes
Major Land Routes
Beijing
Principal Trade Entrepots
ATLANTIC OCEAN
North Sea
Baltic Sea
Black Sea
Adriatic Sea
Mediterranean Sea
Caspian Sea
Red Sea
Persian Gulf
Gulf of Aden
Equator
coal
textiles
tin
iron
copper
lead
silver
wine
textiles
coal
copper
iron
tallow
timber
amber
flax
fur
hemp
honey
slaves
tallow
timber
wax
whalebone
gold
iron
precious stones
horses
carpets
manufactures
mercury
sugar
wine
wool
copper iron
cotton
gold
ivory
salt
slaves
animals
carpets
copper
iron
manufactures
naphtha
paper
textiles
silk
gold
ivory
precious wood
slaves
London
Antwerp
Lubeck
Paris
Novgorod
Tver
Moscow
Kazan
Kiev
Lemberg (Lwow)
Saray
Azov (Tana)
Astrakhan
Moncastro
Kaffa
Venice
Genoa
Marseilles
Ragusa
Barcelona
CORSICA
SARDINIA
Naples
Salonika
Istanbul (Constantinople)
Bursa
Trabzon
Darband
Tabriz
Nishapur
Lisbon
Seville
Granada
Palermo
SICILY
Algiers
Tunis
Oran
Fez
Marrakesh
Agadir
CRETE
Famagusta
CYPRUS
Ayas
Aleppo
Beirut
Damascus
Acre
Baghdad
Isfahan
Yazd
Tripoli
Barqa
Alexandria
Cairo
Qulzum
Basra
Shiraz
Hurmuz
Ghadames
Marzuq
Ghat
Taghaza
Arawan
Agadès
Bilma
Timbuktu
Gao
Sokoto
Kano
El Fasher
Sennar
Aydhab
Jidda
Mecca
Sawakin
Dhotar
Sana'
Shihr
Aden
SOCOTRA
Zeila
Berbera
Mogadishu
Malindi
Mombasa
ZANZIBAR
Kilwa
Mozambique
Quelimane
Sofala
MADAGASCAR

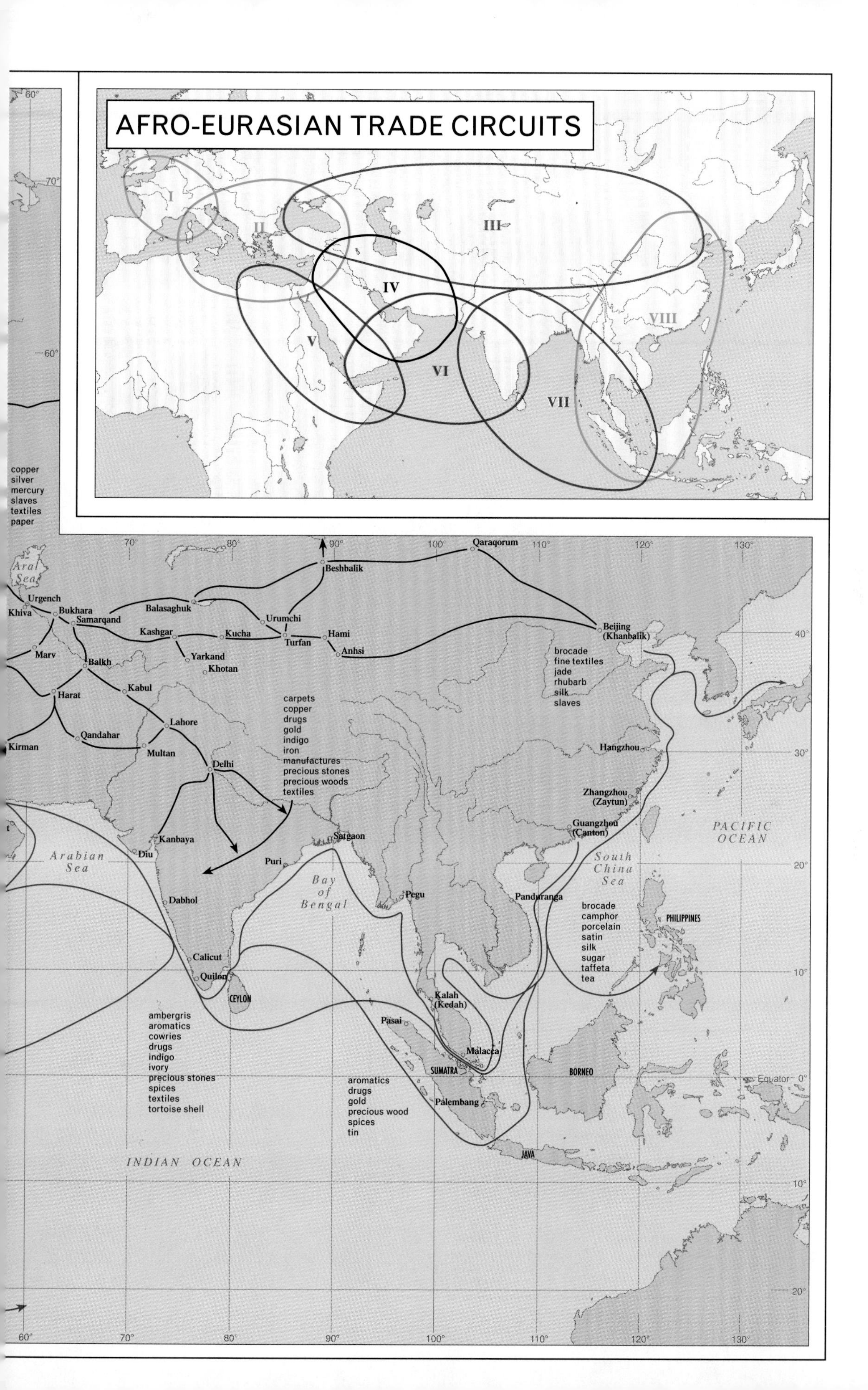

AFRO-EURASIAN TRADE CIRCUITS
I
II
III
IV
V
VI
VII
VIII
copper
silver
mercury
slaves
textiles
paper
Aral Sea
Urgench
Khiva
Bukhara
Samarqand
Marv
Balkh
Harat
Kirman
Qandahar
Kabul
Balasaghuk
Kashgar
Yarkand
Khotan
Kucha
Beshbalik
Urumchi
Turfan
Hami
Anhsi
Qaraqorum
Beijing (Khanbalik)
brocade
fine textiles
jade
rhubarb
silk
slaves
Lahore
Multan
Delhi
carpets
copper
drugs
gold
indigo
iron
manufactures
precious stones
precious woods
textiles
Kanbaya
Diu
Arabian Sea
Puri
Satgaon
Bay of Bengal
Dabhol
Calicut
Quilon
CEYLON
Pegu
Hangzhou
Zhangzhou (Zaytun)
Guangzhou (Canton)
PACIFIC OCEAN
South China Sea
Panduranga
PHILIPPINES
brocade
camphor
porcelain
satin
silk
sugar
taffeta
tea
Kalah (Kedah)
Pasai
Malacca
SUMATRA
BORNEO
Palembang
JAVA
ambergris
aromatics
cowries
drugs
indigo
ivory
precious stones
spices
textiles
tortoise shell
aromatics
drugs
gold
precious wood
spices
tin
INDIAN OCEAN
Equator

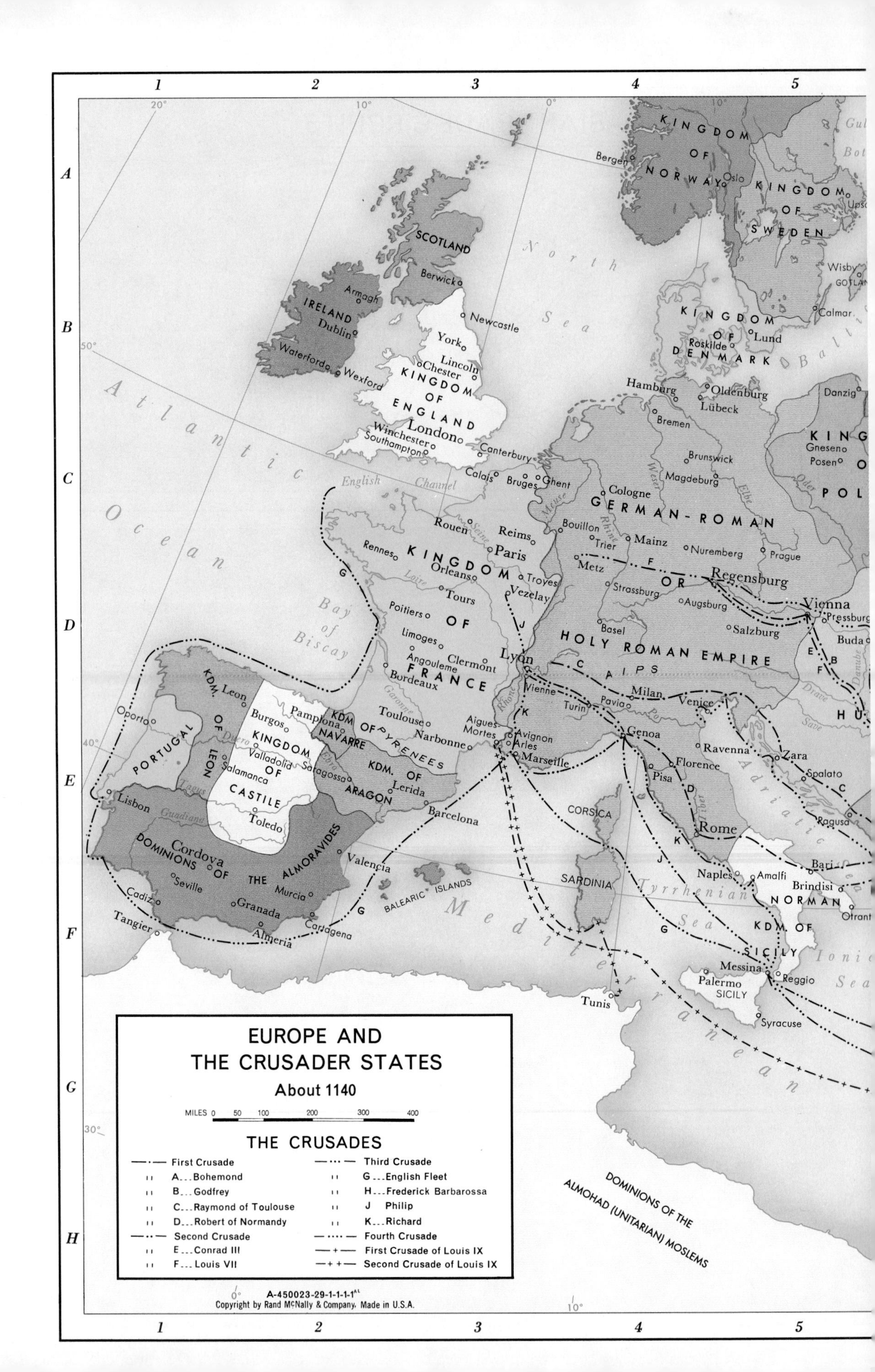
EUROPE AND
THE CRUSADER STATES
About 1140
MILES 0 50 100 200 300 400
THE CRUSADES
First Crusade
A...Bohemond
B...Godfrey
C...Raymond of Toulouse
D...Robert of Normandy
Second Crusade
E...Conrad III
F...Louis VII
Third Crusade
G...English Fleet
H...Frederick Barbarossa
J Philip
K...Richard
Fourth Crusade
First Crusade of Louis IX
Second Crusade of Louis IX
A-450023-29-1-1-1-1
Copyright by Rand McNally & Company. Made in U.S.A.
KINGDOM OF NORWAY
KINGDOM OF SWEDEN
KINGDOM OF DENMARK
SCOTLAND
IRELAND
KINGDOM OF ENGLAND
KINGDOM OF FRANCE
GERMAN-ROMAN OR HOLY ROMAN EMPIRE
KDM. OF LEON
PORTUGAL
KINGDOM OF CASTILE
KDM. OF NAVARRE
KDM. OF ARAGON
PYRENEES
DOMINIONS OF THE ALMORAVIDES
NORMAN KDM. OF SICILY
DOMINIONS OF THE ALMOHAD (UNITARIAN) MOSLEMS
Atlantic Ocean
North Sea
English Channel
Bay of Biscay
Mediterranean
Tyrrhenian Sea
Adriatic
Ionian Sea
ALPS
CORSICA
SARDINIA
SICILY
BALEARIC ISLANDS
Bergen
Oslo
Wisby
Calmar
Lund
Roskilde
Hamburg
Oldenburg
Lübeck
Bremen
Danzig
Gneseno
Posen
Brunswick
Magdeburg
Cologne
Bouillon
Trier
Mainz
Nuremberg
Prague
Metz
Regensburg
Strassburg
Augsburg
Vienna
Pressburg
Basel
Salzburg
Buda
Berwick
Armagh
Dublin
Waterford
Wexford
Newcastle
York
Lincoln
Chester
London
Winchester
Southampton
Canterbury
Calais
Bruges
Ghent
Rouen
Reims
Paris
Rennes
Orleans
Troyes
Vezelay
Tours
Poitiers
Limoges
Clermont
Angouleme
Bordeaux
Lyon
Vienne
Turin
Pavia
Milan
Venice
Genoa
Toulouse
Narbonne
Aigues Mortes
Avignon
Arles
Marseille
Ravenna
Florence
Pisa
Zara
Spalato
Ragusa
Rome
Naples
Amalfi
Bari
Brindisi
Otranto
Messina
Reggio
Palermo
Syracuse
Tunis
Leon
Oporto
Burgos
Pamplona
Valladolid
Saragossa
Salamanca
Lerida
Barcelona
Lisbon
Toledo
Valencia
Cordova
Seville
Murcia
Cadiz
Granada
Cartagena
Almeria
Tangier

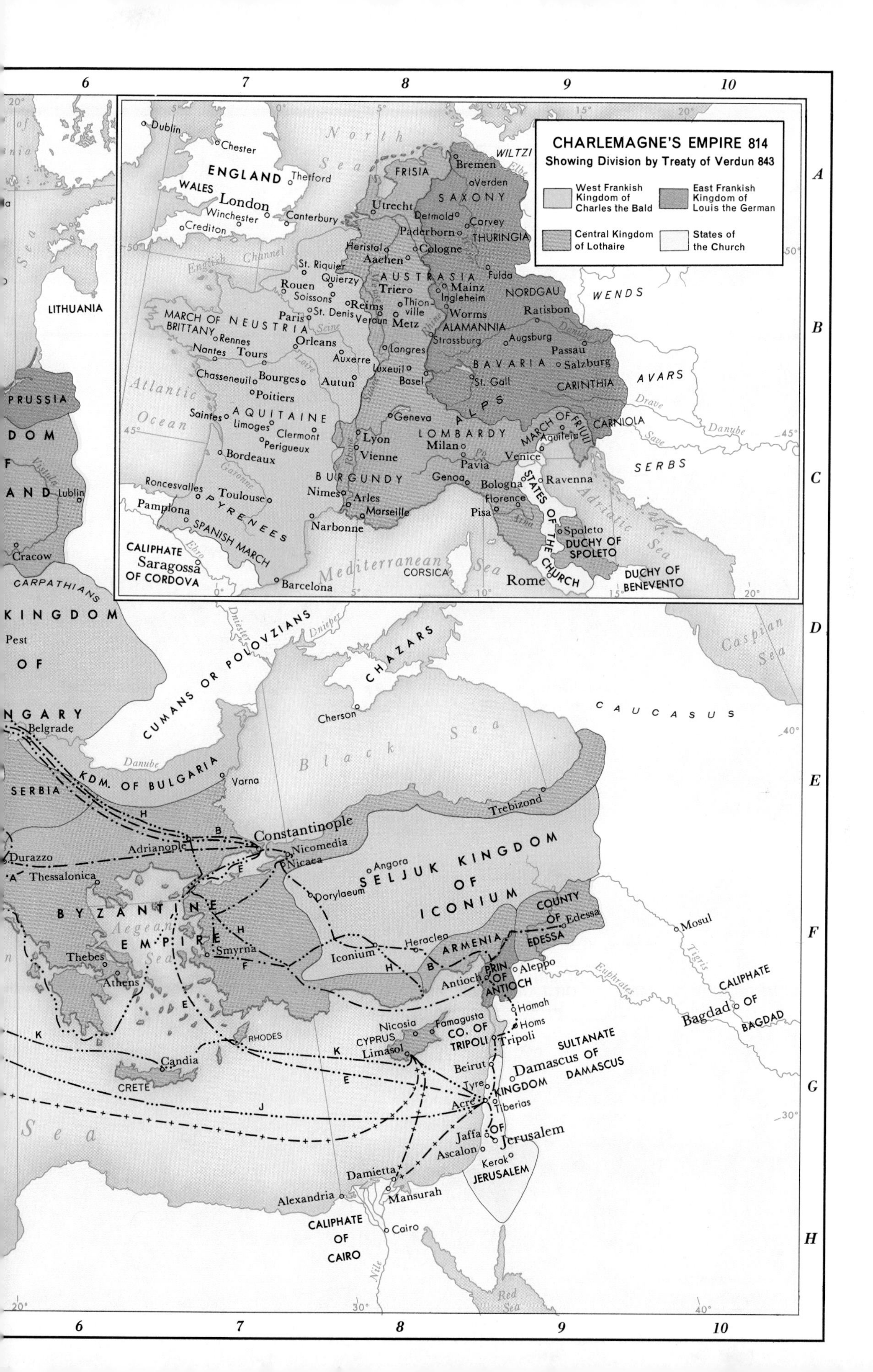

CHARLEMAGNE'S EMPIRE 814
Showing Division by Treaty of Verdun 843
West Frankish Kingdom of Charles the Bald
East Frankish Kingdom of Louis the German
Central Kingdom of Lothaire
States of the Church
6
7
8
9
10
A
B
C
D
E
F
G
H
Dublin
Chester
ENGLAND
Thetford
WALES
London
Winchester
Canterbury
Crediton
North Sea
English Channel
FRISIA
Bremen
Verden
WILTZI
Elbe
SAXONY
Utrecht
Detmold
Corvey
Paderborn
THURINGIA
Heristal
Cologne
Aachen
St. Riquier
Quierzy
AUSTRASIA
Fulda
Rouen
Soissons
Trier
Mainz
Ingleheim
NORDGAU
WENDS
Reims
Thionville
Worms
Ratisbon
St. Denis
Paris
Verdun
Metz
MARCH OF BRITTANY
NEUSTRIA
Seine
ALAMANNIA
Danube
Rennes
Orleans
Strassburg
Augsburg
Nantes
Tours
Langres
Passau
Auxerre
BAVARIA
Salzburg
Loire
Luxeuil
Chasseneuil
Bourges
Autun
Basel
St. Gall
AVARS
Atlantic Ocean
Poitiers
CARINTHIA
Drave
ALPS
Saintes
AQUITAINE
Geneva
Limoges
Clermont
Lyon
LOMBARDY
MARCH OF FRIULI
CARNIOLA
Perigueux
Milan
Aquileia
Danube
Save
Bordeaux
Vienne
Po
Venice
Pavia
SERBS
Garonne
Rhone
BURGUNDY
Genoa
Bologna
Ravenna
Roncesvalles
Toulouse
Nimes
Arles
Florence
STATES OF THE CHURCH
Pamplona
PYRENEES
Marseille
Pisa
Arno
Adriatic Sea
SPANISH MARCH
Narbonne
Spoleto
DUCHY OF SPOLETO
Ebro
CALIPHATE OF CORDOVA
Saragossa
Mediterranean Sea
CORSICA
Rome
DUCHY OF BENEVENTO
Barcelona
LITHUANIA
PRUSSIA
Vistula
Lublin
Cracow
CARPATHIANS
KINGDOM OF HUNGARY
Pest
Dniester
Dnieper
CUMANS OR POLOVZIANS
CHAZARS
Caspian Sea
CAUCASUS
Cherson
Black Sea
Belgrade
Danube
KDM. OF BULGARIA
Varna
SERBIA
Trebizond
Constantinople
Adrianople
Nicomedia
Durazzo
Nicaea
Thessalonica
Angora
SELJUK KINGDOM OF ICONIUM
Dorylaeum
BYZANTINE EMPIRE
Aegean Sea
COUNTY OF EDESSA
Edessa
Mosul
Smyrna
Heraclea
ARMENIA
Iconium
Tigris
Thebes
Athens
Antioch
PRIN. OF ANTIOCH
Aleppo
Euphrates
CALIPHATE OF BAGDAD
Bagdad
Hamah
Homs
RHODES
Nicosia
Famagusta
CYPRUS
CO. OF TRIPOLI
Tripoli
Limasol
SULTANATE OF DAMASCUS
Candia
Beirut
Damascus
CRETE
Tyre
KINGDOM OF JERUSALEM
Acre
Tiberias
Jaffa
Jerusalem
Ascalon
Kerak
Damietta
Mansurah
Alexandria
CALIPHATE OF CAIRO
Cairo
Nile
Red Sea
Sea

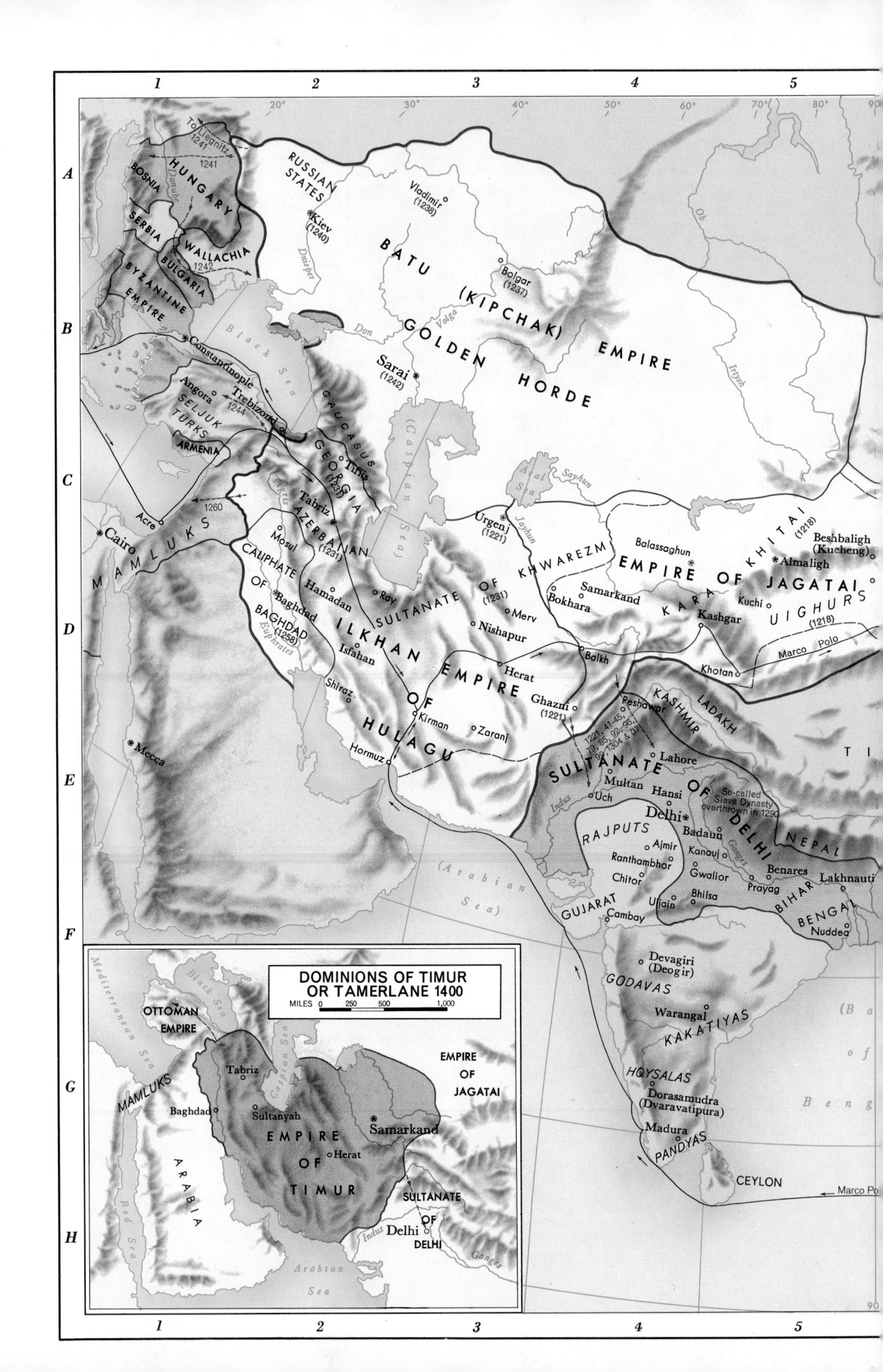

DOMINIONS OF TIMUR OR TAMERLANE 1400
MILES 0 250 500 1,000
HUNGARY
BOSNIA
SERBIA
WALLACHIA
BULGARIA
BYZANTINE EMPIRE
RUSSIAN STATES
Kiev (1240)
Vladimir (1238)
Bolgar (1237)
BATU (KIPCHAK) EMPIRE
GOLDEN HORDE
Sarai (1242)
Constantinople
Angora
Trebizond
SELJUK TURKS
ARMENIA
CAUCASUS
GEORGIA
Tiflis
Tabriz
AZERBAIJAN
Acre
Cairo
MAMLUKS
CALIPHATE OF BAGHDAD (1258)
Mosul
Baghdad
Hamadan
Ray
Isfahan
Shiraz
ILKHAN EMPIRE OF HULAGU
SULTANATE OF KHWAREZM (1231)
Urgenj (1221)
Merv
Nishapur
Herat
Bokhara
Samarkand
Balassaghun
Balkh
Ghazni (1221)
Kirman
Zaranj
Hormuz
Mecca
EMPIRE OF JAGATAI
KARA KHITAI (1218)
Beshbaligh (Kucheng)
Almaligh
Kuchi
Kashgar
UIGHURS (1218)
Khotan
Marco Polo
KASHMIR
LADAKH
Peshawar
Lahore
SULTANATE OF DELHI
Multan
Hansi
Uch
Delhi
So-called Slave Dynasty overthrown in 1290
RAJPUTS
Ajmir
Ranthambhor
Chitor
Badaun
Kanauj
Gwalior
Ujjain
Bhilsa
Benares
Prayag
Lakhnauti
BIHAR
BENGAL
Nuddea
NEPAL
GUJARAT
Cambay
Devagiri (Deogir)
GODAVAS
Warangal
KAKATIYAS
HOYSALAS
Dorasamudra (Dvaravatipura)
Madura
PANDYAS
CEYLON
Arabian Sea
Caspian Sea
Black Sea
Aral Sea
OTTOMAN EMPIRE
MAMLUKS
ARABIA
Tabriz
Sultanyah
Baghdad
EMPIRE OF TIMUR
Herat
Samarkand
EMPIRE OF JAGATAI
SULTANATE OF DELHI
Delhi

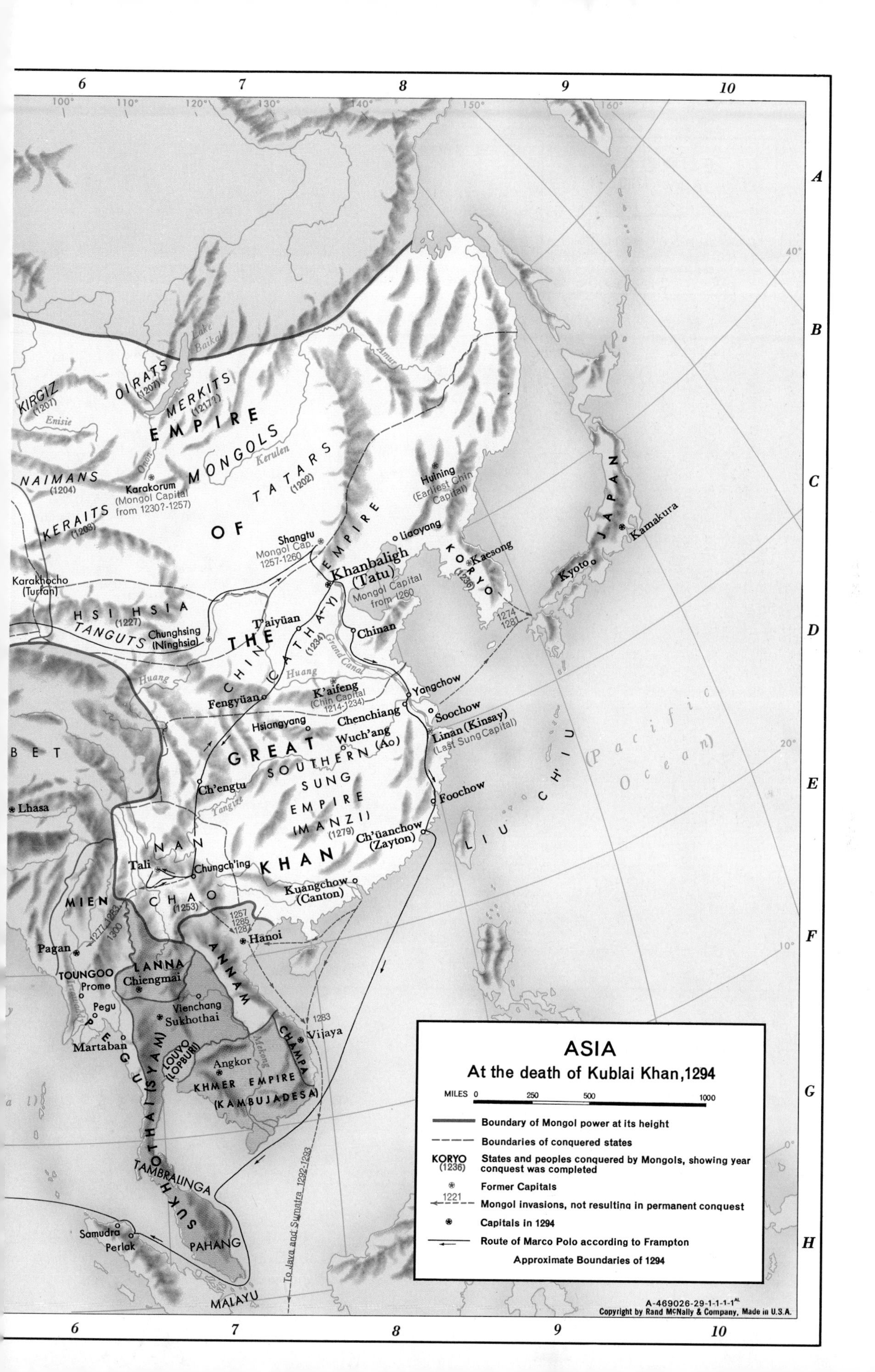
ASIA
At the death of Kublai Khan, 1294
MILES 0 250 500 1000
Boundary of Mongol power at its height
Boundaries of conquered states
KORYO (1236) States and peoples conquered by Mongols, showing year conquest was completed
Former Capitals
1221 Mongol invasions, not resulting in permanent conquest
Capitals in 1294
Route of Marco Polo according to Frampton
Approximate Boundaries of 1294
A-469026-29-1-1-1-1
Copyright by Rand McNally & Company, Made in U.S.A.
6
7
8
9
10
A
B
C
D
E
F
G
H
EMPIRE OF THE GREAT KHAN
MONGOLS
TATARS (1202)
KIRGIZ (1207)
OIRATS (1207)
MERKITS (1217?)
NAIMANS (1204)
KERAITS (1203)
Karakorum (Mongol Capital from 1230?-1257)
Shangtu Mongol Cap. 1257-1260
Khanbaligh (Tatu) Mongol Capital from 1260
Karakhocho (Turfan)
HSI HSIA (1227)
TANGUTS
Chunghsing (Ninghsia)
CHIN (CATHAY) (1234)
T'aiyüan
Chinan
Liaoyang
Huining (Earliest Chin Capital)
KORYO (1236)
Kaesong
JAPAN
Kyoto
Kamakura
1274 1281
K'aifeng (Chin Capital 1214-1234)
Fengyüan
Hsiangyang
Chenchiang
Wuch'ang
Yangchow
Soochow
Linan (Kinsay) (Last Sung Capital)
SOUTHERN SUNG EMPIRE (MANZI) (1279)
Ch'engtu
Foochow
Ch'üanchow (Zayton)
Kuangchow (Canton)
Chungch'ing
NAN CHAO (1253)
Tali
LIU CH'IU
Pacific Ocean
Lhasa
BET
MIEN
1277, 1283, 1300
Pagan
1257 1285 1287
Hanoi
ANNAM
LANNA
Chiengmai
TOUNGOO
Prome
Pegu
PEGU
Martaban
Vienchang
Sukhothai
1283
Vijaya
CHAMPA
LOUVO (LOPBURI)
Angkor
KHMER EMPIRE (KAMBUJADESA)
SUKHOTHAI (SYAM)
TAMBRALINGA
PAHANG
Samudra
Perlak
MALAYU
To Java and Sumatra 1292-1293
Lake Baikal
Enisie
Onon
Kerulen
Amur
Huang
Grand Canal
Yangtze
Mekong
Irawadi

EUROPE
About 1360
MILES 0 50 100 200 300
Boundary of Holy Roman Empire
Boundary of France
FAEROES
NORWAY
SHETLAND ISLANDS
ORKNEY ISLANDS
HEBRIDES
Bergen
Oslo
Upsala
SCOTLAND
Aberdeen
Bannockburn
Edinburgh
Falkirk
Berwick
Armagh
IRELAND
Dublin
Carlisle
North Sea
DENMARK
Copenhagen
Calmar
York
Lincoln
Chester
Wexford
Cork
WALES
ENGLAND
Norwich
Lubeck
Stralsund
POMERANIA
Hamburg
Bremen
Atlantic Ocean
London
Thames
HOLLAND
Bruges
Magdeburg
BRANDENBURG
Gnesen
Posen
English Channel
Agincourt
Calais
BRABANT
Ghent
Rhine
Elbe
SILESIA
Oder
Harfleur
Crecy
HAINAUT
Cologne
HOLY ROMAN EMPIRE
Rouen
Caen
Trier
Frankfurt
Mainz
Prague
BRITTANY
Rennes
Paris
Seine
Reims
Compiegne
Bretigny
Vaucouleurs
LUXEMBURG
PALATINATE
BOHEMIA
MORAVIA
FRANCE
Regensburg
Nantes
Loire
Orleans
Troyes
Domremy
LORRAINE
Strassburg
BAVARIA
Munich
Danube
Chinon
Poitiers
Dijon
BURGUNDY
Basel
Besançon
SWISS CONFED.
Constance
Vienna
Salzburg
Bay of Biscay
Limoges
AUSTRIA
Buda
Bordeaux
AQUITAINE
Lyon
SAVOY
LANDS OF THE VISCONTI
Milan
Turin
Garonne
Rhone
DAUPHINY
Trieste
Drave
Santiago
Bayonne
Toulouse
Ferrara
Venice
Save
Leon
Ebro
Pau
NAVARRE
Avignon
Po
Genoa
REPUBLIC OF VENICE
BOSNIA
PORTUGAL
Duero
Narbonne
PROVENCE
Marseille
Bologna
Florence
Salamanca
Saragossa
PAPAL STATES
Adriatic Sea
Tagus
Toledo
CASTILE
ARAGON
Barcelona
CORSICA
(To Genoa)
Ragusa
Lisbon
Guadiana
Rome
KINGDOM OF NAPLES
Valencia
BALEARIC ISLANDS
(To Aragon)
SARDINIA
(To Aragon)
Naples
Seville
Cordova
Guadalquivir
Taranto
Cadiz
Granada
GRANADA
Mediterranean
Gibraltar
Palermo
Messina
KINGDOM OF SICILY
Reggio
MOSLEM STATES
Algiers
MARINIDS
Tunis
ZIANIDS
HAFSIDS
MALTA
A-450028-29-1-1-1-1

RUSSIAN STATES
PRINCIPALITY OF MOSCOW
White Sea
N. Dvina
Kama
Lake Ladoga
EDEN
Abo
Stockholm
Novgorod
Yaroslavl
Vladimir
Moscow
Kazan
Bulgar
Volga
Wisby
Riga
KNIGHTS
Duna
Vitebsk
Smolensk
Tula
Königsberg
Vilna
Minsk
Orel
Danzig
TEUTONIC
Niemen
Don
Bielystok
Vistula
Warsaw
Pinsk
LITHUANIA
POLAND
KHANATE OF THE GOLDEN HORDE
Sarai
Lublin
Kiev
Dnieper
Cracow
UKRAINE
Astrakhan
Bug
Dniester
Azov
(To Genoa)
Kremnitz
Caspian Sea
Eger
Thiess
Jassy
MOLDAVIA
Pest
Prut
KUBAN
HUNGARY
Arad
Cherson
Belgrade
WALLACHIA
Black Sea
Tiflis
GEORGIA
Bucharest
Vidin
Danube
Nicopolis
Varna
Nissa
Sinope
Trebizond
BULGARIA
EMP. OF TREBIZOND
SERBIAN PRINCES
Sofia
Adrianople
DOMINIONS OF MOHAMMED ARTIN
BYZANTINE EMPIRE
Constantinople
Durazzo
Nicaea
Tabriz
PRIN. OF ALBANIA
Thessalonica
OTTOMAN TURKS
KARA-KUYUNLI
Tigris
Aegean Sea
SELJUK TURKS
Smyrna
ARMENIA
TURKOMENS
Mosul
DUCHY OF ATHENS
Athens
CHIOS
Tarsus
ACHAEA
KNIGHTS OF RHODES
Antioch
Euphrates
RHODES
KINGDOM OF CYPRUS
Nicosia
Tripoli
Damascus
ARABIA
CRETE
(To Venice)

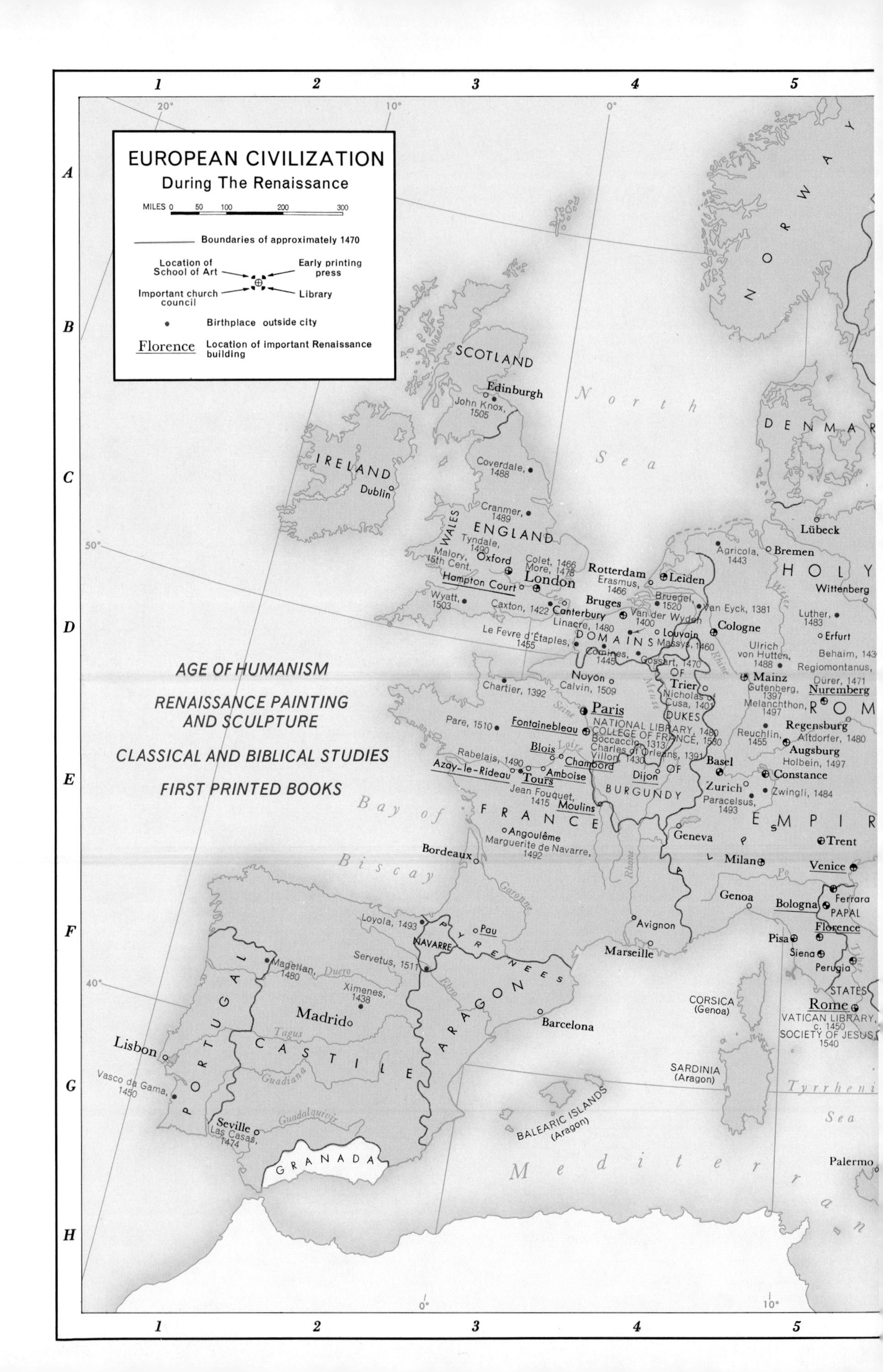
EUROPEAN CIVILIZATION
During The Renaissance
MILES 0 50 100 200 300
Boundaries of approximately 1470
Location of School of Art
Early printing press
Important church council
Library
Birthplace outside city
Florence Location of important Renaissance building
AGE OF HUMANISM
RENAISSANCE PAINTING AND SCULPTURE
CLASSICAL AND BIBLICAL STUDIES
FIRST PRINTED BOOKS
SCOTLAND
Edinburgh
John Knox, 1505
IRELAND
Dublin
Coverdale, 1488
Cranmer, 1489
WALES
ENGLAND
Tyndale, 1490
Malory, 15th Cent.
Oxford
Colet, 1466
More, 1478
London
Hampton Court
Wyatt, 1503
Caxton, 1422
Canterbury
Linacre, 1480
Le Fevre d'Étaples, 1455
North Sea
NORWAY
DENMARK
Lübeck
Agricola, 1443
Bremen
Rotterdam
Erasmus, 1466
Leiden
Bruegel, 1520
Van Eyck, 1381
Bruges
Van der Wyden 1400
Louvain
Massys, 1460
Cologne
DOMAINS
Comines, 1445
Gossart, 1470
OF
Trier
Nicholas of Cusa, 1401
DUKES
OF
BURGUNDY
Noyon
Calvin, 1509
Chartier, 1392
Paris
NATIONAL LIBRARY, 1480
COLLEGE OF FRANCE, 1530
Boccaccio, 1313
Charles of Orleans, 1391
Villon, 1430
Pare, 1510
Fontainebleau
Blois
Chambord
Rabelais, 1490
Amboise
Azay-le-Rideau
Tours
Jean Fouquet, 1415
Moulins
Dijon
FRANCE
Angoulême
Marguerite de Navarre, 1492
Bordeaux
Bay of Biscay
Seine
Loire
Meuse
Rhine
Rhone
Garonne
HOLY ROMAN EMPIRE
Wittenberg
Luther, 1483
Erfurt
Ulrich von Hutten, 1488
Behaim, 143
Regiomontanus,
Mainz
Gutenberg, 1397
Dürer, 1471
Nuremberg
Melanchthon, 1497
Reuchlin, 1455
Regensburg
Altdorfer, 1480
Augsburg
Holbein, 1497
Basel
Constance
Zurich
Zwingli, 1484
Paracelsus, 1493
Geneva
ALPS
Trent
Milan
Venice
Po
Genoa
Bologna
Ferrara
PAPAL STATES
Florence
Pisa
Siena
Perugia
Rome
VATICAN LIBRARY, c. 1450
SOCIETY OF JESUS, 1540
Avignon
Marseille
CORSICA (Genoa)
SARDINIA (Aragon)
Tyrrhenian Sea
Palermo
Mediterranean
Loyola, 1493
Pau
NAVARRE
PYRENEES
Servetus, 1511
Magellan, 1480
Ximenes, 1438
Ducro
Ebro
Madrid
ARAGON
Barcelona
PORTUGAL
Lisbon
CASTILE
Tagus
Guadiana
Guadalquivir
Vasco da Gama, 1450
Seville
Las Casas, 1474
GRANADA
BALEARIC ISLANDS (Aragon)
20°
10°
0°
50°
40°
1 2 3 4 5
A B C D E F G H

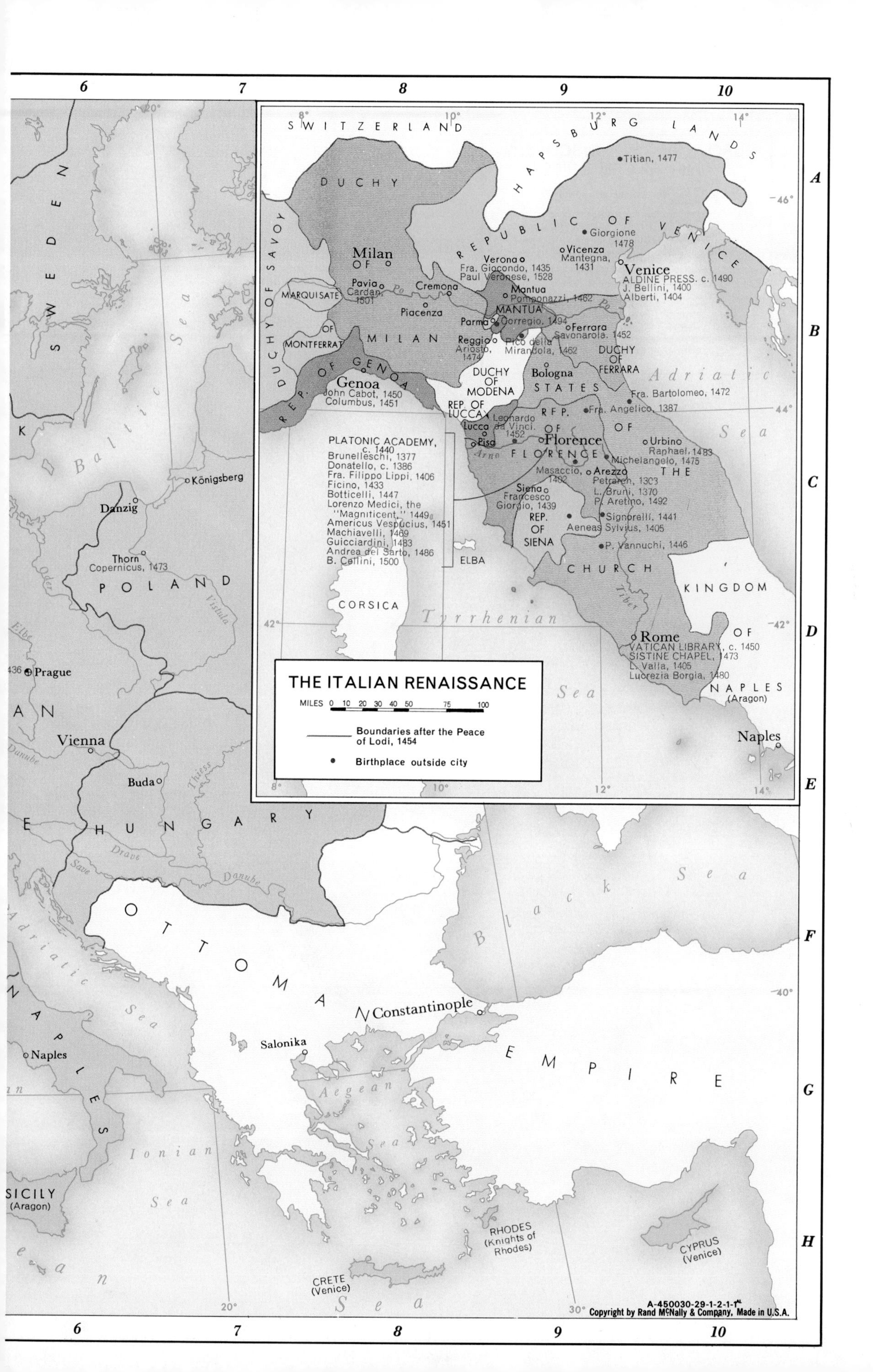

THE ITALIAN RENAISSANCE
MILES 0 10 20 30 40 50 75 100
Boundaries after the Peace of Lodi, 1454
Birthplace outside city
SWITZERLAND
HAPSBURG LANDS
Titian, 1477
DUCHY OF MILAN
Milan
Pavia
Cardan, 1501
Cremona
Piacenza
MARQUISATE OF MONTFERRAT
DUCHY OF SAVOY
REP. OF GENOA
Genoa
John Cabot, 1450
Columbus, 1451
REPUBLIC OF VENICE
Giorgione 1478
Vicenza
Mantegna, 1431
Verona
Fra. Giocondo, 1435
Paul Veronese, 1528
Venice
ALDINE PRESS. c. 1490
J. Bellini, 1400
Alberti, 1404
Mantua
Pomponazzi, 1462
MANTUA
Parma
Correggio, 1494
Reggio
Ariosto, 1474
Pico della Mirandola, 1462
Ferrara
Savonarola, 1452
DUCHY OF FERRARA
DUCHY OF MODENA
Bologna
REP. OF LUCCA
Lucca
Pisa
Leonardo da Vinci, 1452
REP. OF FLORENCE
Florence
Arno
Fra. Bartolomeo, 1472
Fra. Angelico, 1387
PLATONIC ACADEMY, c. 1440
Brunelleschi, 1377
Donatello, c. 1386
Fra. Filippo Lippi, 1406
Ficino, 1433
Botticelli, 1447
Lorenzo Medici, the "Magnificent," 1449
Americus Vespucius, 1451
Machiavelli, 1469
Guicciardini, 1483
Andrea del Sarto, 1486
B. Cellini, 1500
Urbino
Raphael, 1483
Michelangelo, 1475
Masaccio, 1402
Arezzo
Petrarch, 1303
L. Bruni, 1370
P. Aretino, 1492
Siena
Francesco Giorgio, 1439
REP. OF SIENA
Signorelli, 1441
Aeneas Sylvius, 1405
P. Vannuchi, 1446
STATES OF THE CHURCH
ELBA
CORSICA
Tyrrhenian Sea
Tiber
Adriatic Sea
KINGDOM OF NAPLES (Aragon)
Rome
VATICAN LIBRARY, c. 1450
SISTINE CHAPEL, 1473
L. Valla, 1405
Lucrezia Borgia, 1480
Naples
SWEDEN
Baltic Sea
Königsberg
Danzig
Thorn
Copernicus, 1473
POLAND
Oder
Vistula
Elbe
Prague
Vienna
Danube
Buda
Theiss
HUNGARY
Drave
Save
OTTOMAN EMPIRE
Constantinople
Salonika
Black Sea
Adriatic Sea
NAPLES
Naples
Aegean Sea
Ionian Sea
SICILY (Aragon)
RHODES (Knights of Rhodes)
CRETE (Venice)
CYPRUS (Venice)
A-450030-29-1-2-1-1
Copyright by Rand McNally & Company, Made in U.S.A.

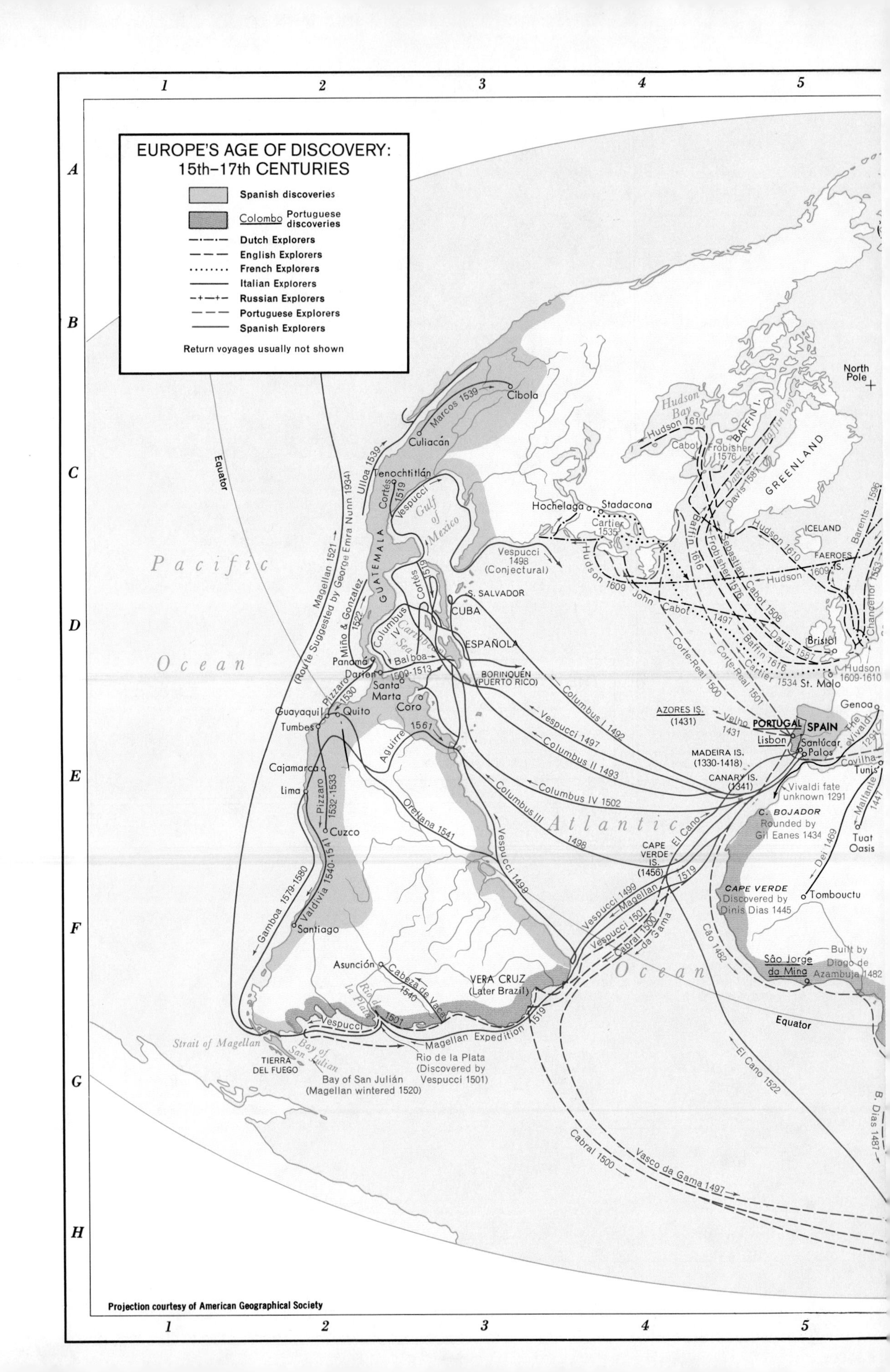

EUROPE'S AGE OF DISCOVERY:
15th–17th CENTURIES
Spanish discoveries
Colombo Portuguese discoveries
Dutch Explorers
English Explorers
French Explorers
Italian Explorers
Russian Explorers
Portuguese Explorers
Spanish Explorers
Return voyages usually not shown
Pacific
Ocean
Equator
Atlantic
Ocean
Magellan 1521
(Route Suggested by George Emra Nunn 1934)
Ulloa 1539
Marcos 1539
Cibola
Culiacán
Tenochtitlán
Cortés 1519
Vespucci
Gulf of Mexico
GUATEMALA
Miño & Gonzalez 1522
Columbus IV
Caribbean Sea
Panamá
Darien
Balboa
1509-1513
Santa Marta
Coro
Pizzaro 1530
Guayaquil
Quito
Tumbes
Cajamarca
Lima
Pizzaro 1532-1533
Cuzco
Aguirre 1561
Orellana 1541
Valdivia 1540-1541
Gamboa 1579-1580
Santiago
Asunción
Cabeza de Vaca 1540
Rio de la Plata
Vespucci
1501
Magellan Expedition
1519
Strait of Magellan
TIERRA DEL FUEGO
Bay of San Julián
Bay of San Julián (Magellan wintered 1520)
Rio de la Plata (Discovered by Vespucci 1501)
VERA CRUZ (Later Brazil)
Vespucci 1499
S. SALVADOR
CUBA
ESPAÑOLA
BORINQUÉN (PUERTO RICO)
Columbus I 1492
Vespucci 1497
Columbus II 1493
Columbus IV 1502
Columbus III 1498
Vespucci 1498 (Conjectural)
Hochelaga
Stadacona
Cartier 1535
Hudson 1609
John Cabot 1497
Hudson Bay
Hudson 1610
Cabot
Frobisher 1576
BAFFIN I.
Baffin Bay
Davis Str.
Davis 1587
GREENLAND
Baffin 1616
Frobisher 1578
Sebastian Cabot 1508
Corte-Real 1500
Corte-Real 1501
Cartier 1534
St. Malo
Davis 1587
Baffin 1616
Bristol
Hudson 1609-1610
Hudson 1610
ICELAND
FAEROES IS.
Hudson 1609
Barents 1596
Chancellor 1553
North Pole
AZORES IS. (1431)
Velho 1431
PORTUGAL
Lisbon
SPAIN
Sanlúcar
Palos
Genoa
The Vivaldi 1291
Covilha
Tunis
MADEIRA IS. (1330-1418)
CANARY IS. (1341)
Vivaldi fate unknown 1291
C. BOJADOR Rounded by Gil Eanes 1434
Malfante 1447
Tuat Oasis
Dei 1469
Tombouctu
El Cano
CAPE VERDE IS. (1456)
1519
CAPE VERDE Discovered by Dinis Dias 1445
Vespucci 1499
Magellan
Vespucci 1501
Cabral 1500
da Gama
Cão 1482
São Jorge da Mina
Built by Diogo de Azambuja 1482
El Cano 1522
B. Dias 1487
Cabral 1500
Vasco da Gama 1497
Projection courtesy of American Geographical Society

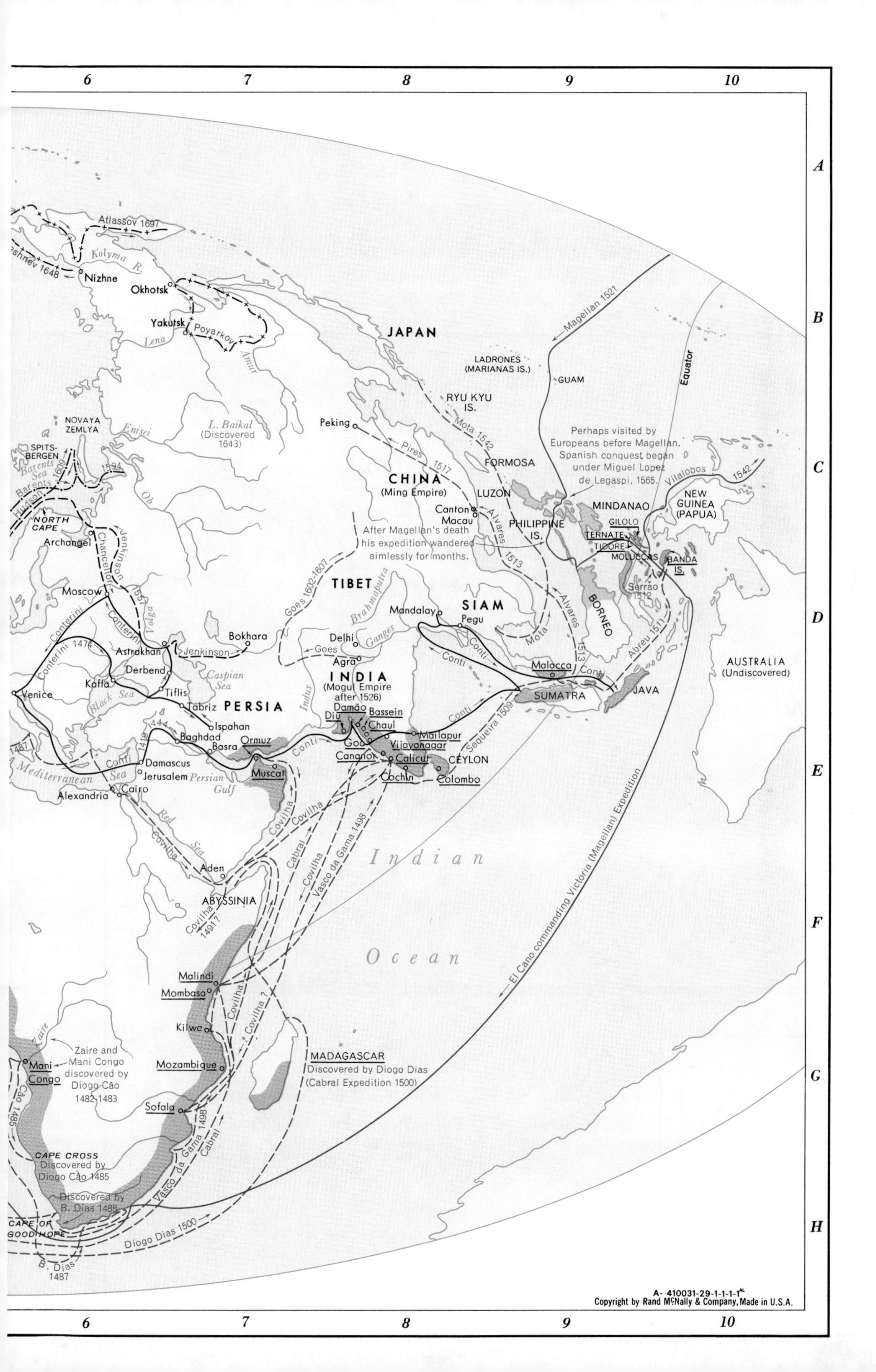
6
7
8
9
10
A
B
C
D
E
F
G
H
Atlassov 1697
Kolyma R.
Nizhne
Okhotsk
Yakutsk
Poyarkov
Lena
Amur
JAPAN
Magellan 1521
LADRONES
(MARIANAS IS.)
GUAM
Equator
RYU KYU
IS.
NOVAYA
ZEMLYA
Enisei
L. Baikal
(Discovered
1643)
Peking
Mota 1542
Pires
1517
FORMOSA
Perhaps visited by
Europeans before Magellan.
Spanish conquest began
under Miguel Lopez
de Legaspi, 1565.
Villalobos
1542
SPITS-
BERGEN
Barents Sea
Barents 1609
1594
Ob
CHINA
(Ming Empire)
LUZON
MINDANAO
NEW
GUINEA
(PAPUA)
NORTH
CAPE
Archangel
Chancellor
Jenkinson
Canton
Macau
Alvares
PHILIPPINE
IS.
GILOLO
TERNATE
TIDORE
MOLUCCAS
BANDA
IS.
After Magellan's death
his expedition wandered
aimlessly for months.
1513
Goes 1602-1607
TIBET
Brahmaputra
Serrão
1512
BORNEO
Moscow
Conterini
Volga
Mandalay
SIAM
Pegu
Mota
Alvares
Bokhara
Delhi
Ganges
Goes
Agra
Conti
Abreu 1511
Conterini 1474
Astrakhan
Jenkinson
Derbend
Caspian
Sea
Kaffa
Tiflis
Black Sea
Venice
Tabriz
PERSIA
INDIA
(Mogul Empire
after 1526)
Indus
Malacca
SUMATRA
JAVA
AUSTRALIA
(Undiscovered)
Diu
Damão
Bassein
Chaul
Ispahan
Baghdad
Basra
Ormuz
Conti
Goa
Mailapur
Vijayanagar
Cananor
Calicut
CEYLON
Cochin
Colombo
Sequeira 1509
Mediterranean Sea
Damascus
Jerusalem
Persian
Gulf
Muscat
Alexandria
Cairo
Red Sea
Covilha
Cabral
Vasco da Gama 1498
Indian
Ocean
Aden
ABYSSINIA
Covilha
1491?
El Cano commanding Victoria (Magellan) Expedition
Malindi
Mombasa
Kilwa
Covilha ?
Zaire
Zaire and
Mani Congo
discovered by
Diogo Cão
1482-1483
Mani
Congo
Mozambique
MADAGASCAR
Discovered by Diogo Dias
(Cabral Expedition 1500)
Sofala
Cão 1485
CAPE CROSS
Discovered by
Diogo Cão 1485
Vasco da Gama 1498
Cabral
Discovered by
B. Dias 1488
CAPE OF
GOOD HOPE
Diogo Dias 1500
B. Dias
1487
A- 410031-29-1-1-1-1

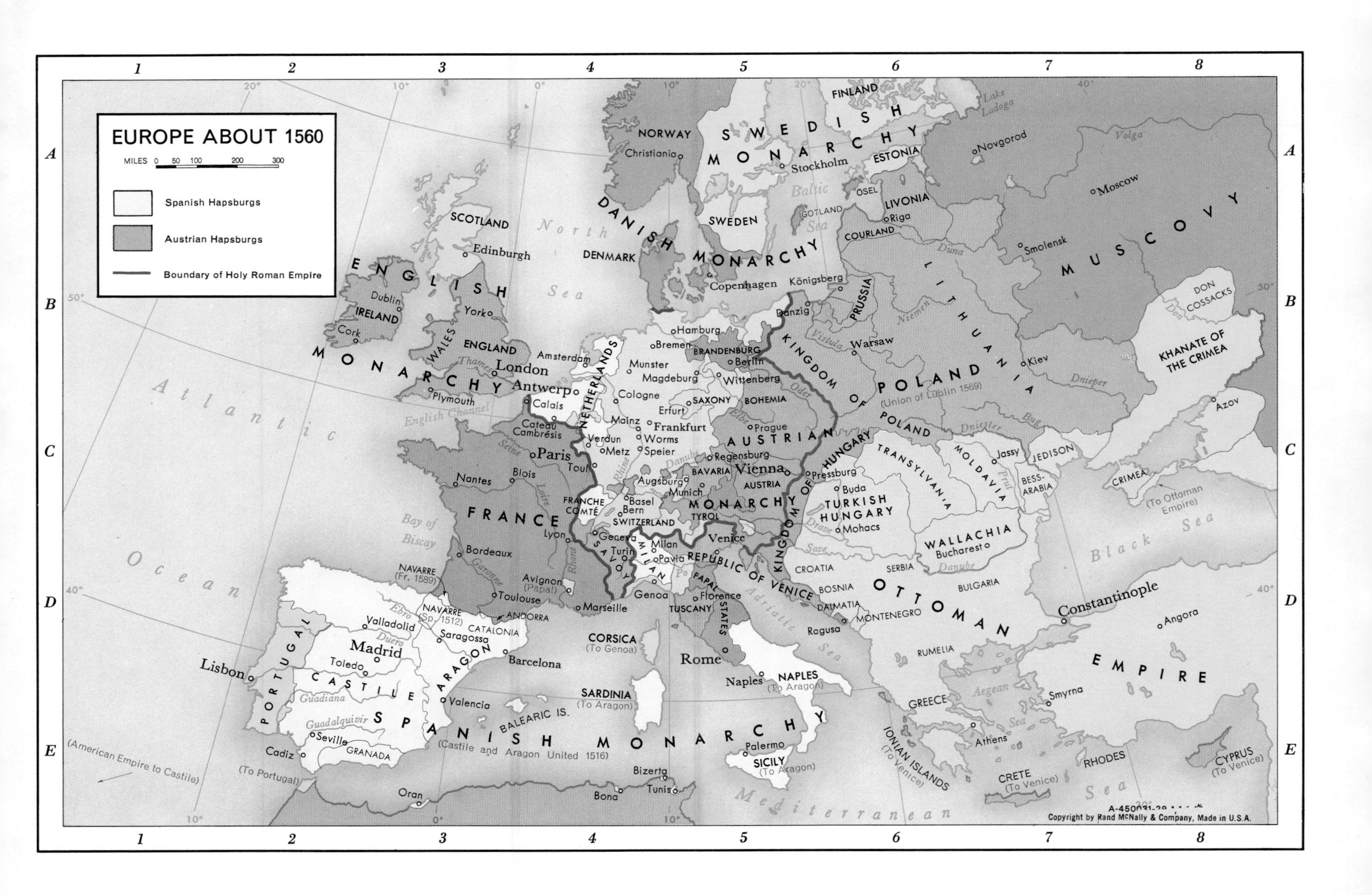

EUROPE ABOUT 1560
MILES 0 50 100 200 300
Spanish Hapsburgs
Austrian Hapsburgs
Boundary of Holy Roman Empire
SWEDISH MONARCHY
DANISH MONARCHY
ENGLISH MONARCHY
SPANISH MONARCHY
(Castile and Aragon United 1516)
AUSTRIAN MONARCHY
KINGDOM OF POLAND
(Union of Lublin 1569)
LITHUANIA
MUSCOVY
OTTOMAN EMPIRE
KINGDOM OF HUNGARY
REPUBLIC OF VENICE
FINLAND
NORWAY
SWEDEN
DENMARK
ESTONIA
LIVONIA
COURLAND
ÖSEL
GOTLAND
PRUSSIA
SCOTLAND
IRELAND
ENGLAND
WALES
NETHERLANDS
FRANCE
FRANCHE COMTÉ
SWITZERLAND
SAVOY
MILAN
TYROL
BAVARIA
AUSTRIA
BOHEMIA
SAXONY
BRANDENBURG
TUSCANY
PAPAL STATES
CORSICA
(To Genoa)
SARDINIA
(To Aragon)
NAPLES
(To Aragon)
SICILY
(To Aragon)
BALEARIC IS.
PORTUGAL
CASTILE
ARAGON
CATALONIA
GRANADA
NAVARRE
(Fr. 1589)
NAVARRE
(Sp. 1512)
ANDORRA
TRANSYLVANIA
TURKISH HUNGARY
MOLDAVIA
WALLACHIA
JEDISON
BESS-ARABIA
CRIMEA
(To Ottoman Empire)
KHANATE OF THE CRIMEA
DON COSSACKS
CROATIA
BOSNIA
SERBIA
DALMATIA
MONTENEGRO
BULGARIA
RUMELIA
GREECE
IONIAN ISLANDS
(To Venice)
CRETE
(To Venice)
RHODES
CYPRUS
(To Venice)
(American Empire to Castile)
(To Portugal)
Christiania
Stockholm
Copenhagen
Königsberg
Danzig
Riga
Novgorod
Moscow
Smolensk
Warsaw
Kiev
Azov
Edinburgh
York
Dublin
Cork
London
Plymouth
Amsterdam
Antwerp
Calais
Cateau Cambrésis
Paris
Nantes
Blois
Tours
Bordeaux
Toulouse
Lyon
Avignon
(Papal)
Marseille
Hamburg
Bremen
Berlin
Munster
Magdeburg
Wittenberg
Cologne
Erfurt
Mainz
Frankfurt
Worms
Speier
Verdun
Metz
Prague
Regensburg
Augsburg
Munich
Vienna
Pressburg
Buda
Mohacs
Basel
Bern
Geneva
Turin
Milan
Pavia
Genoa
Venice
Florence
Rome
Naples
Palermo
Ragusa
Bucharest
Jassy
Constantinople
Angora
Smyrna
Athens
Lisbon
Valladolid
Madrid
Toledo
Saragossa
Barcelona
Valencia
Seville
Cadiz
Oran
Bizerta
Tunis
Bona
North Sea
Baltic Sea
Lake Ladoga
Atlantic Ocean
English Channel
Bay of Biscay
Mediterranean Sea
Adriatic Sea
Aegean Sea
Black Sea
Volga
Don
Dnieper
Dniester
Bug
Duna
Niemen
Vistula
Oder
Elbe
Rhine
Danube
Drave
Save
Prut
Po
Rhone
Loire
Seine
Garonne
Thames
Ebro
Duero
Guadiana
Guadalquivir
Copyright by Rand McNally & Company, Made in U.S.A.

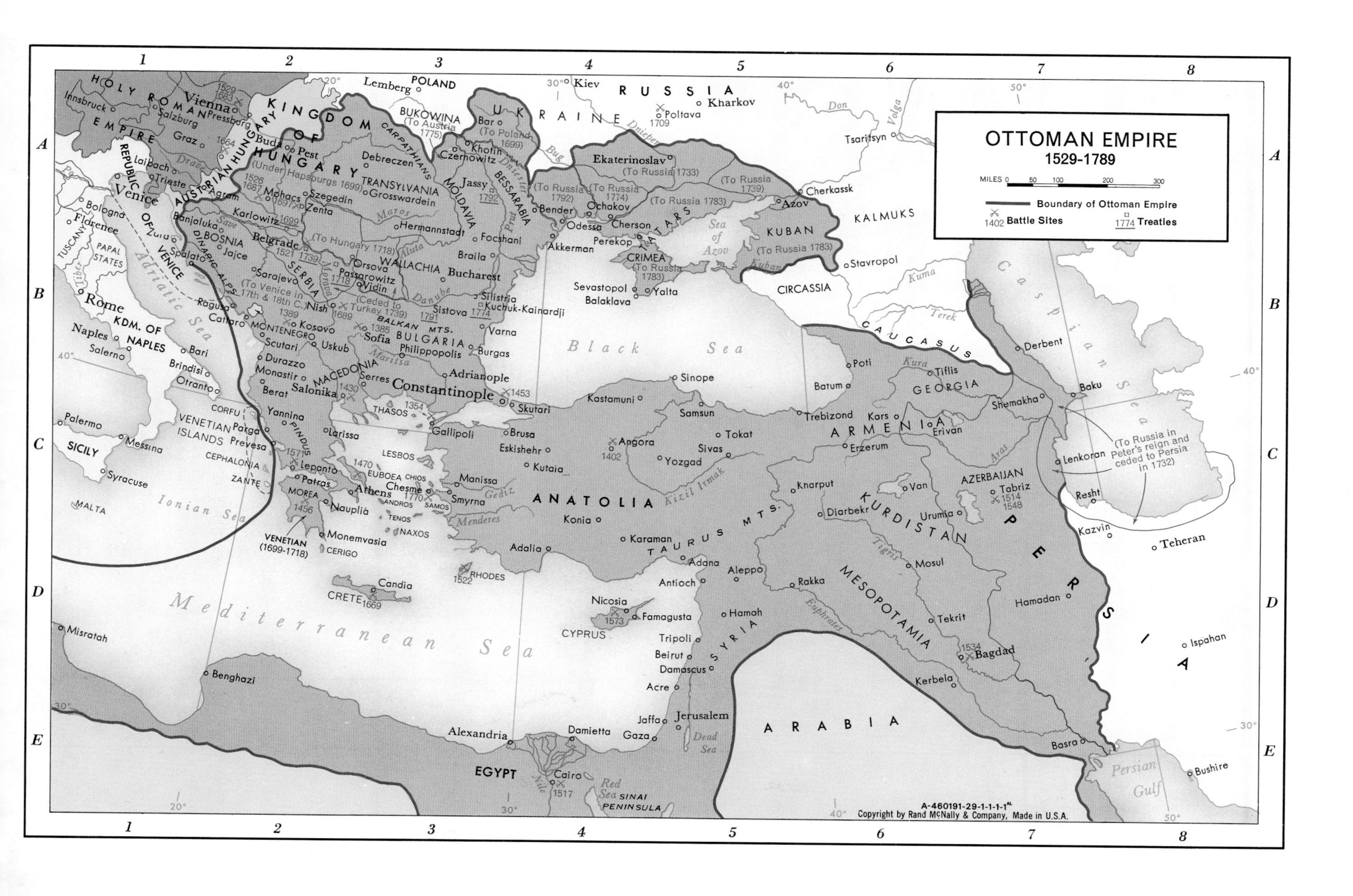
OTTOMAN EMPIRE
1529-1789
MILES 0 50 100 200 300
Boundary of Ottoman Empire
1402 Battle Sites
1774 Treaties
RUSSIA
UKRAINE
POLAND
KINGDOM OF HUNGARY
HOLY ROMAN EMPIRE
AUSTRIAN HUNGARY
REPUBLIC OF VENICE
KDM. OF NAPLES
PAPAL STATES
TUSCANY
SICILY
MALTA
BUKOWINA (To Austria 1775)
MOLDAVIA
BESSARABIA
TRANSYLVANIA
WALLACHIA
BOSNIA
SERBIA
MONTENEGRO
BULGARIA
MACEDONIA
CRIMEA (To Russia 1783)
KUBAN (To Russia 1783)
TATARS
CIRCASSIA
KALMUKS
CAUCASUS
GEORGIA
ARMENIA
AZERBAIJAN
KURDISTAN
MESOPOTAMIA
ANATOLIA
TAURUS MTS.
SYRIA
ARABIA
PERSIA
EGYPT
CYPRUS
CRETE
RHODES
Black Sea
Sea of Azov
Caspian Sea
Mediterranean Sea
Adriatic Sea
Ionian Sea
Persian Gulf
Red Sea
Dead Sea
SINAI PENINSULA
(To Russia in Peter's reign and ceded to Persia in 1732)
VENETIAN (1699-1718)
Constantinople
Vienna
Belgrade
Adrianople
Athens
Smyrna
Angora
Bagdad
Jerusalem
Damascus
Cairo
Alexandria
Teheran
Ispahan
A-460191-29-1-1-1
Copyright by Rand McNally & Company, Made in U.S.A.

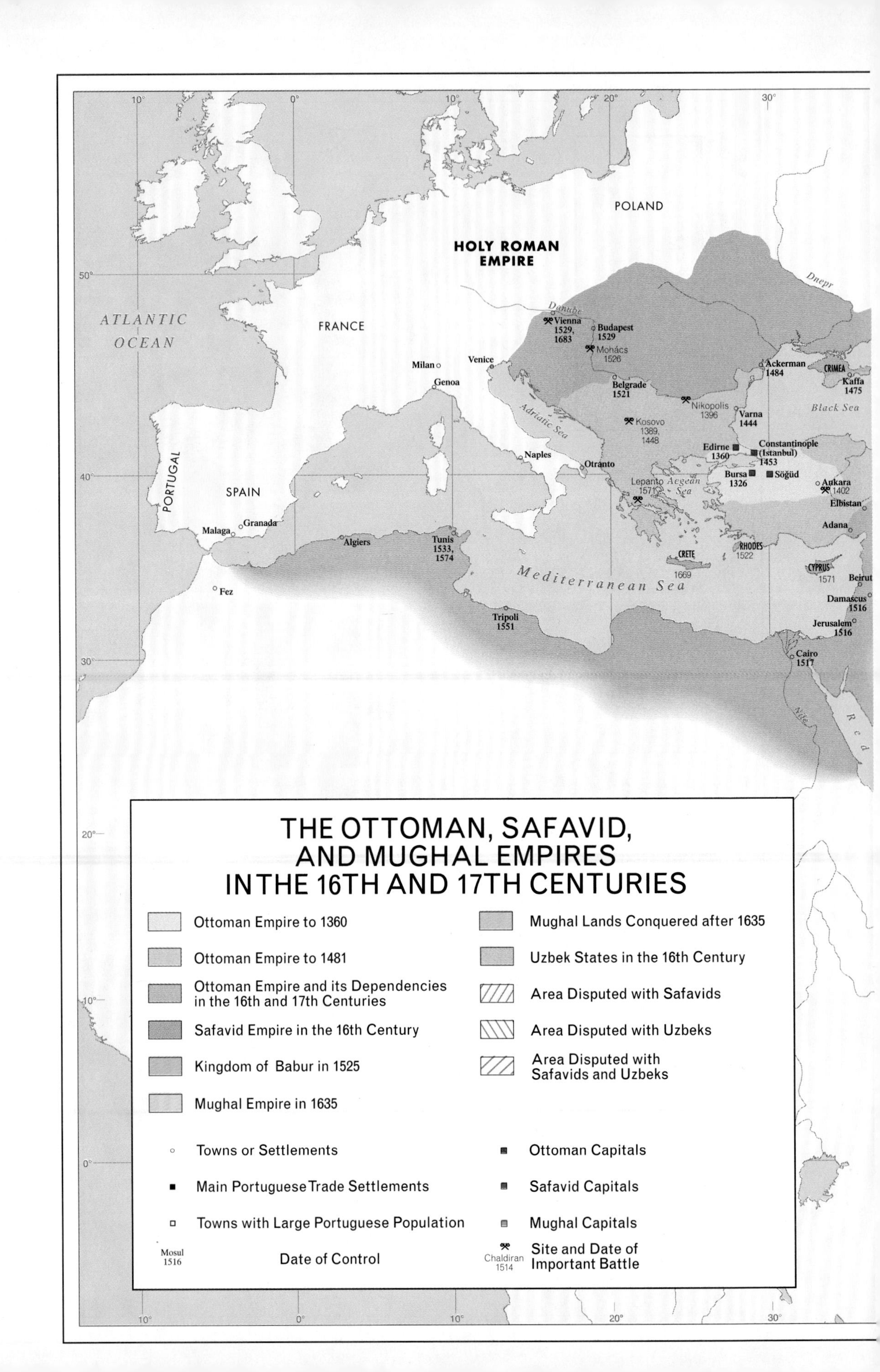

THE OTTOMAN, SAFAVID, AND MUGHAL EMPIRES IN THE 16TH AND 17TH CENTURIES
Ottoman Empire to 1360
Ottoman Empire to 1481
Ottoman Empire and its Dependencies in the 16th and 17th Centuries
Safavid Empire in the 16th Century
Kingdom of Babur in 1525
Mughal Empire in 1635
Mughal Lands Conquered after 1635
Uzbek States in the 16th Century
Area Disputed with Safavids
Area Disputed with Uzbeks
Area Disputed with Safavids and Uzbeks
Towns or Settlements
Main Portuguese Trade Settlements
Towns with Large Portuguese Population
Mosul 1516
Date of Control
Ottoman Capitals
Safavid Capitals
Mughal Capitals
Chaldiran 1514
Site and Date of Important Battle
ATLANTIC OCEAN
FRANCE
SPAIN
PORTUGAL
HOLY ROMAN EMPIRE
POLAND
Mediterranean Sea
Black Sea
Adriatic Sea
Aegean Sea
Danube
Dnepr
Nile
Red
Vienna 1529, 1683
Budapest 1529
Mohács 1526
Belgrade 1521
Nikopolis 1396
Kosovo 1389, 1448
Varna 1444
Ackerman 1484
CRIMEA
Kaffa 1475
Edirne 1360
Constantinople (Istanbul) 1453
Bursa 1326
Söğüd
Ankara 1402
Elbistan
Adana
Lepanto 1571
RHODES 1522
CRETE 1669
CYPRUS 1571
Beirut
Damascus 1516
Jerusalem 1516
Cairo 1517
Tripoli 1551
Tunis 1533, 1574
Algiers
Malaga
Granada
Fez
Milan
Genoa
Venice
Naples
Otranto

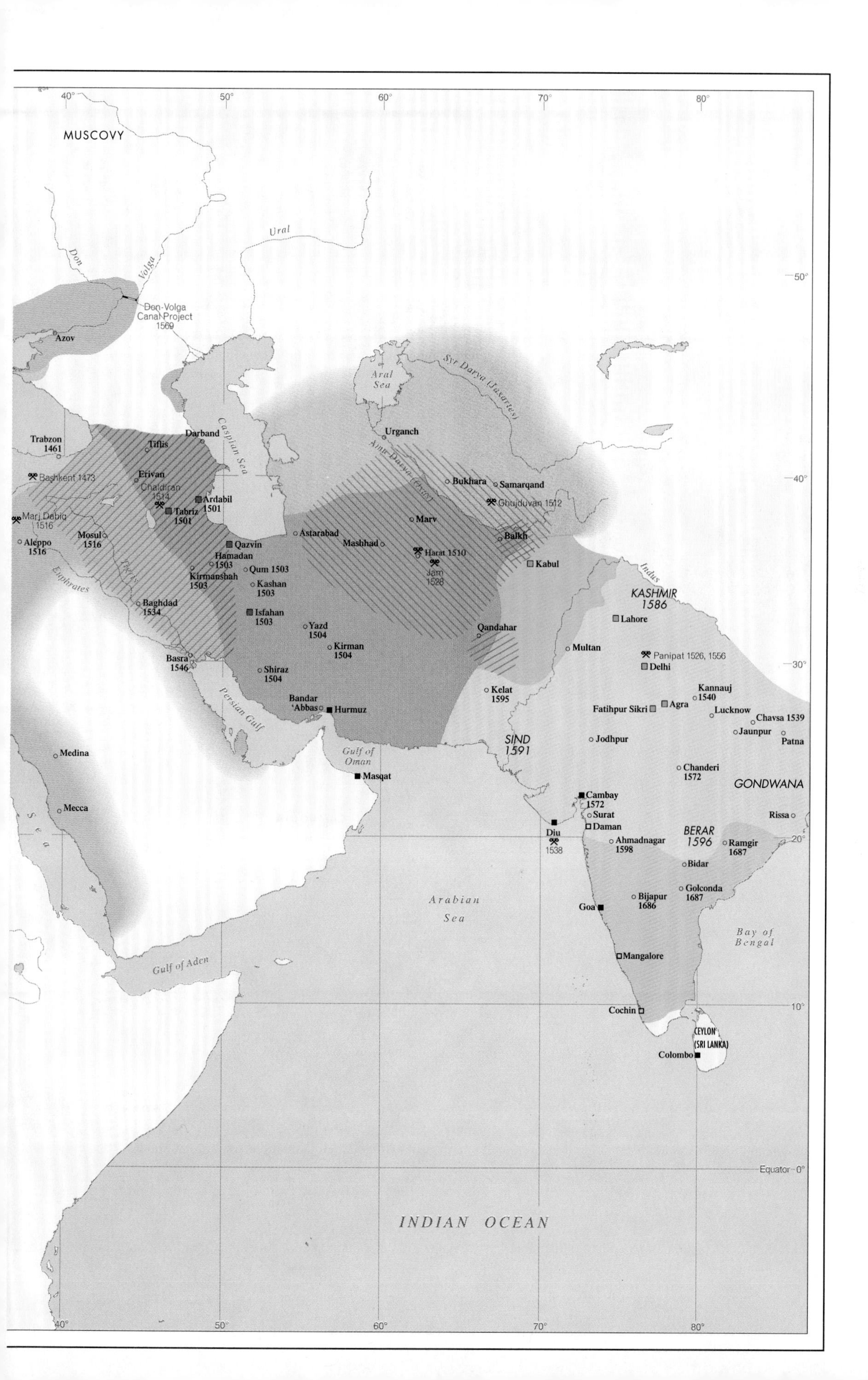

MUSCOVY
Ural
Don
Volga
Don-Volga
Canal Project
1569
Azov
Aral
Sea
Syr Darya (Jaxartes)
Amu Darya (Oxus)
Urganch
Caspian Sea
Trabzon
1461
Darband
Tiflis
Bashkent 1473
Erivan
Chaldiran
1514
Ardabil
1501
Tabriz
1501
Marj Dabiq
1516
Aleppo
1516
Mosul
1516
Qazvin
Hamadan
1503
Kirmanshah
1503
Qum 1503
Kashan
1503
Astarabad
Mashhad
Bukhara
Samarqand
Ghujduvan 1512
Marv
Balkh
Harat 1510
Jam
1528
Kabul
Euphrates
Tigris
Baghdad
1534
Isfahan
1503
Yazd
1504
Kirman
1504
Qandahar
Basra
1546
Shiraz
1504
Persian Gulf
Bandar
'Abbas
Hurmuz
Gulf of
Oman
Masqat
Medina
Mecca
Sea
Indus
KASHMIR
1586
Lahore
Multan
Panipat 1526, 1556
Delhi
Kelat
1595
Kannauj
1540
Fatihpur Sikri
Agra
Lucknow
Chavsa 1539
Jaunpur
Patna
Jodhpur
SIND
1591
Chanderi
1572
GONDWANA
Cambay
1572
Surat
Daman
Diu
1538
Rissa
Ahmadnagar
1598
BERAR
1596
Ramgir
1687
Bidar
Golconda
1687
Bijapur
1686
Goa
Arabian
Sea
Bay of
Bengal
Mangalore
Gulf of Aden
Cochin
CEYLON
(SRI LANKA)
Colombo
INDIAN OCEAN
Equator 0°
40°
50°
60°
70°
80°
10°
20°
30°
40°
50°

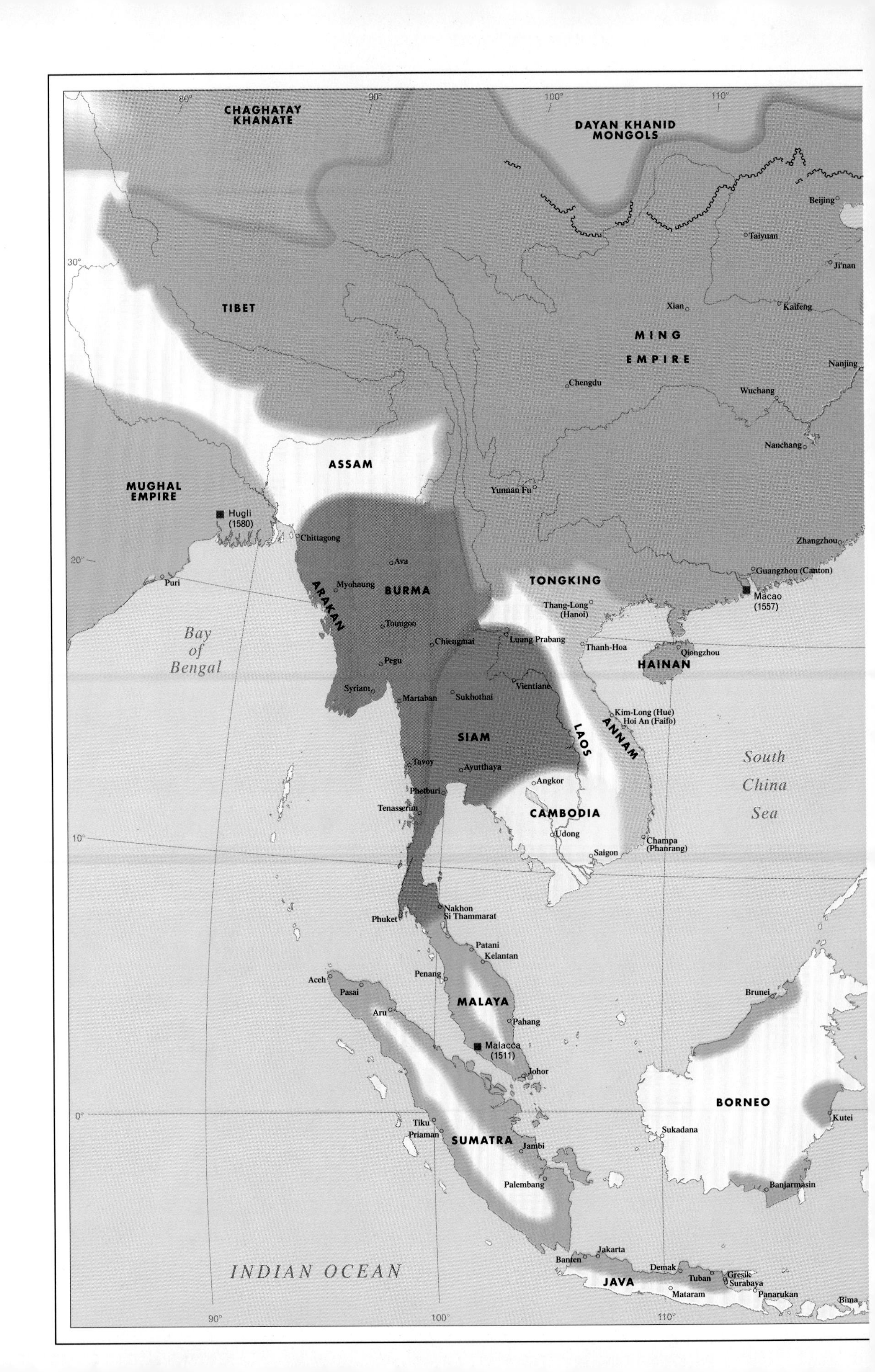

CHAGHATAY KHANATE
DAYAN KHANID MONGOLS
TIBET
MING EMPIRE
ASSAM
MUGHAL EMPIRE
Hugli (1580)
Chittagong
Ava
Myohaung
ARAKAN
BURMA
Toungoo
Chiengmai
Pegu
Syriam
Martaban
Sukhothai
SIAM
Tavoy
Ayutthaya
Phetburi
Tenasserim
Bay of Bengal
Puri
TONGKING
Thang-Long (Hanoi)
Luang Prabang
Thanh-Hoa
HAINAN
Qiongzhou
Vientiane
LAOS
ANNAM
Kim-Long (Hue)
Hoi An (Faifo)
Angkor
CAMBODIA
Udong
Saigon
Champa (Phanrang)
South China Sea
Beijing
Taiyuan
Ji'nan
Xian
Kaifeng
Chengdu
Nanjing
Wuchang
Nanchang
Yunnan Fu
Zhangzhou
Guangzhou (Canton)
Macao (1557)
Nakhon Si Thammarat
Phuket
Patani
Kelantan
Penang
MALAYA
Pahang
Malacca (1511)
Johor
Aceh
Pasai
Aru
Tiku
Priaman
SUMATRA
Jambi
Palembang
Brunei
BORNEO
Kutei
Sukadana
Banjarmasin
Jakarta
Banten
Demak
Tuban
Gresik
Surabaya
JAVA
Mataram
Panarukan
Bima
INDIAN OCEAN
80°
90°
100°
110°
30°
20°
10°
0°

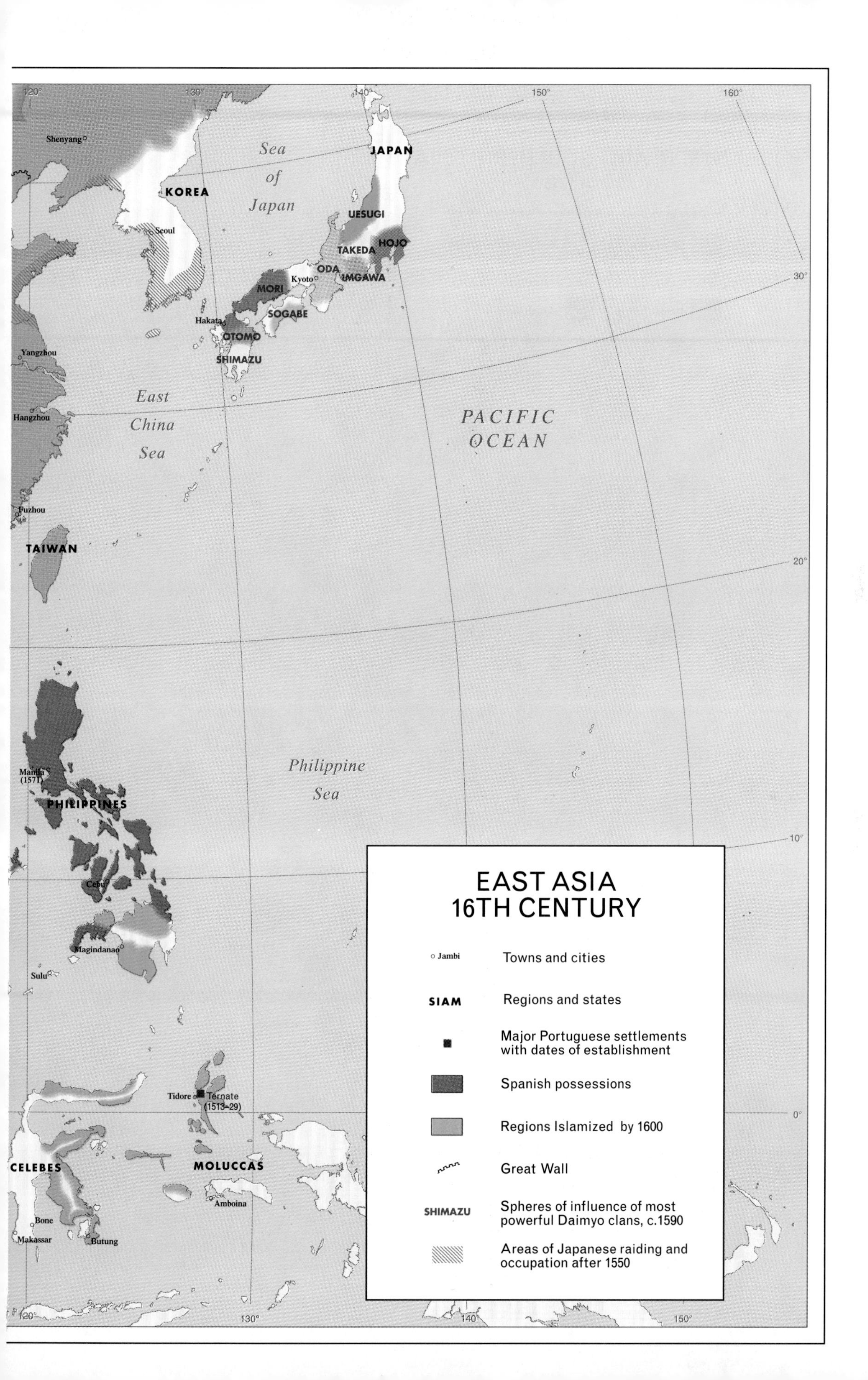

EAST ASIA
16TH CENTURY
Jambi
Towns and cities
SIAM
Regions and states
Major Portuguese settlements with dates of establishment
Spanish possessions
Regions Islamized by 1600
Great Wall
SHIMAZU
Spheres of influence of most powerful Daimyo clans, c.1590
Areas of Japanese raiding and occupation after 1550
Shenyang
KOREA
Seoul
Sea of Japan
JAPAN
UESUGI
HOJO
TAKEDA
ODA
IMGAWA
Kyoto
MORI
SOGABE
Hakata
OTOMO
SHIMAZU
Yangzhou
Hangzhou
East China Sea
PACIFIC OCEAN
Fuzhou
TAIWAN
Philippine Sea
Manila (1571)
PHILIPPINES
Cebu
Magindanao
Sulu
Tidore
Ternate (1513–29)
CELEBES
MOLUCCAS
Amboina
Bone
Makassar
Butung

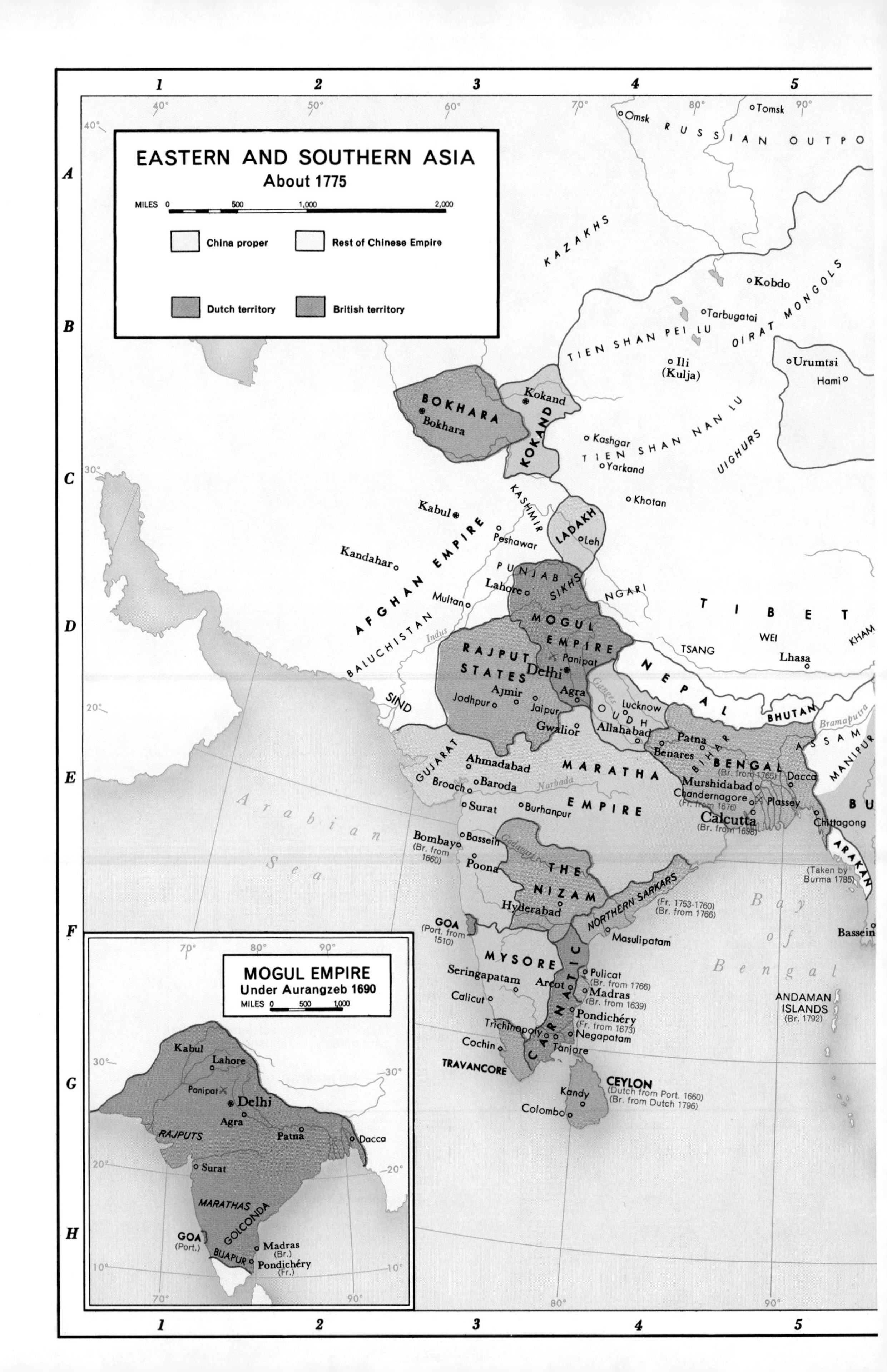
EASTERN AND SOUTHERN ASIA
About 1775
MILES 0 500 1,000 2,000
China proper
Rest of Chinese Empire
Dutch territory
British territory
Omsk
Tomsk
RUSSIAN OUTPO
KAZAKHS
Kobdo
OIRAT MONGOLS
Tarbugatai
TIEN SHAN PEI LU
Ili (Kulja)
Urumtsi
Hami
BOKHARA
Bokhara
Kokand
KOKAND
Kashgar
TIEN SHAN NAN LU
UIGHURS
Yarkand
Khotan
KASHMIR
Kabul
LADAKH
Leh
Peshawar
AFGHAN EMPIRE
Kandahar
PUNJAB
SIKHS
Lahore
Multan
NGARI
TIBET
BALUCHISTAN
Indus
MOGUL EMPIRE
WEI
TSANG
KHAM
Lhasa
RAJPUT STATES
Panipat
Delhi
NEPAL
SIND
Ajmir
Agra
Jodhpur
Jaipur
Ganges
Lucknow
OUDH
BHUTAN
Bramaputra
Gwalior
Allahabad
Patna
BIHAR
ASSAM
MANIPUR
GUJARAT
Ahmadabad
MARATHA
Benares
BENGAL (Br. from 1765)
Dacca
Broach
Baroda
Narbada
Murshidabad
Chandernagore (Fr. from 1676)
Plassey
BU
Surat
Burhanpur
EMPIRE
Calcutta (Br. from 1698)
Chittagong
Arabian Sea
Bombay (Br. from 1660)
Bassein
Godavari
ARAKAN
(Taken by Burma 1785)
Poona
THE NIZAM
NORTHERN SARKARS
(Fr. 1753-1760) (Br. from 1766)
Hyderabad
Bay of Bengal
GOA (Port. from 1510)
Masulipatam
Bassein
MYSORE
CARNATIC
Pulicat (Br. from 1766)
Seringapatam
Arcot
Madras (Br. from 1639)
Calicut
Pondichéry (Fr. from 1673)
ANDAMAN ISLANDS (Br. 1792)
Trichinopoly
Negapatam
Cochin
Tanjore
TRAVANCORE
CEYLON (Dutch from Port. 1660) (Br. from Dutch 1796)
Kandy
Colombo
MOGUL EMPIRE
Under Aurangzeb 1690
MILES 0 500 1,000
Kabul
Lahore
Panipat
Delhi
Agra
RAJPUTS
Patna
Dacca
Surat
MARATHAS
GOLCONDA
GOA (Port.)
BIJAPUR
Madras (Br.)
Pondichéry (Fr.)

Nerchinsk
Irkutsk
BURIAT MONGOLS
Kiakhta
MANCHURIA
Tsitsihar
Kirin
Urga
Uliassutai
OUTER MONGOLIA
KHALKHA MONGOLS
FORTY NINE MONGOL BANNERS OF INNER MONGOLIA
CHAHAR MONGOLS
Great Wall
Jehol
Shengching (Mukden)
MANCHUS
Kalgan
Peking
TORGUT MONGOLS
KANSU
DAM MONGOLS
KOKONOR MONGOLS
Lanchow
Paoting
CHIHLI
Taiyüan
SHANSI
Tsinan
SHANTUNG
SHENSI
Sian
Kaifeng
HONAN
KIANGSU
Grand Canal
Chiangning
ANWEI
Anking
Hangchow
HUPEH
Wuchang
Chengtu
SZECHWAN
Yangtze
Nanchang
CHEKIANG
KIANGSI
Changsha
HUNAN
FUKIEN
Foochow
Kweiyang
KWEICHOW
Kweilin
Yünnan
YUNNAN
KWANGSI
KWANGTUNG
Kwangchow (Canton)
Macao (Port. trading post from 1557)
(Chinese repulsed 1766-1770)
Bhamo
Salween
Irrawaddy
Ava
KOREA
Seoul
JAPAN
YEZO
HONSHU
Yedo
Kyoto
Osaka
Sakai
SHIKOKU
KYUSHU
Nagasaki (Dutch trading post of Deshima from 1641)
LIUCHIU
Pacific Ocean
Zelandia Castel (Dutch, 1624-1662)
FORMOSA
TONGKING
Hanoi
Luang Prabang
Thanh Hoa
(Tongking, Annam and Cochin-China formed Vietnam Empire 1802)
Chiengsen
Toungoo
Chiengmai
Prome
Vientiane
Pegu
Sukhotai
(Laos states of Luang Prabang and Vientiane, under Siamese Suzerainty from 1778)
Rangoon
Syriam
Martaban
SIAM
ANNAM
Hué
Mekong
Lopburi
Ayuthia (Destroyed by Burmese in 1767)
Tavoy
Bangkok (Built 1780's)
Siemreap
CAMBODIA
Phnom Penh
COCHIN-CHINA
Saigon (Taken by Annam 1776)
Mergui
China Sea
Manila
PHILIPPINE ISLANDS (Spain)
Ligor
Patani
KEDAH
PERAK
PAHANG
Acheh
Pedir
Penang (Br. from 1786)
ACHEH
SUMATRA
SELANGOR
Malacca
(Dutch 1641-1795, 1818-1824) (Br. 1795-1818, since 1824)
JOHORE
RIAU ARCH (Center of Bugis power)
Siak
MINANGKABAU
Padang
Jambi
Palembang
BANGKA
BILLITON
BRUNEI
BORNEO
Succadana
Banjermassin
CELEBES
Macassar
Menado
MOLUCCAS
HALMAHERA
CERAM
Amboina
A-469036-29-1-1-1
Copyright by Rand McNally & Company, Made in U.S.A.

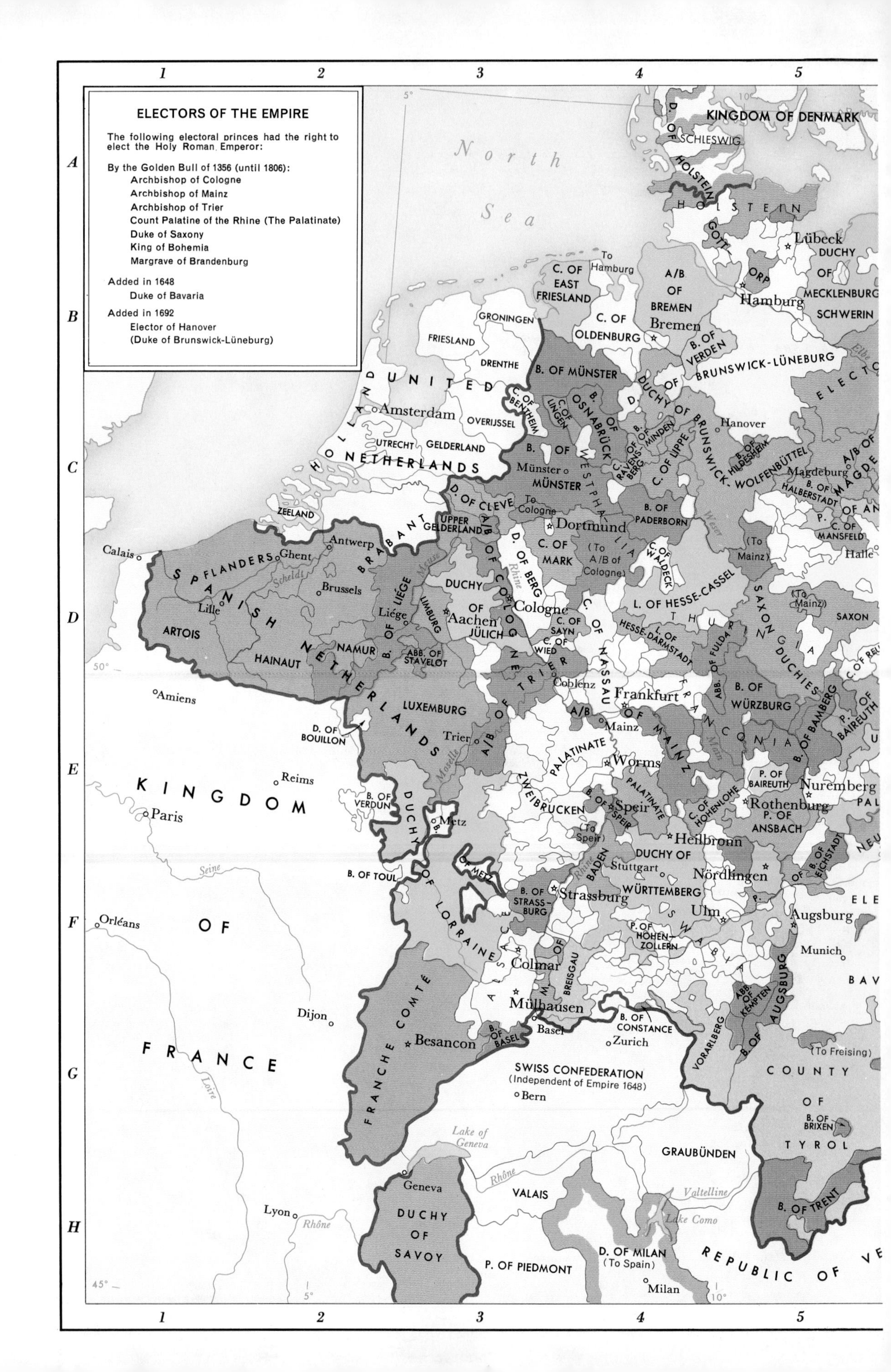
ELECTORS OF THE EMPIRE
The following electoral princes had the right to elect the Holy Roman Emperor:
By the Golden Bull of 1356 (until 1806):
Archbishop of Cologne
Archbishop of Mainz
Archbishop of Trier
Count Palatine of the Rhine (The Palatinate)
Duke of Saxony
King of Bohemia
Margrave of Brandenburg
Added in 1648
Duke of Bavaria
Added in 1692
Elector of Hanover
(Duke of Brunswick-Lüneburg)
1
2
3
4
5
A
B
C
D
E
F
G
H
North Sea
KINGDOM OF DENMARK
D. OF SCHLESWIG
D. OF HOLSTEIN
HOLSTEIN
GOTT.
Lübeck
DUCHY OF MECKLENBURG SCHWERIN
ORP
Hamburg
To Hamburg
C. OF EAST FRIESLAND
A/B OF BREMEN
Bremen
C. OF OLDENBURG
B. OF VERDEN
GRONINGEN
FRIESLAND
DRENTHE
UNITED NETHERLANDS
HOLLAND
Amsterdam
OVERIJSSEL
UTRECHT
GELDERLAND
ZEELAND
B. OF MÜNSTER
C. OF BENTHEIM
C. OF LINGEN
B. OF OSNABRÜCK
DUCHY OF BRUNSWICK-WOLFENBÜTTEL
BRUNSWICK-LÜNEBURG
Hanover
B. OF MINDEN
C. OF LIPPE
B. OF HILDESHEIM
Magdeburg
A/B OF MAGDE
B. OF HALBERSTADT
C. OF MANSFELD
Halle
(To Mainz)
ELECTO
Münster
MÜNSTER
WESTPHALIA
D. OF CLEVE
To Cologne
UPPER GELDERLAND
Dortmund
B. OF PADERBORN
C. OF MARK
(To A/B of Cologne)
C. OF WALDECK
Weser
Calais
SPANISH NETHERLANDS
FLANDERS
Ghent
Antwerp
BRABANT
Scheldt
Brussels
Lille
ARTOIS
HAINAUT
NAMUR
B. OF LIÉGE
Liége
LIMBURG
ABB. OF STAVELOT
DUCHY OF Aachen
JÜLICH
A/B OF COLOGNE
D. OF BERG
Cologne
Rhine
Meuse
C. OF SAYN
C. OF WIED
C. OF NASSAU
L. OF HESSE-CASSEL
L. OF HESSE-DARMSTADT
THURINGIA
SAXON DUCHIES
SAXON
(To Mainz)
ABB. OF FULDA
A/B OF TRIER
Coblenz
Frankfurt
FRANCONIA
B. OF WÜRZBURG
B. OF BAMBERG
P. OF BAIREUTH
Amiens
LUXEMBURG
D. OF BOUILLON
Trier
A/B
A/B OF MAINZ
Mainz
Main
PALATINATE
Worms
Moselle
KINGDOM OF FRANCE
Reims
Paris
B. OF VERDUN
DUCHY OF LORRAINE
Metz
B. OF METZ
B. OF TOUL
ZWEIBRUCKEN
B. OF SPEIR
Speir
(To Speir)
C. OF HOHENLOHE
Rothenburg
P. OF ANSBACH
Nuremberg
Heilbronn
BADEN
DUCHY OF WÜRTTEMBERG
Stuttgart
Nördlingen
B. OF EICHSTADT
Seine
B. OF STRASSBURG
Strassburg
Ulm
SWABIA
Augsburg
P. OF HOHENZOLLERN
Orléans
ALSACE
Colmar
BREISGAU
Munich
BAV
Mülhausen
ABB. OF KEMPTEN
B. OF AUGSBURG
Dijon
FRANCHE COMTÉ
Besancon
B. OF BASEL
Basel
B. OF CONSTANCE
Zurich
VORARLBERG
(To Freising)
SWISS CONFEDERATION
(Independent of Empire 1648)
Bern
COUNTY OF TYROL
B. OF BRIXEN
Loire
Lake of Geneva
Geneva
GRAUBÜNDEN
Rhône
VALAIS
Valtelline
Lake Como
B. OF TRENT
Lyon
DUCHY OF SAVOY
P. OF PIEDMONT
D. OF MILAN
(To Spain)
Milan
REPUBLIC OF VE
50°
45°
5°
10°

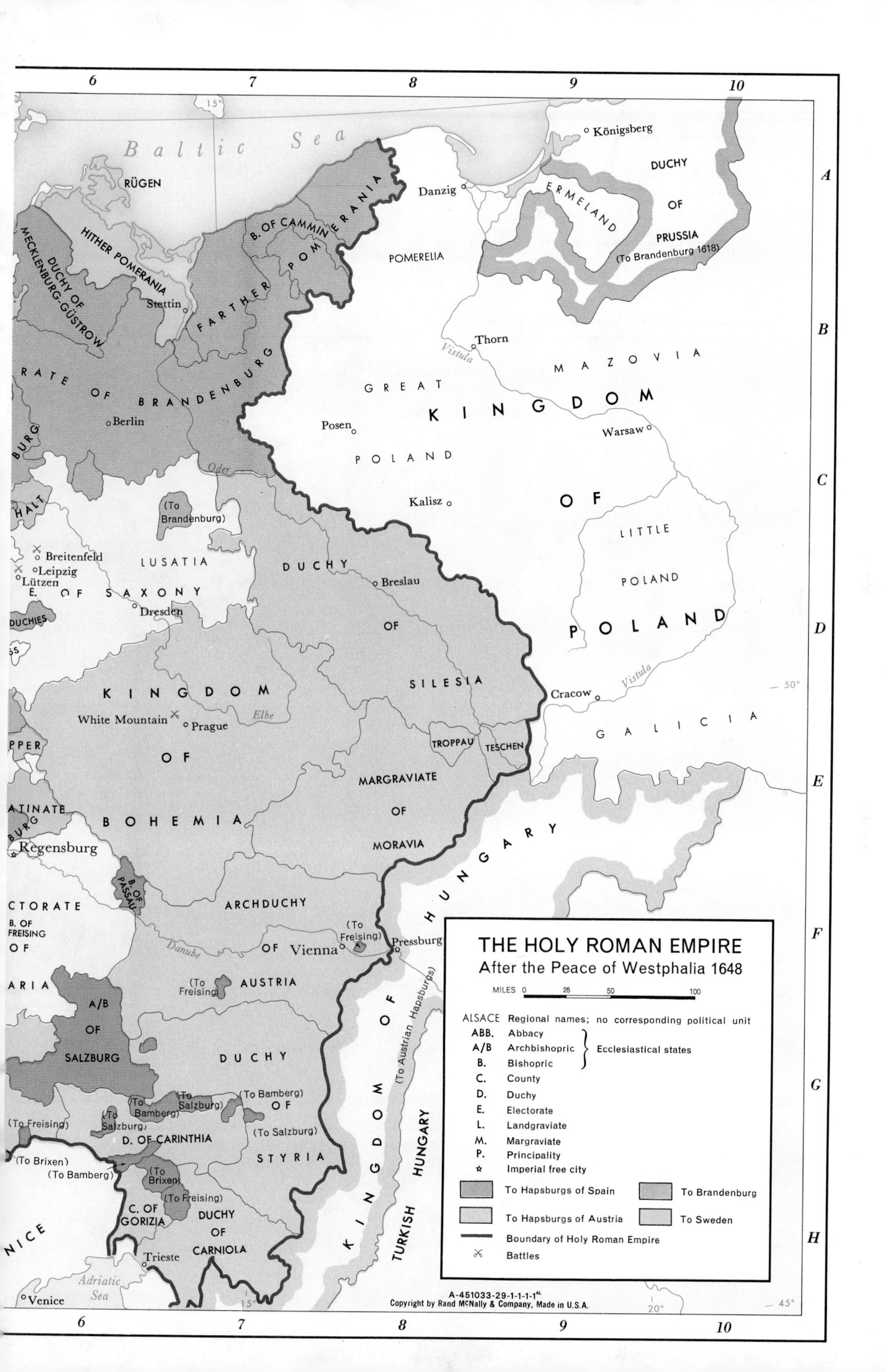
THE HOLY ROMAN EMPIRE
After the Peace of Westphalia 1648
MILES 0 25 50 100
ALSACE Regional names; no corresponding political unit
ABB. Abbacy
A/B Archbishopric
B. Bishopric
Ecclesiastical states
C. County
D. Duchy
E. Electorate
L. Landgraviate
M. Margraviate
P. Principality
Imperial free city
To Hapsburgs of Spain
To Brandenburg
To Hapsburgs of Austria
To Sweden
Boundary of Holy Roman Empire
Battles
Baltic Sea
RÜGEN
HITHER POMERANIA
DUCHY OF MECKLENBURG-GÜSTROW
B. OF CAMMIN
POMERANIA
FARTHER POMERANIA
Stettin
Königsberg
DUCHY OF PRUSSIA
(To Brandenburg 1618)
ERMELAND
Danzig
POMERELIA
Thorn
Vistula
MAZOVIA
GREAT POLAND
KINGDOM OF POLAND
Posen
Warsaw
Kalisz
LITTLE POLAND
Berlin
Oder
(To Brandenburg)
Breitenfeld
Leipzig
Lützen
LUSATIA
E. OF SAXONY
Dresden
DUCHY OF SILESIA
Breslau
KINGDOM OF BOHEMIA
White Mountain
Prague
Elbe
Cracow
GALICIA
TROPPAU
TESCHEN
MARGRAVIATE OF MORAVIA
KINGDOM OF HUNGARY
Regensburg
B. OF PASSAU
ARCHDUCHY OF AUSTRIA
(To Freising)
Vienna
Pressburg
Danube
A/B OF SALZBURG
DUCHY OF STYRIA
(To Bamberg)
(To Salzburg)
(To Freising)
D. OF CARINTHIA
(To Brixen)
C. OF GORIZIA
DUCHY OF CARNIOLA
Trieste
Adriatic Sea
Venice
(To Austrian Hapsburgs)
TURKISH HUNGARY
A-451033-29-1-1-1-1
Copyright by Rand McNally & Company, Made in U.S.A.

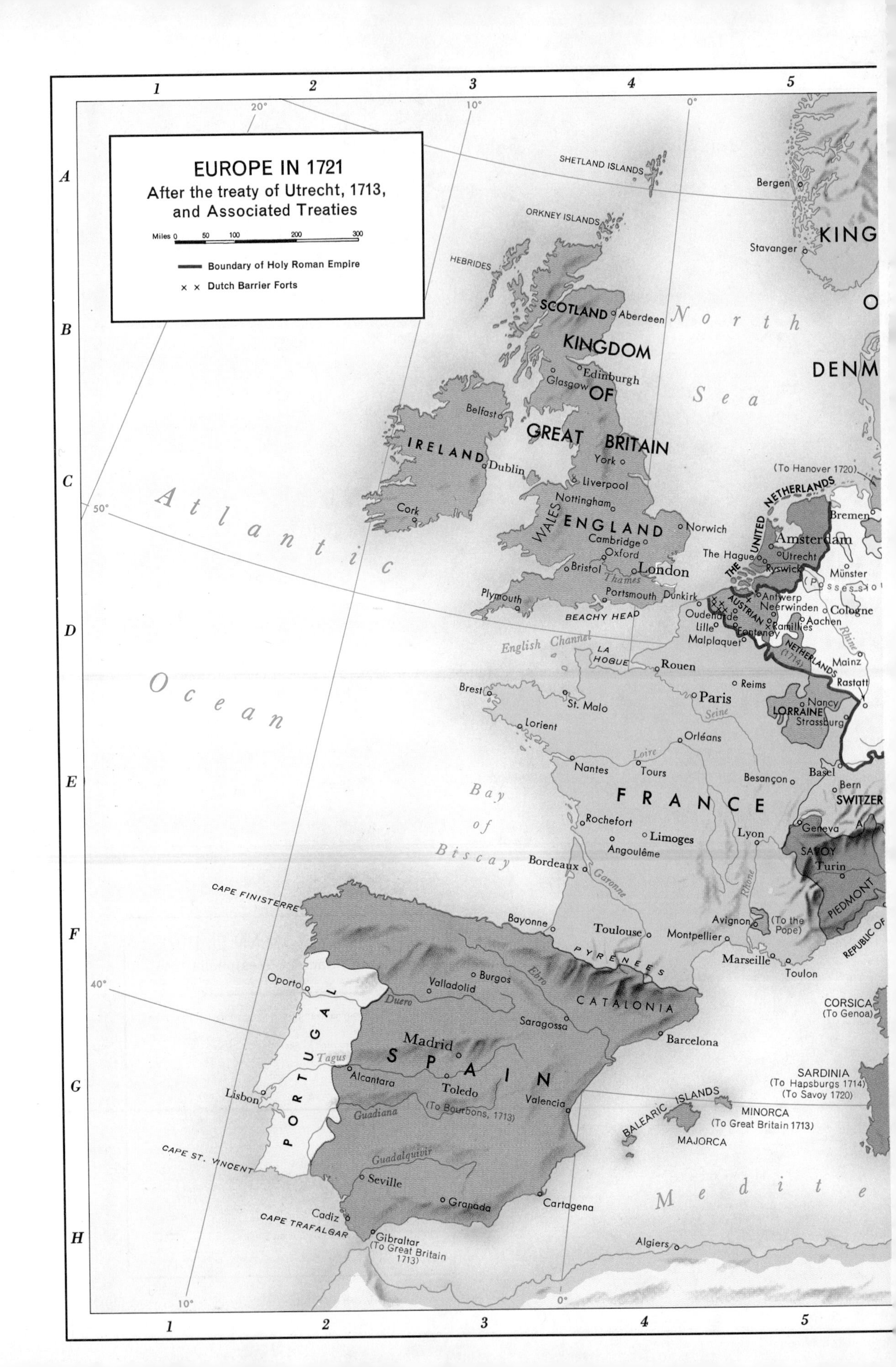

EUROPE IN 1721
After the treaty of Utrecht, 1713, and Associated Treaties
Miles 0 50 100 200 300
Boundary of Holy Roman Empire
× × Dutch Barrier Forts
SHETLAND ISLANDS
ORKNEY ISLANDS
HEBRIDES
SCOTLAND
Aberdeen
KINGDOM OF GREAT BRITAIN
Edinburgh
Glasgow
Belfast
IRELAND
Dublin
Cork
York
Liverpool
Nottingham
WALES
ENGLAND
Norwich
Cambridge
Oxford
Bristol
London
Thames
Plymouth
Portsmouth
BEACHY HEAD
English Channel
North Sea
Atlantic Ocean
Bergen
Stavanger
KING
O
DENM
(To Hanover 1720)
THE UNITED NETHERLANDS
Bremen
Amsterdam
The Hague
Utrecht
Ryswick
Münster
Dunkirk
Antwerp
Neerwinden
Cologne
AUSTRIAN NETHERLANDS (1714)
Oudenarde
Lille
Aachen
Ramillies
Fontenoy
Malplaquet
Rhine
Mainz
Rastatt
LA HOGUE
Rouen
Reims
Brest
St. Malo
Paris
Seine
Nancy
LORRAINE
Strassburg
Lorient
Orléans
Loire
Nantes
Tours
Besançon
Basel
Bern
SWITZER
FRANCE
Bay of Biscay
Rochefort
Limoges
Angoulême
Lyon
Geneva
SAVOY
Turin
PIEDMONT
Bordeaux
Garonne
Rhône
CAPE FINISTERRE
Bayonne
Toulouse
Montpellier
Avignon
(To the Pope)
REPUBLIC OF
PYRENEES
Marseille
Toulon
Oporto
Burgos
Valladolid
Ebro
Duero
CATALONIA
CORSICA (To Genoa)
PORTUGAL
Saragossa
Barcelona
Madrid
Tagus
SPAIN
Alcantara
Toledo
(To Bourbons, 1713)
Valencia
SARDINIA (To Hapsburgs 1714) (To Savoy 1720)
Lisbon
Guadiana
BALEARIC ISLANDS
MINORCA (To Great Britain 1713)
MAJORCA
CAPE ST. VINCENT
Guadalquivir
Seville
Granada
Cartagena
Mediterranean
Cadiz
CAPE TRAFALGAR
Gibraltar (To Great Britain 1713)
Algiers

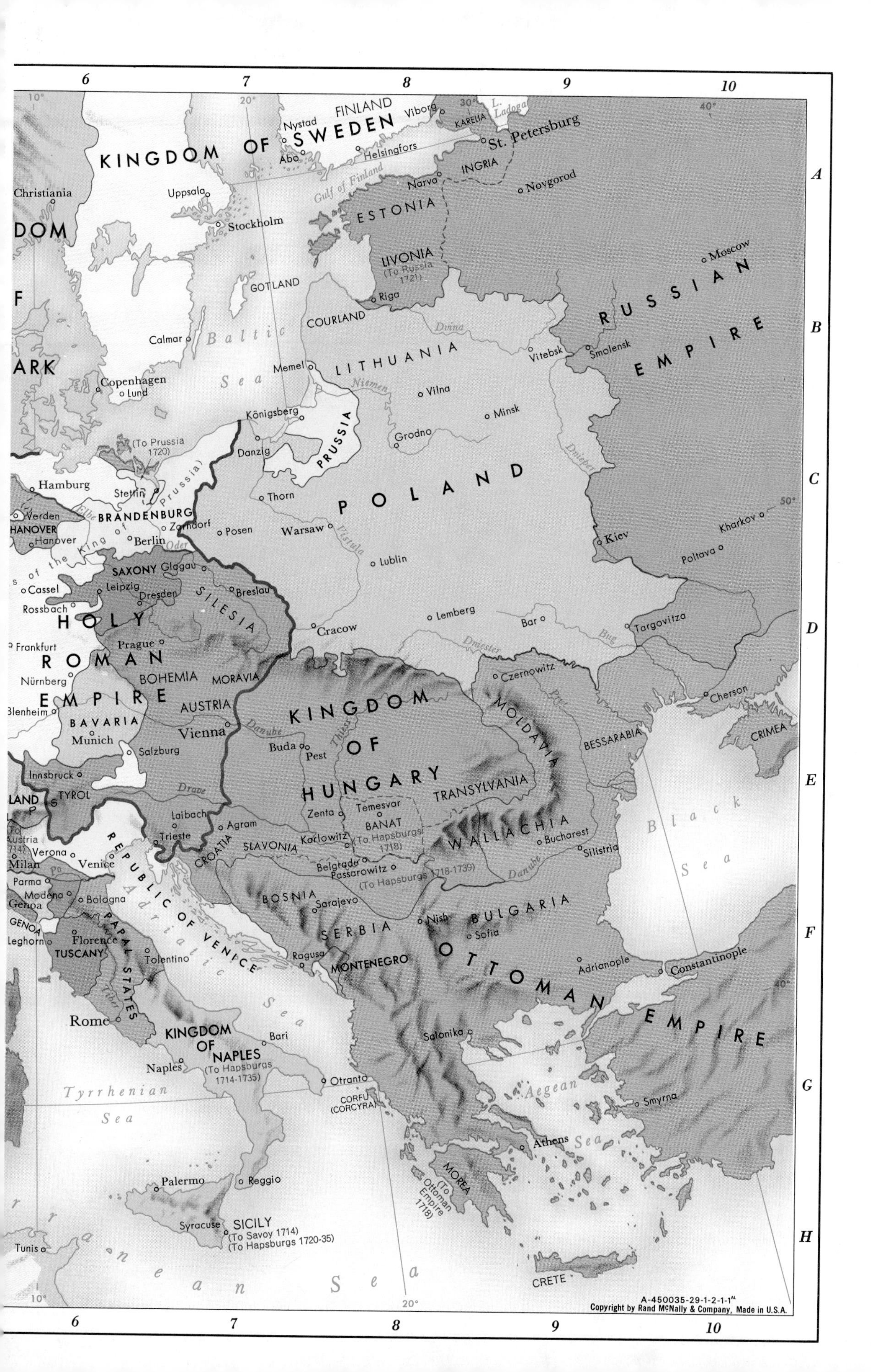

KINGDOM OF SWEDEN
FINLAND
Nystad
Abo
Viborg
KARELIA
L. Ladoga
St. Petersburg
Helsingfors
Gulf of Finland
INGRIA
Narva
Novgorod
Christiania
Uppsala
Stockholm
ESTONIA
LIVONIA
(To Russia 1721)
Moscow
GOTLAND
Riga
COURLAND
Dvina
RUSSIAN EMPIRE
Calmar
Baltic Sea
LITHUANIA
Vitebsk
Smolensk
Memel
Copenhagen
Lund
Niemen
Vilna
Minsk
Königsberg
PRUSSIA
Grodno
(To Prussia 1720)
Danzig
Dnieper
Hamburg
Stettin
Prussia
POLAND
Thorn
Verden
BRANDENBURG
Zorndorf
Posen
Warsaw
Vistula
Kiev
Kharkov
HANOVER
Hanover
Berlin
Oder
Elbe
Lublin
Poltava
SAXONY
Glogau
Cassel
Leipzig
Dresden
SILESIA
Breslau
Rossbach
HOLY ROMAN EMPIRE
Lemberg
Bar
Targovitza
Bug
Frankfurt
Prague
Cracow
Dniester
BOHEMIA
MORAVIA
Nürnberg
Czernowitz
Blenheim
AUSTRIA
KINGDOM OF HUNGARY
MOLDAVIA
Prut
Cherson
BAVARIA
Munich
Vienna
Danube
Thiess
BESSARABIA
CRIMEA
Salzburg
Buda
Pest
Innsbruck
HUNGARY
TRANSYLVANIA
TYROL
Drave
Temesvar
BANAT
(To Hapsburgs 1718)
Zenta
Laibach
Agram
WALLACHIA
Bucharest
Trieste
CROATIA
SLAVONIA
Karlowitz
Silistria
Verona
Venice
REPUBLIC OF VENICE
Belgrade
Passarowitz
(To Hapsburgs 1718-1739)
Black Sea
Milan
Po
Parma
Modena
Bologna
BOSNIA
Sarajevo
Genoa
BULGARIA
Nish
Sofia
Leghorn
Florence
TUSCANY
PAPAL STATES
SERBIA
Ragusa
MONTENEGRO
OTTOMAN EMPIRE
Adrianople
Constantinople
Tolentino
Adriatic Sea
Tiber
Rome
KINGDOM OF NAPLES
(To Hapsburgs 1714-1735)
Bari
Salonika
Naples
Otranto
Tyrrhenian Sea
CORFU (CORCYRA)
Aegean Sea
Smyrna
Athens
MOREA
(To Ottoman Empire 1718)
Palermo
Reggio
SICILY
Syracuse
(To Savoy 1714)
(To Hapsburgs 1720-35)
Tunis
CRETE
A-450035-29-1-2-1-1
Copyright by Rand McNally & Company, Made in U.S.A.

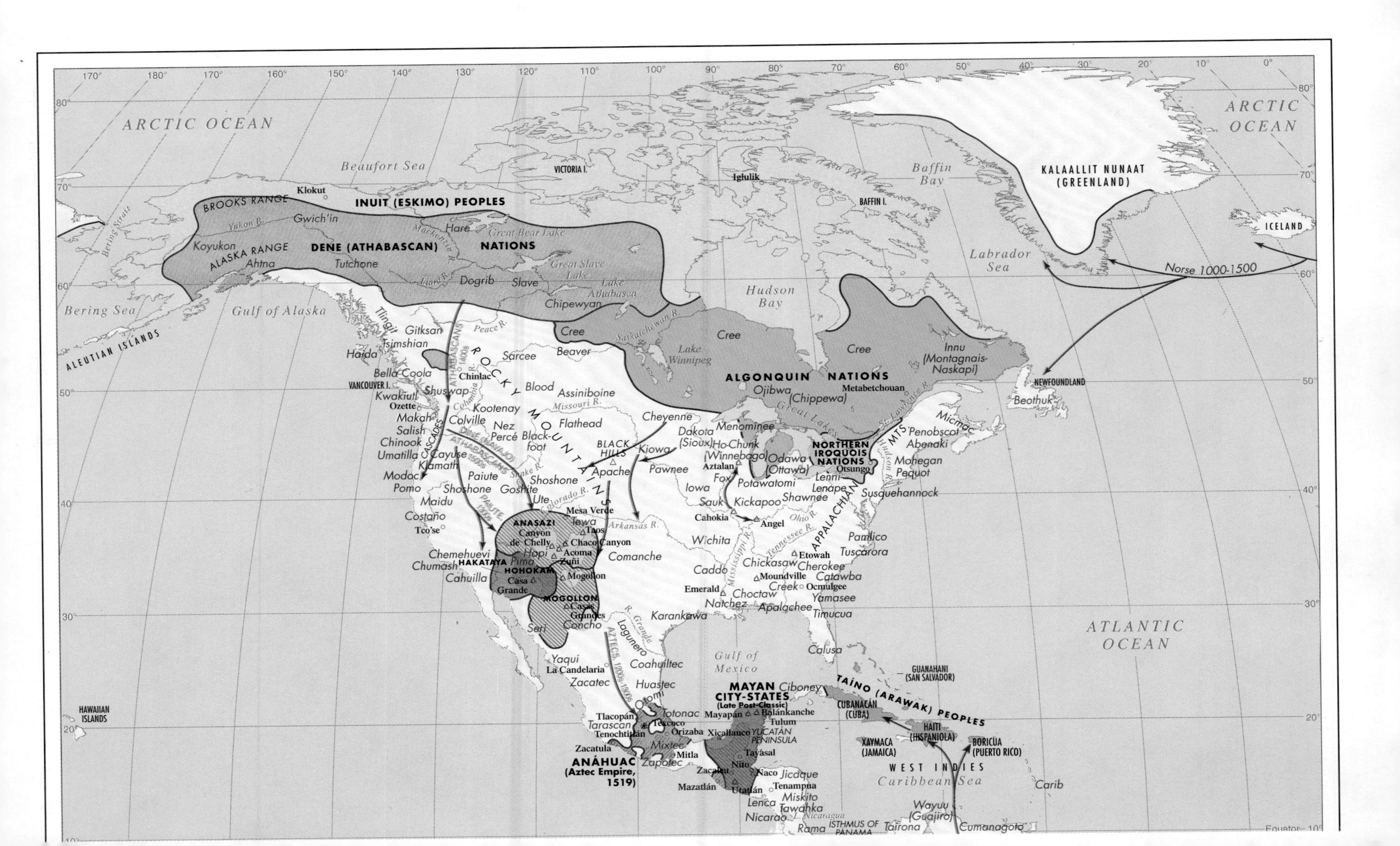

ARCTIC OCEAN
Beaufort Sea
VICTORIA I.
Iglulik
Baffin Bay
BAFFIN I.
KALAALLIT NUNAAT (GREENLAND)
ICELAND
Klokut
BROOKS RANGE
INUIT (ESKIMO) PEOPLES
Gwich'in
Yukon R.
Hare
Great Bear Lake
Koyukon
ALASKA RANGE
DENE (ATHABASCAN)
NATIONS
Ahtna
Tutchone
Great Slave Lake
Labrador Sea
Norse 1000-1500
Dogrib
Slave
Lake Athabasca
Hudson Bay
Bering Sea
Gulf of Alaska
Chipewyan
Bering Strait
ALEUTIAN ISLANDS
Tlingit
Gitksan
Tsimshian
Haida
Peace R.
Cree
Saskatchewan R.
Lake Winnipeg
Innu (Montagnais-Naskapi)
Sarcee
Beaver
ATHABASCANS 1400s
ROCKY MOUNTAINS
ALGONQUIN NATIONS
NEWFOUNDLAND
Bella Coola
Chinlac
VANCOUVER I.
Kwakiutl
Shuswap
Blood
Assiniboine
Ojibwa (Chippewa)
Metabetchouan
Beothuk
Ozette
Makah
Salish
Chinook
Umatilla
Kootenay
Colville
Nez Percé
Black-foot
Flathead
Missouri R.
Cheyenne
Dakota (Sioux)
Menominee
Great Lakes
St. Lawrence R.
Micmac
Penobscot
Abenaki
CASCADES
DINÉ (NAVAJO) ATHABASCANS 1500s
BLACK HILLS
Kiowa
Ho-Chunk (Winnebago)
Odawa (Ottawa)
NORTHERN IROQUOIS NATIONS
Otsungo
Hudson R.
MTS.
Mohegan
Pequot
Cayuse
Klamath
Modoc
Pomo
Paiute
Snake R.
Shoshone
Goshute
Apache
Pawnee
Aztalan
Fox
Potawatomi
Lenni-Lenape
Iowa
Sauk
Kickapoo
Shawnee
Susquehannock
Maidu
Costaño
Tco'se
PAIUTE 1300s
Ute
Colorado R.
Mesa Verde
Tewa
Taos
ANASAZI
Canyon de Chelly
Chaco Canyon
Hopi
Acoma
Zuñi
Arkansas R.
Cahokia
Angel
Ohio R.
Wichita
APPALACHIAN
Pamlico
Tuscarora
Chemehuevi
Chumash
HAKATAYA
Pima
HOHOKAM
Casa Grande
Cahuilla
Mogollon
Comanche
Caddo
Mississippi R.
Chickasaw
Tennessee R.
Etowah
Cherokee
Moundville
Catawba
Creek
Ocmulgee
Emerald
Choctaw
Natchez
Apalachee
Yamasee
Timucua
MOGOLLON
Casas Grandes
Concho
Seri
R. Grande
Karankawa
Lagunero
AZTECS, 1200s-1300s
ATLANTIC OCEAN
Yaqui
La Candelaria
Zacatec
Coahuiltec
Gulf of Mexico
Calusa
GUANAHANI (SAN SALVADOR)
Huastec
Otomi
MAYAN CITY-STATES (Late Post-Classic)
Ciboney
TAÍNO (ARAWAK) PEOPLES
CUBANACÁN (CUBA)
HAWAIIAN ISLANDS
Tlacopán
Tarascan
Tenochtitlán
Texcoco
Totonac
Orizaba
Mayapán
Balánkanche
Tulum
Xicallanco
YUCATÁN PENINSULA
HAITI (HISPANIOLA)
XAYMACA (JAMAICA)
BORICUA (PUERTO RICO)
Zacatula
Mixtec
Mitla
Tayásal
Nito
ANÁHUAC (Aztec Empire, 1519)
Zapotec
Zacaleu
Naco
Jicaque
WEST INDIES
Caribbean Sea
Carib
Mazatlán
Utatlán
Tenampua
Lenca
Miskito
Tawahka
Wayuu (Guajiro)
Nicarao
Nicaragua
Rama
ISTHMUS OF PANAMA
Tairona
Cumanagoto
Equator

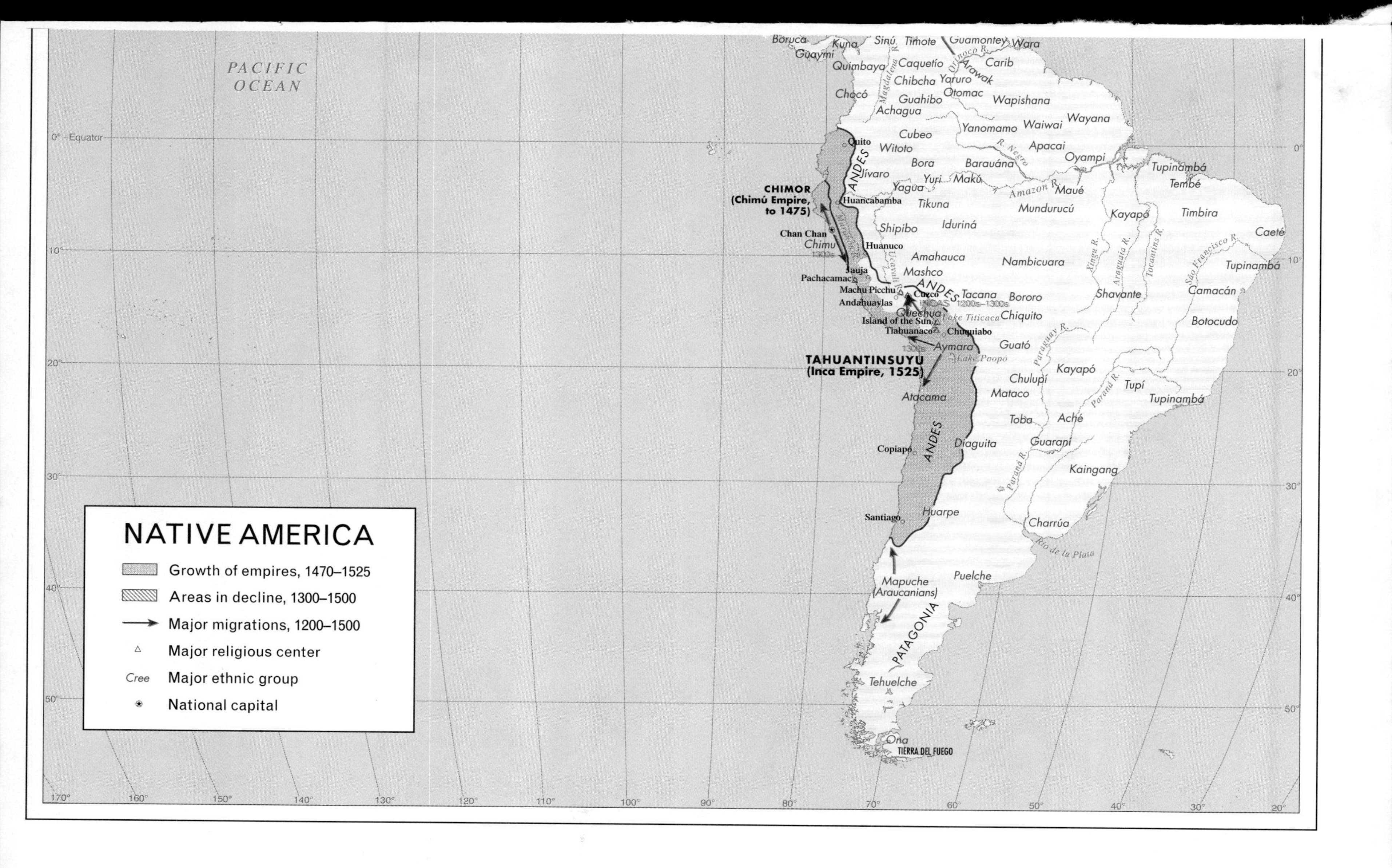
NATIVE AMERICA
Growth of empires, 1470–1525
Areas in decline, 1300–1500
Major migrations, 1200–1500
Major religious center
Cree
Major ethnic group
National capital
PACIFIC OCEAN
0° - Equator
CHIMOR (Chimú Empire, to 1475)
TAHUANTINSUYU (Inca Empire, 1525)
ANDES
PATAGONIA
TIERRA DEL FUEGO
INCAS 1200s–1300s
Chimu 1300s
Quito
Huancabamba
Chan Chan
Huanuco
Jauja
Pachacamac
Machu Picchu
Cuzco
Andahuaylas
Island of the Sun
Tiahuanaco
Chuquiabo
Copiapó
Santiago
Lake Titicaca
Lake Poopó
Amazon R.
R. Negro
Orinoco R.
Magdalena R.
Marañón R.
Ucayali R.
Xingu R.
Araguaia R.
Tocantins R.
São Francisco R.
Paraguay R.
Paraná R.
Río de la Plata
Boruca
Guaymi
Kuna
Sinú
Timote
Guamontey
Wara
Quimbaya
Caquetío
Carib
Arawak
Chibcha
Yaruro
Otomac
Chocó
Guahibo
Achagua
Wapishana
Wayana
Waiwai
Yanomamo
Cubeo
Witoto
Apacai
Oyampi
Bora
Barauána
Jívaro
Yuri
Makú
Yagua
Tikuna
Maué
Mundurucú
Tupinambá
Tembé
Timbira
Kayapó
Caeté
Shipibo
Iduriná
Amahauca
Mashco
Nambicuara
Tacana
Bororo
Quechua
Chiquito
Shavante
Camacán
Botocudo
Aymara
Guató
Kayapó
Chulupí
Mataco
Tupí
Tupinambá
Atacama
Toba
Aché
Diaguita
Guaraní
Kaingang
Huarpe
Charrúa
Puelche
Mapuche (Araucanians)
Tehuelche
Ona

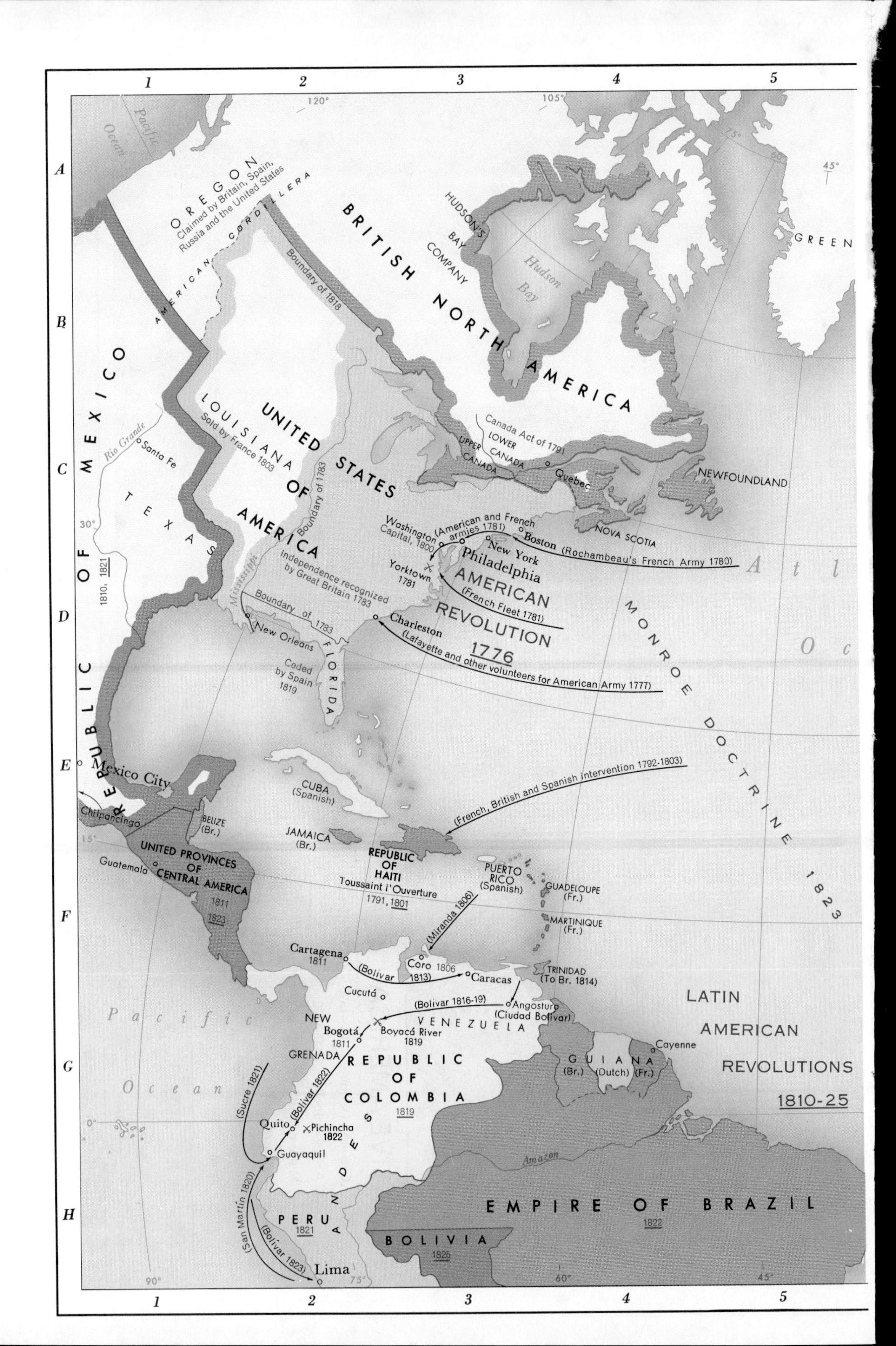

OREGON
Claimed by Britain, Spain, Russia and the United States
AMERICAN CORDILLERA
BRITISH NORTH AMERICA
HUDSON'S BAY COMPANY
Hudson Bay
GREEN
Boundary of 1818
REPUBLIC OF MEXICO
1810, 1821
Rio Grande
Santa Fe
TEXAS
LOUISIANA
Sold by France 1803
UNITED STATES OF AMERICA
Boundary of 1783
Mississippi
Independence recognized by Great Britain 1783
Canada Act of 1791
UPPER CANADA
LOWER CANADA
Quebec
NEWFOUNDLAND
NOVA SCOTIA
Washington Capital, 1800
(American and French armies 1781)
Boston
(Rochambeau's French Army 1780)
New York
Philadelphia
Yorktown 1781
AMERICAN REVOLUTION 1776
(French Fleet 1781)
Charleston
(Lafayette and other volunteers for American Army 1777)
Boundary of 1783
New Orleans
FLORIDA
Ceded by Spain 1819
MONROE DOCTRINE 1823
Atl
Oc
Mexico City
Chilpancingo
CUBA (Spanish)
(French, British and Spanish intervention 1792-1803)
BELIZE (Br.)
JAMAICA (Br.)
REPUBLIC OF HAITI
Toussaint l'Ouverture
1791, 1801
UNITED PROVINCES OF CENTRAL AMERICA
1811
1823
Guatemala
PUERTO RICO (Spanish)
GUADELOUPE (Fr.)
MARTINIQUE (Fr.)
(Miranda 1806)
Cartagena 1811
(Bolivar 1813)
Coro 1806
Caracas
TRINIDAD (To Br. 1814)
Cucutá
(Bolivar 1816-19)
Angostura (Ciudad Bolívar)
VENEZUELA
NEW GRENADA
Bogotá 1811
Boyacá River 1819
REPUBLIC OF COLOMBIA
1819
GUIANA
(Br.) (Dutch) (Fr.)
Cayenne
LATIN AMERICAN REVOLUTIONS 1810-25
Pacific Ocean
(Sucre 1821)
(Bolivar 1822)
Quito
Pichincha 1822
Guayaquil
ANDES
Amazon
EMPIRE OF BRAZIL
1822
PERU
1821
(San Martín 1820)
(Bolívar 1823)
Lima
BOLIVIA
1825

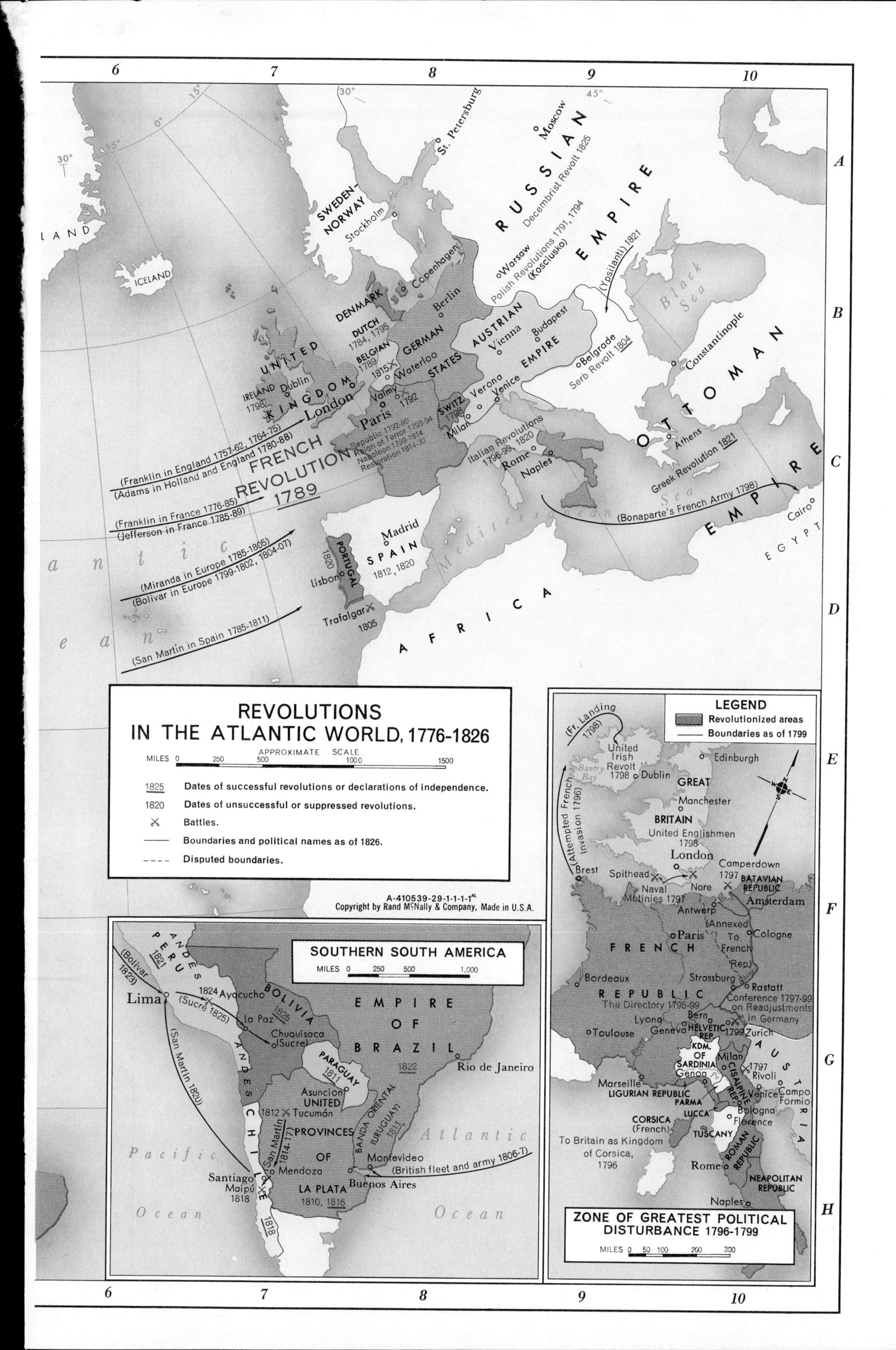

REVOLUTIONS IN THE ATLANTIC WORLD, 1776-1826
APPROXIMATE SCALE
MILES 0 250 500 1000 1500
1825 Dates of successful revolutions or declarations of independence.
1820 Dates of unsuccessful or suppressed revolutions.
Battles.
Boundaries and political names as of 1826.
Disputed boundaries.
A-410539-29-1-1-1-1
Copyright by Rand McNally & Company, Made in U.S.A.
ICELAND
SWEDEN-NORWAY
Stockholm
St. Petersburg
Moscow
RUSSIAN EMPIRE
Decembrist Revolt 1825
Warsaw
Polish Revolutions 1791, 1794 (Kosciusko)
(Ypsilanti) 1821
DENMARK
Copenhagen
Berlin
DUTCH 1784, 1795
BELGIAN 1789
1815 Waterloo
GERMAN STATES
AUSTRIAN EMPIRE
Vienna
Budapest
Belgrade
Serb Revolt 1804
Black Sea
Constantinople
OTTOMAN EMPIRE
UNITED KINGDOM
IRELAND 1798
Dublin
London
Valmy 1792
Paris
Republic 1792-99
Reign of Terror 1793-94
Napoleon 1799-1814
Restoration 1814-30
SWITZ. 1798
Milan
Verona
Venice
Italian Revolutions 1796-99, 1820
Rome
Naples
Athens
Greek Revolution 1821
(Bonaparte's French Army 1798)
Cairo
EGYPT
FRENCH REVOLUTION 1789
(Franklin in England 1757-62, 1764-75)
(Adams in Holland and England 1780-88)
(Franklin in France 1776-85)
(Jefferson in France 1785-89)
(Miranda in Europe 1785-1805)
(Bolivar in Europe 1799-1802, 1804-07)
(San Martin in Spain 1785-1811)
Madrid
SPAIN 1812, 1820
PORTUGAL
1820
Lisbon
Trafalgar 1805
Mediterranean Sea
AFRICA
Atlantic Ocean
SOUTHERN SOUTH AMERICA
MILES 0 250 500 1,000
PERU 1821
ANDES
(Bolivar 1823)
Lima
1824 Ayacucho
(Sucre 1825)
BOLIVIA 1825
La Paz
Chuquisaca (Sucre)
(San Martin 1820)
EMPIRE OF BRAZIL 1822
Rio de Janeiro
PARAGUAY 1811
Asuncion
UNITED PROVINCES OF LA PLATA 1810, 1816
1812 Tucumán
(San Martin 1814-17)
BANDA ORIENTAL (URUGUAY) 1811
Montevideo
(British fleet and army 1806-7)
Buenos Aires
Mendoza
Santiago
Maipú 1818
CHILE 1818
Pacific Ocean
Atlantic Ocean
LEGEND
Revolutionized areas
Boundaries as of 1799
(Fr. Landing 1798)
United Irish Revolt 1798
Dublin
Bantry Bay
(Attempted French Invasion 1796)
Edinburgh
GREAT BRITAIN
Manchester
United Englishmen 1798
London
Brest
Spithead
Nore
Naval Mutinies 1797
Camperdown 1797
BATAVIAN REPUBLIC
Amsterdam
Antwerp
(Annexed To French Rep.)
Cologne
Paris
FRENCH REPUBLIC
The Directory 1795-99
Bordeaux
Strassburg
Rastatt Conference 1797-99 on Readjustments in Germany
Lyons
Bern
Geneva
HELVETIC REP.
1799 Zurich
Toulouse
KDM. OF SARDINIA
Genoa
Milan
CISALPINE REP.
1797 Rivoli
AUSTRIA
Venice
Campo Formio
Marseille
LIGURIAN REPUBLIC
PARMA
LUCCA
Bologna
Florence
CORSICA (French)
TUSCANY
To Britain as Kingdom of Corsica, 1796
ROMAN REPUBLIC
Rome
NEAPOLITAN REPUBLIC
Naples
ZONE OF GREATEST POLITICAL DISTURBANCE 1796-1799
MILES 0 50 100 200 300

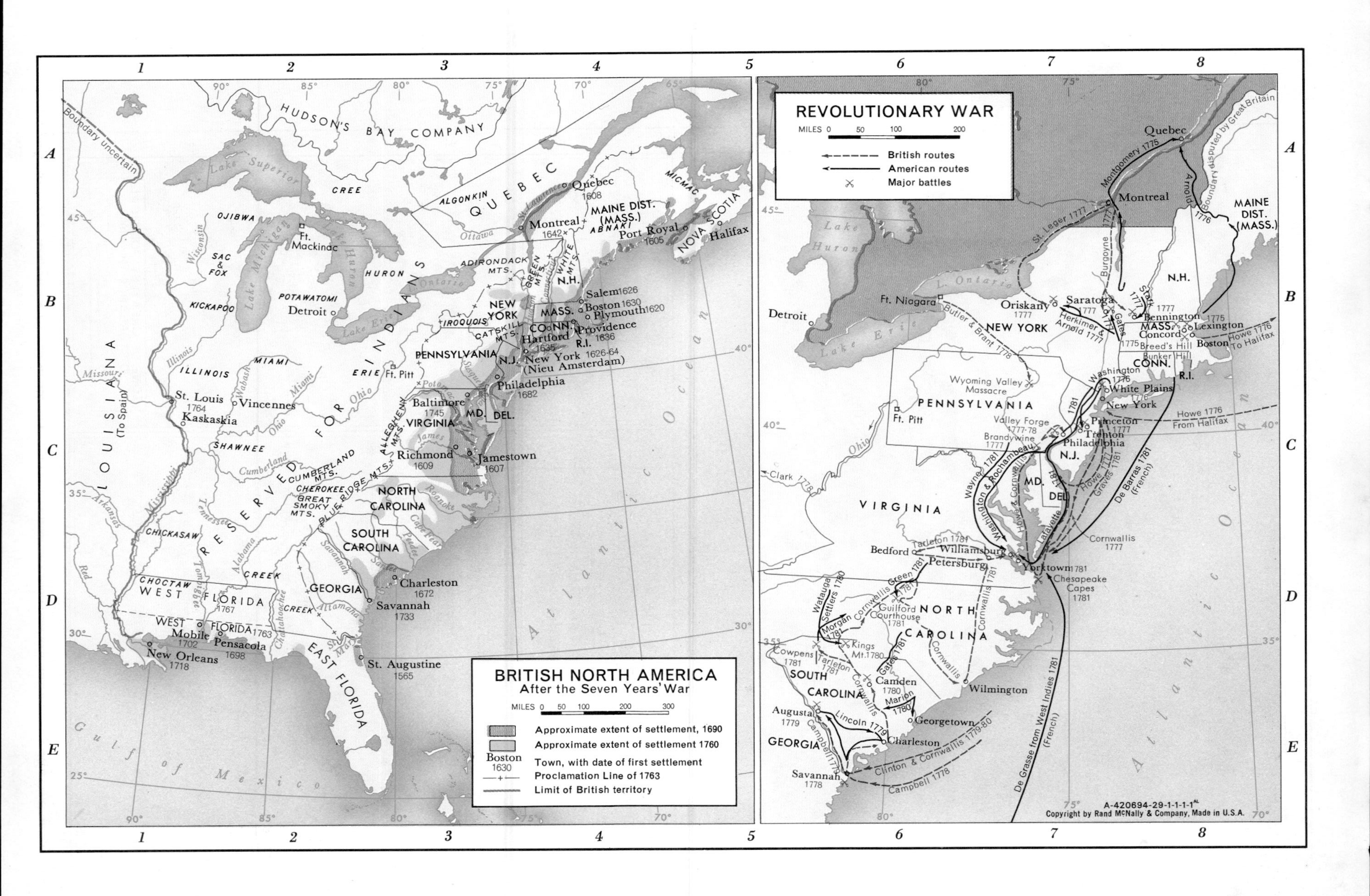

BRITISH NORTH AMERICA
After the Seven Years' War
MILES 0 50 100 200 300
Approximate extent of settlement, 1690
Approximate extent of settlement 1760
Boston 1630
Town, with date of first settlement
Proclamation Line of 1763
Limit of British territory
HUDSON'S BAY COMPANY
QUEBEC
LOUISIANA (To Spain)
RESERVED FOR INDIANS
Boundary uncertain
Lake Superior
Lake Michigan
Lake Huron
Lake Erie
Ontario
CREE
OJIBWA
SAC & FOX
KICKAPOO
ILLINOIS
MIAMI
POTAWATOMI
HURON
ERIE
SHAWNEE
ALGONKIN
ABNAKI
MICMAC
IROQUOIS
CHEROKEE
CHICKASAW
CHOCTAW
CREEK
ADIRONDACK MTS.
GREEN MTS.
WHITE MTS.
CATSKILL MTS.
ALLEGHENY MTS.
CUMBERLAND MTS.
GREAT SMOKY MTS.
BLUE RIDGE MTS.
Ft. Mackinac
Detroit
Ft. Pitt
St. Louis 1764
Kaskaskia
Vincennes
Quebec 1608
Montreal 1642
MAINE DIST. (MASS.)
Port Royal 1605
NOVA SCOTIA
Halifax
N.H.
MASS.
Salem 1626
Boston 1630
Plymouth 1620
Providence 1636
R.I.
CONN.
Hartford 1635
NEW YORK
New York 1626-64 (Nieu Amsterdam)
N.J.
PENNSYLVANIA
Philadelphia 1682
Baltimore 1745
MD.
DEL.
VIRGINIA
Richmond 1609
Jamestown 1607
NORTH CAROLINA
SOUTH CAROLINA
Charleston 1672
GEORGIA
Savannah 1733
St. Augustine 1565
EAST FLORIDA
WEST FLORIDA 1767
WEST FLORIDA 1763
Mobile 1702
Pensacola 1698
New Orleans 1718
Gulf of Mexico
Atlantic Ocean
Mississippi
Missouri
Ohio
Illinois
Wisconsin
Wabash
Tennessee
Cumberland
Arkansas
Red
Alabama
Tombigbee
Chattahoochee
Altamaha
Savannah
Santee
Pee Dee
Cape Fear
Roanoke
James
Potomac
Susquehanna
Connecticut
St. Lawrence
Ottawa
REVOLUTIONARY WAR
MILES 0 50 100 200
British routes
American routes
Major battles
Quebec
Montreal
Montgomery 1775
Arnold 1776
Boundary disputed by Great Britain
MAINE DIST. (MASS.)
St. Leger 1777
Burgoyne 1777
Oriskany 1777
Saratoga 1777
Herkimer & Arnold 1777
Gates 1777
Stark 1777
Bennington 1777
N.H.
MASS.
Lexington 1775
Concord
Breed's Hill
Bunker Hill
1775
Boston
Howe 1776 To Halifax
Howe 1776 From Halifax
CONN.
R.I.
Washington 1776
White Plains
New York
Princeton 1777
Trenton 1777
Philadelphia
N.J.
Valley Forge 1777-78
Brandywine 1777
Wyoming Valley Massacre
Butler & Brant 1778
Ft. Niagara
Detroit
Ft. Pitt
Clark 1778
PENNSYLVANIA
NEW YORK
MD.
DEL.
De Barras 1781 (French)
Howe 1777
Graves 1781
Cornwallis 1777
Washington & Rochambeau 1781
Wayne 1781
Howe & Cornwallis
Lafayette
Yorktown 1781
Chesapeake Capes 1781
VIRGINIA
Bedford
Tarleton 1781
Williamsburg
Petersburg
Cornwallis 1781
Green 1781
Watauga Settlers 1780
Morgan 1781
Guilford Courthouse 1781
Kings Mt. 1780
Cowpens 1781
Tarleton 1781
Gates 1781
Camden 1780
Marion 1780
Georgetown
Wilmington
NORTH CAROLINA
SOUTH CAROLINA
Augusta 1779
GEORGIA
Lincoln 1779
Charleston
Campbell 1779
Clinton & Cornwallis 1779-80
Campbell 1778
Savannah 1778
De Grasse from West Indies 1781 (French)
Lake Huron
Lake Erie
L. Ontario
Ohio
Atlantic Ocean
A-420694-29-1-1-1-1
Copyright by Rand McNally & Company, Made in U.S.A.

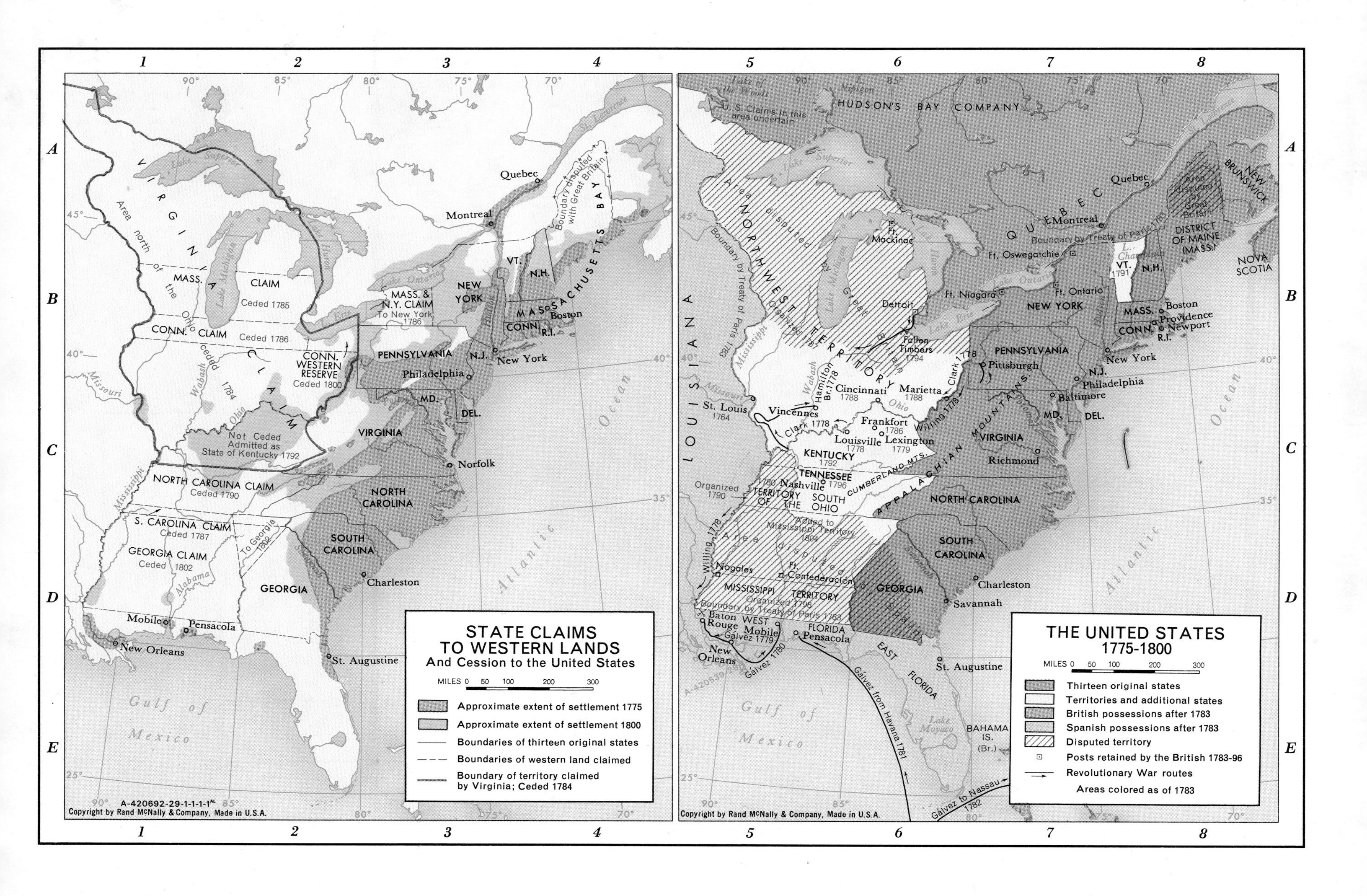

STATE CLAIMS
TO WESTERN LANDS
And Cession to the United States
MILES 0 50 100 200 300
Approximate extent of settlement 1775
Approximate extent of settlement 1800
Boundaries of thirteen original states
Boundaries of western land claimed
Boundary of territory claimed by Virginia; Ceded 1784
VIRGINIA CLAIM
Area north of the Ohio ceded 1784
MASS. CLAIM Ceded 1785
CONN. CLAIM Ceded 1786
CONN. WESTERN RESERVE Ceded 1800
MASS. & N.Y. CLAIM To New York 1786
Not Ceded Admitted as State of Kentucky 1792
NORTH CAROLINA CLAIM Ceded 1790
S. CAROLINA CLAIM Ceded 1787
GEORGIA CLAIM Ceded 1802
To Georgia 1802
Boundary disputed with Great Britain
MASSACHUSETTS BAY
VT.
N.H.
CONN.
R.I.
NEW YORK
PENNSYLVANIA
N.J.
MD.
DEL.
VIRGINIA
NORTH CAROLINA
SOUTH CAROLINA
GEORGIA
Quebec
Montreal
Boston
New York
Philadelphia
Norfolk
Charleston
St. Augustine
Mobile
Pensacola
New Orleans
Gulf of Mexico
Atlantic Ocean
A-420692-29-1-1-1-AL
Copyright by Rand McNally & Company, Made in U.S.A.
THE UNITED STATES
1775-1800
MILES 0 50 100 200 300
Thirteen original states
Territories and additional states
British possessions after 1783
Spanish possessions after 1783
Disputed territory
Posts retained by the British 1783-96
Revolutionary War routes
Areas colored as of 1783
HUDSON'S BAY COMPANY
U. S. Claims in this area uncertain
QUEBEC
NORTHWEST TERRITORY
Organized 1787
Area disputed by Great Britain
Boundary by Treaty of Paris 1783
LOUISIANA
NEW BRUNSWICK
DISTRICT OF MAINE (MASS.)
NOVA SCOTIA
VT. 1791
KENTUCKY 1792
TENNESSEE 1796
TERRITORY SOUTH OF THE OHIO
Organized 1790
MISSISSIPPI TERRITORY
Organized 1798
Added to Mississippi Territory 1804
WEST FLORIDA
EAST FLORIDA
APPALACHIAN MOUNTAINS
CUMBERLAND MTS.
Ft. Mackinac
Detroit
Fallen Timbers 1794
Ft. Niagara
Ft. Oswegatchie
Ft. Ontario
Pittsburgh
Cincinnati 1788
Marietta 1788
St. Louis 1764
Vincennes
Hamilton Br. 1778
Clark 1778
Willing 1778
Frankfort 1786
Louisville 1778
Lexington 1779
Nashville 1780
Nogales
Ft. Confederación
Baton Rouge
Mobile
Pensacola
New Orleans
Gálvez 1779
Gálvez 1780
Gálvez from Havana 1781
Gálvez to Nassau 1782
Savannah
St. Augustine
BAHAMA IS. (Br.)
Lake Moyaco
Richmond
Baltimore
Providence
Newport
Copyright by Rand McNally & Company, Made in U.S.A.

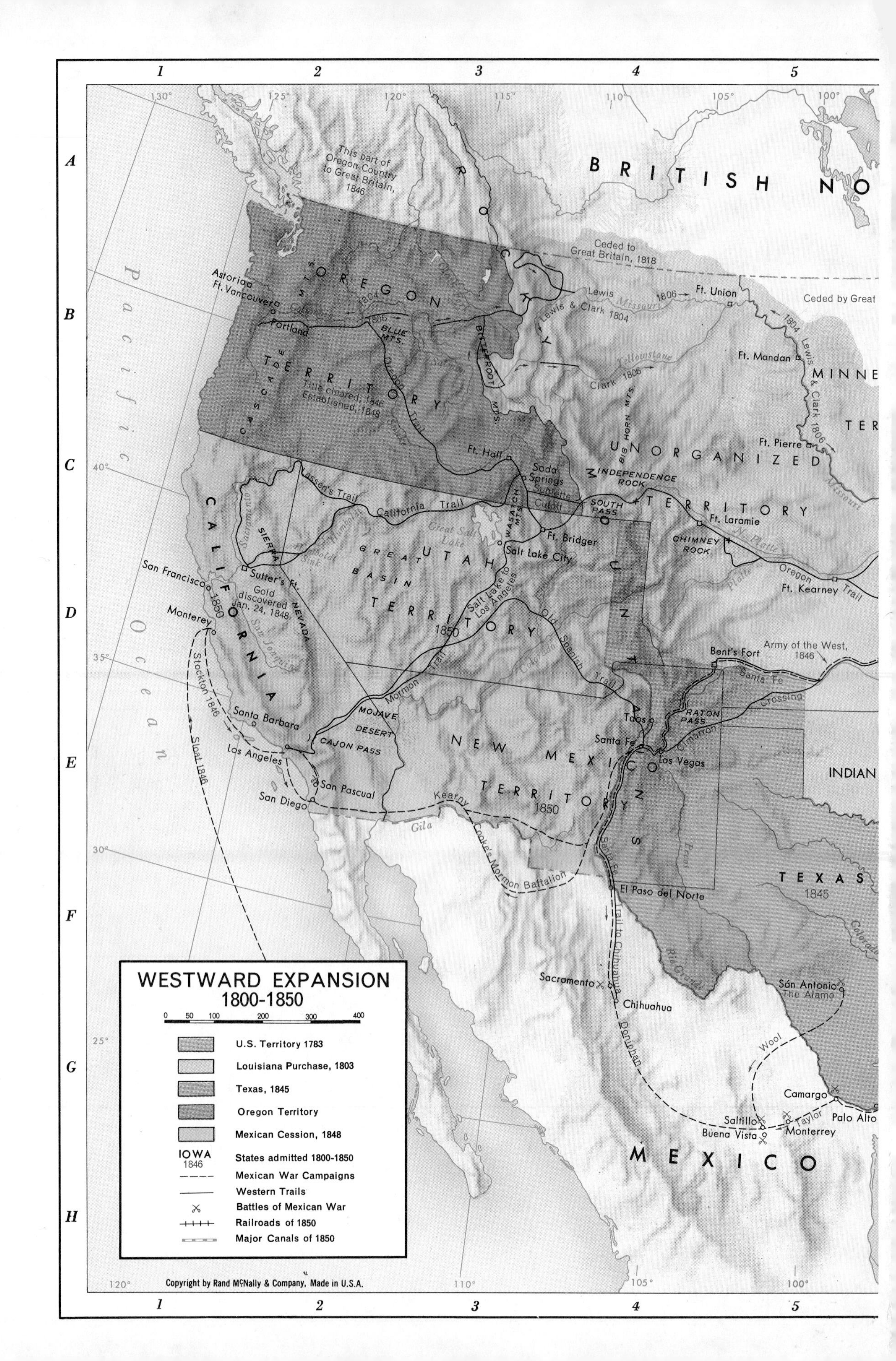
WESTWARD EXPANSION
1800-1850
0 50 100 200 300 400
U.S. Territory 1783
Louisiana Purchase, 1803
Texas, 1845
Oregon Territory
Mexican Cession, 1848
IOWA 1846 States admitted 1800-1850
Mexican War Campaigns
Western Trails
Battles of Mexican War
Railroads of 1850
Major Canals of 1850
BRITISH NO
This part of Oregon Country to Great Britain, 1846
Ceded to Great Britain, 1818
Ceded by Great
OREGON TERRITORY
Title cleared, 1846
Established, 1848
Astoria
Ft. Vancouver
Portland
CASCADE MTS.
BLUE MTS.
BITTERROOT MTS.
ROCKY MOUNTAINS
Oregon Trail
Lewis & Clark 1804
Clark 1806
Ft. Union
Ft. Mandan
Ft. Pierre
Ft. Hall
Soda Springs
Sublette Cutoff
SOUTH PASS
INDEPENDENCE ROCK
UNORGANIZED TERRITORY
Ft. Laramie
CHIMNEY ROCK
Ft. Kearney
Ft. Bridger
Salt Lake City
WASATCH MTS.
MINNE
TER
CALIFORNIA 1850
Lassen's Trail
California Trail
SIERRA NEVADA
Sutter's Ft.
Gold discovered Jan. 24, 1848
San Francisco
Monterey
GREAT BASIN
UTAH TERRITORY 1850
Salt Lake to Los Angeles
Old Spanish Trail
Mormon Trail
MOJAVE DESERT
CAJON PASS
Santa Barbara
Los Angeles
San Pascual
San Diego
Stockton 1846
Sloat 1846
Pacific Ocean
NEW MEXICO TERRITORY 1850
Bent's Fort
Army of the West, 1846
Santa Fe Crossing
RATON PASS
Cimarron
Taos
Santa Fe
Las Vegas
Kearny
Gila
Cooke's Mormon Battalion
El Paso del Norte
Trail to Chihuahua
INDIAN
TEXAS 1845
Rio Grande
Sacramento
Chihuahua
Doniphan
San Antonio
The Alamo
Wool
Camargo
Saltillo
Buena Vista
Monterrey
Taylor
Palo Alto
MEXICO
Copyright by Rand McNally & Company, Made in U.S.A.

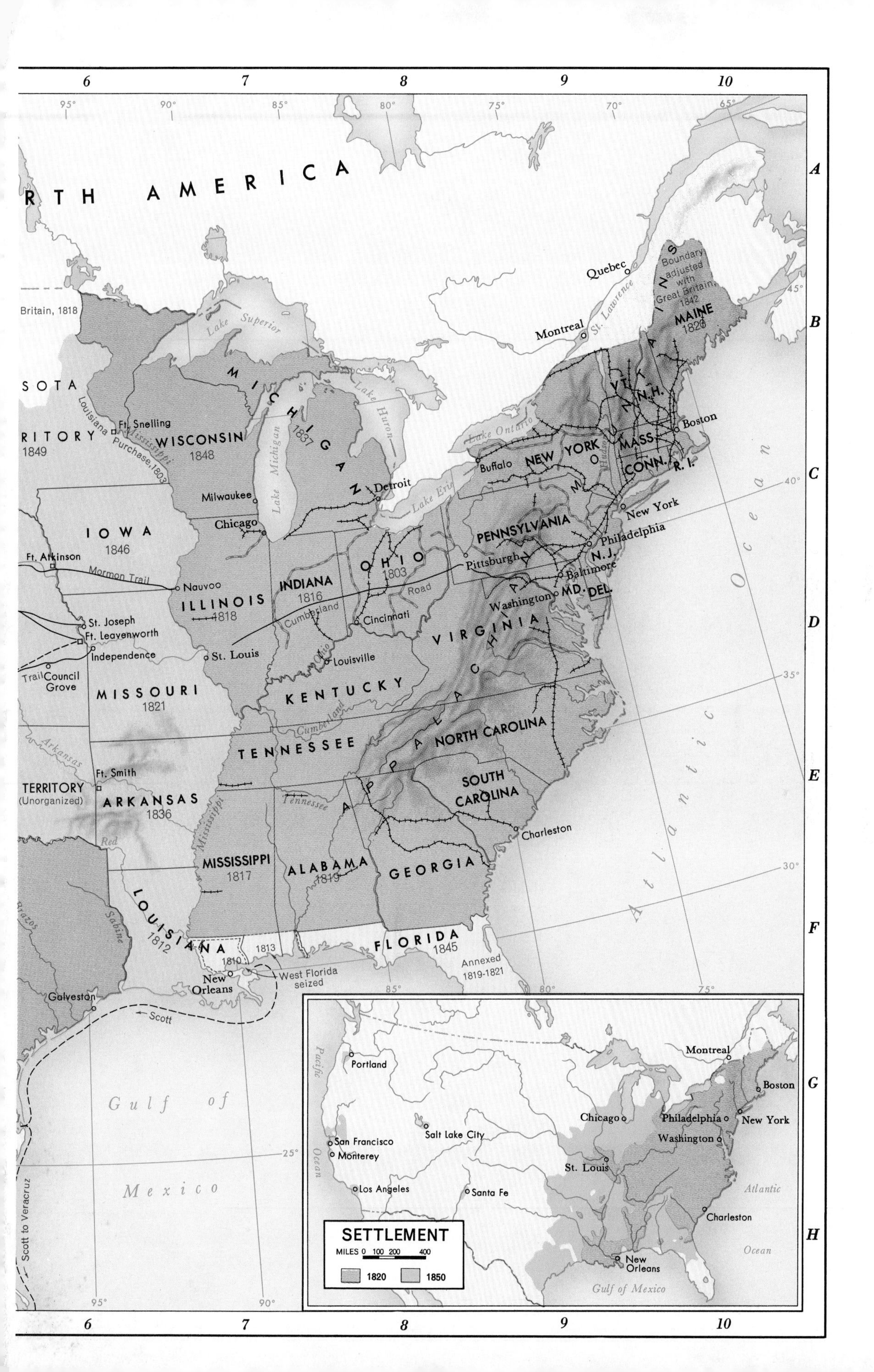

RTH AMERICA
Britain, 1818
SOTA
RITORY
1849
Louisiana Purchase,1803
Ft. Snelling
Mississippi
WISCONSIN
1848
Lake Superior
MICHIGAN
1837
Lake Michigan
Lake Huron
Lake Ontario
Lake Erie
Milwaukee
Chicago
Detroit
IOWA
1846
Ft. Atkinson
Mormon Trail
Nauvoo
ILLINOIS
1818
INDIANA
1816
OHIO
1803
Cumberland
Road
St. Joseph
Ft. Leavenworth
Independence
Trail
Council Grove
St. Louis
Cincinnati
Louisville
Ohio
MISSOURI
1821
KENTUCKY
Cumberland
TENNESSEE
Arkansas
Ft. Smith
TERRITORY
(Unorganized)
ARKANSAS
1836
Red
Tennessee
MISSISSIPPI
1817
ALABAMA
1819
GEORGIA
LOUISIANA
1812
Sabine
Brazos
1810
1813
New Orleans
West Florida seized
FLORIDA
1845
Annexed 1819-1821
Galveston
Scott
Scott to Veracruz
Gulf of Mexico
Quebec
Montreal
St. Lawrence
Boundary adjusted with Great Britain, 1842
MAINE
1820
VT.
N.H.
MASS.
Boston
NEW YORK
Hudson
CONN.
R.I.
Buffalo
New York
PENNSYLVANIA
Philadelphia
Pittsburgh
N.J.
Baltimore
MD.
DEL.
Washington
VIRGINIA
NORTH CAROLINA
SOUTH CAROLINA
Charleston
APPALACHIAN MTS.
Atlantic Ocean
SETTLEMENT
MILES 0 100 200 400
1820
1850
Portland
Pacific Ocean
San Francisco
Monterey
Los Angeles
Salt Lake City
Santa Fe
Chicago
St. Louis
Montreal
Boston
Philadelphia
New York
Washington
Charleston
New Orleans
Gulf of Mexico
Atlantic Ocean

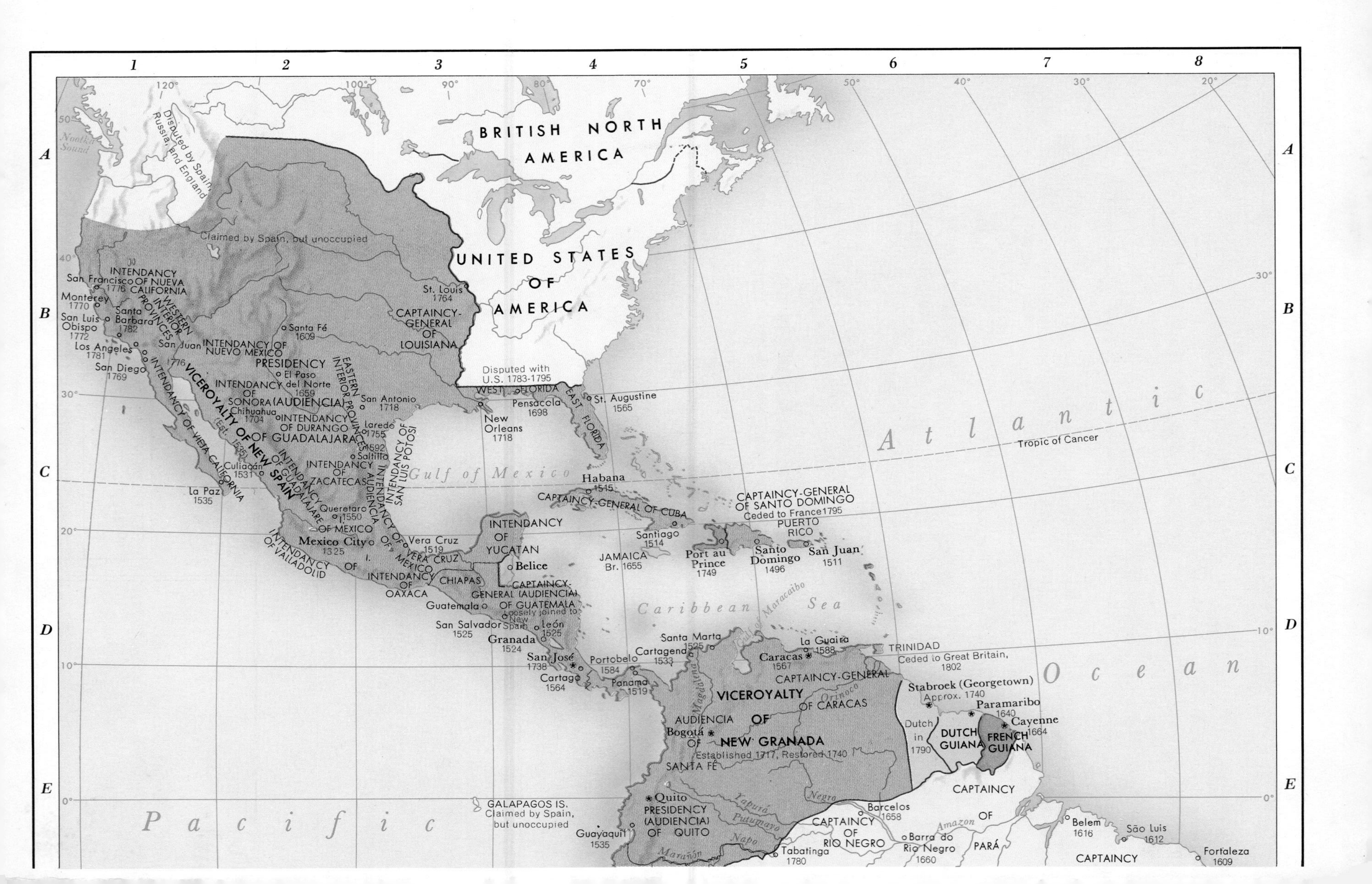

BRITISH NORTH AMERICA
UNITED STATES OF AMERICA
Disputed by Spain, Russia, and England
Nootka Sound
Claimed by Spain, but unoccupied
INTENDANCY OF NUEVA CALIFORNIA
San Francisco 1776
Monterey 1770
San Luis Obispo 1772
Santa Barbara 1782
Los Angeles 1781
San Diego 1769
WESTERN INTERIOR PROVINCES
San Juan
1776
INTENDANCY OF VIEJA CALIFORNIA
La Paz 1535
Santa Fé 1609
INTENDANCY OF NUEVO MEXICO
PRESIDENCY
El Paso
INTENDANCY del Norte 1659
OF SONORA
(AUDIENCIA)
Chihuahua 1704
INTENDANCY OF DURANGO
OF GUADALAJARA
VICEROYALTY OF NEW SPAIN
Culiacán 1531
EASTERN INTERIOR PROVINCES
San Antonio 1718
Laredo 1755
Saltillo 1592
INTENDANCY OF ZACATECAS
INTENDANCY OF SAN LUIS POTOSI
INTENDANCY OF GUADALAJARE
AUDIENCIA
Queretaro 1550
OF MEXICO
Mexico City 1325
INTENDANCY OF VALLADOLID
INTENDANCY OF MEXICO
VERA CRUZ
Vera Cruz 1519
INTENDANCY OF OAXACA
CHIAPAS
St. Louis 1764
CAPTAINCY-GENERAL OF LOUISIANA
Disputed with U.S. 1783-1795
WEST FLORIDA
EAST FLORIDA
Pensacola 1698
New Orleans 1718
St. Augustine 1565
Gulf of Mexico
Habana 1515
CAPTAINCY-GENERAL OF CUBA
INTENDANCY OF YUCATAN
Belice
CAPTAINCY-GENERAL (AUDIENCIA) OF GUATEMALA
Loosely joined to New Spain
Guatemala
San Salvador 1525
León 1525
Granada 1524
San José 1738
Cartago 1564
Portobelo 1584
Panama 1519
Cartagena 1533
Santa Marta 1525
JAMAICA Br. 1655
Santiago 1514
Port au Prince 1749
Santo Domingo 1496
San Juan 1511
CAPTAINCY-GENERAL OF SANTO DOMINGO
Ceded to France 1795
PUERTO RICO
Caribbean Sea
Gulf of Maracaibo
La Guaira 1588
Caracas 1567
CAPTAINCY-GENERAL OF CARACAS
TRINIDAD
Ceded to Great Britain, 1802
Atlantic Ocean
Tropic of Cancer
Magdalena
Orinoco
VICEROYALTY OF NEW GRANADA
AUDIENCIA
Bogotá
OF SANTA FÉ
Established 1717, Restored 1740
Stabroek (Georgetown)
Approx. 1740
Paramaribo 1640
Cayenne 1664
Dutch in 1790
DUTCH GUIANA
FRENCH GUIANA
GALAPAGOS IS.
Claimed by Spain, but unoccupied
Pacific
Quito
PRESIDENCY (AUDIENCIA) OF QUITO
Guayaquil 1535
Tapurá
Putumayo
Napo
Marañon
Negro
Amazon
Tabatinga 1780
CAPTAINCY OF RIO NEGRO
Barcelos 1658
Barra do Rio Negro 1660
CAPTAINCY OF PARÁ
Belem 1616
São Luis 1612
Fortaleza 1609
CAPTAINCY
1 2 3 4 5 6 7 8
A B C D E
120° 100° 90° 80° 70° 50° 40° 30° 20°
40° 30° 20° 10° 0°

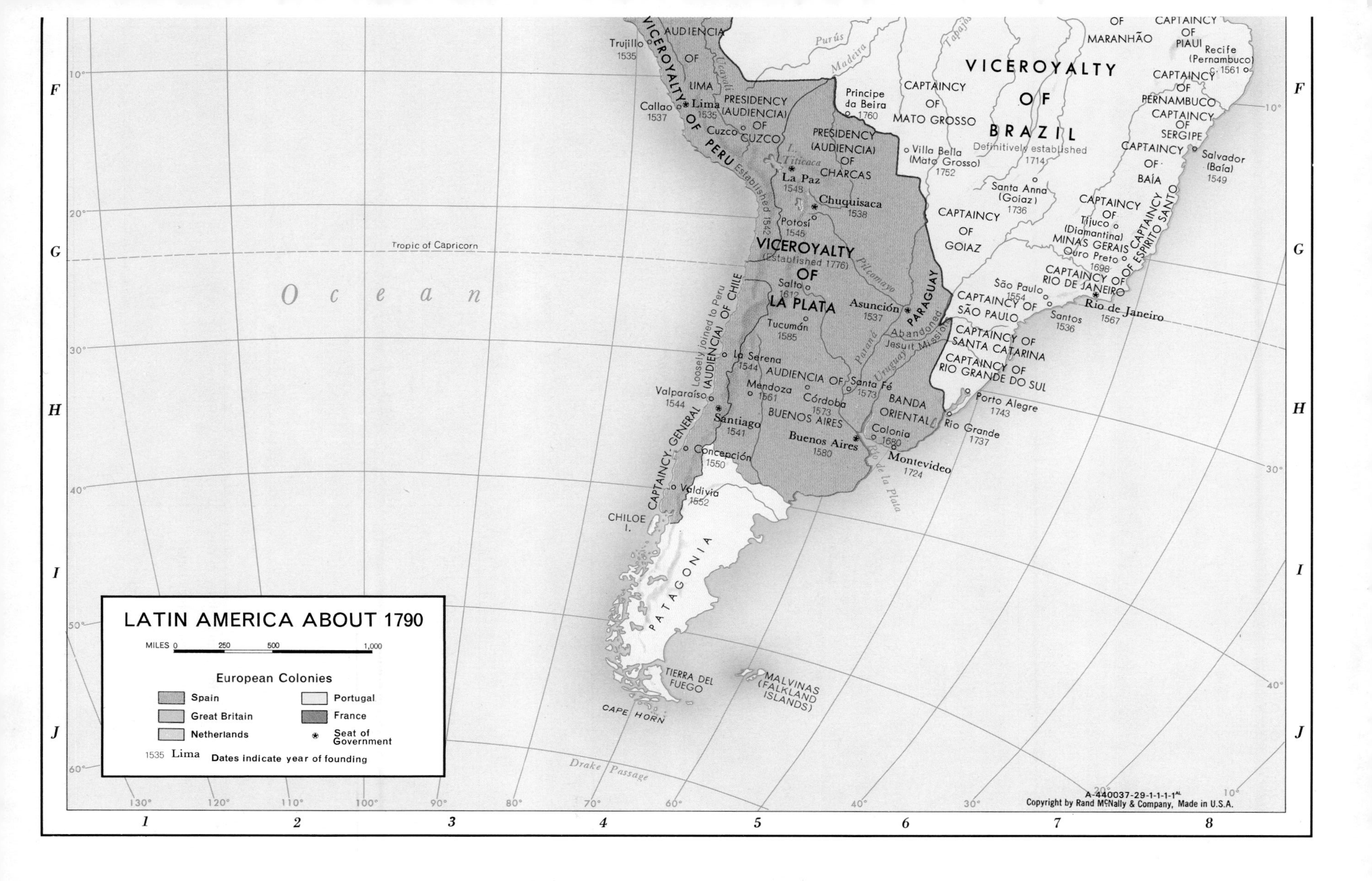

LATIN AMERICA ABOUT 1790
MILES 0 250 500 1,000
European Colonies
Spain
Great Britain
Netherlands
Portugal
France
Seat of Government
1535 Lima Dates indicate year of founding
VICEROYALTY OF PERU
AUDIENCIA OF LIMA
Trujillo 1535
Callao 1537
Lima 1535
PRESIDENCY (AUDIENCIA) OF CUZCO
Cuzco
Established 1542
PRESIDENCY (AUDIENCIA) OF CHARCAS
L. Titicaca
La Paz 1548
Chuquisaca 1538
Potosí 1545
VICEROYALTY OF LA PLATA
(Established 1776)
Salto 1612
Asunción 1537
PARAGUAY
Tucumán 1585
Abandoned Jesuit Missions
AUDIENCIA OF BUENOS AIRES
Santa Fé 1573
Córdoba 1573
Buenos Aires 1580
BANDA ORIENTAL
Colonia 1680
Montevideo 1724
Río de la Plata
Pilcomayo
Paraná
Uruguay
Loosely joined to Peru
CAPTAINCY GENERAL (AUDIENCIA) OF CHILE
La Serena 1544
Mendoza 1561
Valparaíso 1544
Santiago 1541
Concepción 1550
Valdivia 1552
CHILOE I.
PATAGONIA
TIERRA DEL FUEGO
CAPE HORN
MALVINAS (FALKLAND ISLANDS)
Drake Passage
Tropic of Capricorn
Ocean
Purús
Madeira
Tapajós
Ucayali
Principe da Beira 1760
VICEROYALTY OF BRAZIL
Definitively established
CAPTAINCY OF MATO GROSSO
Villa Bella (Mato Grosso) 1752
Santa Anna (Goiaz) 1736
1714
CAPTAINCY OF GOIAZ
OF MARANHÃO
CAPTAINCY OF PIAUI
Recife (Pernambuco) c. 1561
CAPTAINCY OF PERNAMBUCO
CAPTAINCY OF SERGIPE
CAPTAINCY OF BAÍA
Salvador (Baía) 1549
CAPTAINCY OF ESPIRITO SANTO
CAPTAINCY OF MINAS GERAIS
Tijuco (Diamantina)
Ouro Preto 1698
CAPTAINCY OF RIO DE JANEIRO
Rio de Janeiro 1567
São Paulo 1554
Santos 1536
CAPTAINCY OF SÃO PAULO
CAPTAINCY OF SANTA CATARINA
CAPTAINCY OF RIO GRANDE DO SUL
Porto Alegre 1743
Rio Grande 1737
A-440037-29-1-1-1
Copyright by Rand McNally & Company, Made in U.S.A.

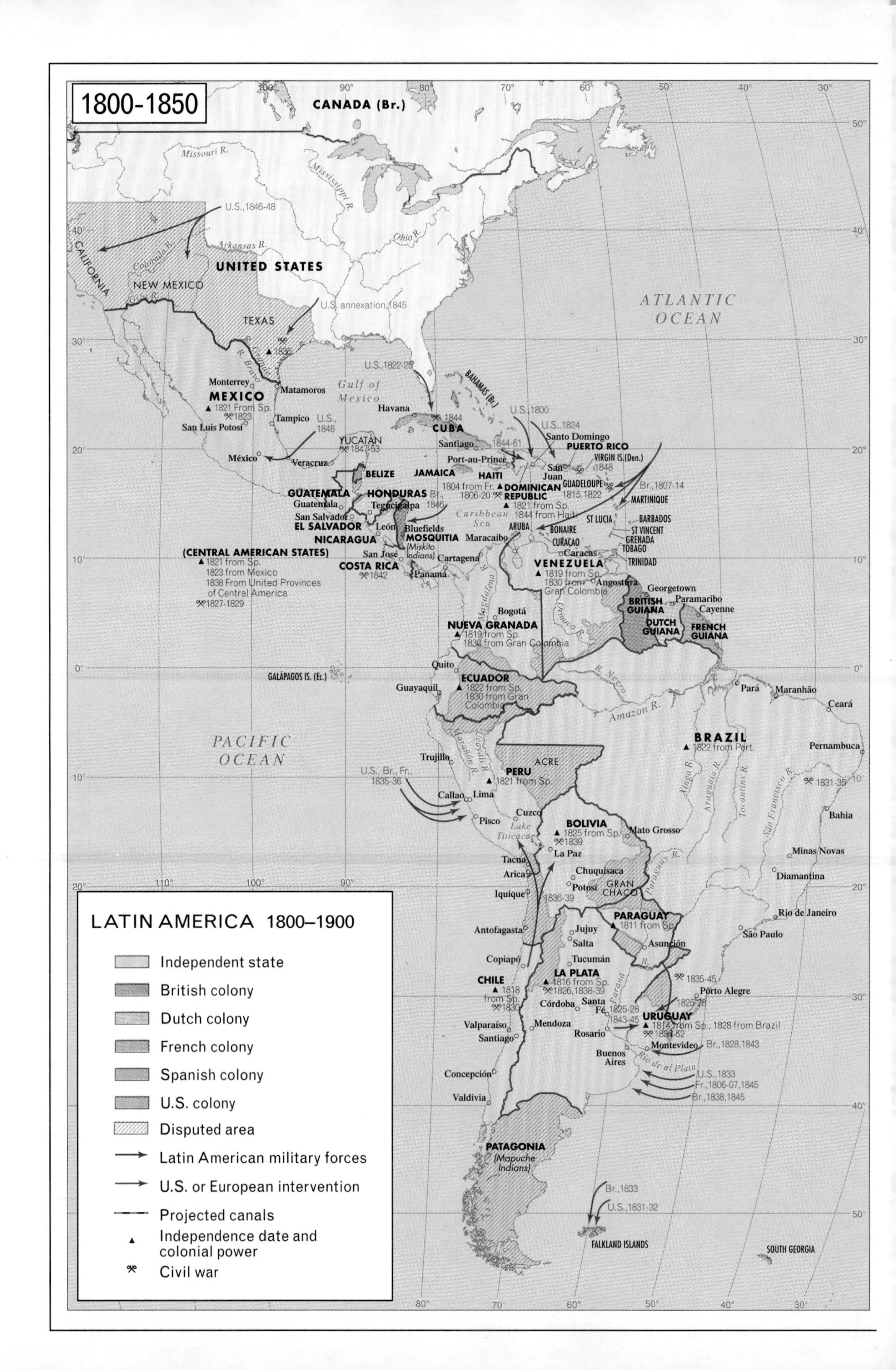
1800-1850
LATIN AMERICA 1800–1900
Independent state
British colony
Dutch colony
French colony
Spanish colony
U.S. colony
Disputed area
Latin American military forces
U.S. or European intervention
Projected canals
Independence date and colonial power
Civil war
CANADA (Br.)
UNITED STATES
ATLANTIC OCEAN
PACIFIC OCEAN
CALIFORNIA
NEW MEXICO
TEXAS
U.S.,1846-48
U.S. annexation,1845
1836
U.S.,1822-25
Missouri R.
Mississippi R.
Ohio R.
Arkansas R.
Colorado R.
R. Grande
R. Bravo
Gulf of Mexico
Monterrey
Matamoros
MEXICO
▲ 1821 From Sp.
1823
Tampico
U.S., 1848
San Luis Potosí
México
Veracruz
YUCATÁN
1847-53
Havana
1844
CUBA
BAHAMAS (Br.)
U.S.,1800
U.S.,1824
Santo Domingo
PUERTO RICO
Santiago
1844-61
Port-au-Prince
San Juan
VIRGIN IS.(Den.)
1848
BELIZE
JAMAICA
HAITI
1804 from Fr.
1806-20
DOMINICAN REPUBLIC
▲ 1821 from Sp.
1844 from Haiti
GUADELOUPE
1815,1822
Br.,1807-14
MARTINIQUE
GUATEMALA
Guatemala
HONDURAS
Tegucigalpa
Br., 1846
San Salvador
EL SALVADOR
León
Bluefields
MOSQUITIA
(Miskito Indians)
NICARAGUA
Caribbean Sea
ARUBA
BONAIRE
CURAÇAO
ST LUCIA
BARBADOS
ST VINCENT
GRENADA
TOBAGO
TRINIDAD
Maracaibo
Caracas
(CENTRAL AMERICAN STATES)
▲ 1821 from Sp.
1823 from Mexico
1838 From United Provinces of Central America
1827-1829
San José
COSTA RICA
1842
Cartagena
Panamá
VENEZUELA
▲ 1819 from Sp.
1830 from Gran Colombia
Angostura
Georgetown
BRITISH GUIANA
Paramaribo
DUTCH GUIANA
Cayenne
FRENCH GUIANA
Bogotá
NUEVA GRANADA
▲ 1819 from Sp.
1830 from Gran Colombia
Magdalena R.
Orinoco R.
Quito
GALÁPAGOS IS. (Ec.)
ECUADOR
▲ 1822 from Sp.
1830 from Gran Colombia
Guayaquil
R. Negro
Amazon R.
Pará
Maranhão
Ceará
BRAZIL
▲ 1822 from Port.
Pernambuca
Trujillo
Marañón R.
Ucayali R.
PERU
ACRE
▲ 1821 from Sp.
U.S., Br., Fr., 1835-36
Callao
Lima
Pisco
Cuzco
Lake Titicaca
BOLIVIA
▲ 1825 from Sp.
1839
La Paz
Mato Grosso
Xingu R.
Araguaia R.
Tocantins R.
São Francisco R.
1831-35
Bahia
Minas Novas
Diamantina
Tacna
Arica
Chuquisaca
Potosí
GRAN CHACO
Paraguay R.
Iquique
1836-39
PARAGUAY
▲ 1811 from Sp.
Rio de Janeiro
São Paulo
Antofagasta
Jujuy
Salta
Asunción
Copiapó
Tucumán
CHILE
▲ 1818 from Sp.
1830
LA PLATA
▲ 1816 from Sp.
1826,1838-39
1835-45
Pôrto Alegre
1825-28
Córdoba
Santa Fé
1825-28
1843-45
URUGUAY
▲ 1814 from Sp., 1828 from Brazil
1836-52
Valparaíso
Mendoza
Santiago
Rosario
Montevideo
Br.,1828,1843
Buenos Aires
Río de al Plata
U.S.,1833
Fr.,1806-07,1845
Br.,1838,1845
Concepción
Valdivia
PATAGONIA
(Mapuche Indians)
Br.,1833
U.S.,1831-32
FALKLAND ISLANDS
SOUTH GEORGIA

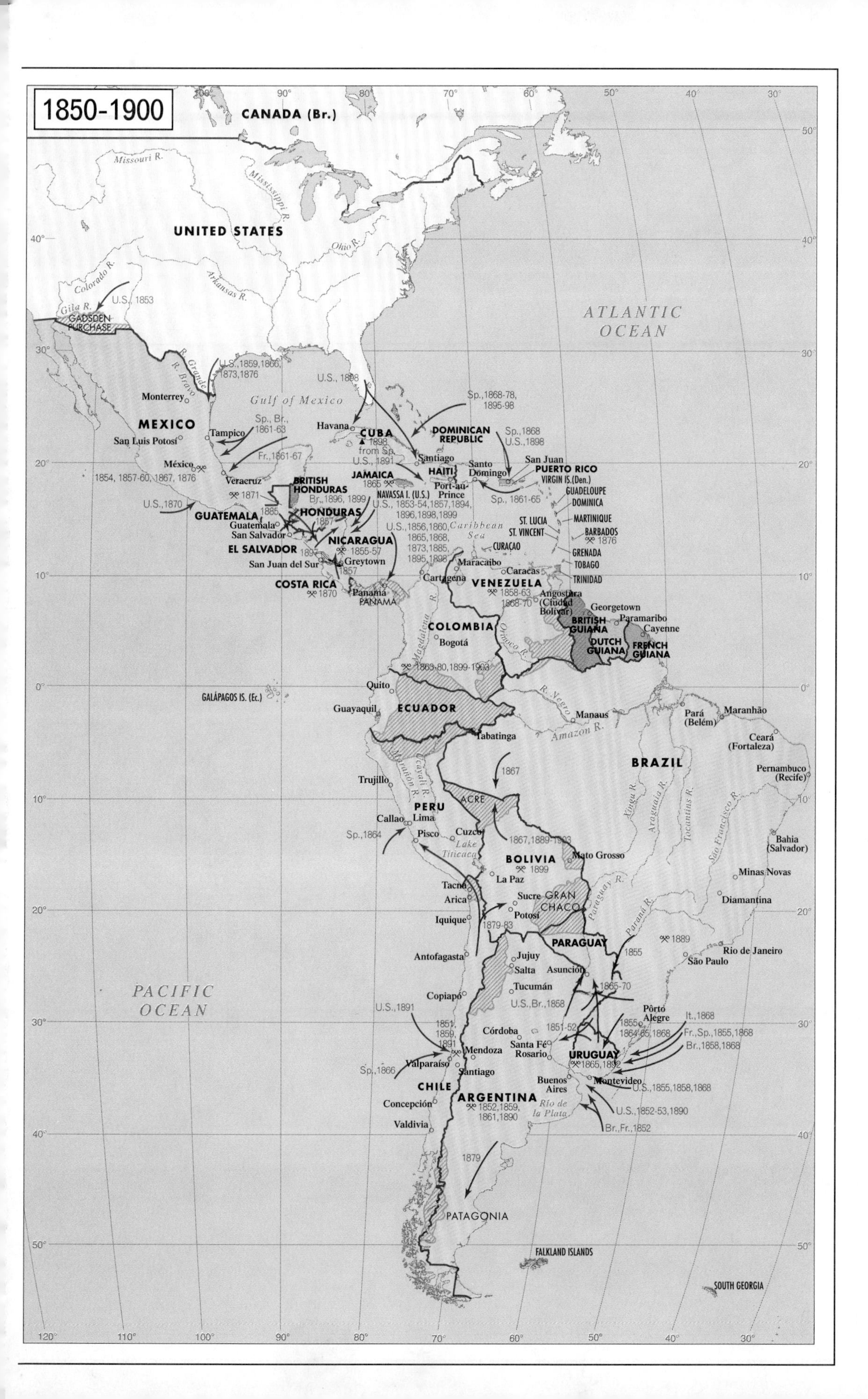

1850-1900
CANADA (Br.)
UNITED STATES
MEXICO
GUATEMALA
BRITISH HONDURAS
HONDURAS
EL SALVADOR
NICARAGUA
COSTA RICA
PANAMA
CUBA
HAITI
DOMINICAN REPUBLIC
JAMAICA
PUERTO RICO
COLOMBIA
VENEZUELA
BRITISH GUIANA
DUTCH GUIANA
FRENCH GUIANA
ECUADOR
PERU
BOLIVIA
BRAZIL
PARAGUAY
URUGUAY
CHILE
ARGENTINA
ACRE
GRAN CHACO
PATAGONIA
GADSDEN PURCHASE
ATLANTIC OCEAN
PACIFIC OCEAN
Gulf of Mexico
Caribbean Sea
Río de la Plata
GALÁPAGOS IS. (Ec.)
FALKLAND ISLANDS
SOUTH GEORGIA
NAVASSA I. (U.S.)
VIRGIN IS.(Den.)
GUADELOUPE
DOMINICA
MARTINIQUE
ST. LUCIA
ST. VINCENT
BARBADOS
GRENADA
TOBAGO
TRINIDAD
CURAÇAO
U.S., 1853
U.S.,1859,1866, 1873,1876
U.S., 1898
Sp.,1868-78, 1895-98
Sp., Br., 1861-63
Fr.,1861-67
1854, 1857-60, 1867, 1876
U.S.,1870
1871
1885
1898 from Sp. U.S., 1891
1865
Br.,1896, 1899
U.S., 1853-54,1857,1894, 1896,1898,1899
U.S.,1856,1860, 1865,1868, 1873,1885, 1895,1898
1855-57
1857
1870
Sp.,1868 U.S.,1898
Sp., 1861-65
1876
1858-63 1868-70
1863-80,1899-1903
1867
1867,1889-1903
1899
Sp.,1864
1879-83
1889
1855
1865-70
U.S.,Br.,1858
U.S.,1891
1851, 1859, 1891
1851-52
Sp.,1866
1855, 1864, 65, 1868
It.,1868
Fr.,Sp.,1855,1868
Br.,1858,1868
1865,1892
U.S.,1855,1858,1868
U.S.,1852-53,1890
Br.,Fr.,1852
1852,1859, 1861,1890
1879
Monterrey
Tampico
San Luis Potosí
México
Veracruz
Havana
Santiago
Port-au-Prince
Santo Domingo
San Juan
Guatemala
San Salvador
San Juan del Sur
Greytown
Panamá
Cartagena
Maracaibo
Caracas
Angostura (Ciudad Bolívar)
Georgetown
Paramaribo
Cayenne
Bogotá
Quito
Guayaquil
Manaus
Pará (Belém)
Maranhão
Ceará (Fortaleza)
Pernambuco (Recife)
Tabatinga
Trujillo
Callao
Lima
Pisco
Cuzco
Lake Titicaca
La Paz
Mato Grosso
Tacna
Arica
Iquique
Sucre
Potosí
Antofagasta
Jujuy
Salta
Tucumán
Asunción
Bahia (Salvador)
Minas Novas
Diamantina
Rio de Janeiro
São Paulo
Pôrto Alegre
Copiapó
Córdoba
Santa Fé
Rosario
Mendoza
Valparaíso
Santiago
Buenos Aires
Montevideo
Concepción
Valdivia
Missouri R.
Mississippi R.
Ohio R.
Arkansas R.
Colorado R.
Gila R.
R. Grande
R. Bravo
Magdalena R.
Orinoco R.
R. Negro
Amazon R.
Ucayali R.
Marañón R.
Xingu R.
Araguaia R.
Tocantins R.
São Francisco R.
Paraguay R.
Paraná R.

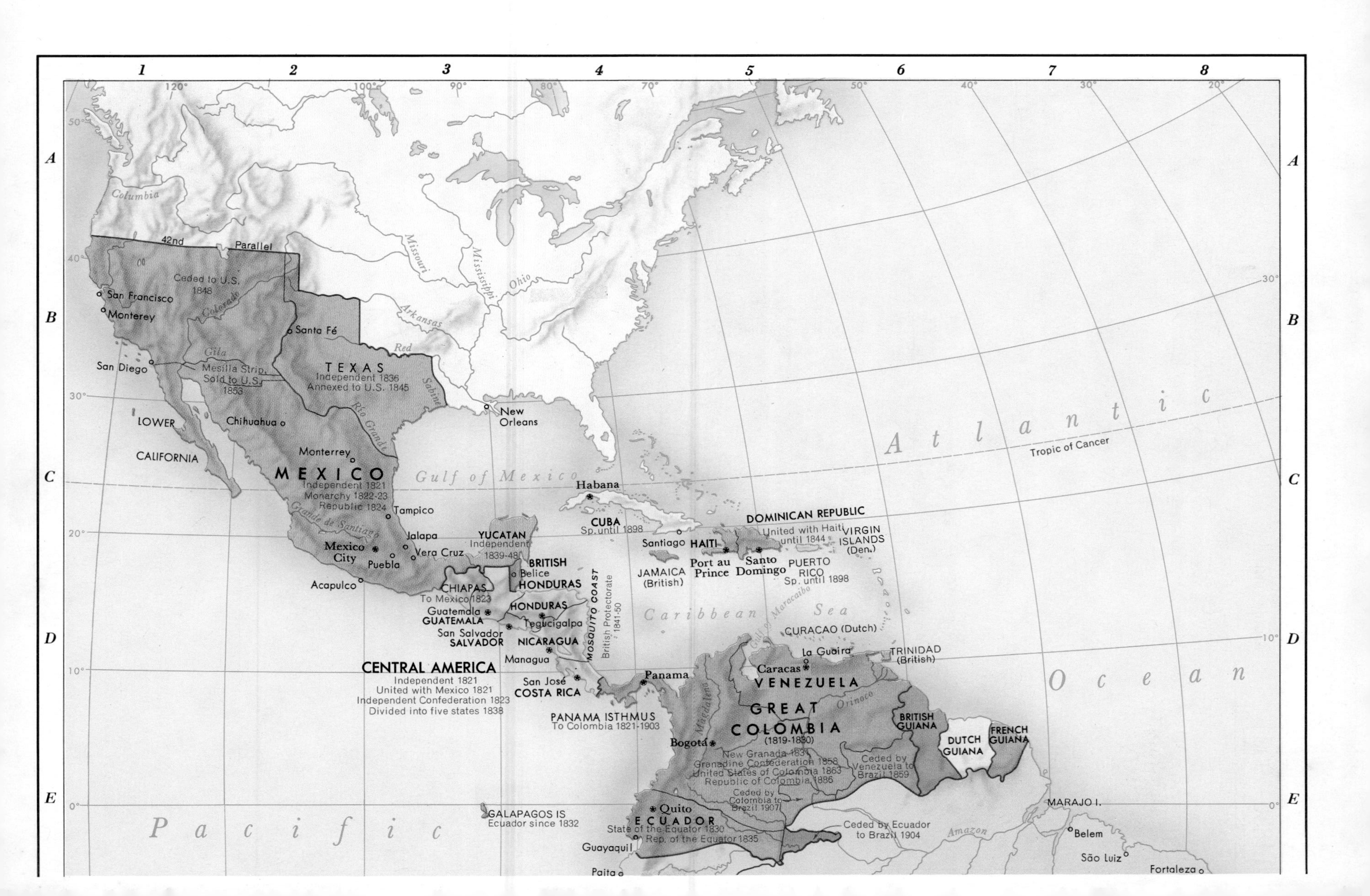

Pacific
Atlantic
Ocean
Gulf of Mexico
Caribbean Sea
Gulf of Maracaibo
Tropic of Cancer
42nd Parallel
Ceded to U.S. 1848
San Francisco
Monterey
San Diego
LOWER CALIFORNIA
Mesilla Strip Sold to U.S. 1853
Santa Fé
TEXAS
Independent 1836
Annexed to U.S. 1845
Chihuahua
Monterrey
MEXICO
Independent 1821
Monarchy 1822-23
Republic 1824
Tampico
Jalapa
Mexico City
Puebla
Vera Cruz
Acapulco
Columbia
Colorado
Gila
Rio Grande
Grande de Santiago
Missouri
Mississippi
Ohio
Arkansas
Red
Sabine
New Orleans
YUCATAN
Independent 1839-48
BRITISH HONDURAS
Belice
CHIAPAS
To Mexico 1823
Guatemala
GUATEMALA
San Salvador
SALVADOR
HONDURAS
Tegucigalpa
NICARAGUA
Managua
MOSQUITO COAST
British Protectorate 1841-50
San José
COSTA RICA
CENTRAL AMERICA
Independent 1821
United with Mexico 1821
Independent Confederation 1823
Divided into five states 1838
PANAMA ISTHMUS
To Colombia 1821-1903
Panama
Habana
CUBA
Sp. until 1898
Santiago
JAMAICA (British)
HAITI
Port au Prince
DOMINICAN REPUBLIC
United with Haiti until 1844
Santo Domingo
PUERTO RICO
Sp. until 1898
VIRGIN ISLANDS (Den.)
CURACAO (Dutch)
TRINIDAD (British)
La Guaira
Caracas
VENEZUELA
GREAT COLOMBIA
(1819-1830)
New Granada 1831
Granadine Confederation 1858
United States of Colombia 1863
Republic of Colombia 1886
Bogotá
Magdalena
Orinoco
Ceded by Venezuela to Brazil 1859
Ceded by Colombia to Brazil 1907
BRITISH GUIANA
DUTCH GUIANA
FRENCH GUIANA
Quito
ECUADOR
State of the Equator 1830
Rep. of the Equator 1835
Guayaquil
Paita
Ceded by Ecuador to Brazil 1904
GALAPAGOS IS
Ecuador since 1832
Amazon
MARAJO I.
Belem
São Luiz
Fortaleza

LATIN AMERICA AFTER INDEPENDENCE: 1821–1929
MILES 0 250 500 1,000
BRAZIL
Empire of Brazil, Monarchy 1822-1889
United States of Brazil since 1889
Recife (Pernambuco)
São Salvador (Baia)
Belo Horizonte
Rio de Janeiro
São Paulo
Santos
To Brazil 1895
Ceded to Brazil 1907
PERU (1824)
Trujillo
Callao
Lima
CHINCHA IS. (Peru)
Cuzco
Peru and Bolivia Confederated 1836-1839
Arequipa
Mollendo
Ceded by Bol. to Braz. 1867 Claim relinquished by Peru 1909
Ceded by Bol. to Braz. 1903
To Peru 1909
BOLIVIA
Republic of Bolivar 1825, Later Bolivia
La Paz
Sucre
Lake Titicaca
TACNA To Chile 1883 To Peru 1929
ARICA To Chile 1883
Arica
TARAPACÁ To Chile 1883
Iquique
ATACAMA To Chile 1884, 1894
Antofagasta
Tropic of Capricorn
Ocean
CHACO Claimed by Bolivia and Paraguay
PARAGUAY 1811
Asunción
Ceded to Brazil 1870
To Argentina 1870
To Arg. 1870
ARGENTINA
United Provinces of Rio de la Plata 1816
Argentine Confederation 1825
Argentine Republic 1853
Salta
Tucumán
Córdoba
Santa Fé
Mendoza
Rosario
Buenos Aires
Federal District since 1880
PROVINCE OF BUENOS AIRES Independent 1853-1859
Argentine Nation 1860
PAMPAS
Bahia Blanca
URUGUAY
To Brazil 1851
Cisplatine Province Spanish expelled 1814 To Portugal 1817 To Brazil 1822 Republic of Uruguay 1828
Montevideo
Río de la Plata
CHILE
Original Republic of Chile 1818
Valparaíso
Santiago
JUAN FERNANDEZ ISLANDS Chile since 1818
CHILOÉ
PATAGONIA
Conquered by Argentina 1878-1879
Boundary adjusted by treaty 1881
Strait of Magellan
TIERRA DEL FUEGO Disputed between Argentina and Chile Divided 1902
FALKLAND IS. Held by Great Britain since 1833 Claimed by Argentina
Madeira
Tapajóz
Tocantins
São Francisco
Paraguay
Paraná
Iguassú
Pilcomayo
Uruguay
A-440039-29-1-1-1

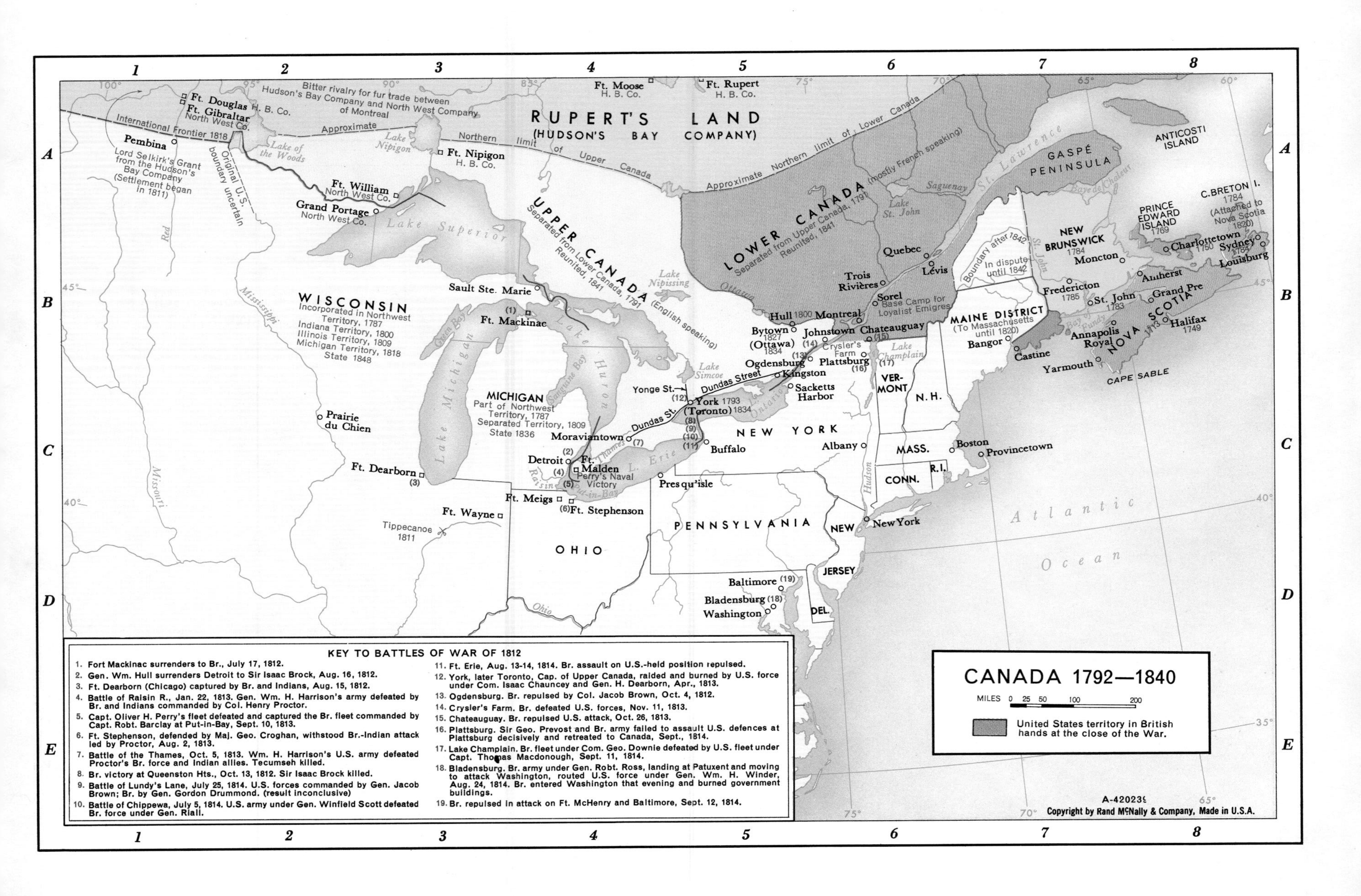

CANADA 1792—1840
MILES 0 25 50 100 200
United States territory in British hands at the close of the War.
RUPERT'S LAND
(HUDSON'S BAY COMPANY)
Ft. Moose
H. B. Co.
Ft. Rupert
H. B. Co.
Ft. Douglas H. B. Co.
Ft. Gibraltar
North West Co.
Bitter rivalry for fur trade between Hudson's Bay Company and North West Company of Montreal
International Frontier 1818
Pembina
Lord Selkirk's Grant from the Hudson's Bay Company (Settlement began in 1811)
Original U.S. boundary uncertain
Approximate Northern limit of Upper Canada
Approximate Northern limit of Lower Canada
Ft. Nipigon
H. B. Co.
Ft. William
North West Co.
Grand Portage
North West Co.
UPPER CANADA
Separated from Lower Canada, 1791
Reunited, 1841
(English speaking)
LOWER CANADA
Separated from Upper Canada, 1791
Reunited, 1841
(mostly French speaking)
GASPÉ PENINSULA
ANTICOSTI ISLAND
C.BRETON I.
1784
(Attached to Nova Scotia 1820)
PRINCE EDWARD ISLAND
1769
NEW BRUNSWICK
1784
Moncton
Charlottetown
Sydney
Louisburg
Amherst
Grand Pre
NOVA SCOTIA
Halifax
1749
Fredericton
1785
St. John
1783
Annapolis Royal
Yarmouth
CAPE SABLE
Boundary after 1842
In dispute until 1842
MAINE DISTRICT
(To Massachusetts until 1820)
Bangor
Castine
Quebec
Lévis
Trois Rivières
Sorel
Base Camp for Loyalist Emigres
Hull 1800
Montreal
Bytown 1827
(Ottawa) 1834
Johnstown
Chateauguay
Crysler's Farm
Plattsburg
Ogdensburg
Kingston
Sacketts Harbor
Yonge St.
Dundas Street
York 1793
(Toronto) 1834
Dundas St.
Moraviantown
Buffalo
Detroit
Ft. Malden
Perry's Naval Victory
Ft. Meigs
Ft. Stephenson
Pres qu'isle
Sault Ste. Marie
Ft. Mackinac
WISCONSIN
Incorporated in Northwest Territory, 1787
Indiana Territory, 1800
Illinois Territory, 1809
Michigan Territory, 1818
State 1848
MICHIGAN
Part of Northwest Territory, 1787
Separated Territory, 1809
State 1836
Prairie du Chien
Ft. Dearborn
Ft. Wayne
Tippecanoe
1811
OHIO
PENNSYLVANIA
NEW YORK
VER-MONT
N. H.
MASS.
CONN.
R.I.
NEW JERSEY
DEL.
Albany
Boston
Provincetown
New York
Baltimore
Bladensburg
Washington
Lake Superior
Lake Michigan
Lake Huron
Lake Nipissing
Lake Simcoe
Ontario
L. Erie
Lake Champlain
Lake of the Woods
Lake Nipigon
Lake St. John
Green Bay
Saginaw Bay
St. Lawrence
Saguenay
Ottawa
Hudson
St. John
Bay of Fundy
Baie de Chaleur
Mississippi
Missouri
Red
Ohio
Thames
Raisin
Put-in-Bay
Atlantic Ocean
KEY TO BATTLES OF WAR OF 1812
1. Fort Mackinac surrenders to Br., July 17, 1812.
2. Gen. Wm. Hull surrenders Detroit to Sir Isaac Brock, Aug. 16, 1812.
3. Ft. Dearborn (Chicago) captured by Br. and Indians, Aug. 15, 1812.
4. Battle of Raisin R., Jan. 22, 1813. Gen. Wm. H. Harrison's army defeated by Br. and Indians commanded by Col. Henry Proctor.
5. Capt. Oliver H. Perry's fleet defeated and captured the Br. fleet commanded by Capt. Robt. Barclay at Put-in-Bay, Sept. 10, 1813.
6. Ft. Stephenson, defended by Maj. Geo. Croghan, withstood Br.-Indian attack led by Proctor, Aug. 2, 1813.
7. Battle of the Thames, Oct. 5, 1813. Wm. H. Harrison's U.S. army defeated Proctor's Br. force and Indian allies. Tecumseh killed.
8. Br. victory at Queenston Hts., Oct. 13, 1812. Sir Isaac Brock killed.
9. Battle of Lundy's Lane, July 25, 1814. U.S. forces commanded by Gen. Jacob Brown; Br. by Gen. Gordon Drummond. (result inconclusive)
10. Battle of Chippewa, July 5, 1814. U.S. army under Gen. Winfield Scott defeated Br. force under Gen. Riall.
11. Ft. Erie, Aug. 13-14, 1814. Br. assault on U.S.-held position repulsed.
12. York, later Toronto, Cap. of Upper Canada, raided and burned by U.S. force under Com. Isaac Chauncey and Gen. H. Dearborn, Apr., 1813.
13. Ogdensburg. Br. repulsed by Col. Jacob Brown, Oct. 4, 1812.
14. Crysler's Farm. Br. defeated U.S. forces, Nov. 11, 1813.
15. Chateauguay. Br. repulsed U.S. attack, Oct. 26, 1813.
16. Plattsburg. Sir Geo. Prevost and Br. army failed to assault U.S. defences at Plattsburg decisively and retreated to Canada, Sept., 1814.
17. Lake Champlain. Br. fleet under Com. Geo. Downie defeated by U.S. fleet under Capt. Thomas Macdonough, Sept. 11, 1814.
18. Bladensburg. Br. army under Gen. Robt. Ross, landing at Patuxent and moving to attack Washington, routed U.S. force under Gen. Wm. H. Winder, Aug. 24, 1814. Br. entered Washington that evening and burned government buildings.
19. Br. repulsed in attack on Ft. McHenry and Baltimore, Sept. 12, 1814.
A-42023

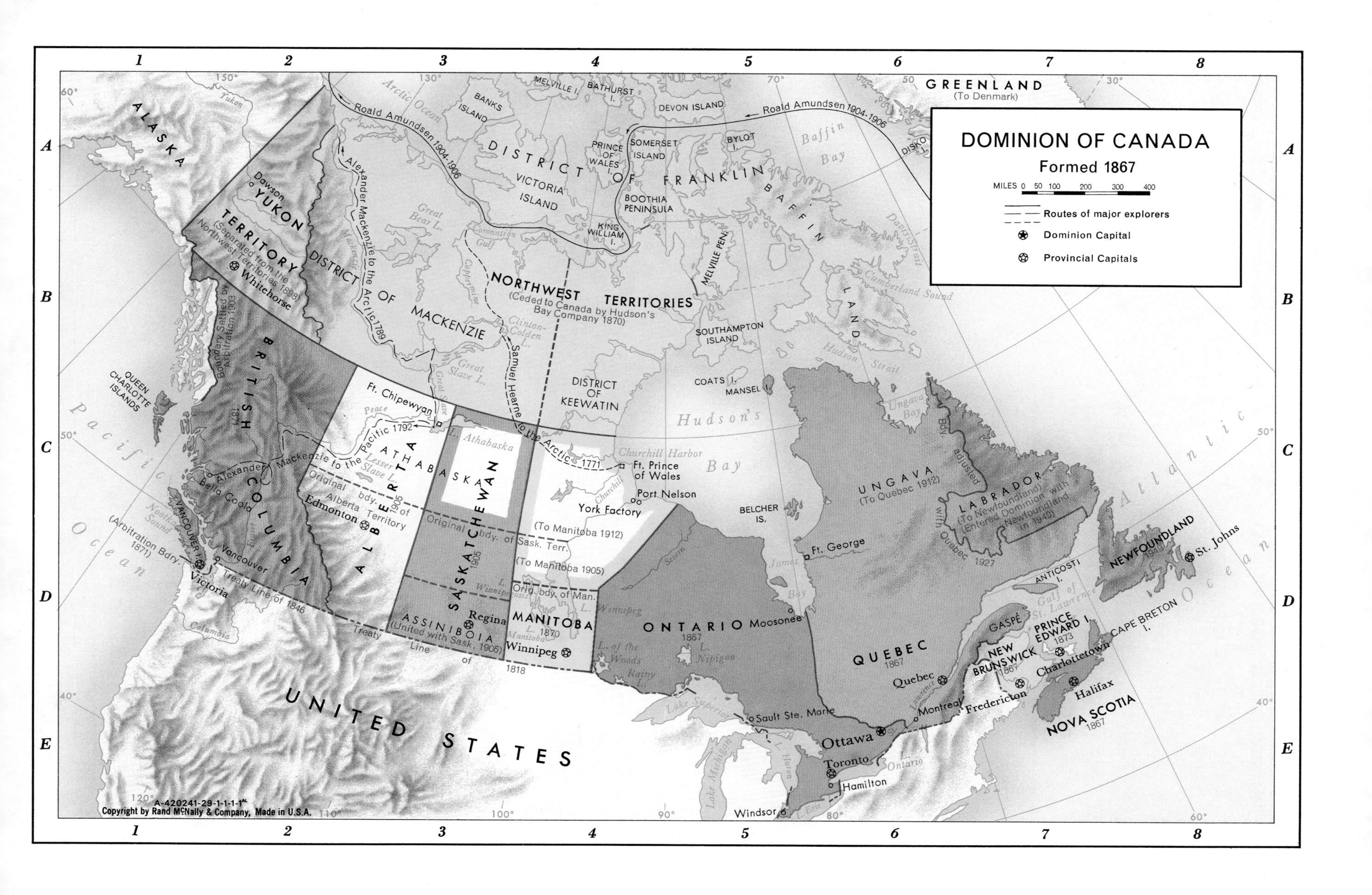
DOMINION OF CANADA
Formed 1867
MILES 0 50 100 200 300 400
Routes of major explorers
Dominion Capital
Provincial Capitals
GREENLAND
(To Denmark)
ALASKA
YUKON TERRITORY
(Separated from the Northwest Territories 1898)
Dawson
Whitehorse
BRITISH COLUMBIA
1871
Boundary Settled by Arbitration 1903
QUEEN CHARLOTTE ISLANDS
VANCOUVER I.
Vancouver
Victoria
Bella Coola
Alexander Mackenzie to the Pacific 1792
Alexander Mackenzie to the Arctic 1789
(Arbitration Bdry. 1871)
Treaty Line of 1846
Treaty Line of 1818
DISTRICT OF MACKENZIE
DISTRICT OF FRANKLIN
DISTRICT OF KEEWATIN
NORTHWEST TERRITORIES
(Ceded to Canada by Hudson's Bay Company 1870)
Roald Amundsen 1904-1906
Samuel Hearne to the Arctic 1771
BANKS ISLAND
MELVILLE I.
BATHURST I.
DEVON ISLAND
VICTORIA ISLAND
PRINCE OF WALES I.
SOMERSET ISLAND
BOOTHIA PENINSULA
KING WILLIAM I.
BYLOT I.
BAFFIN LAND
MELVILLE PEN.
SOUTHAMPTON ISLAND
COATS I.
MANSEL
BELCHER IS.
Ft. Chipewyan
ATHABASKA
ALBERTA
Original bdy. of Alberta Territory
1905
Edmonton
SASKATCHEWAN
Original bdy. of Sask. Terr.
Regina
ASSINIBOIA
(United with Sask. 1905)
MANITOBA
1870
Orig. bdy. of Man.
Winnipeg
(To Manitoba 1912)
(To Manitoba 1905)
Ft. Prince of Wales
Port Nelson
York Factory
ONTARIO
1867
Moosonee
Ft. George
Sault Ste. Marie
Ottawa
Toronto
Hamilton
Windsor
UNGAVA
(To Quebec 1912)
LABRADOR
(To Newfoundland)
(Entered Dominion with Newfoundland in 1949)
Bdy. adjusted with Quebec 1927
QUEBEC
1867
Quebec
Montreal
ANTICOSTI I.
GASPÉ
NEW BRUNSWICK
1867
Fredericton
PRINCE EDWARD I.
1873
Charlottetown
NOVA SCOTIA
1867
Halifax
CAPE BRETON I.
NEWFOUNDLAND
1949
St. Johns
UNITED STATES
Pacific Ocean
Atlantic Ocean
Arctic Ocean
Hudson's Bay
Baffin Bay
Davis Strait
Hudson Strait
Cumberland Sound
Ungava Bay
James Bay
Churchill Harbor
Gulf of St. Lawrence
Great Bear L.
Great Slave L.
L. Athabaska
Lesser Slave L.
L. Winnipeg
L. of the Woods
L. Nipigon
Lake Superior
Lake Michigan
L. Huron
L. Erie
Ontario
DISKO I.
A-420241-29-1-1-1

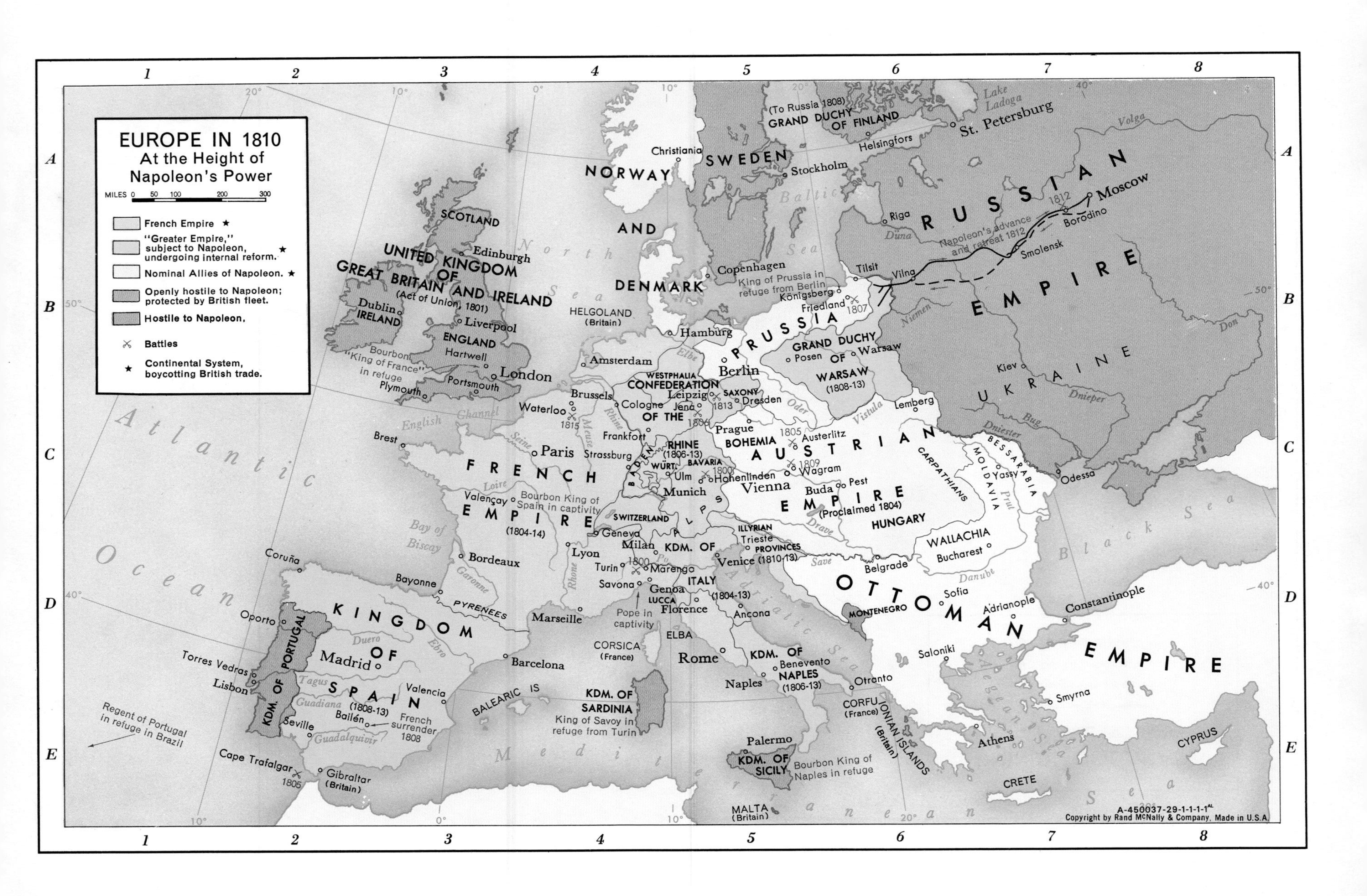
EUROPE IN 1810
At the Height of
Napoleon's Power
MILES 0 50 100 200 300
French Empire ★
"Greater Empire," subject to Napoleon, undergoing internal reform. ★
Nominal Allies of Napoleon. ★
Openly hostile to Napoleon; protected by British fleet.
Hostile to Napoleon.
Battles
Continental System, boycotting British trade.
SCOTLAND
Edinburgh
UNITED KINGDOM OF GREAT BRITAIN AND IRELAND
(Act of Union, 1801)
Dublin
IRELAND
Liverpool
ENGLAND
Hartwell
London
Portsmouth
Plymouth
Bourbon "King of France" in refuge
North Sea
HELGOLAND (Britain)
NORWAY AND DENMARK
Christiania
Copenhagen
SWEDEN
Stockholm
Baltic Sea
(To Russia 1808) GRAND DUCHY OF FINLAND
Helsingfors
St. Petersburg
Lake Ladoga
Volga
RUSSIAN EMPIRE
Moscow
1812
Borodino
Napoleon's advance and retreat 1812
Smolensk
Riga
Duna
Tilsit
Vilna
Niemen
UKRAINE
Kiev
Dnieper
Bug
Dniester
Don
Odessa
King of Prussia in refuge from Berlin
Königsberg
Friedland 1807
PRUSSIA
Hamburg
Berlin
GRAND DUCHY OF WARSAW (1808-13)
Posen
Warsaw
Lemberg
Amsterdam
Elbe
WESTPHALIA
CONFEDERATION OF THE RHINE (1806-13)
Leipzig 1813
SAXONY
Dresden
Jena 1806
Oder
Vistula
Cologne
Brussels
Waterloo 1815
Meuse
Rhine
Frankfort
Prague
BOHEMIA
1805 Austerlitz
AUSTRIAN EMPIRE
1809 Wagram
Vienna
Buda Pest
(Proclaimed 1804)
HUNGARY
CARPATHIANS
MOLDAVIA
BESSARABIA
Yassy
Prut
WALLACHIA
Bucharest
Danube
Black Sea
BADEN
WÜRT.
BAVARIA
Ulm
1800 Hohenlinden
Munich
ALPS
Brest
English Channel
Seine
Paris
Strassburg
FRENCH EMPIRE (1804-14)
Loire
Valençay
Bourbon King of Spain in captivity
Bay of Biscay
Atlantic Ocean
Bordeaux
Garonne
Lyon
Rhone
SWITZERLAND
Geneva
Milan
KDM. OF ITALY (1804-13)
Turin
1800 Marengo
Savona
Genoa
LUCCA
Florence
Pope in captivity
ILLYRIAN PROVINCES (1810-13)
Trieste
Venice
Drave
Save
Belgrade
Adriatic Sea
Ancona
OTTOMAN EMPIRE
MONTENEGRO
Sofia
Adrianople
Constantinople
Saloniki
Aegean Sea
Smyrna
Athens
CRETE
CYPRUS
Coruña
Bayonne
PYRENEES
Oporto
KDM. OF PORTUGAL
Torres Vedras
Lisbon
KINGDOM OF SPAIN (1808-13)
Duero
Ebro
Madrid
Tagus
Guadiana
Valencia
Bailén
French surrender 1808
Seville
Guadalquivir
Regent of Portugal in refuge in Brazil
Cape Trafalgar 1805
Gibraltar (Britain)
Marseille
Barcelona
BALEARIC IS
CORSICA (France)
ELBA
KDM. OF SARDINIA
King of Savoy in refuge from Turin
Rome
KDM. OF NAPLES (1806-13)
Benevento
Naples
Otranto
CORFU (France)
IONIAN ISLANDS (Britain)
Palermo
KDM. OF SICILY
Bourbon King of Naples in refuge
MALTA (Britain)
Mediterranean Sea
A-450037-29-1-1-1-1
Copyright by Rand McNally & Company, Made in U.S.A.

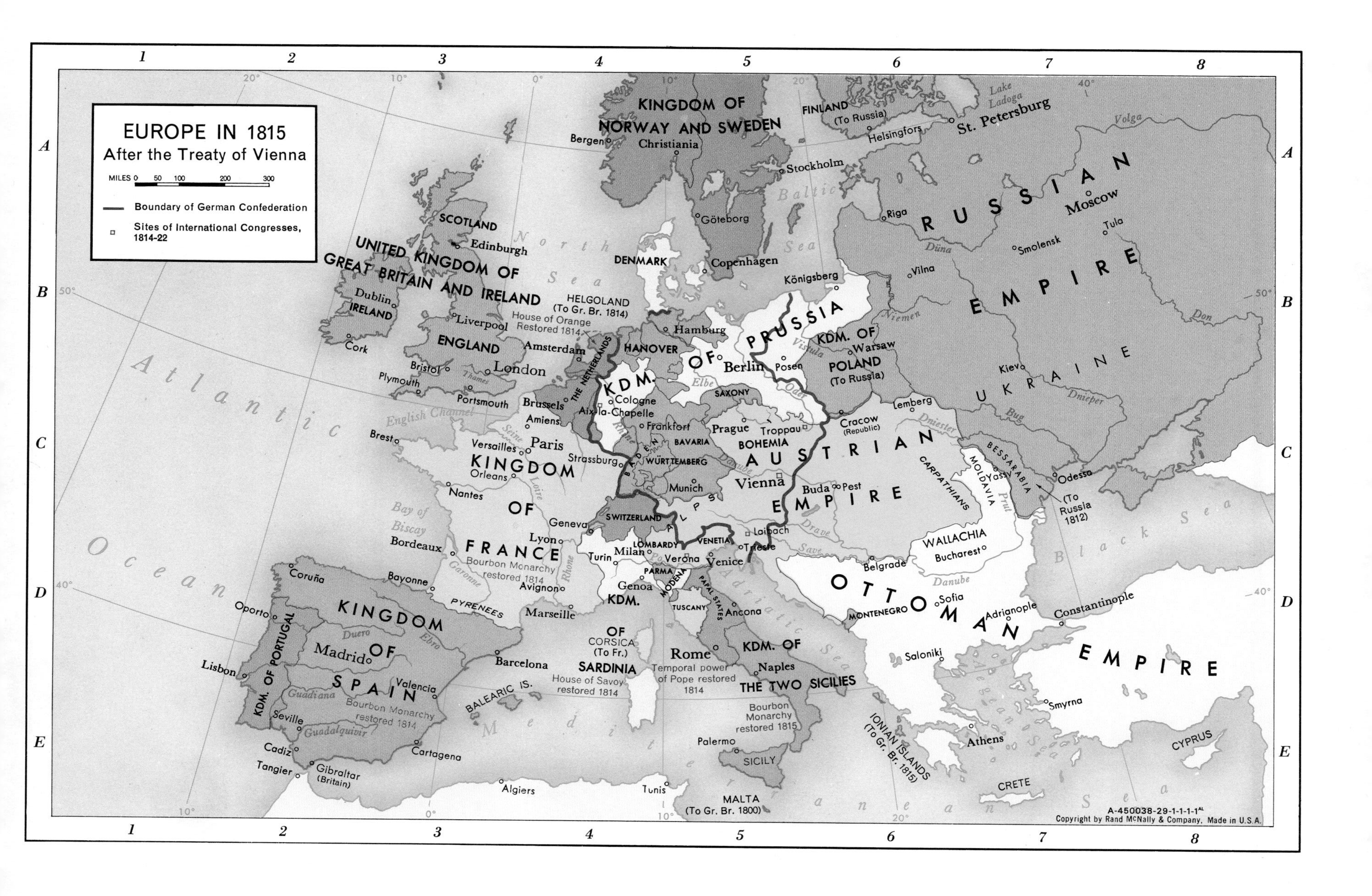
EUROPE IN 1815
After the Treaty of Vienna
MILES 0 50 100 200 300
Boundary of German Confederation
Sites of International Congresses, 1814-22
KINGDOM OF NORWAY AND SWEDEN
Bergen
Christiania
Stockholm
Göteborg
Copenhagen
DENMARK
FINLAND (To Russia)
Helsingfors
St. Petersburg
Lake Ladoga
Volga
RUSSIAN EMPIRE
Moscow
Tula
Smolensk
Riga
Vilna
Düna
Niemen
Don
Kiev
UKRAINE
Dnieper
Bug
Dniester
Baltic Sea
North Sea
SCOTLAND
Edinburgh
UNITED KINGDOM OF GREAT BRITAIN AND IRELAND
Dublin
IRELAND
Cork
Liverpool
ENGLAND
London
Thames
Bristol
Plymouth
Portsmouth
English Channel
HELGOLAND (To Gr. Br. 1814)
House of Orange Restored 1814
Amsterdam
THE NETHERLANDS
Brussels
Hamburg
HANOVER
KDM. OF PRUSSIA
Königsberg
Berlin
Posen
Elbe
Oder
Vistula
KDM. OF POLAND (To Russia)
Warsaw
KDM.
Cologne
Aix-la-Chapelle
Frankfort
Rhine
SAXONY
Prague
Troppau
BOHEMIA
BAVARIA
BADEN
WÜRTTEMBERG
Munich
Danube
AUSTRIAN EMPIRE
Vienna
Cracow (Republic)
Lemberg
CARPATHIANS
Buda
Pest
Laibach
Trieste
Drave
Save
ALPS
Atlantic Ocean
Brest
Amiens
Seine
Paris
Versailles
KINGDOM OF FRANCE
Orleans
Loire
Nantes
Strassburg
Bay of Biscay
Bordeaux
Bourbon Monarchy restored 1814
Garonne
Lyon
Geneva
Rhone
Avignon
Bayonne
PYRENEES
Marseille
SWITZERLAND
Turin
Milan
LOMBARDY
VENETIA
Verona
Venice
PARMA
MODENA
Genoa
KDM. OF SARDINIA
CORSICA (To Fr.)
House of Savoy restored 1814
TUSCANY
PAPAL STATES
Ancona
Rome
Temporal power of Pope restored 1814
KDM. OF THE TWO SICILIES
Naples
Bourbon Monarchy restored 1815
Palermo
SICILY
MALTA (To Gr. Br. 1800)
Tunis
Algiers
Adriatic Sea
Mediterranean Sea
Coruña
Oporto
KDM. OF PORTUGAL
Lisbon
KINGDOM OF SPAIN
Duero
Ebro
Madrid
Guadiana
Guadalquivir
Valencia
Bourbon Monarchy restored 1814
Seville
Cadiz
Gibraltar (Britain)
Tangier
Cartagena
Barcelona
BALEARIC IS.
MOLDAVIA
Yassy
Prut
BESSARABIA
Odessa
(To Russia 1812)
WALLACHIA
Bucharest
Belgrade
MONTENEGRO
OTTOMAN EMPIRE
Sofia
Adrianople
Constantinople
Saloniki
Smyrna
Athens
Aegean Sea
IONIAN ISLANDS (To Gr. Br. 1815)
CRETE
CYPRUS
Black Sea
A-450038-29-1-1-1
Copyright by Rand McNally & Company. Made in U.S.A.

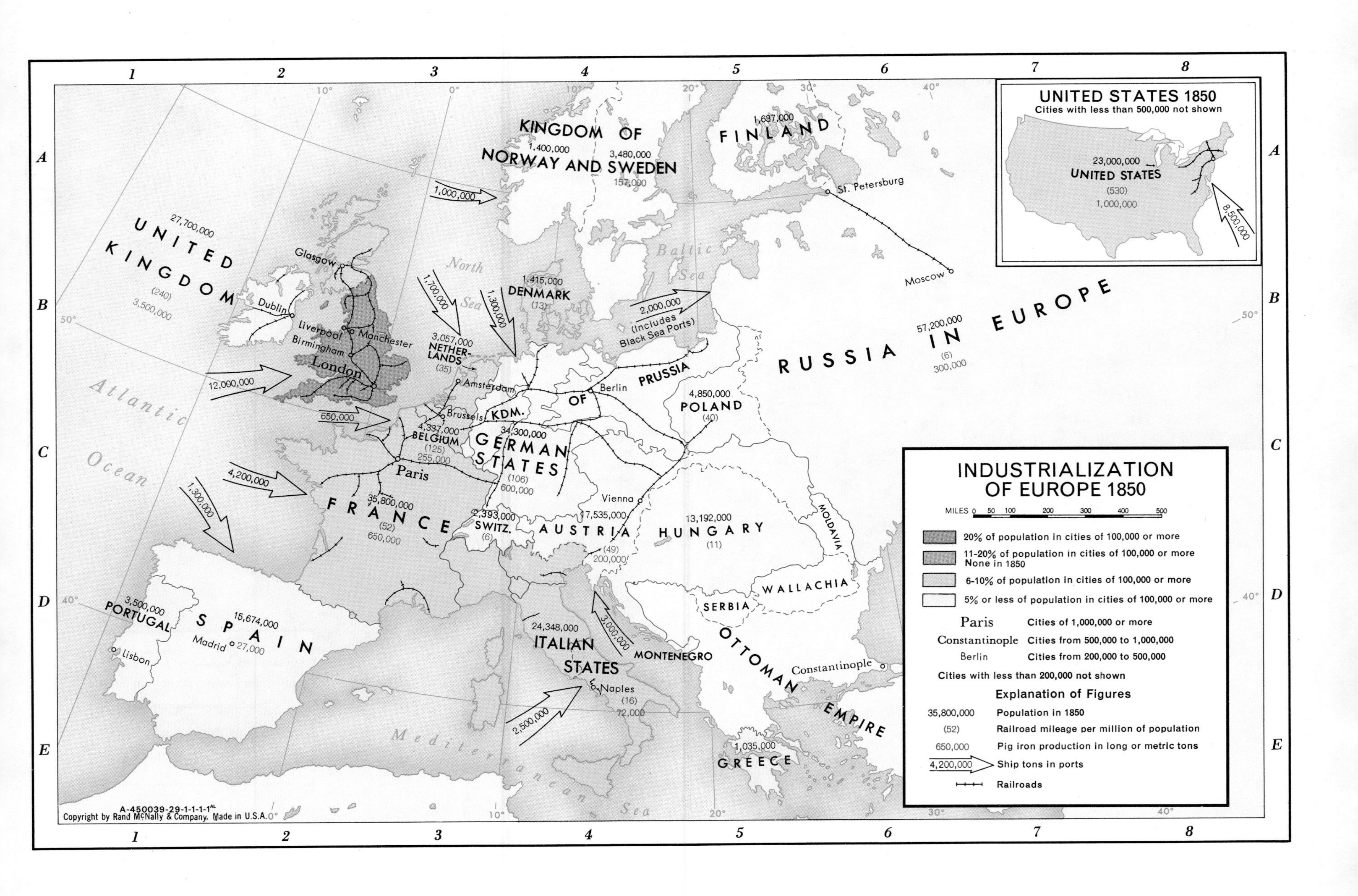

INDUSTRIALIZATION OF EUROPE 1850
MILES 0 50 100 200 300 400 500
20% of population in cities of 100,000 or more
11-20% of population in cities of 100,000 or more
None in 1850
6-10% of population in cities of 100,000 or more
5% or less of population in cities of 100,000 or more
Paris Cities of 1,000,000 or more
Constantinople Cities from 500,000 to 1,000,000
Berlin Cities from 200,000 to 500,000
Cities with less than 200,000 not shown
Explanation of Figures
35,800,000 Population in 1850
(52) Railroad mileage per million of population
650,000 Pig iron production in long or metric tons
4,200,000 Ship tons in ports
Railroads
UNITED STATES 1850
Cities with less than 500,000 not shown
23,000,000
UNITED STATES
(530)
1,000,000
8,500,000
UNITED KINGDOM
27,700,000
(240)
3,500,000
Glasgow
Dublin
Liverpool
Manchester
Birmingham
London
12,000,000
KINGDOM OF NORWAY AND SWEDEN
1,400,000
3,480,000
157,000
1,000,000
FINLAND
1,637,000
St. Petersburg
Moscow
RUSSIA IN EUROPE
57,200,000
(6)
300,000
North Sea
Baltic Sea
1,700,000
1,300,000
DENMARK
1,415,000
(13)
2,000,000
(Includes Black Sea Ports)
NETHER-LANDS
3,057,000
(35)
Amsterdam
Brussels
BELGIUM
4,337,000
(125)
255,000
650,000
KDM. OF PRUSSIA
Berlin
GERMAN STATES
34,300,000
(106)
600,000
POLAND
4,850,000
(40)
Paris
FRANCE
35,800,000
(52)
650,000
4,200,000
1,300,000
SWITZ.
2,393,000
(6)
AUSTRIA
17,535,000
(49)
200,000
Vienna
HUNGARY
13,192,000
(11)
MOLDAVIA
WALLACHIA
SERBIA
MONTENEGRO
OTTOMAN EMPIRE
Constantinople
GREECE
1,035,000
PORTUGAL
3,500,000
Lisbon
SPAIN
15,674,000
Madrid
27,000
ITALIAN STATES
24,348,000
Naples
(16)
72,000
3,000,000
2,500,000
Atlantic Ocean
Mediterranean Sea

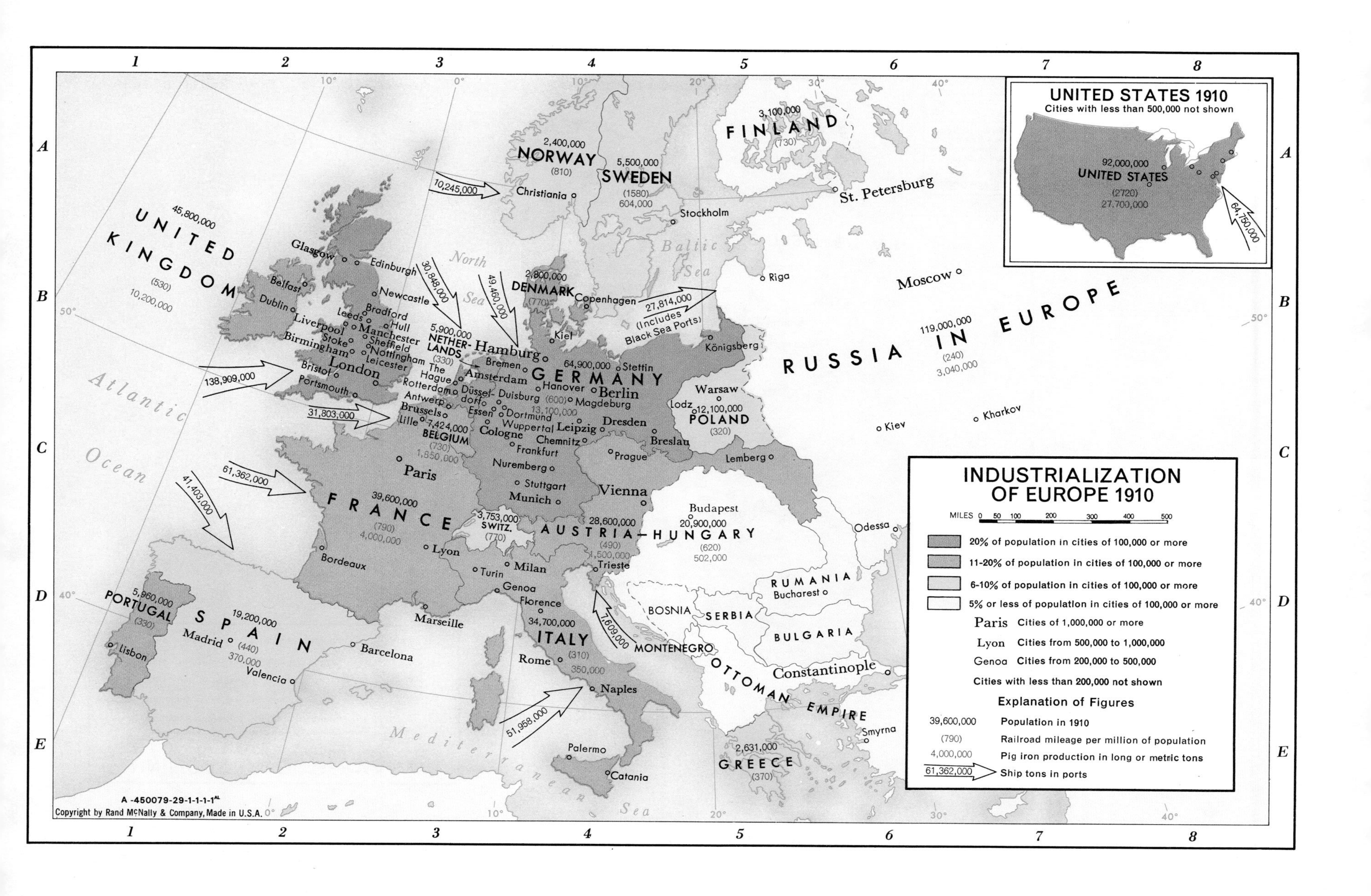
INDUSTRIALIZATION OF EUROPE 1910
MILES 0 50 100 200 300 400 500
20% of population in cities of 100,000 or more
11-20% of population in cities of 100,000 or more
6-10% of population in cities of 100,000 or more
5% or less of population in cities of 100,000 or more
Paris Cities of 1,000,000 or more
Lyon Cities from 500,000 to 1,000,000
Genoa Cities from 200,000 to 500,000
Cities with less than 200,000 not shown
Explanation of Figures
39,600,000 Population in 1910
(790) Railroad mileage per million of population
4,000,000 Pig iron production in long or metric tons
61,362,000 Ship tons in ports
UNITED STATES 1910
Cities with less than 500,000 not shown
92,000,000
UNITED STATES
(2720)
27,700,000
64,750,000
UNITED KINGDOM
45,800,000
(530)
10,200,000
NORWAY
2,400,000
(810)
SWEDEN
5,500,000
(1580)
604,000
FINLAND
3,100,000
(730)
DENMARK
2,800,000
(770)
NETHER-LANDS
5,900,000
(330)
BELGIUM
7,424,000
(730)
1,850,000
GERMANY
64,900,000
(600)
13,100,000
FRANCE
39,600,000
(790)
4,000,000
SWITZ.
3,753,000
(770)
AUSTRIA-HUNGARY
28,600,000
(490)
1,500,000
20,900,000
(620)
502,000
POLAND
12,100,000
(320)
RUSSIA IN EUROPE
119,000,000
(240)
3,040,000
PORTUGAL
5,960,000
(330)
SPAIN
19,200,000
(440)
370,000
ITALY
34,700,000
(310)
350,000
GREECE
2,631,000
(370)
RUMANIA
BOSNIA
SERBIA
BULGARIA
MONTENEGRO
OTTOMAN EMPIRE
10,245,000
30,848,000
49,460,000
27,814,000 (Includes Black Sea Ports)
138,909,000
31,803,000
61,362,000
41,403,000
7,609,000
51,958,000
Glasgow
Edinburgh
Belfast
Dublin
Newcastle
Bradford
Leeds
Hull
Liverpool
Manchester
Stoke
Sheffield
Nottingham
Birmingham
Leicester
London
Bristol
Portsmouth
Christiania
Stockholm
St. Petersburg
Copenhagen
Kiel
Hamburg
Bremen
Amsterdam
The Hague
Rotterdam
Antwerp
Brussels
Lille
Düssel-dorf
Duisburg
Essen
Dortmund
Wuppertal
Cologne
Hanover
Magdeburg
Berlin
Stettin
Königsberg
Leipzig
Dresden
Chemnitz
Frankfurt
Nuremberg
Stuttgart
Munich
Breslau
Prague
Vienna
Budapest
Trieste
Warsaw
Lodz
Lemberg
Riga
Moscow
Kiev
Kharkov
Odessa
Bucharest
Constantinople
Smyrna
Paris
Lyon
Bordeaux
Marseille
Turin
Milan
Genoa
Florence
Rome
Naples
Palermo
Catania
Lisbon
Madrid
Barcelona
Valencia
North Sea
Baltic Sea
Atlantic Ocean
Mediterranean Sea
A -450079-29-1-1-1-1AL
Copyright by Rand McNally & Company, Made in U.S.A.

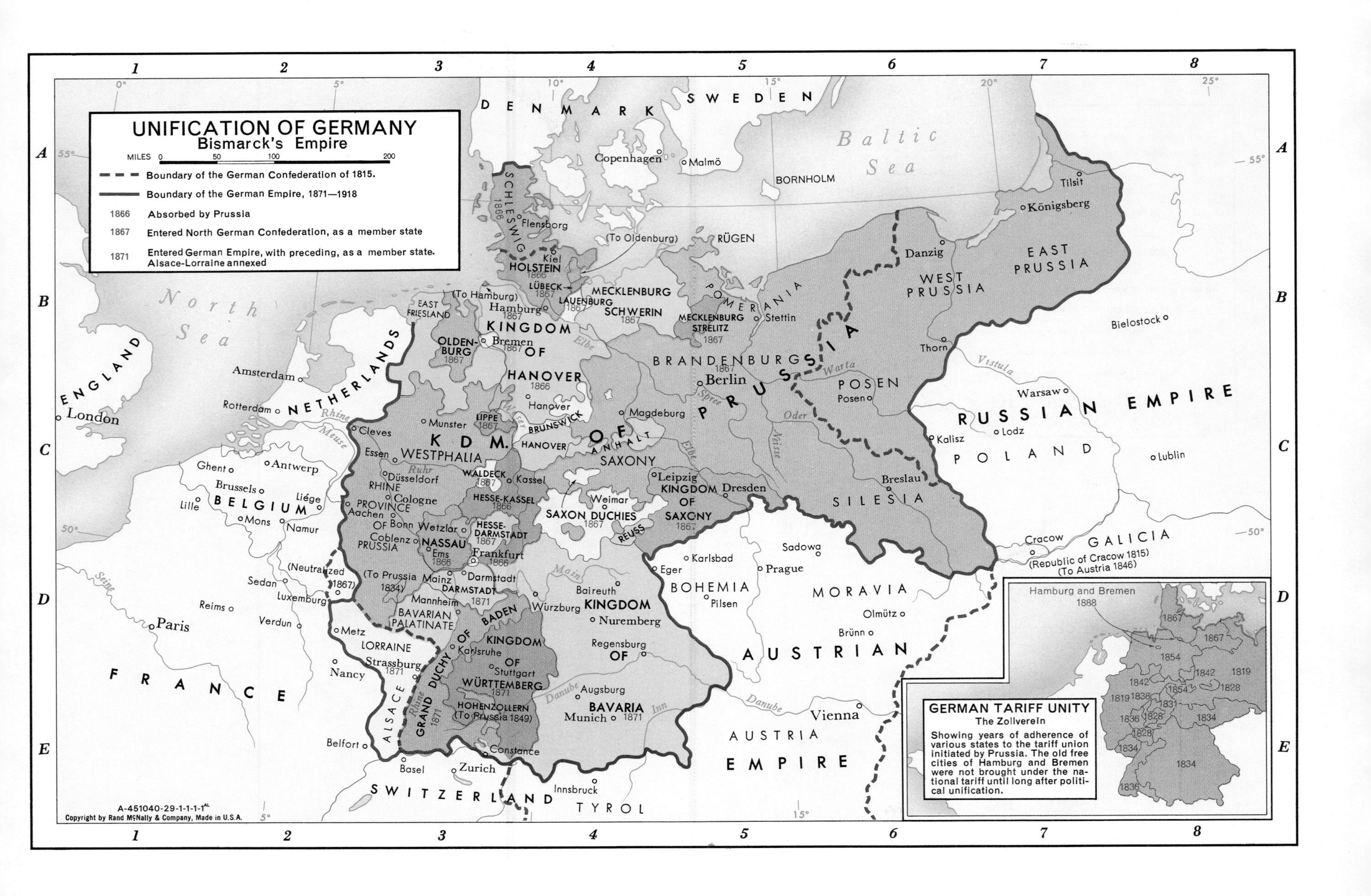

UNIFICATION OF GERMANY
Bismarck's Empire
MILES 0 50 100 200
Boundary of the German Confederation of 1815.
Boundary of the German Empire, 1871—1918
1866 Absorbed by Prussia
1867 Entered North German Confederation, as a member state
1871 Entered German Empire, with preceding, as a member state. Alsace-Lorraine annexed
GERMAN TARIFF UNITY
The Zollverein
Showing years of adherence of various states to the tariff union initiated by Prussia. The old free cities of Hamburg and Bremen were not brought under the national tariff until long after political unification.
Hamburg and Bremen 1888
DENMARK
SWEDEN
Baltic Sea
North Sea
ENGLAND
London
NETHERLANDS
Amsterdam
Rotterdam
BELGIUM
Antwerp
Ghent
Brussels
Lille
Liége
Mons
Namur
FRANCE
Paris
Reims
Sedan
Verdun
Nancy
Belfort
(Neutralized 1867)
Luxemburg
SWITZERLAND
Basel
Zurich
Constance
TYROL
Innsbruck
AUSTRIAN EMPIRE
AUSTRIA
BOHEMIA
MORAVIA
Prague
Pilsen
Karlsbad
Eger
Sadowa
Brünn
Olmütz
Vienna
GALICIA
Cracow
(Republic of Cracow 1815)
(To Austria 1846)
RUSSIAN EMPIRE
POLAND
Warsaw
Lodz
Kalisz
Lublin
Bielostock
KINGDOM OF PRUSSIA
EAST PRUSSIA
Königsberg
Tilsit
WEST PRUSSIA
Danzig
Thorn
POMERANIA
Stettin
POSEN
Posen
SILESIA
Breslau
BRANDENBURG
Berlin
Magdeburg
SAXONY
ANHALT
KINGDOM OF SAXONY 1867
Leipzig
Dresden
SAXON DUCHIES 1867
Weimar
REUSS
SCHLESWIG 1866
Flensburg
HOLSTEIN 1866
Kiel
LÜBECK 1867
LAUENBURG 1867
MECKLENBURG SCHWERIN 1867
MECKLENBURG STRELITZ 1867
(To Oldenburg)
RÜGEN
BORNHOLM
Copenhagen
Malmö
(To Hamburg)
Hamburg 1867
EAST FRIESLAND
OLDENBURG 1867
Bremen 1867
KINGDOM OF HANOVER 1866
Hanover
BRUNSWICK
HANOVER
LIPPE 1867
Munster
WESTPHALIA
WALDECK 1867
Kassel
HESSE-KASSEL 1866
HESSE-DARMSTADT 1867
NASSAU 1866
Ems
Frankfurt 1866
Wetzlar
RHINE PROVINCE OF PRUSSIA
Cleves
Essen
Düsseldorf
Cologne
Aachen
Bonn
Coblenz
(To Prussia 1834)
Mainz
Darmstadt
DARMSTADT 1871
Mannheim
BAVARIAN PALATINATE
LORRAINE
Metz
Strassburg 1871
ALSACE
GRAND DUCHY OF BADEN 1871
Karlsruhe
KINGDOM OF WÜRTTEMBERG 1871
Stuttgart
HOHENZOLLERN (To Prussia 1849)
KINGDOM OF BAVARIA 1871
Würzburg
Baireuth
Nuremberg
Regensburg
Augsburg
Munich
Rhine
Meuse
Ruhr
Weser
Elbe
Main
Spree
Oder
Warta
Neisse
Vistula
Danube
Inn
Seine
A-451040-29-1-1-1
Copyright by Rand McNally & Company, Made in U.S.A.

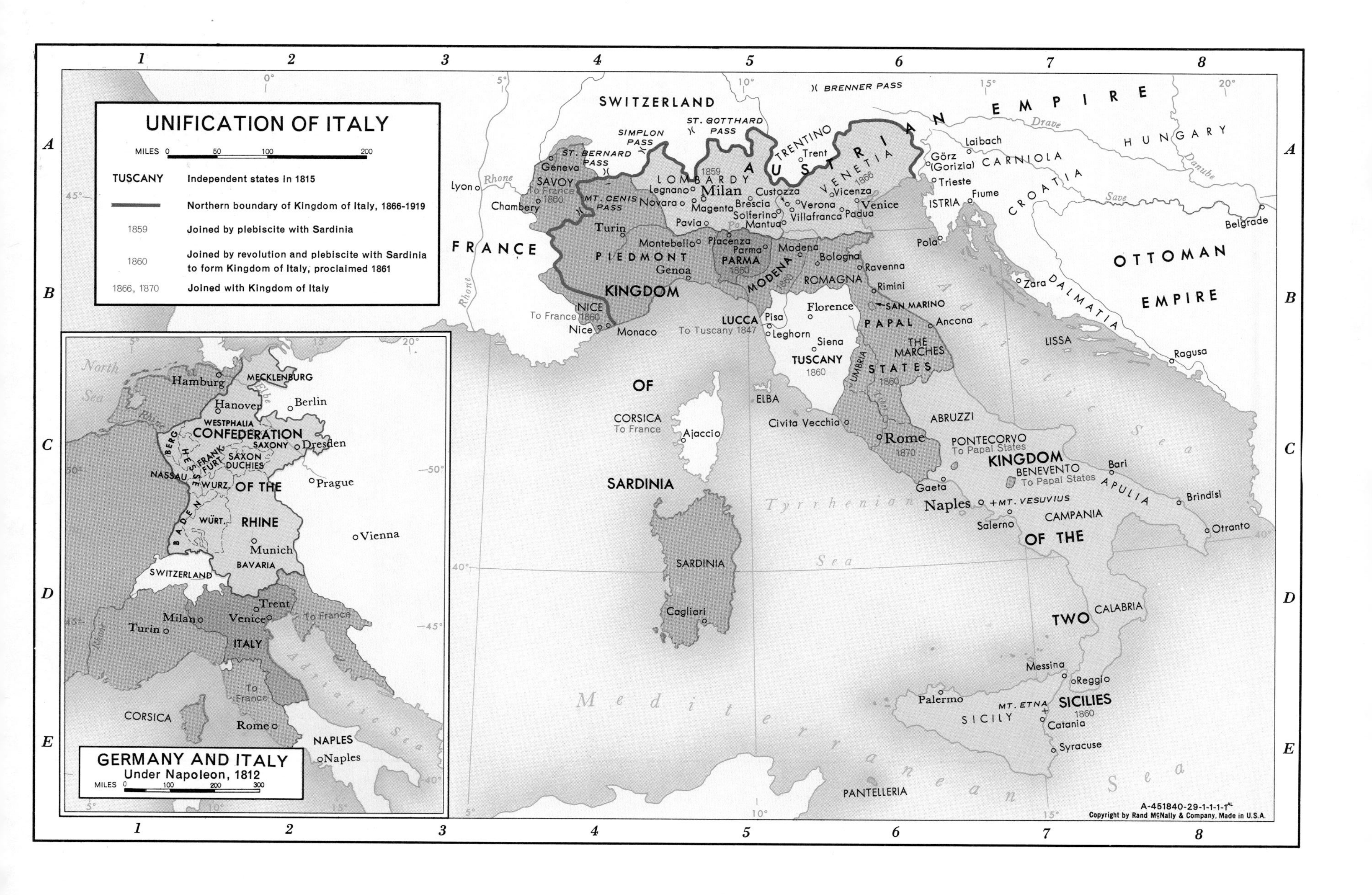

UNIFICATION OF ITALY
MILES 0 50 100 200
TUSCANY Independent states in 1815
Northern boundary of Kingdom of Italy, 1866-1919
1859 Joined by plebiscite with Sardinia
1860 Joined by revolution and plebiscite with Sardinia to form Kingdom of Italy, proclaimed 1861
1866, 1870 Joined with Kingdom of Italy
SWITZERLAND
BRENNER PASS
ST. GOTTHARD PASS
SIMPLON PASS
ST. BERNARD PASS
MT. CENIS PASS
AUSTRIAN EMPIRE
HUNGARY
OTTOMAN EMPIRE
FRANCE
Lyon
Rhone
Chambery
Geneva
SAVOY
To France 1860
Turin
PIEDMONT
KINGDOM OF SARDINIA
Montebello
Genoa
NICE
To France 1860
Nice
Monaco
LOMBARDY
1859
Legnano
Milan
Novara
Magenta
Pavia
Po
Brescia
Solferino
Mantua
Custozza
Verona
Villafranca
TRENTINO
Trent
VENETIA
1866
Vicenza
Venice
Padua
Piacenza
Parma
PARMA
1860
MODENA
1860
Modena
Bologna
ROMAGNA
Ravenna
Rimini
SAN MARINO
LUCCA
To Tuscany 1847
Pisa
Leghorn
Florence
Siena
TUSCANY
1860
ELBA
PAPAL STATES
1860
THE MARCHES
UMBRIA
Tiber
Ancona
Civita Vecchia
Rome
1870
ABRUZZI
PONTECORVO
To Papal States
KINGDOM OF THE TWO SICILIES
BENEVENTO
To Papal States
Gaeta
Naples
MT. VESUVIUS
Salerno
CAMPANIA
APULIA
Bari
Brindisi
Otranto
CALABRIA
Messina
Reggio
Palermo
SICILY
MT. ETNA
SICILIES
1860
Catania
Syracuse
PANTELLERIA
CORSICA
To France
Ajaccio
SARDINIA
Cagliari
Tyrrhenian Sea
Mediterranean Sea
Adriatic Sea
Görz
(Gorizia)
Laibach
CARNIOLA
Trieste
Fiume
ISTRIA
Pola
CROATIA
Drave
Save
Danube
Belgrade
Zara
DALMATIA
LISSA
Ragusa
GERMANY AND ITALY
Under Napoleon, 1812
MILES 0 100 200 300
North Sea
Hamburg
MECKLENBURG
Elbe
Hanover
Berlin
WESTPHALIA
CONFEDERATION OF THE RHINE
SAXONY
Dresden
BERG
HESSE
FRANKFURT
SAXON DUCHIES
NASSAU
WURZ.
Prague
BADEN
WÜRT.
Munich
BAVARIA
Vienna
SWITZERLAND
Trent
Milan
Venice
Turin
Rhone
ITALY
To France
To France
CORSICA
Rome
NAPLES
Naples
Adriatic Sea
A-451840-29-1-1-1
Copyright by Rand McNally & Company, Made in U.S.A.

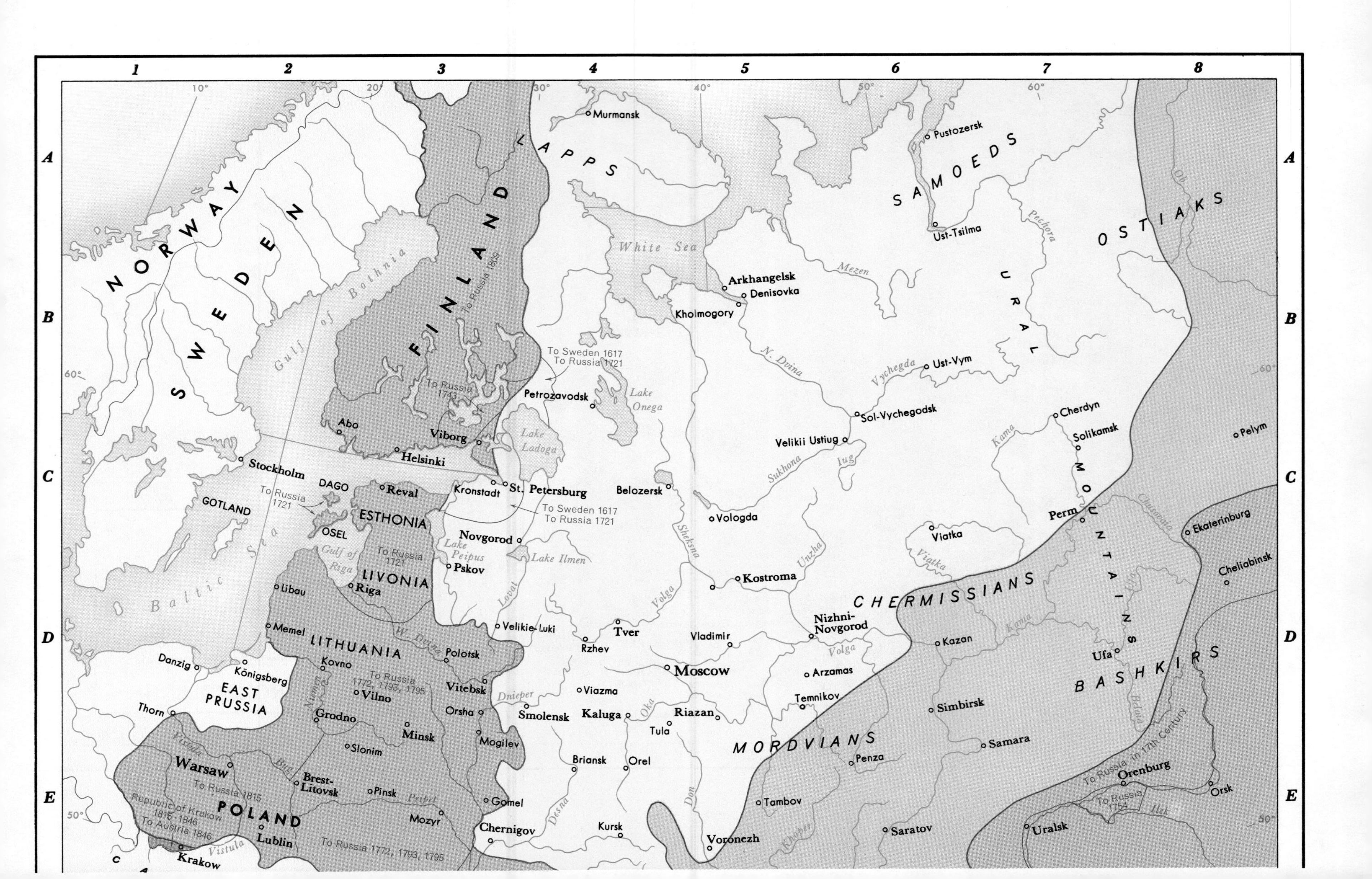

1
2
3
4
5
6
7
8
A
B
C
D
E
10°
20°
30°
40°
50°
60°
NORWAY
SWEDEN
FINLAND
LAPPS
SAMOEDS
OSTIAKS
URAL MOUNTAINS
CHERMISSIANS
BASHKIRS
MORDVIANS
ESTHONIA
LIVONIA
LITHUANIA
EAST PRUSSIA
POLAND
GOTLAND
DAGO
OSEL
Gulf of Bothnia
Gulf of Riga
Baltic Sea
White Sea
Lake Onega
Lake Ladoga
Lake Peipus
Lake Ilmen
To Russia 1809
To Russia 1743
To Russia 1721
To Sweden 1617
To Russia 1721
To Russia 1772, 1793, 1795
To Russia 1815
Republic of Krakow 1815-1846
To Austria 1846
To Russia in 17th Century
To Russia 1754
Murmansk
Pustozersk
Ust-Tsilma
Arkhangelsk
Denisovka
Kholmogory
Ust-Vym
Sol-Vychegodsk
Velikii Ustiug
Cherdyn
Solikamsk
Pelym
Petrozavodsk
Abo
Viborg
Helsinki
Stockholm
Reval
Kronstadt
St. Petersburg
Belozersk
Vologda
Perm
Ekaterinburg
Cheliabinsk
Viatka
Novgorod
Pskov
Riga
Libau
Memel
Kostroma
Velikie-Luki
Tver
Rzhev
Vladimir
Nizhni-Novgorod
Kazan
Ufa
Moscow
Arzamas
Polotsk
Vitebsk
Kovno
Vilno
Danzig
Königsberg
Thorn
Grodno
Minsk
Orsha
Smolensk
Viazma
Kaluga
Tula
Riazan
Temnikov
Simbirsk
Samara
Mogilev
Slonim
Briansk
Orel
Penza
Warsaw
Brest-Litovsk
Pinsk
Gomel
Mozyr
Chernigov
Kursk
Tambov
Saratov
Voronezh
Uralsk
Orenburg
Orsk
Lublin
Krakow
Mezen
Pechora
Ob
N. Dvina
Vychegda
Sukhona
Iug
Kama
Chusovaia
Sheksna
Unzha
Viatka
Volga
Ufa
Belaia
Ilek
Lovat
W. Dvina
Dnieper
Oka
Don
Khoper
Desna
Niemen
Bug
Pripet
Vistula

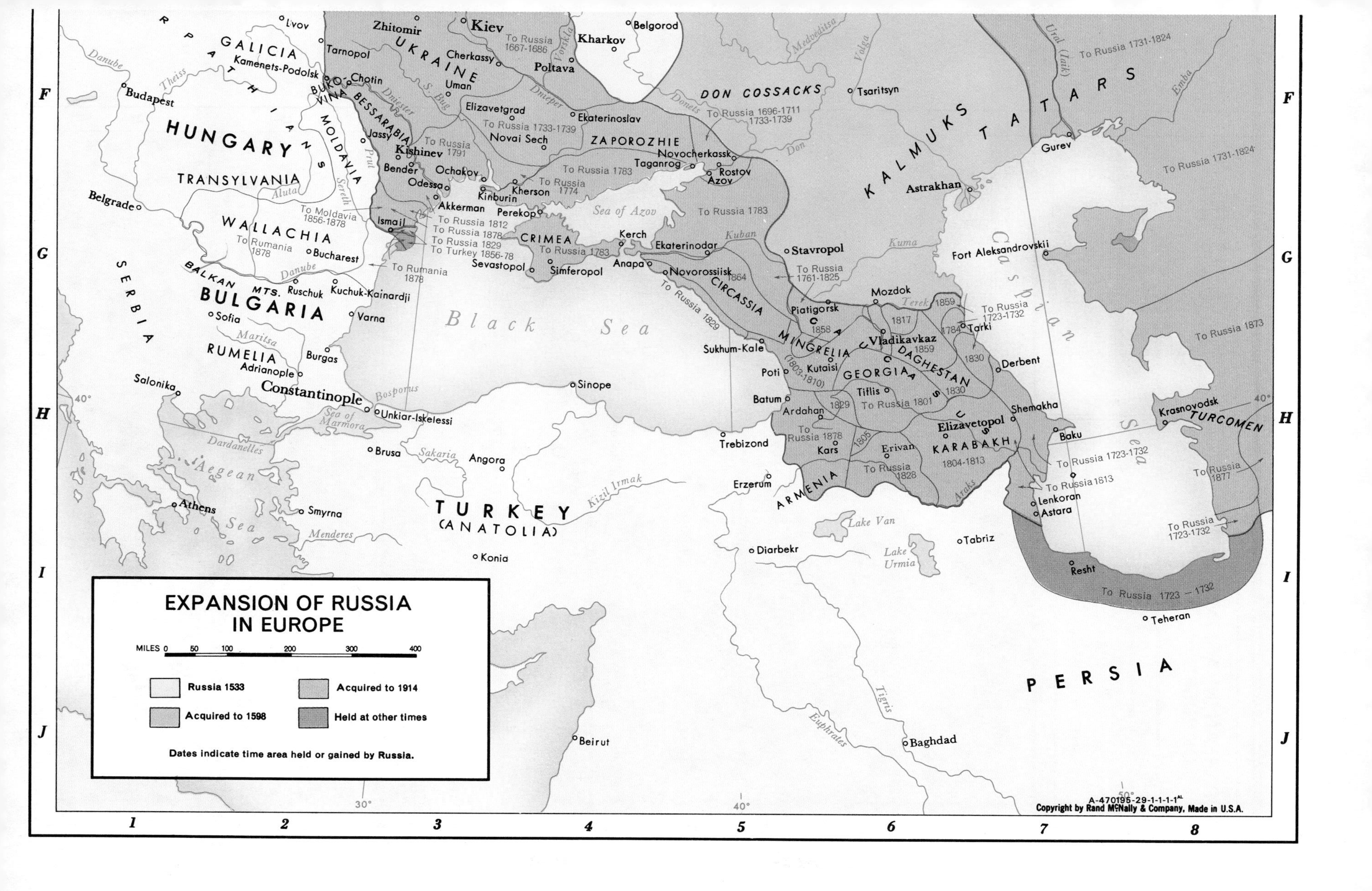
EXPANSION OF RUSSIA
IN EUROPE
MILES 0 50 100 200 300 400
Russia 1533
Acquired to 1598
Acquired to 1914
Held at other times
Dates indicate time area held or gained by Russia.
HUNGARY
TRANSYLVANIA
WALLACHIA
MOLDAVIA
BULGARIA
BALKAN MTS.
SERBIA
RUMELIA
GALICIA
BUKOVINA
BESSARABIA
UKRAINE
ZAPOROZHIE
CRIMEA
DON COSSACKS
KALMUKS
TATARS
CIRCASSIA
MINGRELIA
GEORGIA
DAGHESTAN
KARABAKH
ARMENIA
TURCOMEN
TURKEY
(ANATOLIA)
PERSIA
Black Sea
Sea of Azov
Caspian Sea
Aegean Sea
Sea of Marmora
Bosporus
Dardanelles
Lake Van
Lake Urmia
Danube
Theiss
Aluta
Sereth
Prut
Dniester
S. Bug
Dnieper
Vorskla
Donets
Don
Medveditsa
Volga
Kuma
Kuban
Terek
Ural (Iaik)
Emba
Araks
Tigris
Euphrates
Kizil Irmak
Sakaria
Menderes
Maritsa
Lvov
Tarnopol
Kamenets-Podolsk
Chotin
Budapest
Jassy
Kishinev
Bender
Belgrade
Bucharest
Ruschuk
Kuchuk-Kainardji
Varna
Sofia
Burgas
Adrianople
Constantinople
Unkiar-Iskelessi
Salonika
Athens
Brusa
Smyrna
Angora
Konia
Beirut
Sinope
Trebizond
Erzerum
Diarbekr
Baghdad
Tabriz
Teheran
Resht
Zhitomir
Kiev
Cherkassy
Uman
Kharkov
Belgorod
Poltava
Elizavetgrad
Ekaterinoslav
Novai Sech
Ochakov
Odessa
Akkerman
Ismail
Kinburin
Kherson
Perekop
Sevastopol
Simferopol
Kerch
Novocherkassk
Taganrog
Rostov
Azov
Ekaterinodar
Anapa
Novorossiisk
Sukhum-Kale
Poti
Batum
Ardahan
Kars
Kutaisi
Tiflis
Erivan
Elizavetopol
Shemakha
Baku
Lenkoran
Astara
Derbent
Tarki
Vladikavkaz
Mozdok
Piatigorsk
Stavropol
Tsaritsyn
Astrakhan
Fort Aleksandrovskii
Gurev
Krasnovodsk
To Russia 1667-1686
To Russia 1696-1711 1733-1739
To Russia 1733-1739
To Russia 1791
To Russia 1783
To Russia 1774
To Moldavia 1856-1878
To Russia 1812
To Russia 1878
To Russia 1829
To Turkey 1856-78
To Rumania 1878
To Russia 1761-1825
To Russia 1829
To Russia 1723-1732
To Russia 1801
To Russia 1828
To Russia 1813
To Russia 1873
To Russia 1877
To Russia 1731-1824
To Russia 1723 — 1732
1804-1813
(1803-1810)
1858
1859
1817
1784
1830
1829
1805
1864
40°
30°
50°
F
G
H
I
J
1
2
3
4
5
6
7
8
A-470195-29-1-1-1-1

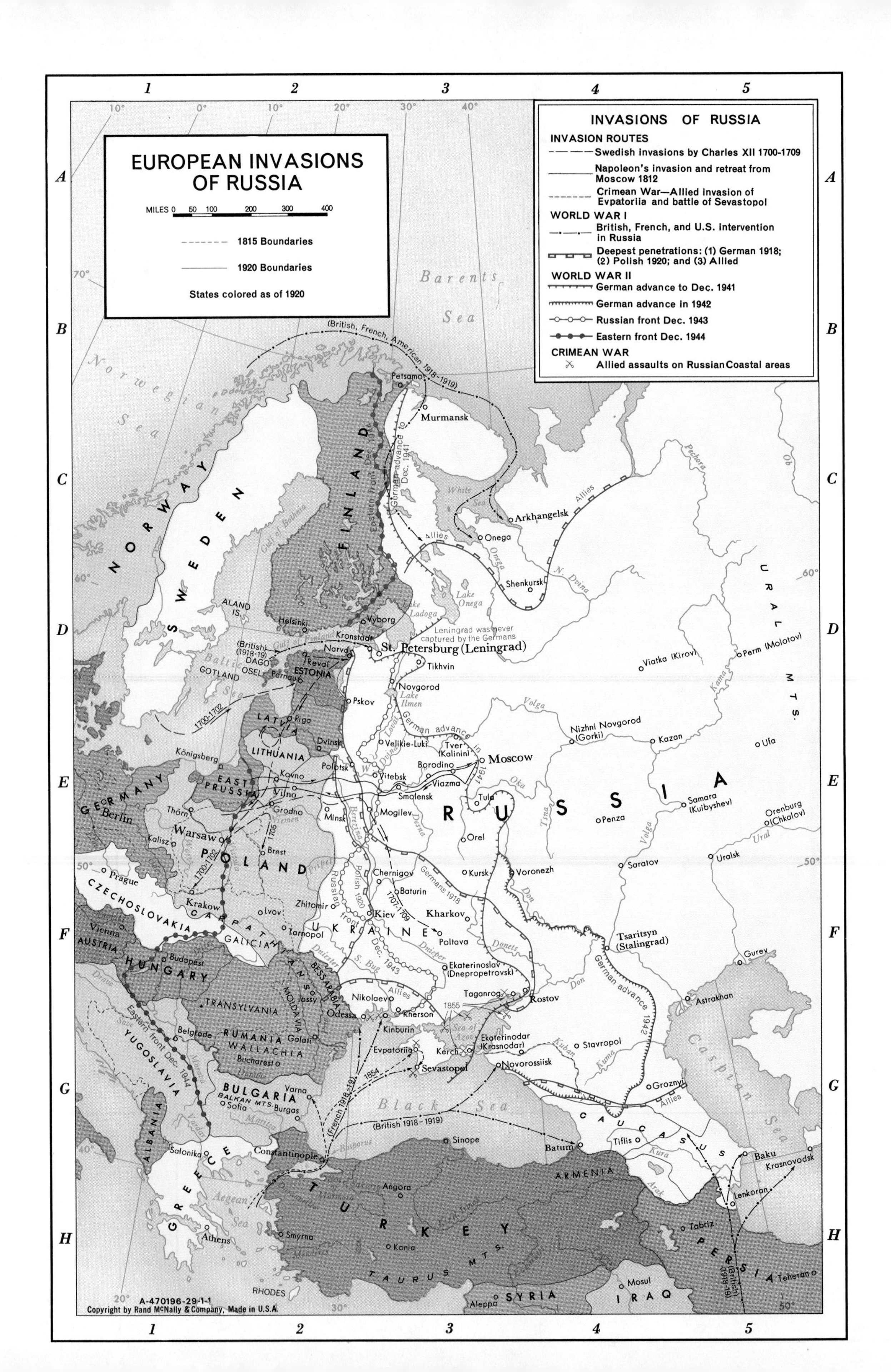

EUROPEAN INVASIONS OF RUSSIA
MILES 0 50 100 200 300 400
1815 Boundaries
1920 Boundaries
States colored as of 1920
INVASIONS OF RUSSIA
INVASION ROUTES
Swedish invasions by Charles XII 1700-1709
Napoleon's invasion and retreat from Moscow 1812
Crimean War—Allied invasion of Evpatoriia and battle of Sevastopol
WORLD WAR I
British, French, and U.S. intervention in Russia
Deepest penetrations: (1) German 1918; (2) Polish 1920; and (3) Allied
WORLD WAR II
German advance to Dec. 1941
German advance in 1942
Russian front Dec. 1943
Eastern front Dec. 1944
CRIMEAN WAR
Allied assaults on Russian Coastal areas
Barents Sea
Norwegian Sea
NORWAY
SWEDEN
FINLAND
Eastern front Dec. 1944
German advance to Dec. 1941
(British, French, American 1918-1919)
Petsamo
Murmansk
White Sea
Arkhangelsk
Allies
Onega
Shenkursk
N. Dvina
Pechora
URAL MTS.
Gulf of Bothnia
ALAND IS.
Helsinki
Vyborg
Lake Ladoga
Lake Onega
Leningrad was never captured by the Germans
Kronstadt
St. Petersburg (Leningrad)
(British) (1918-19)
DAGO
OSEL
GOTLAND
Narva
Reval
ESTONIA
Parnau
Baltic Sea
Tikhvin
Novgorod
Lake Ilmen
Pskov
1700-1702
Riga
LATVIA
Dvinsk
LITHUANIA
Königsberg
EAST PRUSSIA
Kovno
Vilno
Grodno
Niemen
Polotsk
Velikie-Luki
Tver (Kalinin)
Moscow
German advance in 1941
Borodino
Vitebsk
Viazma
Smolensk
Oka
Tula
Minsk
Mogilev
Berezina
Desna
RUSSIA
Orel
Penza
Tsna
Volga
Viatka (Kirov)
Perm (Molotov)
Kama
Nizhni Novgorod (Gorki)
Kazan
Ufa
Samara (Kuibyshev)
Orenburg (Chkalov)
Ural
Uralsk
Saratov
GERMANY
Berlin
Elbe
Oder
Thorn
Warsaw
Kalisz
Warta
Vistula
1705
POLAND
Brest
1700-1702
Pripet
Prague
CZECHOSLOVAKIA
Krakow
CARPATHIANS
Lvov
GALICIA
Tarnopol
Zhitomir
Chernigov
Baturin
Germans 1918
Polish 1920
Russian front Dec. 1943
1707-1709
Kiev
Kursk
Voronezh
Don
Kharkov
UKRAINE
Poltava
Dnieper
Donets
Tsaritsyn (Stalingrad)
Gurev
Vienna
AUSTRIA
Danube
Theiss
Budapest
HUNGARY
Drave
Dniester
BESSARABIA
S. Bug
Ekaterinoslav (Dnepropetrovsk)
German advance 1942
Taganrog
Rostov
Astrakhan
TRANSYLVANIA
MOLDAVIA
Jassy
Nikolaev
Allies
Odessa
Kherson
1855
Prut
Kinburn
Sea of Azov
Belgrade
Save
RUMANIA
WALLACHIA
Galati
Evpatoriia
Kerch
Ekaterinodar (Krasnodar)
Kuban
Stavropol
Kuma
Caspian Sea
Bucharest
1854
Sevastopol
Novorossiisk
YUGOSLAVIA
Eastern front Dec. 1944
Morava
BULGARIA
BALKAN MTS.
Varna
Sofia
Burgas
Maritsa
(French 1918-19)
Black Sea
(British 1918-1919)
Grozny
Allies
CAUCASUS
ALBANIA
Vardar
Salonika
Constantinople
Bosporus
Sinope
Batum
Tiflis
Kura
Baku
Krasnovodsk
GREECE
Aegean Sea
Dardanelles
Sea of Marmora
Sakarya
Angora
TURKEY
Kizil Irmak
ARMENIA
Arax
Lenkoran
Athens
Smyrna
Konia
Menderes
TAURUS MTS.
Euphrates
Tigris
Tabriz
PERSIA
(British) (1918-19)
Teheran
Mosul
RHODES
Aleppo
SYRIA
IRAQ
A-470196-29-1-1
Copyright by Rand McNally & Company, Made in U.S.A.

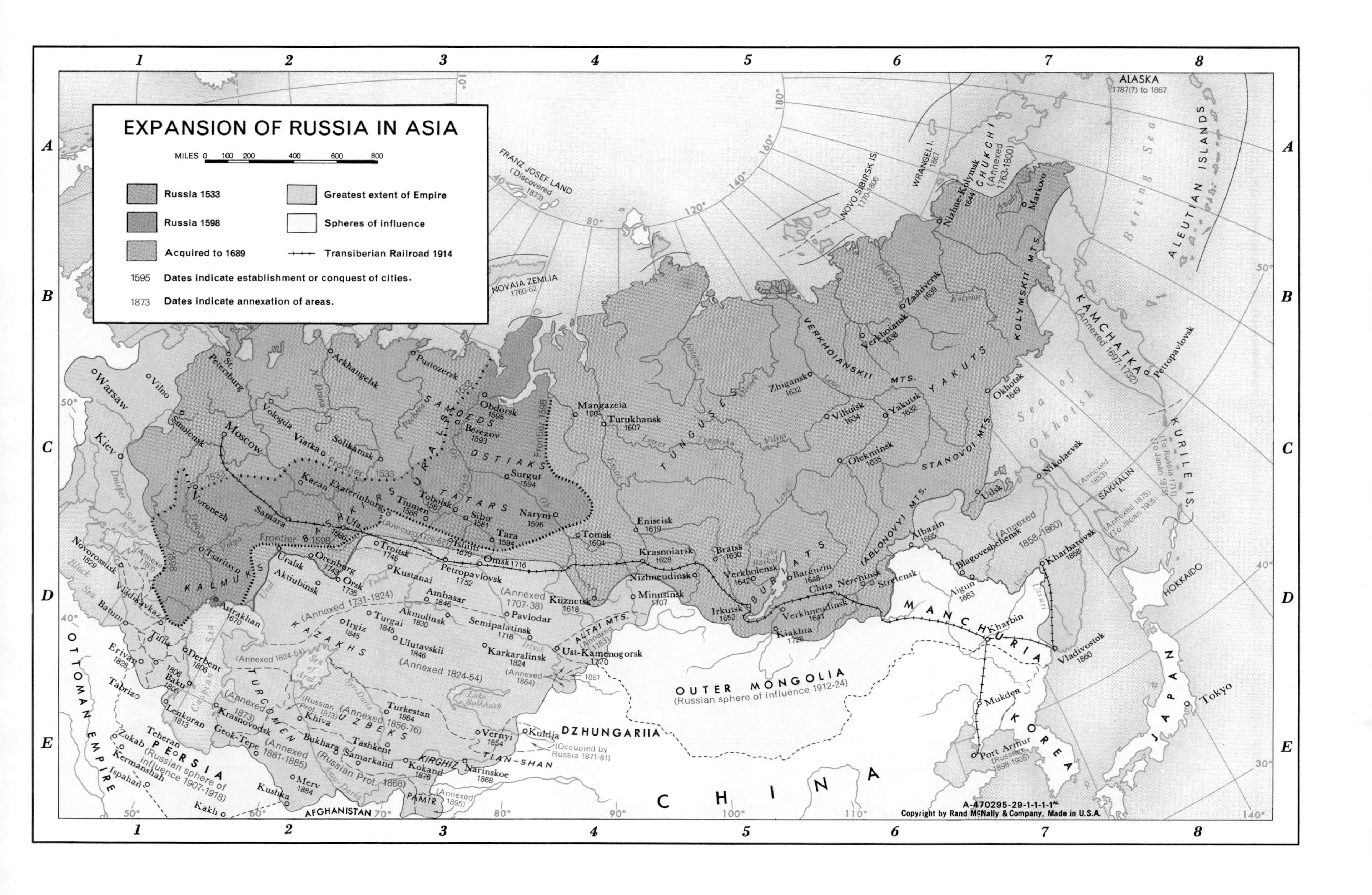

EXPANSION OF RUSSIA IN ASIA
MILES 0 100 200 400 600 800
Russia 1533
Russia 1598
Acquired to 1689
Greatest extent of Empire
Spheres of influence
Transiberian Railroad 1914
1595 Dates indicate establishment or conquest of cities.
1873 Dates indicate annexation of areas.
ALASKA 1787(?) to 1867
ALEUTIAN ISLANDS
Bering Sea
CHUKCHI (Annexed 1763-1800)
WRANGEL I. 1867
NOVO SIBIRSK IS. 1770-1806
FRANZ JOSEF LAND (Discovered 1873)
NOVAIA ZEMLIA 1760-62
KAMCHATKA (Annexed 1697-1732)
Petropavlovsk
KURILE IS. (To Russia 1711) (To Japan 1875)
SAKHALIN I. (Annexed 1853) (Annexed 1875) (To Japan 1905)
Sea of Okhotsk
HOKKAIDO
JAPAN
Tokyo
KOREA
Port Arthur (Russian 1898-1905)
Mukden
MANCHURIA
Kharbin
Vladivostok 1860
Kharbarovsk 1858
(Annexed 1858-1860)
Blagoveshchensk
Aigun 1683
Albazin 1665
Nizhne-Kolymsk 1644
Markovo
Zashiversk 1639
Verkhoiansk 1638
Zhigansk 1632
Yakutsk 1632
Viliuisk 1634
Olekminsk 1635
Okhotsk 1649
Udsk
Nikolaevsk
KOLYMSKII MTS.
VERKHOIANSKII MTS.
YAKUTS
STANOVOI MTS.
IABLONOVYI MTS.
TUNGUSES
BURIATS
Mangazeia 1601
Turukhansk 1607
Eniseisk 1619
Krasnoiarsk 1628
Bratsk 1630
Verkholensk 1642
Barguzin 1648
Chita
Nerchinsk
Stretensk
Irkutsk 1652
Verkhneudinsk 1641
Kiakhta 1728
Nizhneudinsk
Minusinsk 1707
Tomsk 1604
Kuznetsk 1618
ALTAI MTS.
(Annexed 1763)
Ust-Kamenogorsk 1720
OUTER MONGOLIA (Russian sphere of influence 1912-24)
DZHUNGARIIA
(Occupied by Russia 1871-81)
Kuldja
CHINA
TIAN-SHAN
Vernyi 1854
Narinskoe 1868
KIRGHIZ
Kokand 1876
PAMIR (Annexed 1895)
AFGHANISTAN
Obdorsk 1595
Berezov 1593
Surgut 1594
Narym 1596
Tara 1594
Sibir 1581
Tobolsk 1587
Tiumen 1586
Ishim 1670
Omsk 1716
SAMOEDS
OSTIAKS
TATARS
URALS
BASHKIRS
Frontier 1533
Frontier 1598
(Annexed 1726-62)
Pustozersk
Arkhangelsk
Solikamsk
Viatka
Vologda
St. Petersburg
Moscow
Smolensk
Vilno
Warsaw
Kiev
Kazan
Ekaterinburg
Ufa 1586
Samara
Voronezh
Tsaritsyn
KALMUKS
Astrakhan 1670
Uralsk
Orenburg 1743
Orsk 1735
Aktiubinsk
Troitsk 1745
Kustanai
Petropavlovsk 1752
Ambasar 1846
Akmolinsk 1830
Pavlodar
(Annexed 1707-38)
Semipalatinsk 1718
Karkaralinsk 1824
(Annexed 1864)
1881
Irgiz 1845
Turgai 1845
Ulutavskii 1846
(Annexed 1731-1824)
KAZAKHS
(Annexed 1824-54)
Sea of Aral
Lake Balkhash
Turkestan 1864
(Annexed 1856-76)
UZBEKS
(Russian Prot. 1873)
Khiva
Tashkent
Samarkand
Bukhara (Russian Prot. 1868)
TURCOMEN
(Annexed 1873)
Krasnovodsk
Geok-Tepe (Annexed 1881-1885)
Merv 1884
Kushka
Caspian Sea
Derbent 1806
Baku 1806
Lenkoran 1813
Tiflis
Vladikavkaz
Novorossiisk 1829
Batum
Erivan 1828
Tabriz
(Annexed 1783)
Sea of Azov
Black Sea
OTTOMAN EMPIRE
PERSIA (Russian sphere of influence 1907-1918)
Teheran
Zukab
Kermanshah
Ispahan
Kakh
Dnieper
Don
Volga
Ural
Tobol
Irtysh
Ob
Pechora
N. Dvina
Enisei
Lower Tunguska
Khatanga
Olenek
Viliui
Lena
Indigirka
Kolyma
Anadyr
Amur
Ussuri
Syr-Daria
Amu-Daria
A-470295-29-1-1-1
Copyright by Rand McNally & Company, Made in U.S.A.

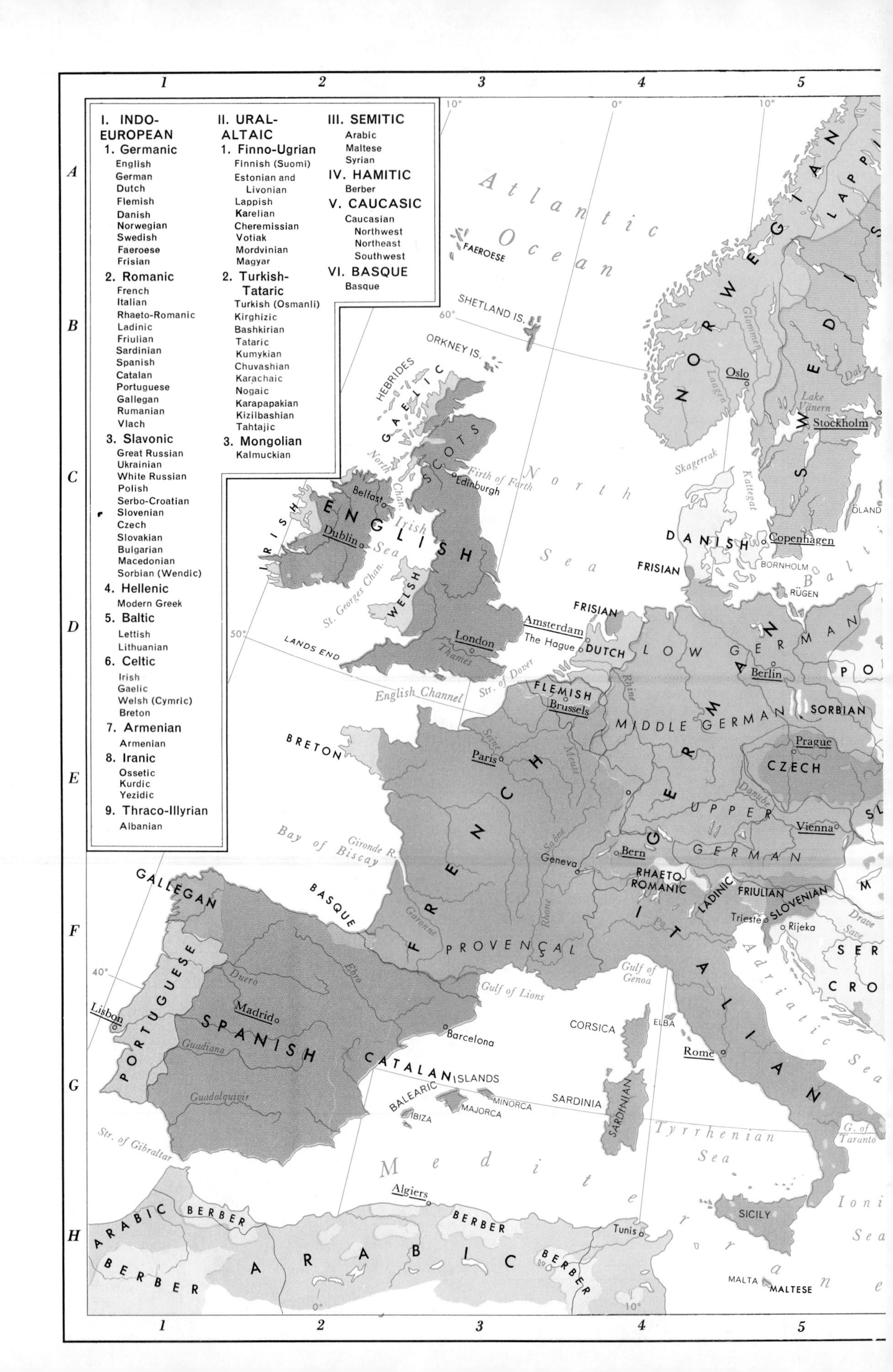
I. INDO-EUROPEAN
1. Germanic
English
German
Dutch
Flemish
Danish
Norwegian
Swedish
Faeroese
Frisian
2. Romanic
French
Italian
Rhaeto-Romanic
Ladinic
Friulian
Sardinian
Spanish
Catalan
Portuguese
Gallegan
Rumanian
Vlach
3. Slavonic
Great Russian
Ukrainian
White Russian
Polish
Serbo-Croatian
Slovenian
Czech
Slovakian
Bulgarian
Macedonian
Sorbian (Wendic)
4. Hellenic
Modern Greek
5. Baltic
Lettish
Lithuanian
6. Celtic
Irish
Gaelic
Welsh (Cymric)
Breton
7. Armenian
Armenian
8. Iranic
Ossetic
Kurdic
Yezidic
9. Thraco-Illyrian
Albanian
II. URAL-ALTAIC
1. Finno-Ugrian
Finnish (Suomi)
Estonian and Livonian
Lappish
Karelian
Cheremissian
Votiak
Mordvinian
Magyar
2. Turkish-Tataric
Turkish (Osmanli)
Kirghizic
Bashkirian
Tataric
Kumykian
Chuvashian
Karachaic
Nogaic
Karapapakian
Kizilbashian
Tahtajic
3. Mongolian
Kalmuckian
III. SEMITIC
Arabic
Maltese
Syrian
IV. HAMITIC
Berber
V. CAUCASIC
Caucasian
Northwest
Northeast
Southwest
VI. BASQUE
Basque
Atlantic Ocean
FAEROESE
SHETLAND IS.
ORKNEY IS.
HEBRIDES
GAELIC
SCOTS
IRISH
ENGLISH
WELSH
North Chan.
Irish Sea
St. Georges Chan.
Belfast
Dublin
Edinburgh
Firth of Forth
London
Thames
LANDS END
North Sea
NORWEGIAN
LAPPISH
SWEDISH
Oslo
Stockholm
Lake Vänern
Glommen
Laagen
Dal
Skagerrak
Kattegat
DANISH
Copenhagen
BORNHOLM
ÖLAND
RÜGEN
Baltic
FRISIAN
Amsterdam
The Hague
DUTCH
LOW GERMAN
Berlin
GERMAN
MIDDLE GERMAN
SORBIAN
Prague
CZECH
UPPER GERMAN
Danube
Vienna
Str. of Dover
English Channel
FLEMISH
Brussels
Rhine
Meuse
Seine
Paris
BRETON
FRENCH
Bay of Biscay
Gironde R.
Saône
Geneva
Bern
RHAETO-ROMANIC
LADINIC
FRIULIAN
SLOVENIAN
Trieste
Rijeka
Drave
Save
SER
CRO
Adriatic Sea
Po
ITALIAN
Gulf of Genoa
BASQUE
GALLEGAN
PORTUGUESE
Lisbon
SPANISH
Madrid
Duero
Ebro
Guadiana
Guadalquivir
Garonne
Rhone
PROVENÇAL
Gulf of Lions
Barcelona
CATALAN
BALEARIC ISLANDS
IBIZA
MAJORCA
MINORCA
CORSICA
ELBA
SARDINIA
SARDINIAN
Rome
Tyrrhenian Sea
G. of Taranto
SICILY
Ionian Sea
Str. of Gibraltar
Mediterranean
Algiers
Tunis
MALTA
MALTESE
ARABIC
BERBER
40°
50°
60°
10°
0°

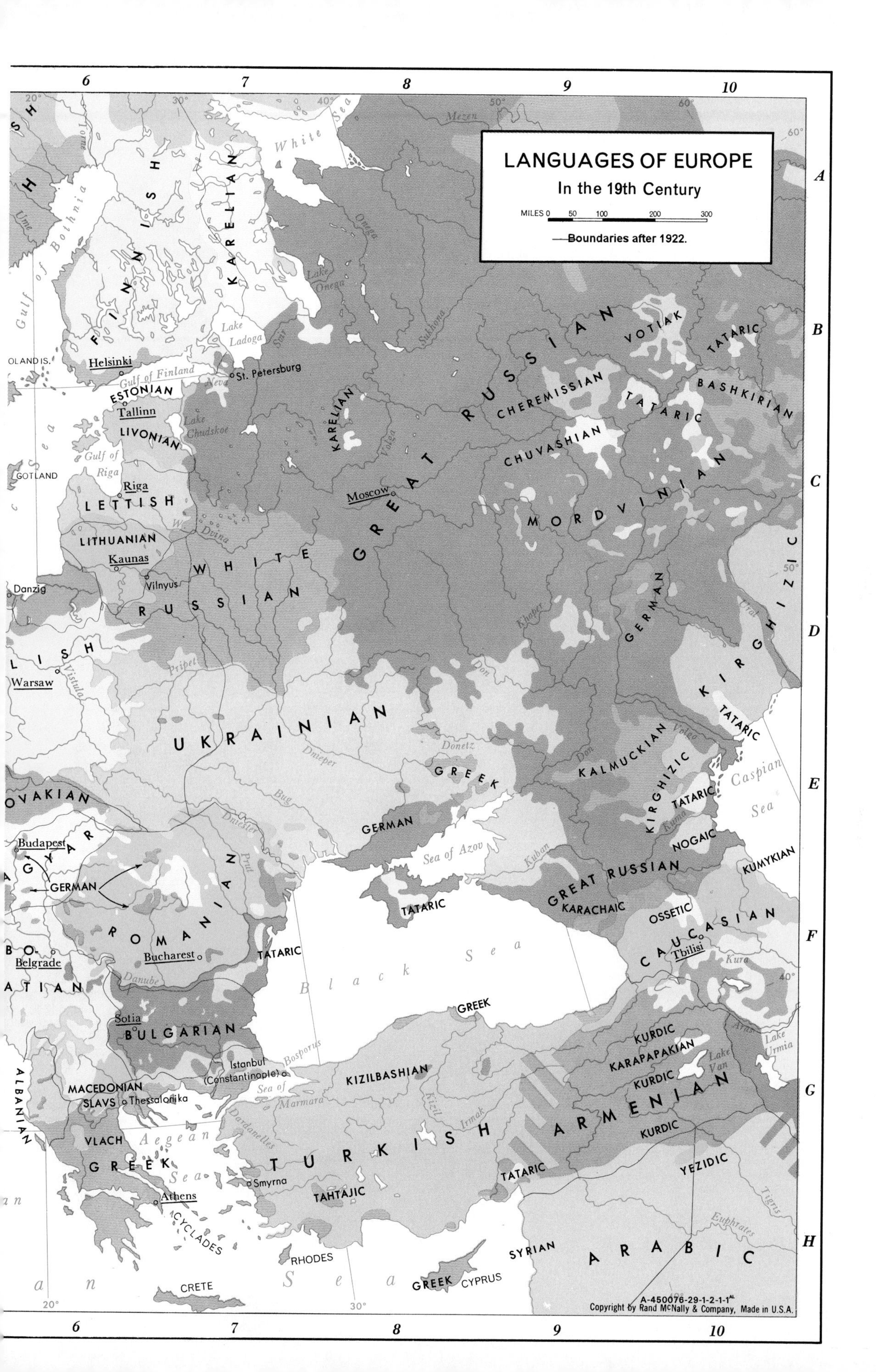
LANGUAGES OF EUROPE
In the 19th Century
MILES 0 50 100 200 300
Boundaries after 1922.
FINNISH
KARELIAN
ESTONIAN
LIVONIAN
LETTISH
LITHUANIAN
WHITE RUSSIAN
GREAT RUSSIAN
VOTIAK
TATARIC
BASHKIRIAN
CHEREMISSIAN
CHUVASHIAN
MORDVINIAN
GERMAN
KIRGHIZIC
UKRAINIAN
GREEK
KALMUCKIAN
NOGAIC
KUMYKIAN
KARACHAIC
OSSETIC
CAUCASIAN
ROMANIAN
BULGARIAN
MACEDONIAN SLAVS
VLACH
ALBANIAN
KIZILBASHIAN
KURDIC
KARAPAPAKIAN
ARMENIAN
TURKISH
TAHTAJIC
YEZIDIC
SYRIAN
ARABIC
Helsinki
St. Petersburg
Tallinn
Riga
Kaunas
Vilnyus
Danzig
Warsaw
Moscow
Budapest
Belgrade
Bucharest
Sofia
Istanbul (Constantinople)
Thessalonika
Smyrna
Athens
Tbilisi
White Sea
Black Sea
Caspian Sea
Sea of Azov
Aegean Sea
Sea of Marmara
CRETE
RHODES
CYPRUS
CYCLADES
A-450076-29-1-2-1-1
Copyright by Rand McNally & Company, Made in U.S.A.

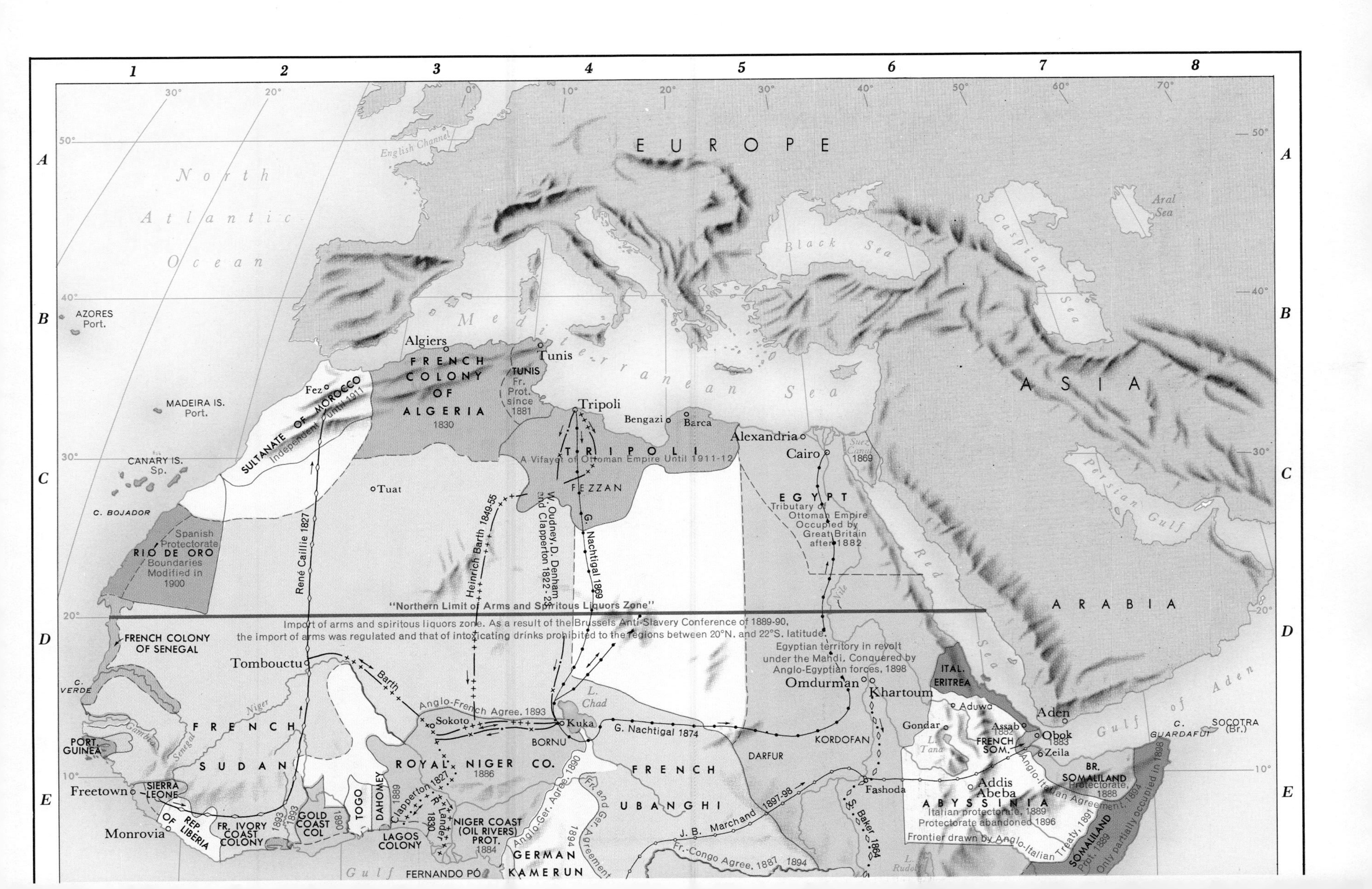

EUROPE
ASIA
ARABIA
North Atlantic Ocean
Mediterranean Sea
Black Sea
Caspian Sea
Aral Sea
Persian Gulf
Red Sea
Gulf of Aden
English Channel
AZORES Port.
MADEIRA IS. Port.
CANARY IS. Sp.
C. BOJADOR
C. VERDE
RIO DE ORO Spanish Protectorate Boundaries Modified in 1900
SULTANATE OF MOROCCO Independent until 1911
Fez
Algiers
FRENCH COLONY OF ALGERIA 1830
Tunis
TUNIS Fr. Prot. since 1881
Tripoli
Bengazi
Barca
TRIPOLI A Vilayet of Ottoman Empire Until 1911-12
FEZZAN
Alexandria
Cairo
Suez Canal 1869
EGYPT Tributary of Ottoman Empire Occupied by Great Britain after 1882
Nile
Tuat
René Caillie 1827
Heinrich Barth 1849-55
W. Oudney, D. Denham and Clapperton 1822-23
G. Nachtigal 1869
"Northern Limit of Arms and Spiritous Liquors Zone"
Import of arms and spiritous liquors zone. As a result of the Brussels Anti-Slavery Conference of 1889-90, the import of arms was regulated and that of intoxicating drinks prohibited to the regions between 20°N. and 22°S. latitude.
Egyptian territory in revolt under the Mahdi. Conquered by Anglo-Egyptian forces, 1898
Omdurman
Khartoum
FRENCH COLONY OF SENEGAL
Tombouctu
Barth
Niger
Gambia
Senegal
FRENCH SUDAN
PORT GUINEA
Freetown
SIERRA LEONE
Monrovia
REP. OF LIBERIA
FR. IVORY COAST COLONY
1893
GOLD COAST COL.
1890
TOGO
DAHOMEY 1889
Anglo-French Agree. 1893
Sokoto
ROYAL NIGER CO. 1886
Clapperton 1827
Lander 1830
LAGOS COLONY
NIGER COAST (OIL RIVERS) PROT. 1884
Gulf
FERNANDO PÓ
L. Chad
Kuka
BORNU
G. Nachtigal 1874
KORDOFAN
DARFUR
FRENCH UBANGHI
Anglo-Ger. Agree. 1890
Fr. and Ger. Agreement 1894
GERMAN KAMERUN
J. B. Marchand 1897-98
Fr.-Congo Agree. 1887, 1894
Fashoda
S. Baker 1864
L. Rudolf
ITAL. ERITREA
Aduwa
Gondar
L. Tana
Assab 1882
FRENCH SOM.
Aden
Obok 1883
Zeila
Addis Abeba
ABYSSINIA
Italian protectorate, 1889 Protectorate abandoned 1896
Frontier drawn by Anglo-Italian Treaty, 1891
Anglo-Italian Agreement, 1894
BR. SOMALILAND Protectorate, 1888
SOMALILAND Prot. 1889
Only partially occupied in 1898
C. GUARDAFUI
SOCOTRA (Br.)
1 2 3 4 5 6 7 8
A B C D E
50° 40° 30° 20° 10°
30° 20° 0° 10° 20° 30° 40° 50° 60° 70°

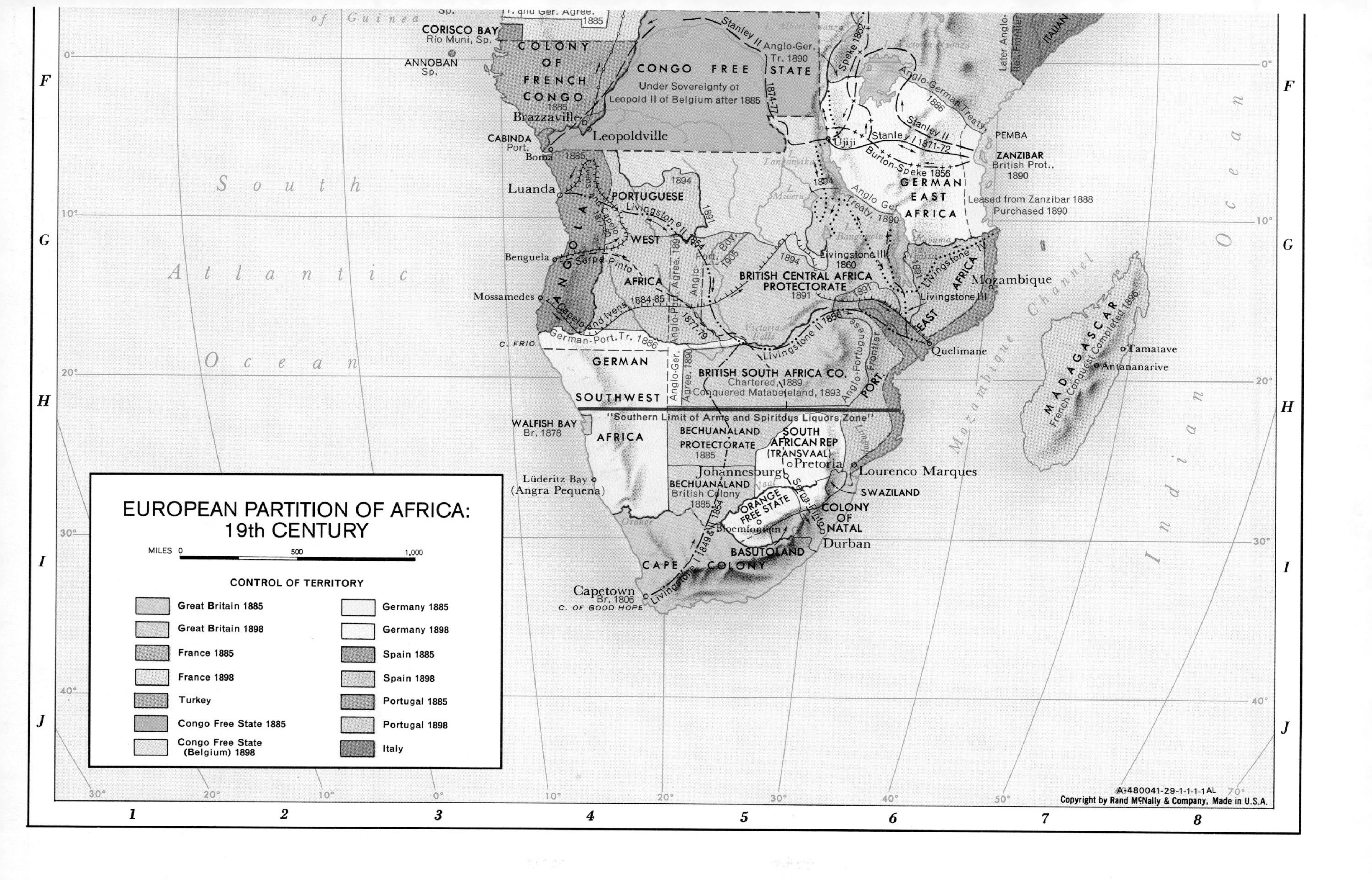

EUROPEAN PARTITION OF AFRICA:
19th CENTURY
MILES 0 500 1,000
CONTROL OF TERRITORY
Great Britain 1885
Great Britain 1898
France 1885
France 1898
Turkey
Congo Free State 1885
Congo Free State (Belgium) 1898
Germany 1885
Germany 1898
Spain 1885
Spain 1898
Portugal 1885
Portugal 1898
Italy
South Atlantic Ocean
Indian Ocean
Mozambique Channel
CORISCO BAY
Río Muni, Sp.
ANNOBAN
Sp.
COLONY OF FRENCH CONGO
1885
Brazzaville
CONGO FREE STATE
Under Sovereignty of Leopold II of Belgium after 1885
Leopoldville
CABINDA
Port.
Boma
Luanda
Benguela
Mossamedes
ANGOLA
PORTUGUESE WEST AFRICA
C. FRIO
GERMAN SOUTHWEST AFRICA
WALFISH BAY
Br. 1878
Lüderitz Bay
(Angra Pequena)
Capetown
Br. 1806
C. OF GOOD HOPE
CAPE COLONY
BASUTOLAND
ORANGE FREE STATE
Bloemfontein
COLONY OF NATAL
Durban
SWAZILAND
Lourenco Marques
SOUTH AFRICAN REP
(TRANSVAAL)
Pretoria
Johannesburg
BECHUANALAND
British Colony
1885
BECHUANALAND PROTECTORATE
1885
"Southern Limit of Arms and Spiritous Liquors Zone"
BRITISH SOUTH AFRICA CO.
Chartered 1889
Conquered Matabeleland, 1893
BRITISH CENTRAL AFRICA PROTECTORATE
1891
Victoria Falls
PORT. EAST AFRICA
Mozambique
Quelimane
GERMAN EAST AFRICA
Ujiji
Stanley II
Stanley I 1871-72
Burton-Speke 1856
Speke 1862
Anglo-German Treaty 1886
Anglo Ger. Treaty, 1890
Anglo-Ger. Tr. 1890
Livingstone III 1860
Livingstone II 1854
Livingstone II 1856
Livingstone III
Livingstone I 1849 & 1854
Capelo and Ivens 1884-85
Capelo and Ivens 1877-80
Serpa Pinto
German-Port. Tr. 1886
Anglo-Port. Agree. 1891
Anglo-Port. Bdy. 1905
Anglo-Ger. Agree. 1890
Anglo-Portuguese Frontier
ZANZIBAR
British Prot., 1890
PEMBA
Leased from Zanzibar 1888
Purchased 1890
Later Anglo-Ital. Frontier
ITALIAN
MADAGASCAR
French Conquest Completed 1896
Tamatave
Antananarive
L. Tanganyika
L. Mweru
L. Bangweolu
L. Nyassa
L. Victoria Nyanza
L. Albert Nyanza
Congo
Zambezi
Limpopo
Orange
Vaal
Rovuma
A-480041-29-1-1-1-1AL
Copyright by Rand McNally & Company, Made in U.S.A.

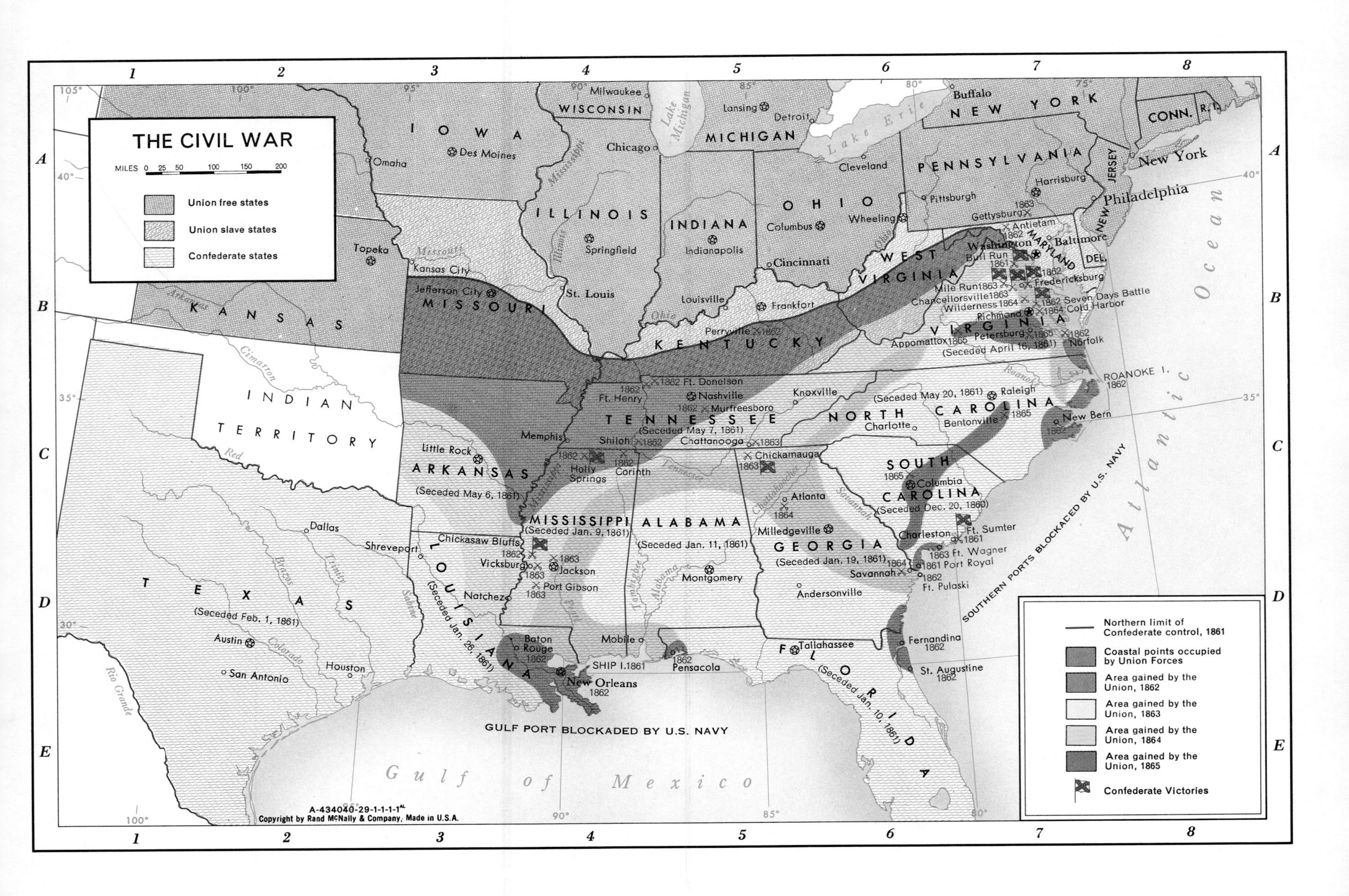
THE CIVIL WAR
MILES 0 25 50 100 150 200
Union free states
Union slave states
Confederate states
Northern limit of Confederate control, 1861
Coastal points occupied by Union Forces
Area gained by the Union, 1862
Area gained by the Union, 1863
Area gained by the Union, 1864
Area gained by the Union, 1865
Confederate Victories
IOWA
WISCONSIN
MICHIGAN
ILLINOIS
INDIANA
OHIO
PENNSYLVANIA
NEW YORK
CONN.
R.I.
NEW JERSEY
DEL.
MARYLAND
KANSAS
MISSOURI
KENTUCKY
WEST VIRGINIA
VIRGINIA
(Seceded April 16, 1861)
INDIAN TERRITORY
ARKANSAS
(Seceded May 6, 1861)
TENNESSEE
(Seceded May 7, 1861)
NORTH CAROLINA
(Seceded May 20, 1861)
SOUTH CAROLINA
(Seceded Dec. 20, 1860)
MISSISSIPPI
(Seceded Jan. 9, 1861)
ALABAMA
(Seceded Jan. 11, 1861)
GEORGIA
(Seceded Jan. 19, 1861)
FLORIDA
(Seceded Jan. 10, 1861)
LOUISIANA
(Seceded Jan. 26, 1861)
TEXAS
(Seceded Feb. 1, 1861)
Omaha
Des Moines
Topeka
Kansas City
Jefferson City
Milwaukee
Chicago
Springfield
St. Louis
Lansing
Detroit
Indianapolis
Cincinnati
Louisville
Frankfort
Columbus
Cleveland
Wheeling
Buffalo
Pittsburgh
Harrisburg
Gettysburg 1863
Antietam 1862
Baltimore
Washington
Bull Run 1861
Fredericksburg 1862
Mile Run 1863
Chancellorsville 1863
Wilderness 1864
Seven Days Battle 1862
Cold Harbor 1864
Richmond
Petersburg 1865
Appomattox 1865
Norfolk 1862
New York
Philadelphia
ROANOKE I. 1862
New Bern 1862
Raleigh
Bentonville 1865
Charlotte
Columbia 1865
Charleston
Ft. Sumter 1861
Ft. Wagner 1863
Port Royal 1861
Savannah 1864
Ft. Pulaski 1862
Fernandina 1862
St. Augustine 1862
Tallahassee
Andersonville
Milledgeville
Atlanta 1864
Chickamauga 1863
Chattanooga 1863
Knoxville
Nashville
Murfreesboro 1862
Ft. Donelson 1862
Ft. Henry 1862
Perryville 1862
Shiloh 1862
Corinth 1862
Memphis
Holly Springs 1862
Little Rock
Chickasaw Bluffs 1862
Vicksburg 1863
Jackson 1863
Port Gibson 1863
Natchez
Montgomery
Mobile
Pensacola 1862
SHIP I. 1861
New Orleans 1862
Baton Rouge 1862
Shreveport
Dallas
Houston
Austin
San Antonio
GULF PORT BLOCKADED BY U.S. NAVY
SOUTHERN PORTS BLOCKADED BY U.S. NAVY
Atlantic Ocean
Gulf of Mexico
Lake Michigan
Lake Erie
Mississippi
Missouri
Ohio
Tennessee
Arkansas
Cimarron
Red
Rio Grande
A-434040-29-1-1-1-1
Copyright by Rand McNally & Company, Made in U.S.A.

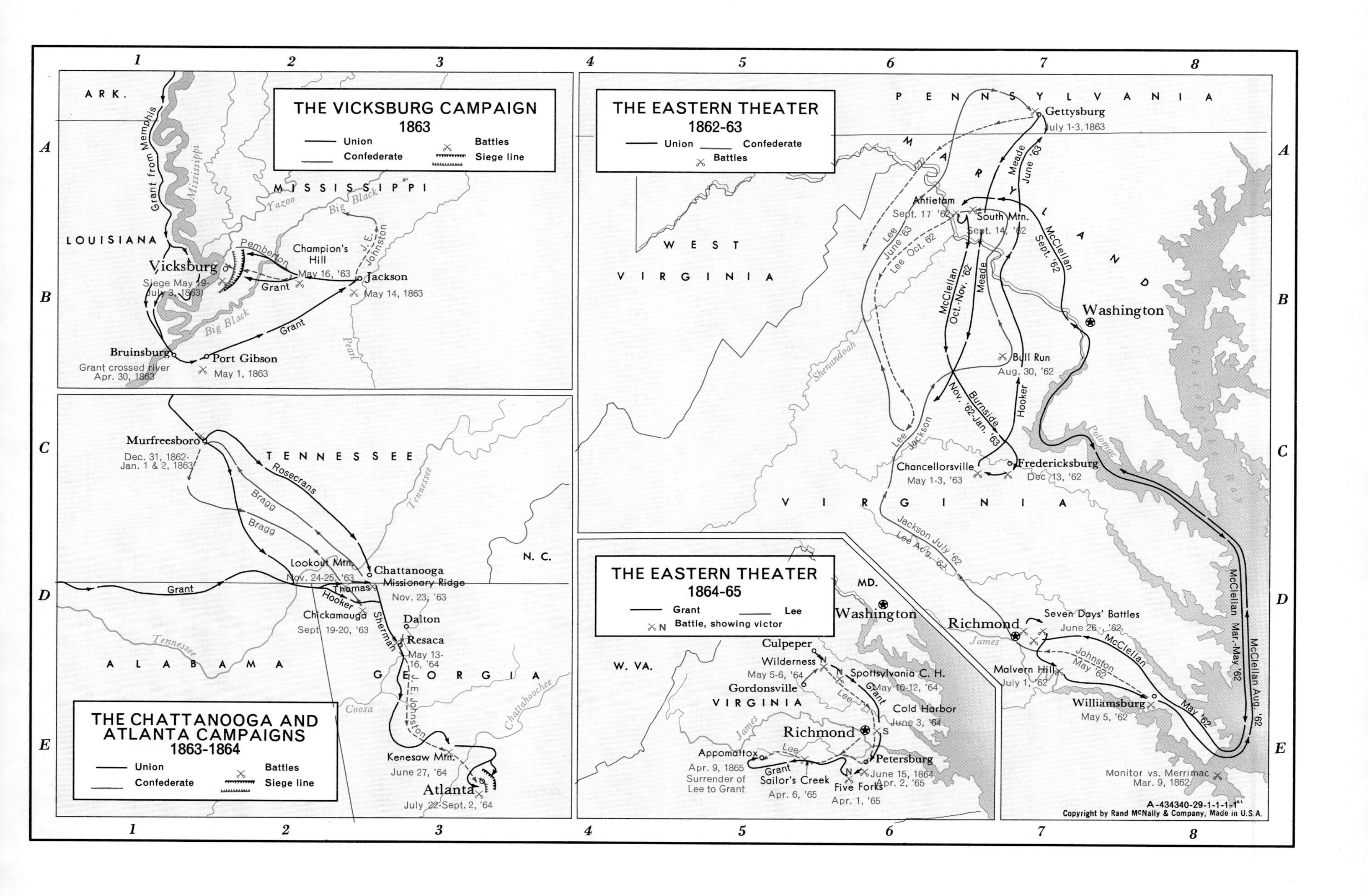
THE VICKSBURG CAMPAIGN
1863
Union
Confederate
Battles
Siege line
ARK.
LOUISIANA
MISSISSIPPI
Grant from Memphis
Mississippi
Yazoo
Big Black
Pearl
Vicksburg
Siege May 19-July 3, 1863
Pemberton
Champion's Hill
May 16, '63
Grant
J. E. Johnston
Jackson
May 14, 1863
Bruinsburg
Grant crossed river
Apr. 30, 1863
Port Gibson
May 1, 1863
THE CHATTANOOGA AND ATLANTA CAMPAIGNS
1863-1864
Union
Confederate
Battles
Siege line
TENNESSEE
Tennessee
N. C.
ALABAMA
GEORGIA
Murfreesboro
Dec. 31, 1862-
Jan. 1 & 2, 1863
Rosecrans
Bragg
Bragg
Lookout Mtn.
Nov. 24-25, '63
Chattanooga
Missionary Ridge
Nov. 23, '63
Grant
Thomas
Hooker
Chickamauga
Sept. 19-20, '63
Sherman
Dalton
Resaca
May 13-16, '64
J. E. Johnston
Coosa
Chattahoochee
Kenesaw Mtn.
June 27, '64
Atlanta
July 22-Sept. 2, '64
THE EASTERN THEATER
1862-63
Union
Confederate
Battles
PENNSYLVANIA
MARYLAND
WEST VIRGINIA
VIRGINIA
Gettysburg
July 1-3, 1863
Meade
June '63
Antietam
Sept. 17 '62
South Mtn.
Sept. 14, '62
McClellan
Sept. '62
Lee
June '63
Lee Oct. '62
McClellan
Oct.-Nov. '62
Meade
Shenandoah
Washington
Bull Run
Aug. 30, '62
Hooker
Burnside
Nov. '62-Jan. '63
Lee
Jackson
Chancellorsville
May 1-3, '63
Fredericksburg
Dec. 13, '62
Potomac
Chesapeake Bay
Jackson July '62
Lee Aug. '62
McClellan Mar.-May '62
McClellan Aug. '62
Richmond
Seven Days' Battles
June 26-, '62
James
McClellan
Johnston
May '62
Malvern Hill
July 1, '62
Williamsburg
May 5, '62
May '62
Monitor vs. Merrimac
Mar. 9, 1862
THE EASTERN THEATER
1864-65
Grant
Lee
N Battle, showing victor
MD.
Washington
W. VA.
VIRGINIA
Culpeper
Wilderness
May 5-6, '64
Spottsylvania C. H.
May 10-12, '64
Gordonsville
Grant
Lee
Cold Harbor
June 3, '64
Richmond
James
Appomattox
Apr. 9, 1865
Surrender of Lee to Grant
Grant
Lee
Sailor's Creek
Apr. 6, '65
Five Forks
Apr. 1, '65
Petersburg
June 15, 1864-Apr. 2, '65
A-434340-29-1-1-1
Copyright by Rand McNally & Company, Made in U.S.A.

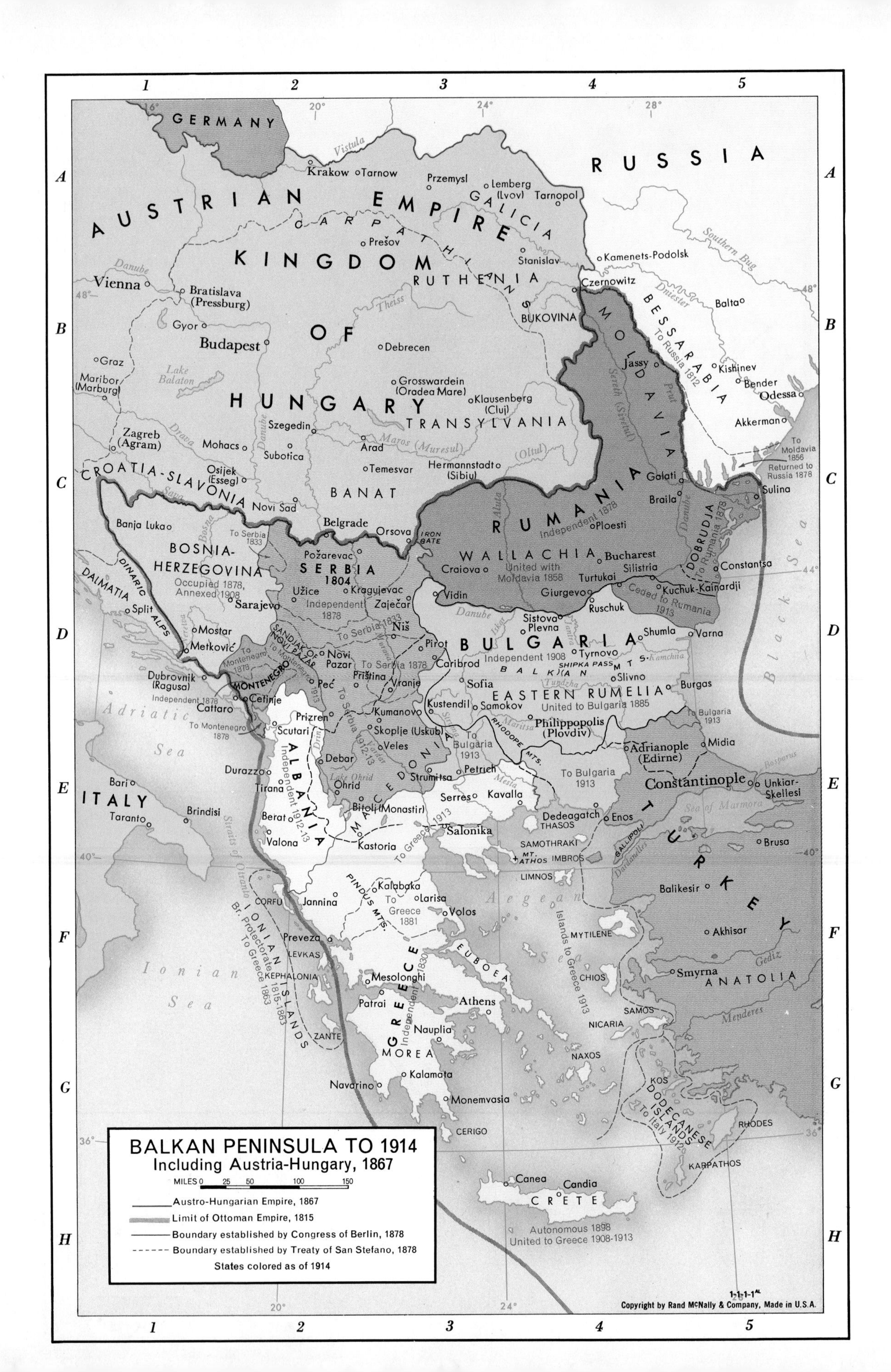

BALKAN PENINSULA TO 1914
Including Austria-Hungary, 1867
MILES 0 25 50 100 150
Austro-Hungarian Empire, 1867
Limit of Ottoman Empire, 1815
Boundary established by Congress of Berlin, 1878
Boundary established by Treaty of San Stefano, 1878
States colored as of 1914
GERMANY
RUSSIA
AUSTRIAN EMPIRE
KINGDOM OF HUNGARY
GALICIA
CARPATHIANS
RUTHENIA
BUKOVINA
MOLDAVIA
BESSARABIA
To Russia 1812
TRANSYLVANIA
BANAT
CROATIA-SLAVONIA
BOSNIA-HERZEGOVINA
Occupied 1878, Annexed 1908
DALMATIA
DINARIC ALPS
SERBIA 1804
Independent 1878
SANDJAK OF NOVI PAZAR
MONTENEGRO
Independent 1878
RUMANIA
Independent 1878
WALLACHIA
United with Moldavia 1858
DOBRUDJA
To Rumania 1878
Ceded to Rumania 1913
BULGARIA
Independent 1908
BALKAN MTS.
SHIPKA PASS
EASTERN RUMELIA
United to Bulgaria 1885
RHODOPE MTS.
MACEDONIA
ALBANIA
Independent 1912-13
GREECE
Independent 1830
PINDUS MTS.
To Greece 1881
MOREA
EUBOEA
IONIAN ISLANDS
Br. Protectorate 1815-1863
To Greece 1863
TURKEY
ANATOLIA
ITALY
DODECANESE ISLANDS
To Italy 1912
CRETE
Autonomous 1898
United to Greece 1908-1913
Islands to Greece 1913
To Bulgaria 1913
To Serbia 1833
To Serbia 1878
To Serbia 1912-13
To Montenegro 1878
To Montenegro 1913
To Greece 1913
To Moldavia 1856
Returned to Russia 1878
Vienna
Bratislava (Pressburg)
Gyor
Budapest
Graz
Maribor (Marburg)
Zagreb (Agram)
Mohacs
Szegedin
Subotica
Osijek (Esseg)
Novi Sad
Belgrade
Orsova
IRON GATE
Arad
Temesvar
Hermannstadt (Sibiu)
Klausenberg (Cluj)
Grosswardein (Oradea Mare)
Debrecen
Krakow
Tarnow
Przemysl
Lemberg (Lvov)
Tarnopol
Prešov
Stanislav
Czernowitz
Kamenets-Podolsk
Balta
Jassy
Kishinev
Bender
Odessa
Akkerman
Galati
Braila
Sulina
Ploesti
Bucharest
Craiova
Turtukai
Silistria
Giurgevo
Constantsa
Kuchuk-Kainardji
Vidin
Ruschuk
Sistova
Plevna
Shumla
Varna
Tyrnovo
Slivno
Burgas
Sofia
Caribrod
Pirot
Samokov
Kustendil
Philippopolis (Plovdiv)
Adrianople (Edirne)
Midia
Constantinople
Unkiar-Skellesi
Enos
Dedeagatch
Gallipoli
Dardanelles
Sea of Marmora
Bosporus
Brusa
Balikesir
Akhisar
Smyrna
Banja Luka
Sarajevo
Split
Mostar
Metković
Dubrovnik (Ragusa)
Cattaro
Cetinje
Požarevac
Užice
Kragujevac
Zaječar
Niš
Novi Pazar
Priština
Peć
Vranje
Kumanovo
Skoplje (Uskub)
Veles
Prizren
Scutari
Debar
Ohrid
Lake Ohrid
Strumitsa
Petrich
Bitolj (Monastir)
Kastoria
Serres
Kavalla
Salonika
Durazzo
Tirana
Berat
Valona
Jannina
Kalabaka
Larisa
Volos
Preveza
Mesolonghi
Patrai
Athens
Nauplia
Kalamata
Navarino
Monemvasia
CORFU
LEVKAS
KEPHALONIA
ZANTE
CERIGO
THASOS
SAMOTHRAKI
IMBROS
MT. ATHOS
LIMNOS
MYTILENE
CHIOS
SAMOS
NICARIA
NAXOS
KOS
RHODES
KARPATHOS
Canea
Candia
Bari
Brindisi
Taranto
Straits of Otranto
Adriatic Sea
Ionian Sea
Aegean Sea
Black Sea
Danube
Vistula
Dniester
Southern Bug
Prut
Sereth (Siretul)
Theiss
Drava
Sava
Maros (Muresul)
Oltul
Aluta
Iskar
Maritsa
Tundzha
Kamchia
Struma
Vardar
Drin
Morava
Bosna
Mesta
Gediz
Menderes
Lake Balaton
1-1-1-1
Copyright by Rand McNally & Company, Made in U.S.A.

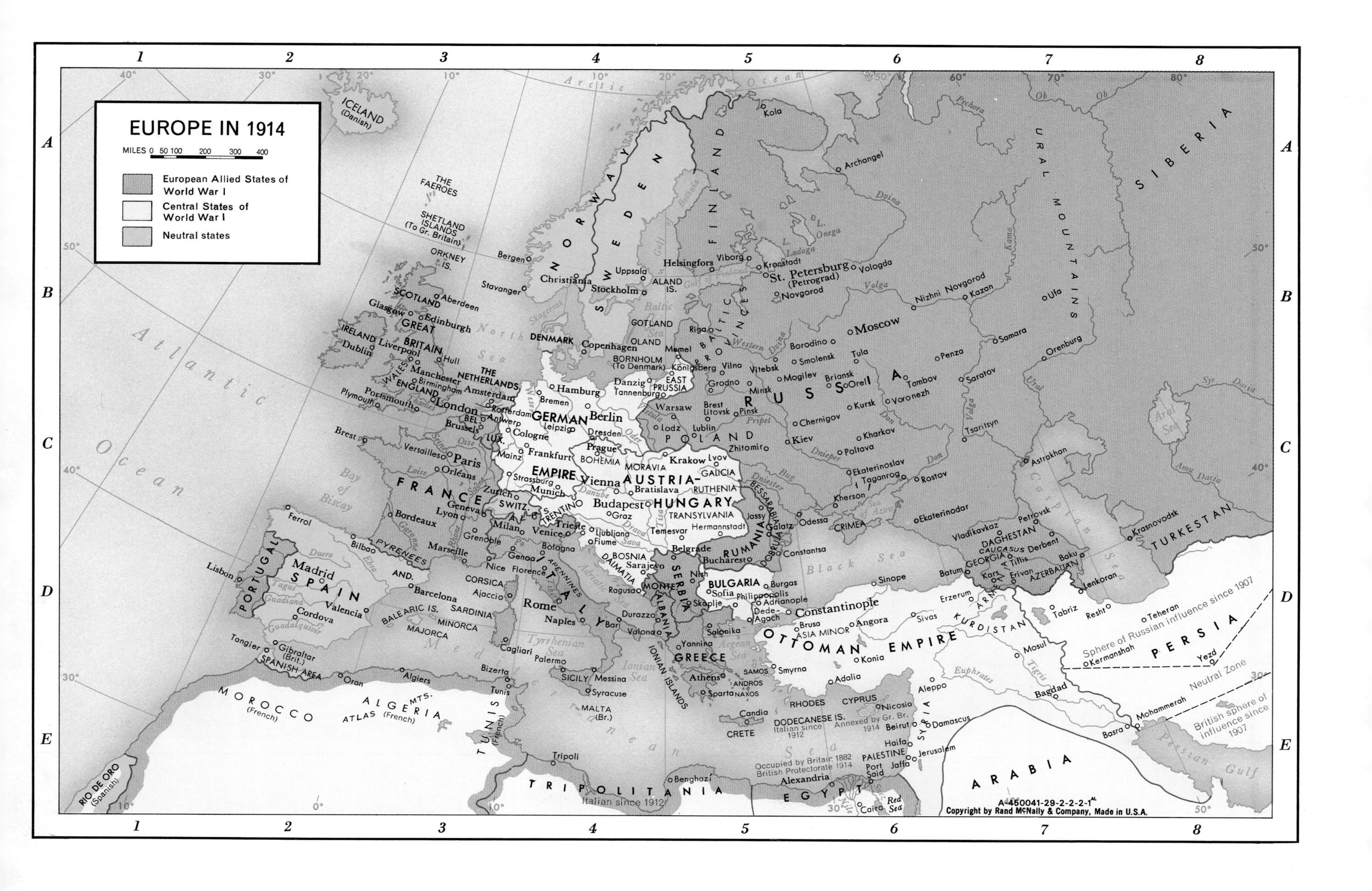

EUROPE IN 1914
MILES 0 50 100 200 300 400
European Allied States of World War I
Central States of World War I
Neutral states
ICELAND (Danish)
THE FAEROES
SHETLAND ISLANDS (To Gr. Britain)
ORKNEY IS.
NORWAY
SWEDEN
FINLAND
SIBERIA
URAL MOUNTAINS
RUSSIA
BALTIC PROVINCES
POLAND
GREAT BRITAIN
SCOTLAND
IRELAND
WALES
ENGLAND
DENMARK
THE NETHERLANDS
BEL.
LUX.
GERMAN EMPIRE
AUSTRIA-HUNGARY
FRANCE
SWITZ.
SPAIN
PORTUGAL
ITALY
RUMANIA
BULGARIA
SERBIA
MONTE.
ALBANIA
GREECE
OTTOMAN EMPIRE
PERSIA
ARABIA
EGYPT
TRIPOLITANIA
Italian since 1912
TUNIS (French)
ALGERIA (French)
MOROCCO (French)
RIO DE ORO (Spanish)
SPANISH AREA
Sphere of Russian influence since 1907
Neutral Zone
British sphere of influence since 1907
Occupied by Britain 1882 British Protectorate 1914
Annexed by Gr. Br. 1914
DODECANESE IS. Italian since 1912
Atlantic Ocean
Arctic Ocean
North Sea
Baltic Sea
Black Sea
Caspian Sea
Mediterranean Sea
Bay of Biscay
Aral Sea
Persian Gulf
Red Sea
A-450041-29-2-2-2-1
Copyright by Rand McNally & Company, Made in U.S.A.

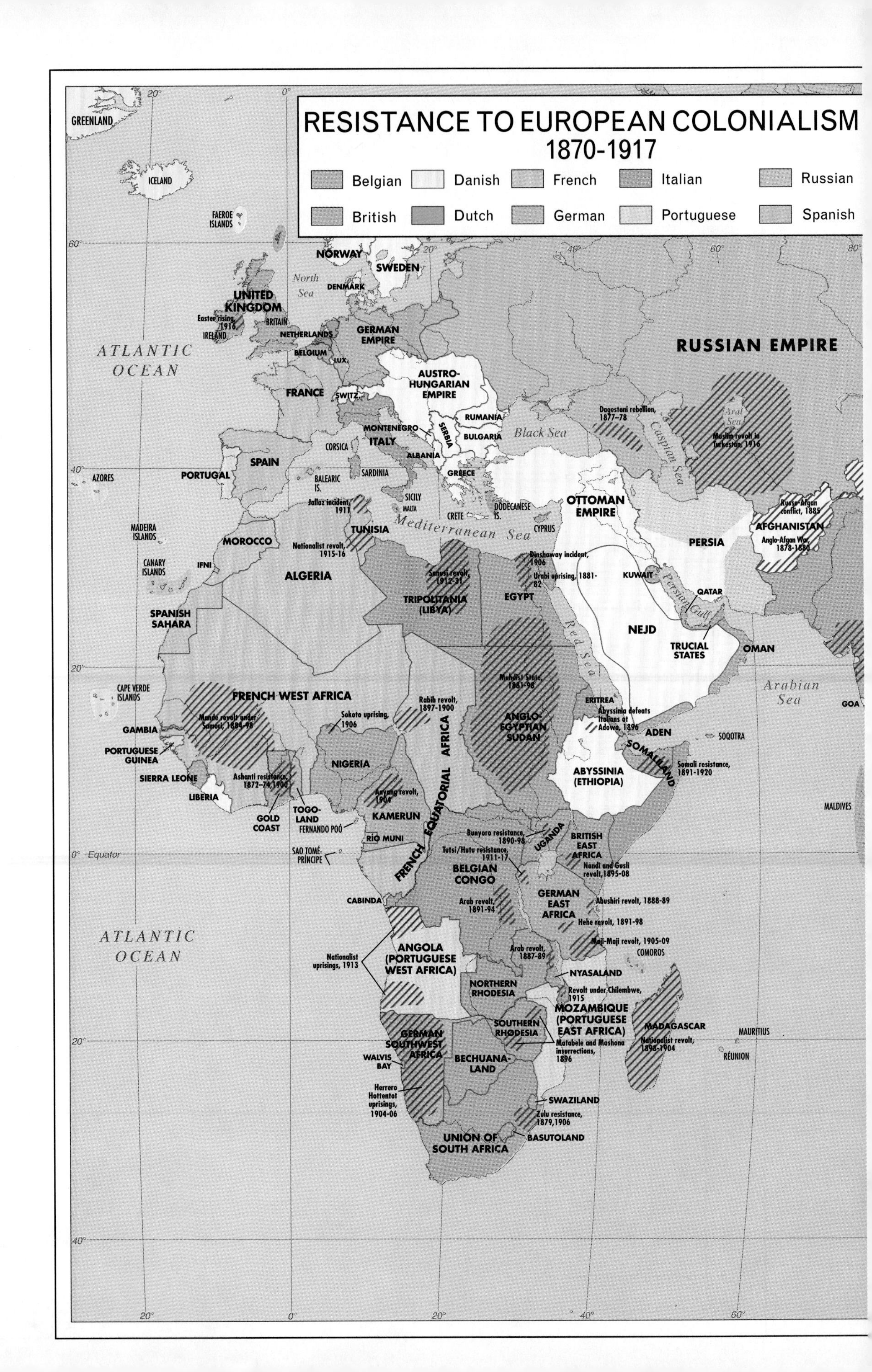

RESISTANCE TO EUROPEAN COLONIALISM
1870-1917
Belgian
Danish
French
Italian
Russian
British
Dutch
German
Portuguese
Spanish
GREENLAND
ICELAND
FAEROE ISLANDS
NORWAY
SWEDEN
North Sea
DENMARK
UNITED KINGDOM
Easter rising, 1916
IRELAND
BRITAIN
NETHERLANDS
GERMAN EMPIRE
BELGIUM
LUX.
ATLANTIC OCEAN
RUSSIAN EMPIRE
AUSTRO-HUNGARIAN EMPIRE
FRANCE
SWITZ.
Dagestani rebellion, 1877–78
Aral Sea
Caspian Sea
Muslim revolt in Turkestan, 1916
RUMANIA
MONTENEGRO
SERBIA
BULGARIA
Black Sea
CORSICA
ITALY
ALBANIA
SPAIN
PORTUGAL
AZORES
SARDINIA
BALEARIC IS.
GREECE
SICILY
MALTA
Jallaz incident, 1911
DODECANESE IS.
CRETE
OTTOMAN EMPIRE
Russo-Afgan conflict, 1885
AFGHANISTAN
Anglo-Afgan War, 1878-1880
MADEIRA ISLANDS
TUNISIA
Mediterranean Sea
CYPRUS
MOROCCO
Nationalist revolt, 1915-16
PERSIA
CANARY ISLANDS
IFNI
ALGERIA
Dinshaway incident, 1906
Urabi uprising, 1881-82
Sanusi revolt, 1912-31
KUWAIT
Persian Gulf
QATAR
TRIPOLITANIA (LIBYA)
EGYPT
SPANISH SAHARA
Red Sea
NEJD
TRUCIAL STATES
OMAN
Mahdist State, 1881-98
Arabian Sea
CAPE VERDE ISLANDS
FRENCH WEST AFRICA
Rabih revolt, 1897-1900
ERITREA
GOA
Abyssinia defeats Italians at Adowa, 1896
Mande revolt under Samori, 1884-98
Sokoto uprising, 1906
ANGLO-EGYPTIAN SUDAN
ADEN
SOQOTRA
GAMBIA
SOMALILAND
PORTUGUESE GUINEA
NIGERIA
EQUATORIAL AFRICA
Somali resistance, 1891-1920
ABYSSINIA (ETHIOPIA)
SIERRA LEONE
Ashanti resistance, 1872-74,1900
LIBERIA
Anyang revolt, 1904
TOGO-LAND
GOLD COAST
KAMERUN
MALDIVES
FERNANDO POÓ
Bunyoro resistance, 1890-98
UGANDA
BRITISH EAST AFRICA
RIO MUNI
Tutsi/Hutu resistance, 1911-17
SAO TOMÉ-PRINCIPE
Equator
FRENCH
BELGIAN CONGO
Nandi and Gusli revolt, 1895-08
CABINDA
Arab revolt, 1891-94
GERMAN EAST AFRICA
Abushiri revolt, 1888-89
Hehe revolt, 1891-98
ATLANTIC OCEAN
Maji-Maji revolt, 1905-09
Arab revolt, 1887-89
COMOROS
Nationalist uprisings, 1913
ANGOLA (PORTUGUESE WEST AFRICA)
NYASALAND
NORTHERN RHODESIA
Revolt under Chilembwe, 1915
MOZAMBIQUE (PORTUGUESE EAST AFRICA)
MADAGASCAR
MAURITIUS
SOUTHERN RHODESIA
GERMAN SOUTHWEST AFRICA
Matabele and Mashona insurrections, 1896
Nationalist revolt, 1898-1904
RÉUNION
WALVIS BAY
BECHUANA-LAND
Herrero Hottentot uprisings, 1904-06
SWAZILAND
Zulu resistance, 1879,1906
UNION OF SOUTH AFRICA
BASUTOLAND

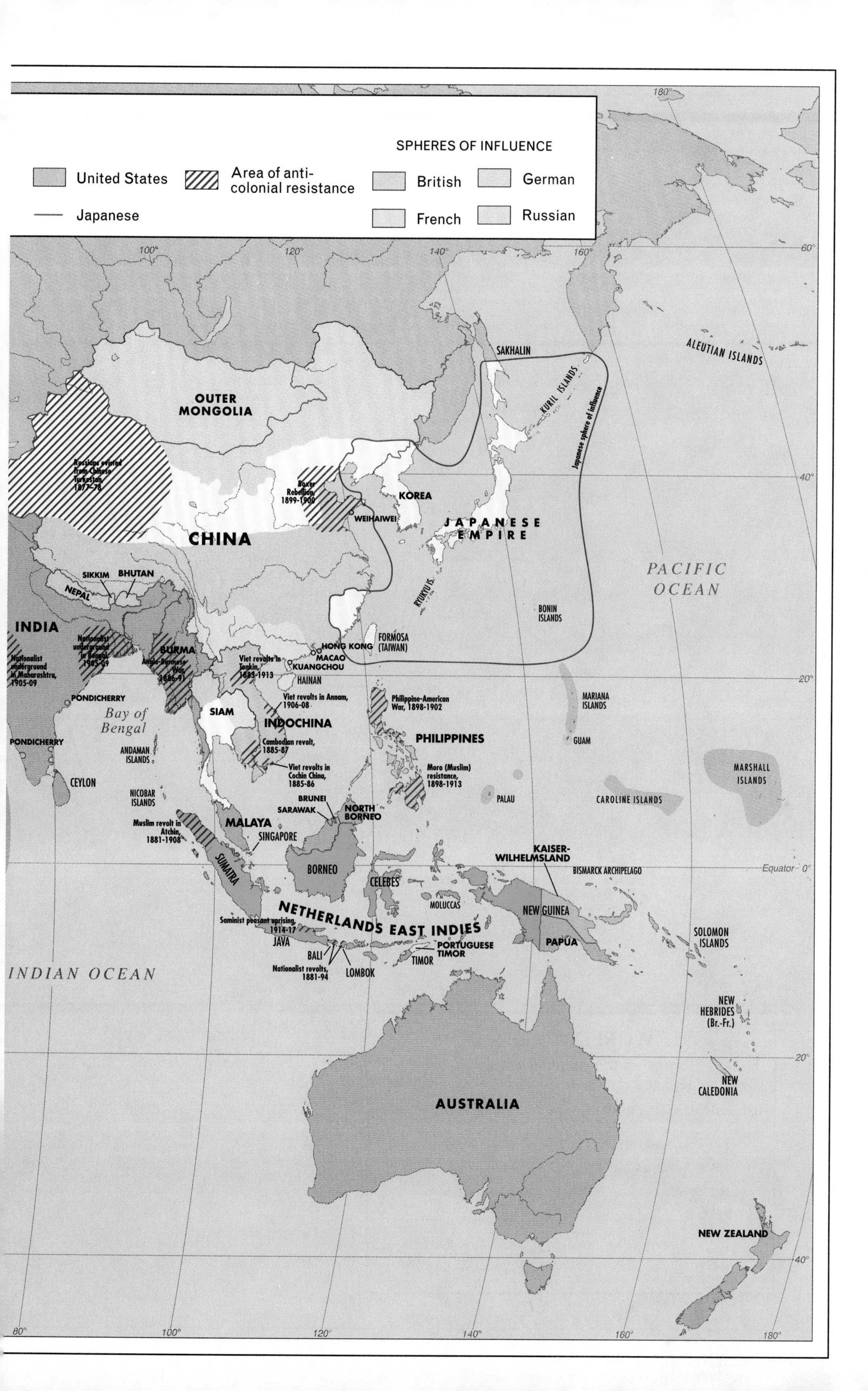
SPHERES OF INFLUENCE
United States
Area of anti-colonial resistance
British
German
Japanese
French
Russian
OUTER MONGOLIA
Russians evicted from Chinese Turkestan, 1877–78
CHINA
Boxer Rebellion, 1899-1900
WEIHAIWEI
KOREA
SAKHALIN
KURIL ISLANDS
Japanese sphere of influence
JAPANESE EMPIRE
RYUKYU IS.
BONIN ISLANDS
FORMOSA (TAIWAN)
HONG KONG
MACAO
KUANGCHOU
HAINAN
ALEUTIAN ISLANDS
PACIFIC OCEAN
SIKKIM
BHUTAN
NEPAL
INDIA
Nationalist underground in Bengal, 1905-09
Nationalist underground in Maharashtra, 1905-09
BURMA
Anglo-Burmese War, 1886-91
Viet revolts in Tonkin, 1885-1913
PONDICHERRY
Bay of Bengal
PONDICHERRY
SIAM
Viet revolts in Annam, 1906-08
INDOCHINA
Cambodian revolt, 1885-87
Viet revolts in Cochin China, 1885-86
ANDAMAN ISLANDS
CEYLON
NICOBAR ISLANDS
Philippine-American War, 1898-1902
PHILIPPINES
Moro (Muslim) resistance, 1898-1913
MARIANA ISLANDS
GUAM
MARSHALL ISLANDS
PALAU
CAROLINE ISLANDS
BRUNEI
SARAWAK
NORTH BORNEO
MALAYA
Muslim revolt in Atchin, 1881-1908
SINGAPORE
SUMATRA
BORNEO
CELEBES
MOLUCCAS
KAISER-WILHELMSLAND
BISMARCK ARCHIPELAGO
NEW GUINEA
PAPUA
NETHERLANDS EAST INDIES
Saminist peasant uprising, 1914-17
JAVA
BALI
LOMBOK
Nationalist revolts, 1881-94
PORTUGUESE TIMOR
TIMOR
SOLOMON ISLANDS
INDIAN OCEAN
NEW HEBRIDES (Br.-Fr.)
NEW CALEDONIA
AUSTRALIA
NEW ZEALAND
Equator 0°
60°
40°
20°
20°
40°
80°
100°
120°
140°
160°
180°

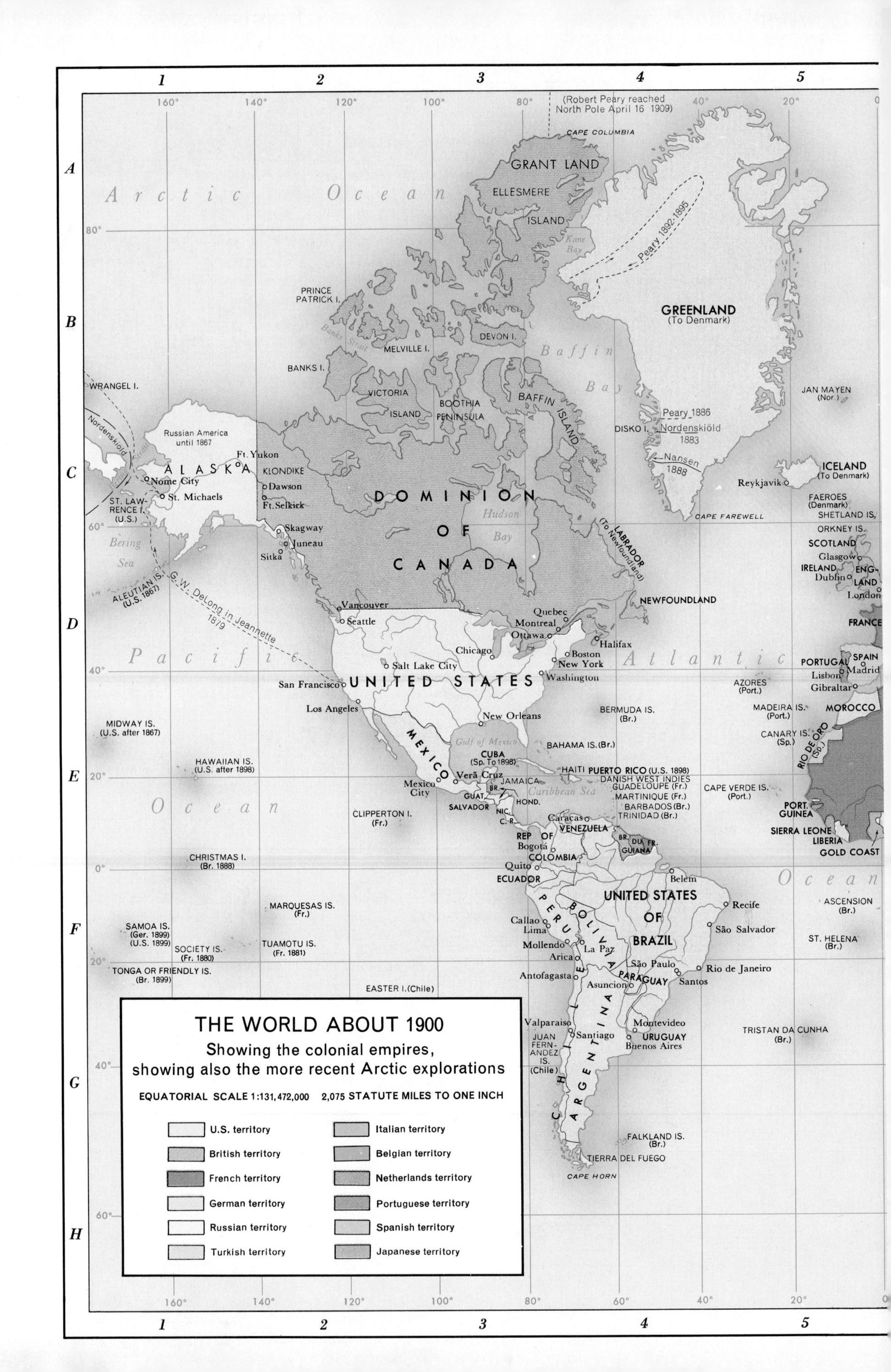
THE WORLD ABOUT 1900
Showing the colonial empires,
showing also the more recent Arctic explorations
EQUATORIAL SCALE 1:131,472,000 2,075 STATUTE MILES TO ONE INCH
U.S. territory
British territory
French territory
German territory
Russian territory
Turkish territory
Italian territory
Belgian territory
Netherlands territory
Portuguese territory
Spanish territory
Japanese territory
(Robert Peary reached North Pole April 16 1909)
CAPE COLUMBIA
GRANT LAND
ELLESMERE ISLAND
Kane Bay
Peary 1892-1895
Arctic Ocean
PRINCE PATRICK I.
GREENLAND (To Denmark)
DEVON I.
MELVILLE I.
BANKS I.
Baffin Bay
WRANGEL I.
VICTORIA ISLAND
BOOTHIA PENINSULA
BAFFIN ISLAND
Peary 1886
DISKO I.
Nordenskiöld 1883
Nansen 1888
JAN MAYEN (Nor.)
Russian America until 1867
Nordenskiöld
ALASKA
Ft. Yukon
KLONDIKE
Nome City
Dawson
St. Michaels
Ft. Selkirk
ST. LAWRENCE I. (U.S.)
DOMINION OF CANADA
Hudson Bay
Skagway
Juneau
Sitka
Bering Sea
LABRADOR (To Newfoundland)
CAPE FAREWELL
ICELAND (To Denmark)
Reykjavik
FAEROES (Denmark)
SHETLAND IS.
ORKNEY IS.
SCOTLAND
Glasgow
IRELAND
Dublin
ENGLAND
London
ALEUTIAN IS. (U.S. 1867)
G. W. DeLong in Jeannette 1879
NEWFOUNDLAND
Vancouver
Seattle
Quebec
Montreal
Ottawa
Halifax
Chicago
Boston
New York
Washington
FRANCE
Pacific Ocean
Salt Lake City
San Francisco
UNITED STATES
Atlantic Ocean
PORTUGAL
SPAIN
Lisbon
Madrid
Gibraltar
AZORES (Port.)
Los Angeles
New Orleans
MIDWAY IS. (U.S. after 1867)
BERMUDA IS. (Br.)
MADEIRA IS. (Port.)
MOROCCO
MEXICO
Gulf of Mexico
CANARY IS. (Sp.)
RIO DE ORO (Sp.)
BAHAMA IS. (Br.)
CUBA (Sp. To 1898)
HAWAIIAN IS. (U.S. after 1898)
HAITI
PUERTO RICO (U.S. 1898)
DANISH WEST INDIES
GUADELOUPE (Fr.)
MARTINIQUE (Fr.)
BARBADOS (Br.)
TRINIDAD (Br.)
Verã Cruz
JAMAICA
Caribbean Sea
Mexico City
BR.
GUAT.
HOND.
SALVADOR
NIC.
C. R.
CAPE VERDE IS. (Port.)
PORT. GUINEA
SIERRA LEONE
LIBERIA
GOLD COAST
CLIPPERTON I. (Fr.)
Caracas
VENEZUELA
BR. DU. FR. GUIANA
REP OF COLOMBIA
Bogotá
CHRISTMAS I. (Br. 1888)
Quito
ECUADOR
Belem
UNITED STATES OF BRAZIL
Recife
ASCENSION (Br.)
MARQUESAS IS. (Fr.)
PERU
BOLIVIA
Callao
Lima
São Salvador
SAMOA IS. (Ger. 1899) (U.S. 1899)
SOCIETY IS. (Fr. 1880)
TUAMOTU IS. (Fr. 1881)
Mollendo
La Paz
Arica
ST. HELENA (Br.)
São Paulo
Rio de Janeiro
Antofagasta
Asuncion
PARAGUAY
Santos
TONGA OR FRIENDLY IS. (Br. 1899)
EASTER I. (Chile)
Valparaiso
Santiago
Montevideo
URUGUAY
Buenos Aires
TRISTAN DA CUNHA (Br.)
JUAN FERNANDEZ IS. (Chile)
CHILE
ARGENTINA
FALKLAND IS. (Br.)
TIERRA DEL FUEGO
CAPE HORN

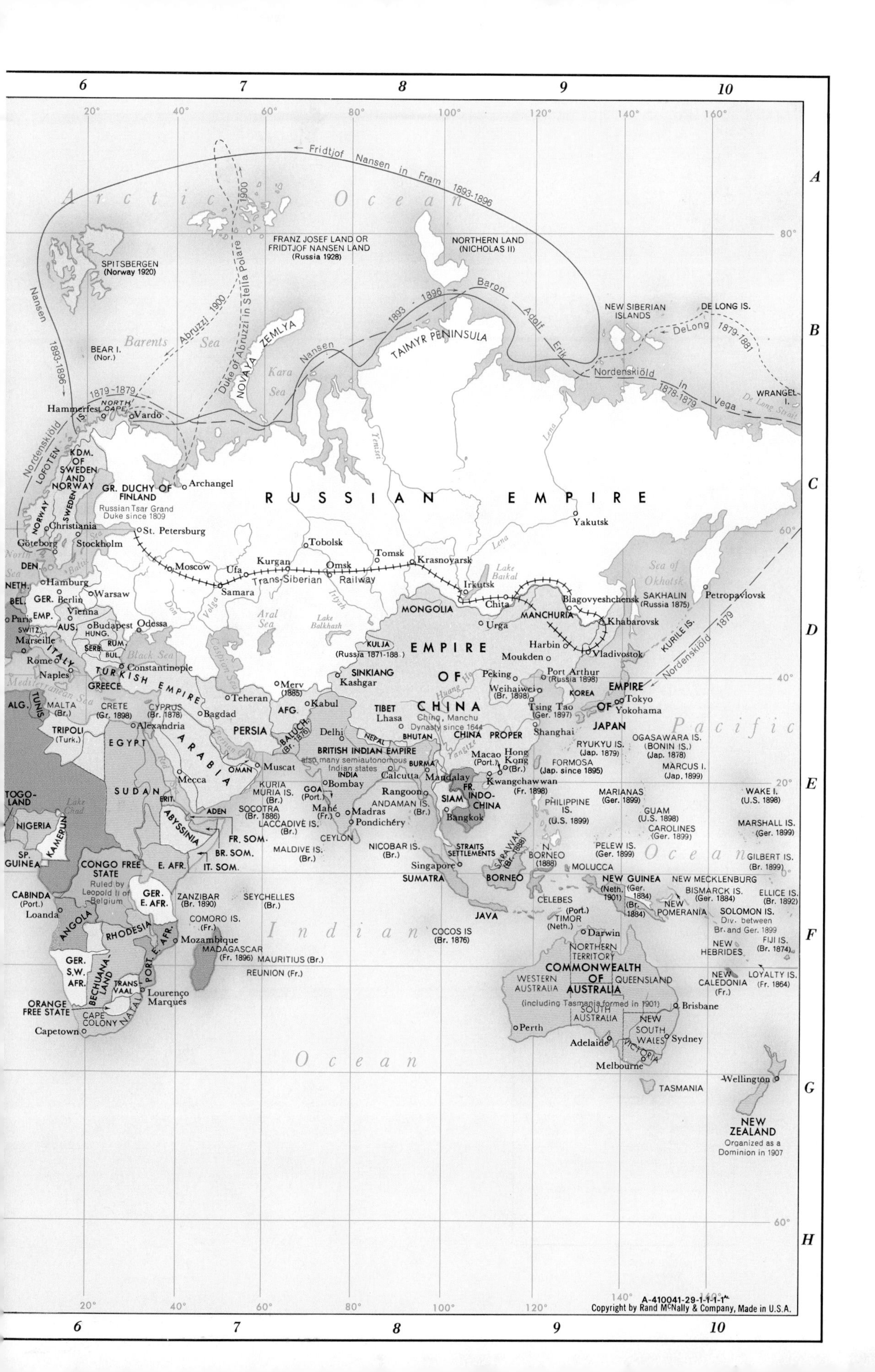

6
7
8
9
10
A
B
C
D
E
F
G
H
20°
40°
60°
80°
100°
120°
140°
160°
Fridtjof Nansen in Fram 1893-1896
Arctic Ocean
FRANZ JOSEF LAND OR
FRIDTJOF NANSEN LAND
(Russia 1928)
NORTHERN LAND
(NICHOLAS II)
SPITSBERGEN
(Norway 1920)
Duke of Abruzzi in Stella Polare 1900
Abruzzi 1900
Nansen 1893-1896
Nansen
Baron Adolf Erik
1893 - 1896
NEW SIBERIAN
ISLANDS
DE LONG IS.
DeLong 1879-1881
BEAR I.
(Nor.)
Barents Sea
NOVAYA ZEMLYA
TAIMYR PENINSULA
Kara Sea
Nordenskiöld in 1878-1879 Vega
WRANGEL I.
De Long Strait
1879 -1879
NORTH CAPE
Hammerfest
Vardö
Nordenskiöld
LOFOTEN IS.
KDM. OF SWEDEN AND NORWAY
NORWAY
SWEDEN
GR. DUCHY OF FINLAND
Russian Tsar Grand Duke since 1809
Archangel
RUSSIAN EMPIRE
Yakutsk
Yenisei
Lena
Christiania
St. Petersburg
Göteborg
Stockholm
North Sea
Baltic Sea
DEN.
Hamburg
NETH.
BEL.
GER. EMP.
Berlin
Warsaw
Paris
Vienna
AUS.
SWITZ.
Budapest
HUNG.
Odessa
Marseille
RUM.
SERB.
BUL.
ITALY
Rome
Naples
Black Sea
Constantinople
TURKISH EMPIRE
GREECE
Mediterranean Sea
TUNIS
ALG.
MALTA
(Br.)
CRETE
(Gr. 1898)
CYPRUS
(Br. 1878)
TRIPOLI
(Turk.)
Alexandria
EGYPT
Moscow
Tobolsk
Tomsk
Krasnoyarsk
Kurgan
Omsk
Ufa
Samara
Trans-Siberian Railway
Irkutsk
Lake Baikal
Chita
Blagovyeshchensk
Sea of Okhotsk
SAKHALIN
(Russia 1875)
Petropavlovsk
Khabarovsk
KURILE IS.
Nordenskiöld 1879
Don
Volga
Aral Sea
Lake Balkhash
Irtysh
Caspian Sea
MONGOLIA
Urga
MANCHURIA
Harbin
Vladivostok
Moukden
KULJA
(Russia 1871-188)
EMPIRE OF CHINA
SINKIANG
Kashgar
Merv
(1885)
Teheran
Bagdad
Peking
Port Arthur
(Russia 1898)
Weihaiwei
(Br. 1898)
KOREA
EMPIRE OF JAPAN
Tokyo
Yokohama
Tsing Tao
(Ger. 1897)
Shanghai
Huang Ho
AFG.
Kabul
TIBET
Lhasa
CHINA PROPER
China, Manchu Dynasty since 1644
PERSIA
BALUCH.
(Br. 1876)
Delhi
NEPAL
BHUTAN
Yangtze
Pacific Ocean
RYUKYU IS.
(Jap. 1879)
OGASAWARA IS.
(BONIN IS.)
(Jap. 1878)
MARCUS I.
(Jap. 1899)
ARABIA
Persian Gulf
Red Sea
OMAN
Muscat
Mecca
BRITISH INDIAN EMPIRE
also many semiautonomous Indian states
INDIA
BURMA
Calcutta
Macao
(Port.)
Hong Kong
(Br.)
FORMOSA
(Jap. since 1895)
KURIA MURIA IS.
(Br.)
Bombay
GOA
(Port.)
Mandalay
FR. INDO-CHINA
Kwangchawwan
(Fr. 1898)
Rangoon
SIAM
Bangkok
ANDAMAN IS.
(Br.)
Mahé
(Fr.)
Madras
Pondichéry
SOCOTRA
(Br. 1886)
LACCADIVE IS.
(Br.)
CEYLON
MALDIVE IS.
(Br.)
NICOBAR IS.
(Br.)
STRAITS SETTLEMENTS
Singapore
SUMATRA
SARAWAK
(Br. 1888)
N. BORNEO
(1888)
BORNEO
PHILIPPINE IS.
(U.S. 1899)
MARIANAS
(Ger. 1899)
GUAM
(U.S. 1898)
CAROLINES
(Ger. 1899)
WAKE I.
(U.S. 1898)
MARSHALL IS.
(Ger. 1899)
PELEW IS.
(Ger. 1899)
GILBERT IS.
(Br. 1899)
MOLUCCA
CELEBES
NEW GUINEA
(Neth. 1901)
(Ger. 1884)
(Br. 1884)
NEW MECKLENBURG
BISMARCK IS.
(Ger. 1884)
NEW POMERANIA
ELLICE IS.
(Br. 1892)
SOLOMON IS.
Div. between Br. and Ger. 1899
JAVA
(Port.)
TIMOR
(Neth.)
Darwin
NORTHERN TERRITORY
COCOS IS
(Br. 1876)
FIJI IS.
(Br. 1874)
NEW HEBRIDES
NEW CALEDONIA
(Fr.)
LOYALTY IS.
(Fr. 1864)
COMMONWEALTH OF AUSTRALIA
(including Tasmania formed in 1901)
WESTERN AUSTRALIA
QUEENSLAND
SOUTH AUSTRALIA
NEW SOUTH WALES
VICTORIA
Brisbane
Perth
Sydney
Adelaide
Melbourne
TASMANIA
Wellington
NEW ZEALAND
Organized as a Dominion in 1907
Indian Ocean
SUDAN
TOGO-LAND
Lake Chad
NIGERIA
KAMERUN
ERIT.
ABYSSINIA
ADEN
FR. SOM.
BR. SOM.
IT. SOM.
SP. GUINEA
CONGO FREE STATE
Ruled by Leopold II of Belgium
E. AFR.
GER. E. AFR.
ZANZIBAR
(Br. 1890)
SEYCHELLES
(Br.)
CABINDA
(Port.)
Loanda
ANGOLA
RHODESIA
COMORO IS.
(Fr.)
PORT. E. AFR.
Mozambique
MADAGASCAR
(Fr. 1896)
MAURITIUS (Br.)
REUNION (Fr.)
GER. S.W. AFR.
BECHUANA-LAND
TRANS-VAAL
Lourenço Marques
ORANGE FREE STATE
NATAL
CAPE COLONY
Capetown
A-410041-29-1-1-1
Copyright by Rand McNally & Company, Made in U.S.A.

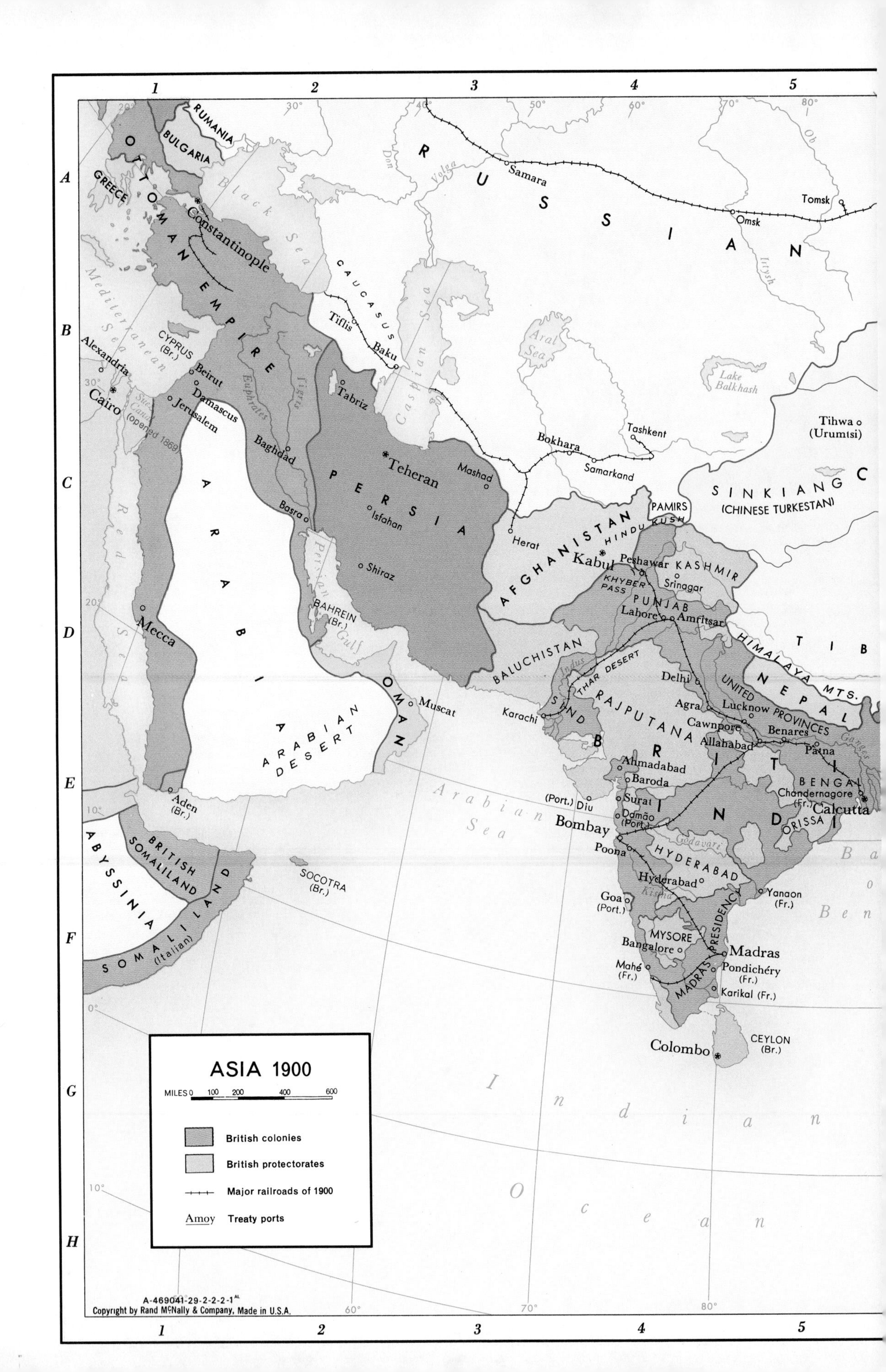

ASIA 1900
MILES 0 100 200 400 600
British colonies
British protectorates
Major railroads of 1900
Amoy Treaty ports
RUMANIA
BULGARIA
GREECE
OTTOMAN EMPIRE
Constantinople
Black Sea
Mediterranean Sea
CYPRUS (Br.)
Alexandria
Cairo
Suez Canal (opened 1869)
Beirut
Damascus
Jerusalem
Euphrates
Tigris
Baghdad
Basra
Red Sea
Mecca
ARABIA
ARABIAN DESERT
Aden (Br.)
BAHREIN (Br.)
Persian Gulf
OMAN
Muscat
RUSSIAN
Don
Volga
Samara
Omsk
Tomsk
Ob
Irtysh
CAUCASUS
Tiflis
Baku
Caspian Sea
Aral Sea
Lake Balkhash
Tabriz
Teheran
PERSIA
Isfahan
Shiraz
Mashad
Bokhara
Samarkand
Tashkent
Herat
AFGHANISTAN
Kabul
HINDU KUSH
PAMIRS
SINKIANG (CHINESE TURKESTAN)
Tihwa (Urumtsi)
KASHMIR
Peshawar
KHYBER PASS
Srinagar
PUNJAB
Lahore
Amritsar
BALUCHISTAN
Indus
THAR DESERT
HIMALAYA MTS.
TIB
NEPAL
Delhi
Agra
UNITED PROVINCES
Lucknow
Cawnpore
Benares
Allahabad
Patna
Ganges
Karachi
SIND
RAJPUTANA
BRITISH INDIA
Ahmadabad
Baroda
Surat
(Port.) Diu
Damão (Port.)
Bombay
Poona
BENGAL
Chandernagore (Fr.)
Calcutta
ORISSA
Godavari
HYDERABAD
Hyderabad
Kistna
Goa (Port.)
Yanaon (Fr.)
MYSORE
Bangalore
MADRAS PRESIDENCY
Madras
Mahé (Fr.)
Pondichéry (Fr.)
Karikal (Fr.)
CEYLON (Br.)
Colombo
Arabian Sea
Bay of Bengal
Indian Ocean
SOCOTRA (Br.)
ABYSSINIA
BRITISH SOMALILAND
SOMALILAND (Italian)
A-469041-29-2-2-2-1
Copyright by Rand McNally & Company, Made in U.S.A.

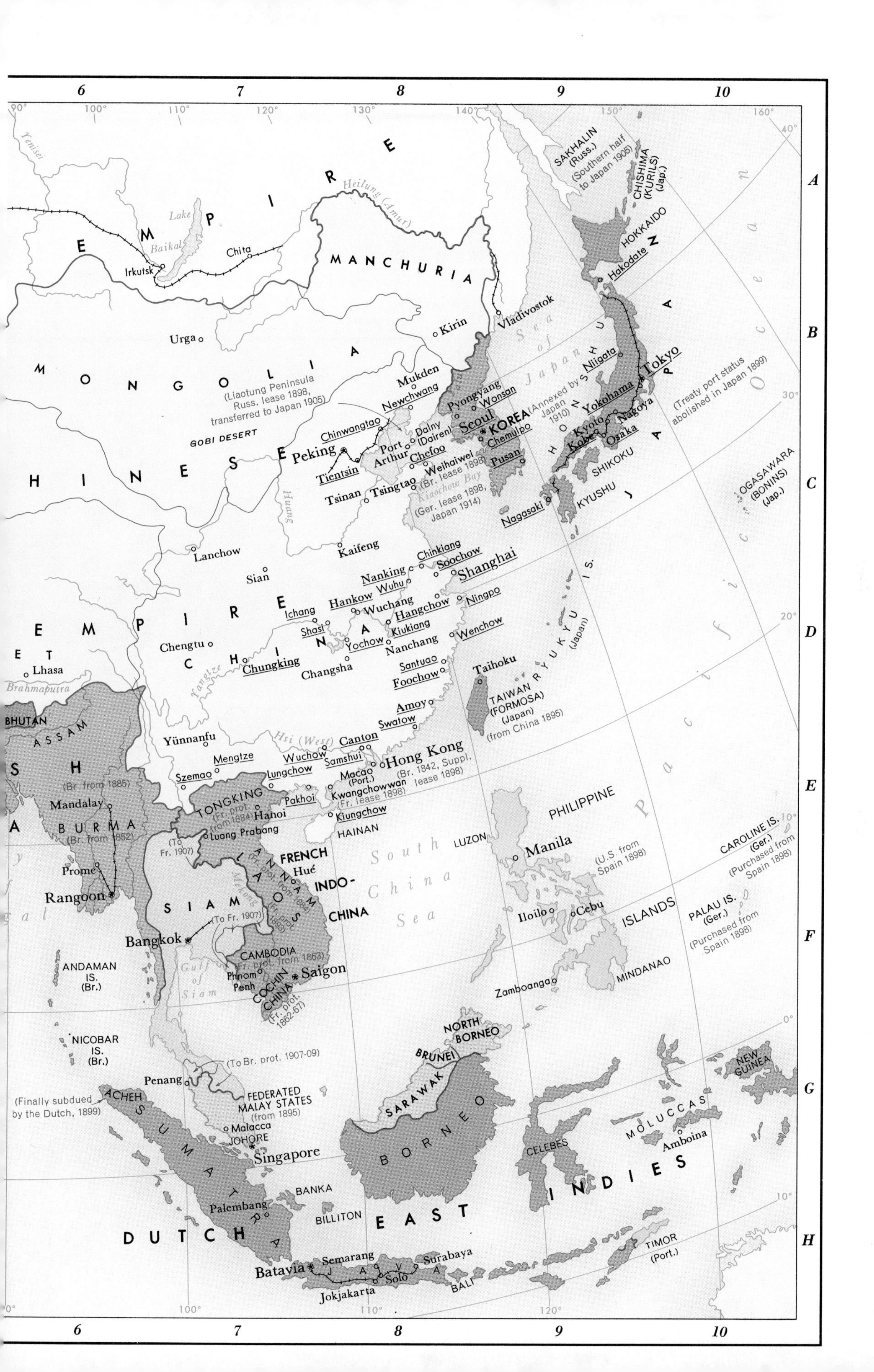

MANCHURIA
MONGOLIA
CHINESE EMPIRE
KOREA
JAPAN
SAKHALIN (Russ.) (Southern half to Japan 1905)
CHISHIMA (KURILS) (Jap.)
HOKKAIDO
HONSHU
SHIKOKU
KYUSHU
Sea of Japan
Pacific Ocean
Vladivostok
Irkutsk
Chita
Lake Baikal
Heilung (Amur)
Urga
Kirin
Mukden
Newchwang
(Liaotung Peninsula Russ. lease 1898, transferred to Japan 1905)
GOBI DESERT
Chinwangtao
Peking
Tientsin
Port Arthur
Dalny (Dairen)
Chefoo
Weihaiwei (Br. lease 1898)
Kiaochow Bay (Ger. lease 1898, Japan 1914)
Tsingtao
Tsinan
Pyongyang
Wonsan
Seoul
Chemulpo
Pusan
(Annexed by Japan 1910)
Niigata
Tokyo
Yokohama
Nagoya
Kyoto
Kobe
Osaka
Hakodate
Nagasaki
(Treaty port status abolished in Japan 1899)
OGASAWARA (BONINS) (Jap.)
Lanchow
Sian
Kaifeng
Chinkiang
Soochow
Shanghai
Nanking
Wuhu
Hankow
Wuchang
Hangchow
Ningpo
Ichang
Shasi
Kiukiang
Yochow
Nanchang
Wenchow
Chengtu
Chungking
Changsha
Santuao
Foochow
Lhasa
TIBET
Yangtze
Huang
Brahmaputra
RYUKYU IS. (Japan)
Taihoku
TAIWAN (FORMOSA) (Japan) (from China 1895)
Amoy
Swatow
Canton
Hsi (West)
Samshui
Wuchow
Yünnanfu
Mengtze
Szemao
Lungchow
Macao (Port.)
Hong Kong (Br. 1842, Suppl. lease 1898)
Pakhoi
Kwangchowwan (Fr. lease 1898)
Kiungchow
HAINAN
BHUTAN
ASSAM
BRITISH
(Br. from 1885)
Mandalay
BURMA (Br. from 1852)
Prome
Rangoon
TONGKING (Fr. prot. from 1884)
Hanoi
Luang Prabang
(To Fr. 1907)
LAOS (Fr. prot. 1893)
ANNAM (Fr. prot. from 1884)
FRENCH INDO-CHINA
Hué
Mekong
SIAM
(To Fr. 1907)
Bangkok
CAMBODIA (Fr. prot. from 1863)
Phnom Penh
Saigon
COCHIN CHINA (Fr. prot. 1862-67)
Gulf of Siam
South China Sea
ANDAMAN IS. (Br.)
NICOBAR IS. (Br.)
LUZON
Manila
PHILIPPINE ISLANDS
(U.S. from Spain 1898)
Iloilo
Cebu
MINDANAO
Zamboanga
CAROLINE IS. (Ger.) (Purchased from Spain 1898)
PALAU IS. (Ger.) (Purchased from Spain 1898)
NORTH BORNEO
BRUNEI
SARAWAK
BORNEO
(To Br. prot. 1907-09)
Penang
FEDERATED MALAY STATES (from 1895)
Malacca
JOHORE
Singapore
ACHEH
(Finally subdued by the Dutch, 1899)
SUMATRA
Palembang
BANKA
BILLITON
CELEBES
MOLUCCAS
Amboina
NEW GUINEA
DUTCH EAST INDIES
Batavia
Semarang
JAVA
Surabaya
Solo
Jokjakarta
BALI
TIMOR (Port.)

1
2
3
4
5
A
B
C
D
E
F
G
H
30°
10°
0°
10°
20°
50°
40°
30°
Arctic
ICELAND
Reykjavik
Atlantic Ocean
TH
SHETLAND ISLANDS
HEBRIDES
ORKNEY IS.
SCOTLAND
Aberdeen
Glasgow
Edinburgh
North Sea
IRISH FREE STATE
Dublin
Belfast
Cork
GREAT BRITAIN
Liverpool
Manchester
Leeds
Hull
Sheffield
WALES
ENGLAND
Birmingham
Cardiff
Oxford
Bristol
London
Plymouth
Portsmouth
Thames
Dover
English Channel
CHANNEL IS.
Brest
Havre
Caen
Rennes
Amiens
Dunkirk
Lille
Rotterdam
Brussels
BEL.
Occ. by Ger. 1940
NETHERLANDS
Occ. by Ger. 1940
Amsterdam
HELGOLAND
DENMARK
Occupied by Germany 1940
Aalborg
Copenhagen
Bergen
NORWAY
Occupied by Germany 1940
Oslo
Stavanger
SWEDEN
Uppsala
Stockholm
Göteborg
Hälsingborg
ÖLAND
GOTLAND
BORNHOLM
Baltic Sea
Gulf of Bothnia
Gulf of Finland
ALAND IS.
Tornio
Vaasa (Vasa)
Helsingfors (Helsinki)
Revel
ESTON
Annexed by USSR
LATV
Riga
Annexed by USSR
LITHUANIA
Annexed by USSR 1940
Memel
MEMELAND
To Ger. 1939
Königsberg
Kovno (Kaunas)
Vilna
EAST PRUSSIA
Danzig
Tannenberg
Grodno
Bialystok
Nazi-Soviet Pact Annexed by Germany 1939
Posen
Warsaw
POLAND
Vistula
Brest Litovsk
Lublin
Curzon Line 1919-1920
Annexed by USSR 1939
Nazi-Soviet Pact
Lemberg (Lwow)
Przemysl
Tarnopol
Kiel
Lübeck
Hamburg
Bremen
Stettin
Elbe
Weser
Hanover
Berlin
Magdeburg
Potsdam
GERMANY
Essen
Cassel
Cologne
Weimar
Leipzig
Dresden
Frankfurt
Oder
Breslau
SILESIA
LUX.
Occ. by Ger. 1940
SAAR
To Germany Plebescite 1935
Mainz
Nürnberg
Mannheim
BAVARIA
Stuttgart
Strassburg
Munich
Danube
ALSACE
LORRAINE
Reims
Verdun
Paris
Versailles
Seine
Fontainbleau
Occupied by Germany 1940
Orleans
Loire
Nantes
St. Nazaire
La Rochelle
Bay of Biscay
FRANCE
Dijon
Saône
Bordeaux
Limoges
Lyon
Garonne
Rhone
VICHY FRANCE 1940
Grenoble
Montpellier
Toulouse
Avignon
Marseille
Nice
Toulon
PYRENEES
Bayonne
ANDORRA
To Ger. at Munich 1938
Pilsen
Prague
CZECHOSLOVAKIA
To Pol. 1938
Tesin
Vienna
AUSTRIA
To Germany Anschluss 1938
Bratislava (Pressburg)
Annexed by Hungary 1938
Kosice
RUTHENIA
Basel
Zürich
Berne
SWITZERLAND
LIECH.
Geneva
Innsbruck
TRENTINO
Drava
Graz
Budapest
Annexed by Hungary 1939
HUNGARY
Oradea
Mohacs
Annexed by Hungary 1940
BUKOVINA
Cluj
TRANSYLVANIA
RUMANIA
Temisoara
Sibiu
WALLACHIA
Bucharest
Ruschuk
Milan
Verona
Turin
Parma
Po
Genoa
Venice
Trieste
Ljubljana
Zagreb
Fiume
Italy 1924
CROATIA
YUGOSLAVIA
Sava
Bologna
Ravenna
SAN MARINO
San Remo
Florence
Ancona
ITALY
Adriatic Sea
Tiber
Rome
Naples
Bari
Taranto
Brindisi
Zara
BOSNIA
Sarajevo
DALMATIA
Split
LAGOSTA (To Italy)
Dubrovnik (Ragusa)
MONTENEGRO
Cattaro
Antivari
Durazzo
Tirana
ALBANIA
Valona
Belgrade
SERBIA
Morava
Nish
Novi Pazar
Skoplje
MACEDONIA
Sistova
BULGARIA
Sofia
Philippopolis
Adrianople
Maritsa
Dede-Agach
Kavala
Enos
Salonika
Dardanelles
LESBOS
CORFU
Yannina
CEPHALLENIA
IONIAN ISLANDS
GREECE
Messolongi
Patras
Athens
Sparta
Aegean Sea
Candia
CRETE
Ionian Sea
Corunna
Oporto
Coimbra
PORTUGAL
Lisbon
Burgos
Santander
Valladolid
Duero
Salamanca
Madrid
Tagus
Toledo
Guadiana
SPAIN
Ebro
Saragossa
Barcelona
Cordoba
Guadalquivir
Seville
Granada
Cadiz
Almeria
Cartagena
Valencia
BALERIC ISLANDS (To Spain)
MINORCA
MAJORCA
Gibralter (To Great Britain)
Tangier
SPANISH AREA
Rabat
MOROCCO
To France
ATLAS MOUNTAINS
Oran
Algiers
Ajaccio
CORSICA (To France)
SARDINIA (To Italy)
Cagliari
Tyrrhenian Sea
Mediterranean
Palermo
Messina
SICILY
Syracuse
MALTA (Br.)
Tunis
TUNIS
French Protectorate
ALGERIA
To France
AFRICA
Tripoli
TRIPOLITANIA
To Italy
Bengazi
Gulf of Sidra
CYRENAICA
To Italy
LIBYA

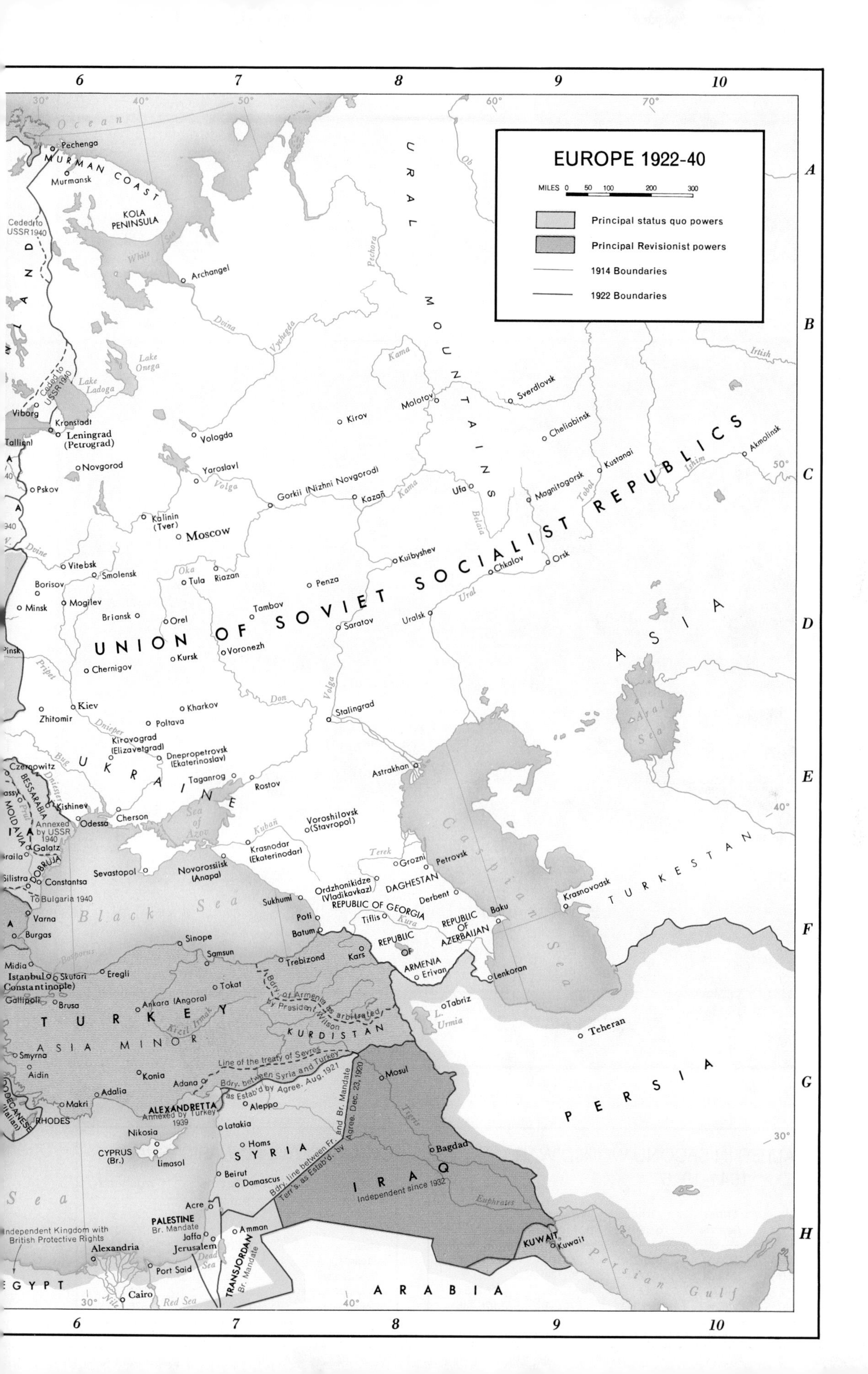
EUROPE 1922-40
MILES 0 50 100 200 300
Principal status quo powers
Principal Revisionist powers
1914 Boundaries
1922 Boundaries
UNION OF SOVIET SOCIALIST REPUBLICS
UKRAINE
ASIA
TURKESTAN
PERSIA
TURKEY
ASIA MINOR
KURDISTAN
SYRIA
IRAQ
Independent since 1932
ARABIA
KUWAIT
PALESTINE
Br. Mandate
TRANSJORDAN
Br. Mandate
EGYPT
Independent Kingdom with British Protective Rights
CYPRUS (Br.)
ALEXANDRETTA
Annexed by Turkey 1939
REPUBLIC OF GEORGIA
REPUBLIC OF ARMENIA
REPUBLIC OF AZERBAIJAN
DAGHESTAN
BESSARABIA
Annexed by USSR 1940
To Bulgaria 1940
Ceded to USSR 1940
KOLA PENINSULA
MURMAN COAST
URAL MOUNTAINS
Line of the treaty of Sevres
Bdry. between Syria and Turkey as Estab'd by Agree. Aug. 1921
Bdry. of Armenia as arbitrated by President Wilson
Bdry. line between Fr. and Br. Mandate Terr's as Estab'd. by Agree. Dec. 23, 1920
Moscow
Leningrad (Petrograd)
Stalingrad
Teheran
Bagdad
Constantinople

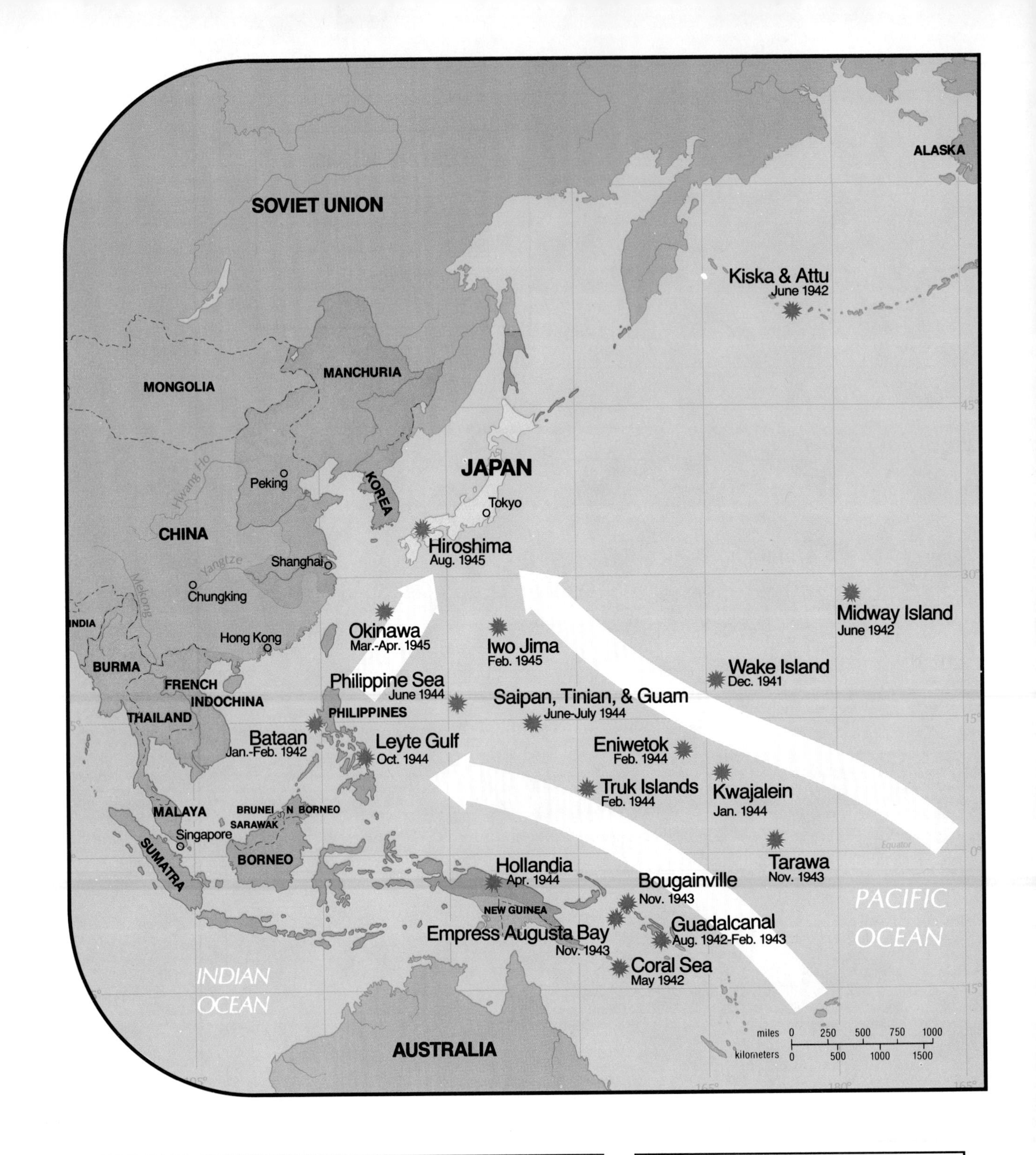

U. S. CASUALTIES IN SECOND WORLD WAR
1941-1946

Branch	Numbers engaged	Battle deaths	Other deaths	Total deaths	Wounds not mortal	Total casualties
Army*	11,260,000	234,874	83,400	318,274	565,861	884,135
Navy	4,183,466	36,950	25,664	62,614	37,778	100,392
Marines	669,100	19,773	4,778	24,511	67,207	91,718
Total	16,112,566	291,557	113,842	405,399	670,846	1,076,245

*Includes Air Force

Source: *Information Please Almanac* (Boston: Houghton Mifflin Co., 1988)

SECOND WORLD WAR CASUALTIES

Country	Battle Deaths	Wounded
Australia	26,976	180,684
China	1,324,516	1,762,006
India	32,121	64,354
Japan	1,270,000	140,000
New Zealand	11,625	17,000
United Kingdom	357,116	369,267
United States	291,557	670,846

Source: *Information Please Almanac* (Boston: Houghton Mifflin Co., 1988)

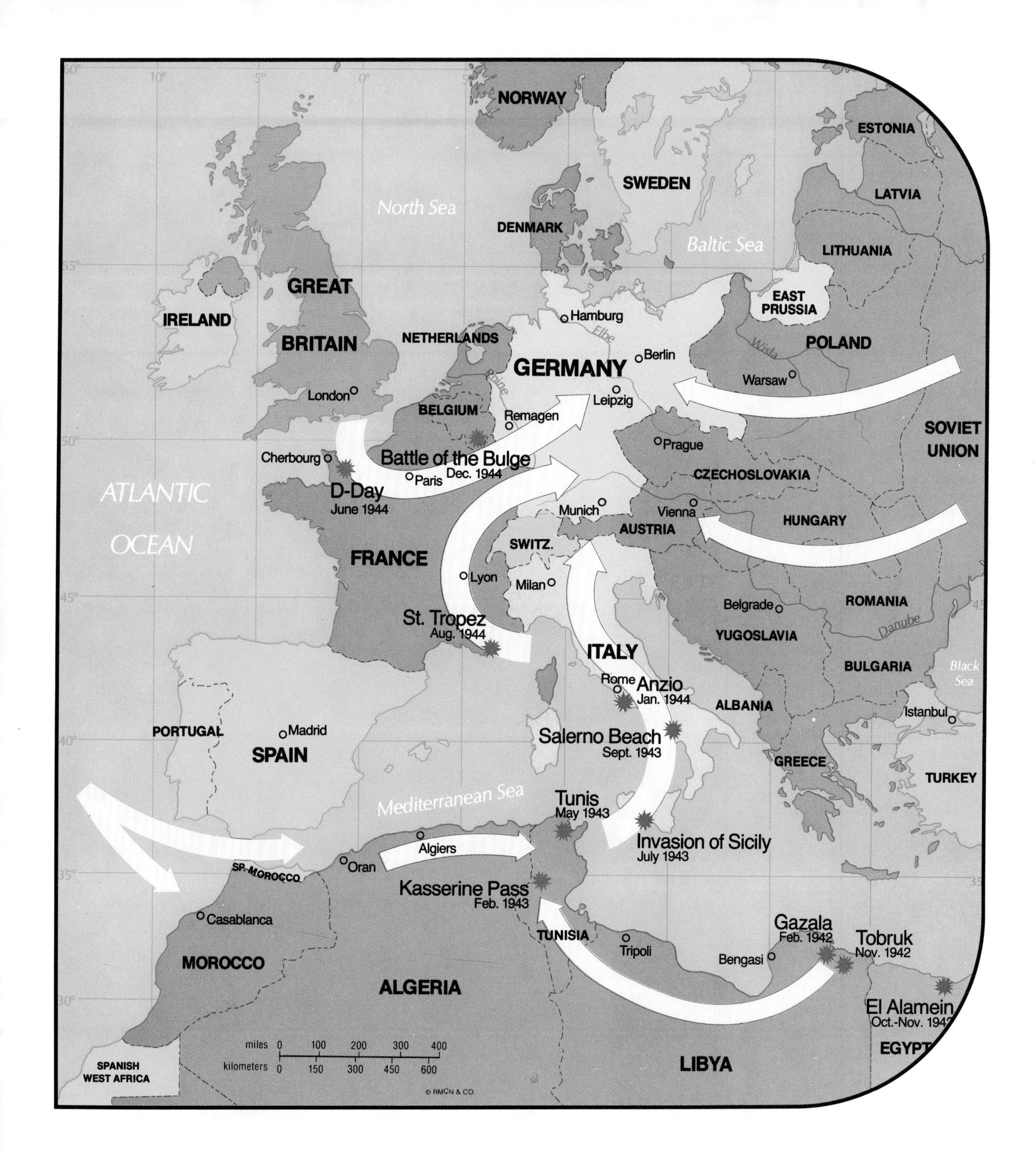

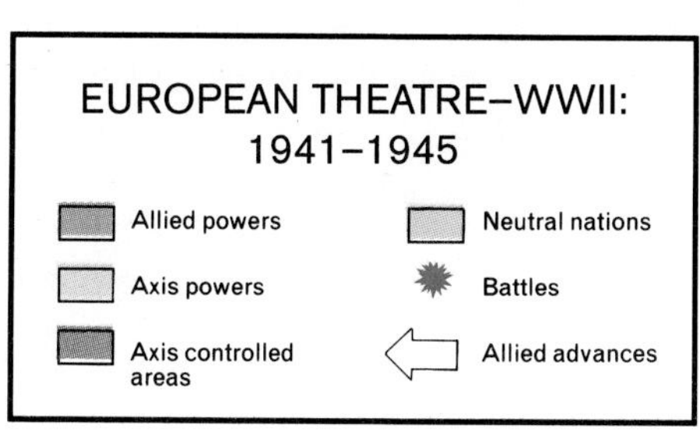

SECOND WORLD WAR CASUALTIES

Country	Battle Deaths	Wounded
Austria	280,000	350,117
Canada	32,714	53,145
France	201,568	400,000
Germany	3,250,000	7,250,000
Hungary	147,435	89,313
Italy	149,496	66,716
Poland	320,000	530,000
U.S.S.R.	6,115,000	14,012,000

Source: Information Please Almanac (Boston: Houghton Mifflin Co., 1988)

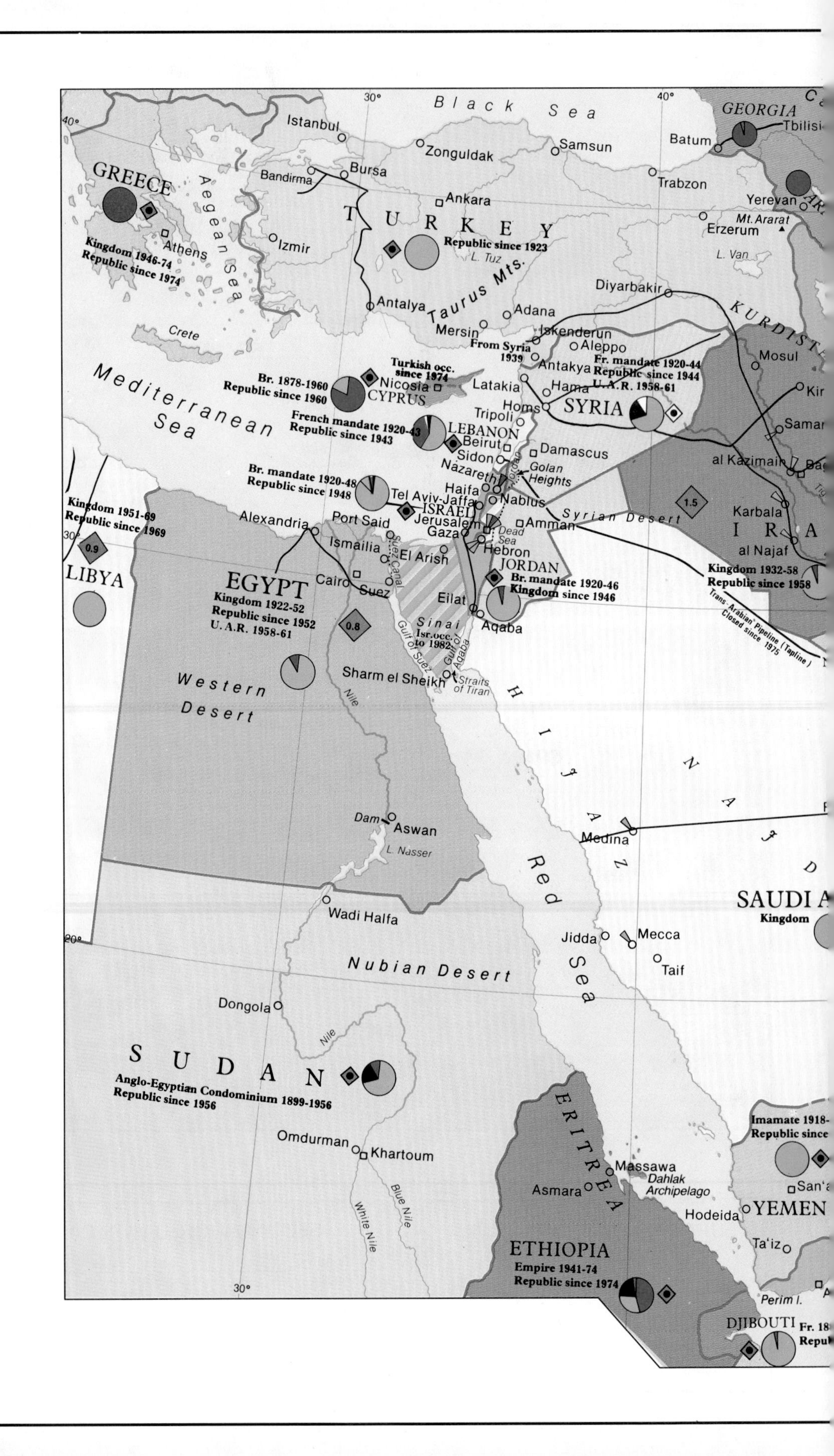

Black Sea
GEORGIA
Tbilisi
Batum
Istanbul
Zonguldak
Samsun
Bandirma
Bursa
Trabzon
GREECE
Ankara
Yerevan
Mt. Ararat
Erzerum
T U R K E Y
Republic since 1923
Aegean Sea
Izmir
Athens
Kingdom 1946-74
Republic since 1974
L. Tuz
L. Van
Taurus Mts.
Diyarbakir
Antalya
Adana
KURDISTAN
Mersin
Iskenderun
Aleppo
Crete
From Syria 1939
Antakya
Fr. mandate 1920-44
Republic since 1944
U.A.R. 1958-61
Mosul
Turkish occ. since 1974
Br. 1878-1960
Republic since 1960
Nicosia
CYPRUS
Latakia
Hama
Mediterranean Sea
Homs
SYRIA
Tripoli
French mandate 1920-43
Republic since 1943
LEBANON
Beirut
Damascus
Sidon
Nazareth
Golan Heights
al Kazimain
Br. mandate 1920-48
Republic since 1948
Haifa
Tel Aviv-Jaffa
Nablus
ISRAEL
1.5
Kingdom 1951-69
Republic since 1969
Alexandria
Port Said
Jerusalem
Amman
Syrian Desert
Karbala
I R A
Gaza
Dead Sea
Ismailia
Hebron
al Najaf
0.9
El Arish
JORDAN
Suez Canal
LIBYA
EGYPT
Cairo
Suez
Br. mandate 1920-46
Kingdom since 1946
Kingdom 1932-58
Republic since 1958
Kingdom 1922-52
Republic since 1952
U.A.R. 1958-61
Eilat
Aqaba
Trans-Arabian Pipeline (Tapline) Closed since 1975
0.8
Sinai
Isr. occ. to 1982
Gulf of Suez
Gulf of Aqaba
Sharm el Sheikh
Straits of Tiran
Western Desert
Nile
H I J A Z
N A J D
Dam
Aswan
Medina
L. Nasser
Red Sea
SAUDI A
Kingdom
Wadi Halfa
Jidda
Mecca
Taif
Nubian Desert
Dongola
S U D A N
Anglo-Egyptian Condominium 1899-1956
Republic since 1956
Imamate 1918-
Republic since
Omdurman
Khartoum
Blue Nile
White Nile
ERITREA
Massawa
Dahlak Archipelago
Asmara
San'a
Hodeida
YEMEN
ETHIOPIA
Empire 1941-74
Republic since 1974
Ta'iz
Perim I.
DJIBOUTI
40°
30°
20°

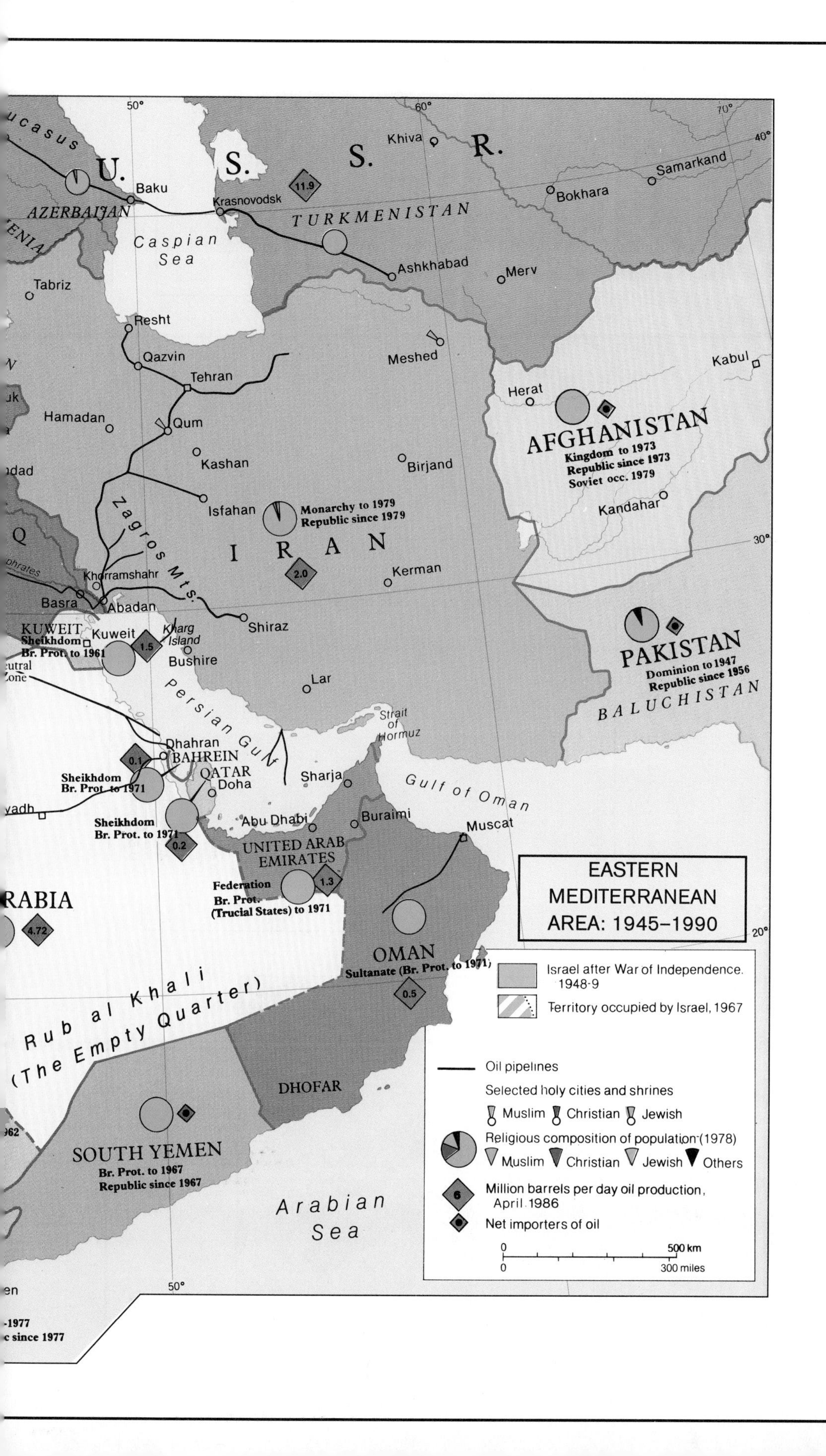
EASTERN MEDITERRANEAN AREA: 1945–1990
U. S. S. R.
AZERBAIJAN
TURKMENISTAN
Baku
Krasnovodsk
Khiva
Bokhara
Samarkand
Ashkhabad
Merv
Caspian Sea
Tabriz
Resht
Qazvin
Tehran
Meshed
Hamadan
Qum
Kashan
Birjand
Isfahan
Zagros Mts.
Monarchy to 1979
Republic since 1979
I R A N
Kerman
Khorramshahr
Abadan
Basra
Shiraz
KUWEIT
Sheikhdom
Br. Prot. to 1961
Kuweit
Kharg Island
Bushire
Lar
Persian Gulf
Strait of Hormuz
Dhahran
BAHREIN
Sheikhdom
Br. Prot. to 1971
QATAR
Doha
Sheikhdom
Br. Prot. to 1971
Sharja
Abu Dhabi
Buraimi
Muscat
Gulf of Oman
UNITED ARAB EMIRATES
Federation
Br. Prot.
(Trucial States) to 1971
OMAN
Sultanate (Br. Prot. to 1971)
DHOFAR
Rub al Khali
(The Empty Quarter)
SOUTH YEMEN
Br. Prot. to 1967
Republic since 1967
Arabian Sea
Herat
Kabul
AFGHANISTAN
Kingdom to 1973
Republic since 1973
Soviet occ. 1979
Kandahar
PAKISTAN
Dominion to 1947
Republic since 1956
BALUCHISTAN
11.9
2.0
1.5
0.1
0.2
1.3
4.72
0.5
Israel after War of Independence. 1948-9
Territory occupied by Israel, 1967
Oil pipelines
Selected holy cities and shrines
Muslim
Christian
Jewish
Religious composition of population (1978)
Muslim
Christian
Jewish
Others
Million barrels per day oil production, April 1986
Net importers of oil
0
500 km
0
300 miles
50°
60°
70°
40°
30°
20°

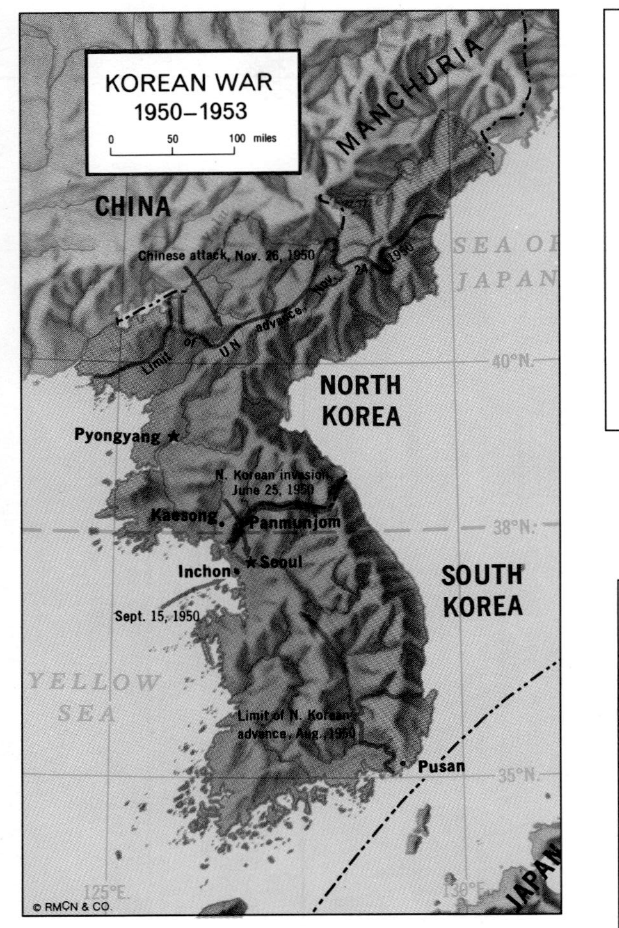

VIETNAM WAR CASUALTIES

United States	
Battle deaths	47,382
Wounded	153,303
Died, non-combat	1,811
Missing, captured	10,753
South Vietnam	
Military killed in action	110,357
Military wounded	499,026
Civilian killed	415,000
Civilian wounded	913,000
Communists Regulars and Guerillas	
Killed in action	666,000

Source: U.S. Department of Defense

KOREAN WAR CASUALTIES

United States	
Killed	54,246
Wounded	103,284
Republic of Korea	
Killed	415,004
Wounded	428,568
United Nations	
Killed and wounded	15,465
China	
Killed and wounded	900,000
North Korea	
Killed and wounded	520,000

Source: U.S. Department of Defense

The Vietnam War
1957-1975
0 100 200
Place of conflict
Tropic of Cancer
Nanning
CHINA
NORTH VIETNAM
Ha Noi
Hai Phong
LAOS
GULF OF TONKIN
Gulf of Tonkin incident
HAINAN ISLAND
Vinh
Vientiane
Mu Gia Pass
DEMILITARIZED ZONE (DMZ)
Quang Tri
Hue
Khe Sanh
Da Nang
THAILAND
My Lai
DacTo
Kontum
HO CHI MINH TRAIL
Pleiku
Qui Nhon
SOUTH VIETNAM
CAMBODIA
Nha Trang
Cam Ranh Bay Naval Base
Loc Ninh
Phnum Pénh
Bien Hoa
Tan Son Nhut Air Base
Saigon (Ho Chi Minh City)
Mekong Delta
GULF OF THAILAND
SOUTH CHINA SEA
M-663000-9H-AH1-1
© Rand McNally & Co.

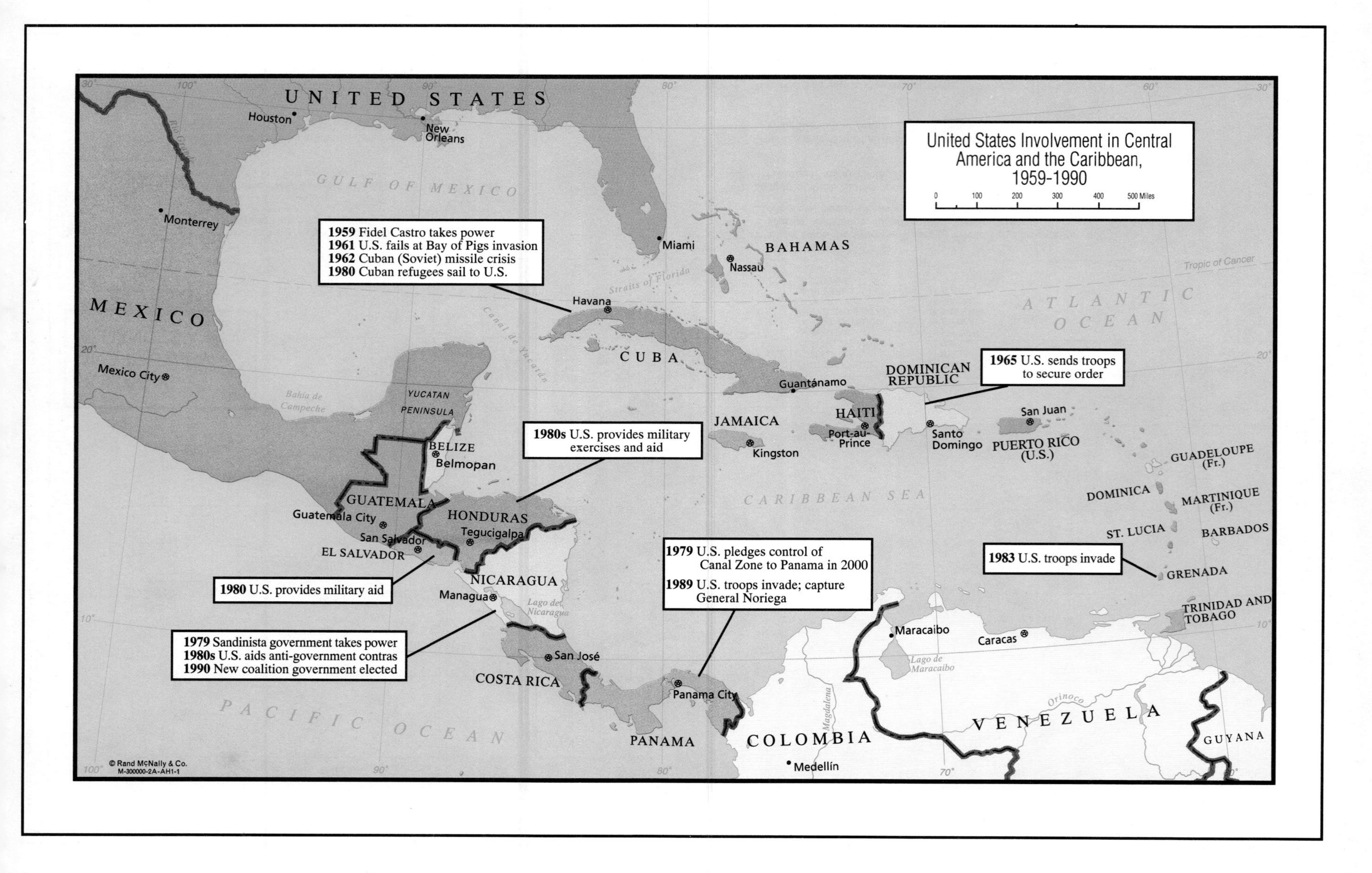
United States Involvement in Central America and the Caribbean, 1959-1990
0 100 200 300 400 500 Miles
1959 Fidel Castro takes power
1961 U.S. fails at Bay of Pigs invasion
1962 Cuban (Soviet) missile crisis
1980 Cuban refugees sail to U.S.
1965 U.S. sends troops to secure order
1980s U.S. provides military exercises and aid
1980 U.S. provides military aid
1979 Sandinista government takes power
1980s U.S. aids anti-government contras
1990 New coalition government elected
1979 U.S. pledges control of Canal Zone to Panama in 2000
1989 U.S. troops invade; capture General Noriega
1983 U.S. troops invade
UNITED STATES
MEXICO
GULF OF MEXICO
Houston
New Orleans
Monterrey
Mexico City
Miami
BAHAMAS
Nassau
Straits of Florida
Havana
CUBA
Canal de Yucatán
Bahía de Campeche
YUCATAN PENINSULA
BELIZE
Belmopan
GUATEMALA
Guatemala City
San Salvador
EL SALVADOR
HONDURAS
Tegucigalpa
NICARAGUA
Managua
Lago de Nicaragua
COSTA RICA
San José
PANAMA
Panama City
PACIFIC OCEAN
Guantánamo
JAMAICA
Kingston
HAITI
Port-au-Prince
DOMINICAN REPUBLIC
Santo Domingo
San Juan
PUERTO RICO (U.S.)
ATLANTIC OCEAN
Tropic of Cancer
CARIBBEAN SEA
GUADELOUPE (Fr.)
DOMINICA
MARTINIQUE (Fr.)
ST. LUCIA
BARBADOS
GRENADA
TRINIDAD AND TOBAGO
Maracaibo
Lago de Maracaibo
Caracas
VENEZUELA
Orinoco
GUYANA
COLOMBIA
Magdalena
Medellín
© Rand McNally & Co.
M-300000-2A-AH1-1

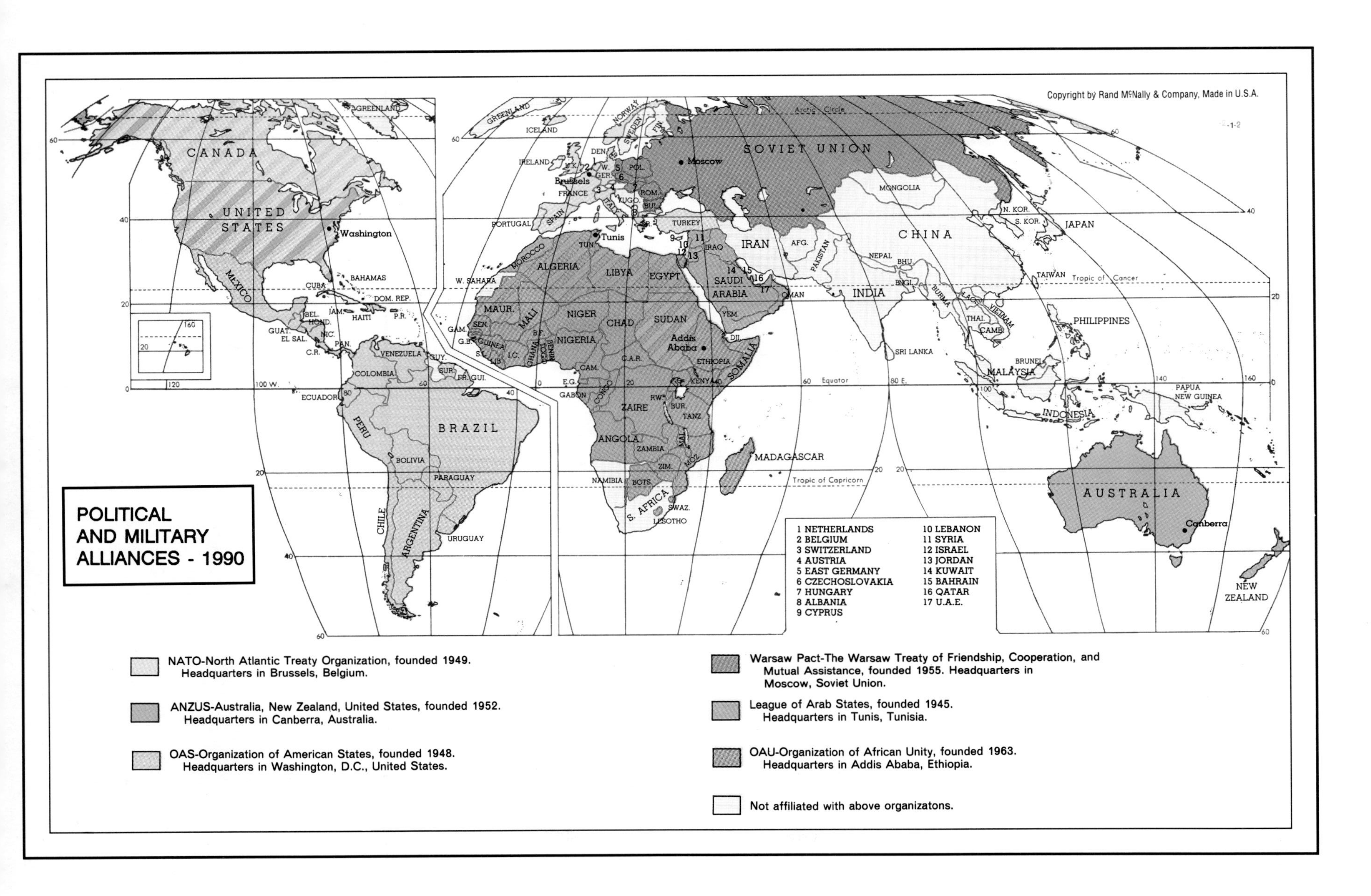

POLITICAL AND MILITARY ALLIANCES - 1990
CANADA
UNITED STATES
Washington
MEXICO
BAHAMAS
CUBA
DOM. REP.
HAITI
P.R.
JAM.
BEL.
HOND.
GUAT.
EL SAL.
NIC.
C.R.
PAN.
VENEZUELA
GUY.
SUR.
FR. GUI.
COLOMBIA
ECUADOR
PERU
BRAZIL
BOLIVIA
PARAGUAY
CHILE
ARGENTINA
URUGUAY
GREENLAND
ICELAND
IRELAND
U.K.
DEN.
NORWAY
SWEDEN
FIN.
Brussels
FRANCE
W. GER.
POL.
ROM.
BUL.
YUGO.
ITALY
SPAIN
PORTUGAL
TURKEY
SOVIET UNION
Moscow
Arctic Circle
MONGOLIA
CHINA
N. KOR.
S. KOR.
JAPAN
TAIWAN
Tropic of Cancer
IRAN
AFG.
PAKISTAN
NEPAL
BHU.
BNGL.
INDIA
SRI LANKA
BURMA
LAOS
VIETNAM
THAI.
CAMB.
PHILIPPINES
BRUNEI
MALAYSIA
INDONESIA
PAPUA NEW GUINEA
AUSTRALIA
Canberra
NEW ZEALAND
Tunis
TUN.
MOROCCO
ALGERIA
LIBYA
EGYPT
W. SAHARA
MAUR.
MALI
NIGER
CHAD
SUDAN
SEN.
GAM.
G.B.
GUINEA
S.L.
LIB.
I.C.
GHANA
B.F.
TOGO
BENIN
NIGERIA
CAM.
C.A.R.
E.G.
GABON
CONGO
ZAIRE
RW.
BUR.
KENYA
TANZ.
Addis Ababa
ETHIOPIA
DJI.
SOMALIA
IRAQ
SAUDI ARABIA
YEM.
OMAN
ANGOLA
ZAMBIA
MAL.
MOZ.
ZIM.
NAMIBIA
BOTS.
S. AFRICA
SWAZ.
LESOTHO
MADAGASCAR
Equator
Tropic of Capricorn
100 W.
60 E.
80 E.
Copyright by Rand McNally & Company, Made in U.S.A.
1 NETHERLANDS
2 BELGIUM
3 SWITZERLAND
4 AUSTRIA
5 EAST GERMANY
6 CZECHOSLOVAKIA
7 HUNGARY
8 ALBANIA
9 CYPRUS
10 LEBANON
11 SYRIA
12 ISRAEL
13 JORDAN
14 KUWAIT
15 BAHRAIN
16 QATAR
17 U.A.E.
NATO-North Atlantic Treaty Organization, founded 1949. Headquarters in Brussels, Belgium.
ANZUS-Australia, New Zealand, United States, founded 1952. Headquarters in Canberra, Australia.
OAS-Organization of American States, founded 1948. Headquarters in Washington, D.C., United States.
Warsaw Pact-The Warsaw Treaty of Friendship, Cooperation, and Mutual Assistance, founded 1955. Headquarters in Moscow, Soviet Union.
League of Arab States, founded 1945. Headquarters in Tunis, Tunisia.
OAU-Organization of African Unity, founded 1963. Headquarters in Addis Ababa, Ethiopia.
Not affiliated with above organizatons.

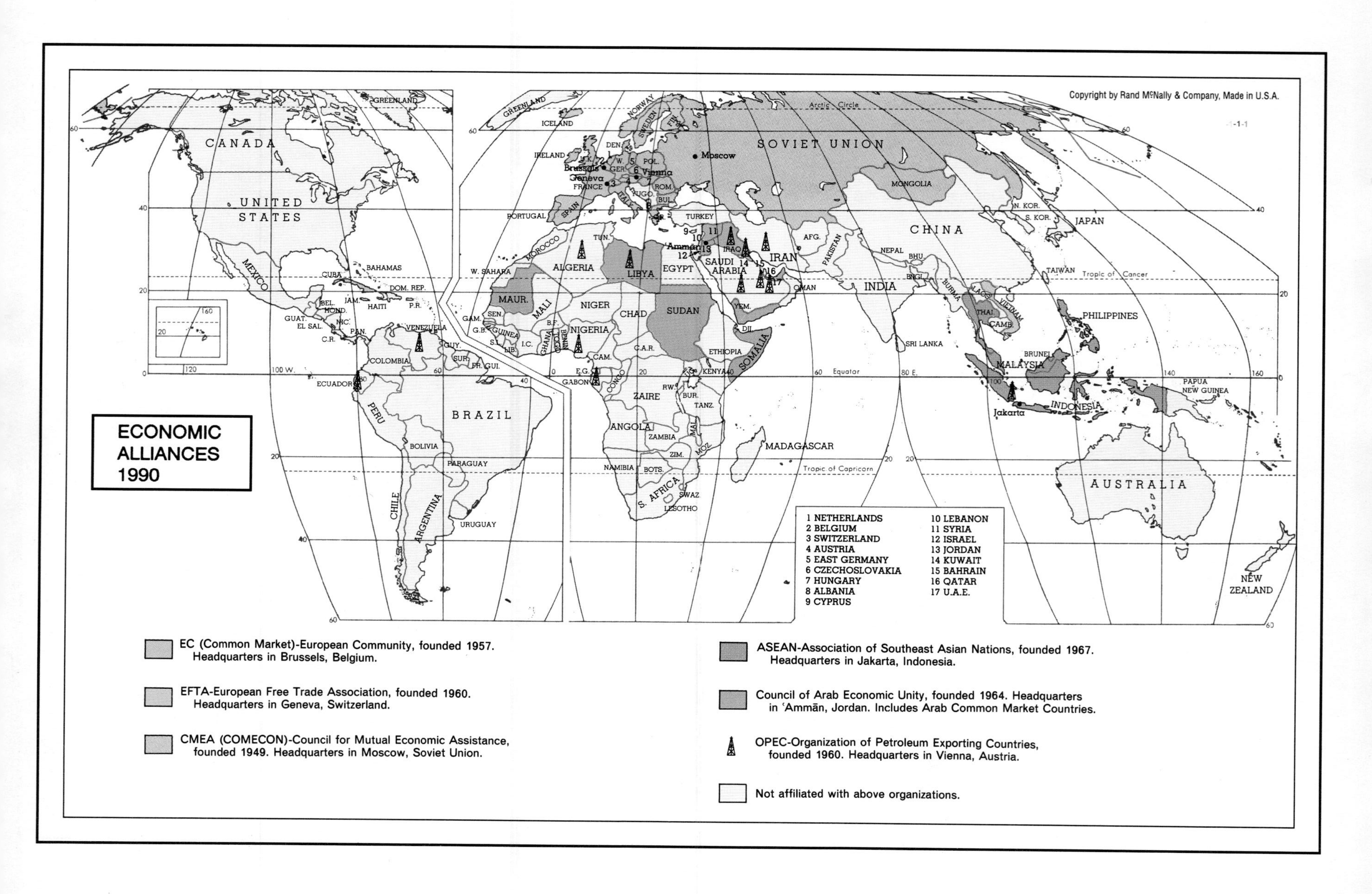
ECONOMIC ALLIANCES 1990
Copyright by Rand McNally & Company, Made in U.S.A.
EC (Common Market)-European Community, founded 1957. Headquarters in Brussels, Belgium.
EFTA-European Free Trade Association, founded 1960. Headquarters in Geneva, Switzerland.
CMEA (COMECON)-Council for Mutual Economic Assistance, founded 1949. Headquarters in Moscow, Soviet Union.
ASEAN-Association of Southeast Asian Nations, founded 1967. Headquarters in Jakarta, Indonesia.
Council of Arab Economic Unity, founded 1964. Headquarters in 'Ammān, Jordan. Includes Arab Common Market Countries.
OPEC-Organization of Petroleum Exporting Countries, founded 1960. Headquarters in Vienna, Austria.
Not affiliated with above organizations.
1 NETHERLANDS
2 BELGIUM
3 SWITZERLAND
4 AUSTRIA
5 EAST GERMANY
6 CZECHOSLOVAKIA
7 HUNGARY
8 ALBANIA
9 CYPRUS
10 LEBANON
11 SYRIA
12 ISRAEL
13 JORDAN
14 KUWAIT
15 BAHRAIN
16 QATAR
17 U.A.E.
GREENLAND
CANADA
UNITED STATES
MEXICO
CUBA
BAHAMAS
DOM. REP.
P.R.
JAM.
HAITI
BEL.
HOND.
GUAT.
EL SAL.
NIC.
C.R.
PAN.
VENEZUELA
COLOMBIA
GUY.
SUR.
FR. GUI.
ECUADOR
PERU
BRAZIL
BOLIVIA
PARAGUAY
CHILE
ARGENTINA
URUGUAY
ICELAND
IRELAND
U.K.
DEN.
NORWAY
SWEDEN
FIN.
W. GER.
POL.
Brussels
Geneva
Vienna
FRANCE
PORTUGAL
SPAIN
ITALY
YUGO.
ROM.
BUL.
TURKEY
Moscow
SOVIET UNION
MONGOLIA
CHINA
N. KOR.
S. KOR.
JAPAN
TAIWAN
Tropic of Cancer
Arctic Circle
W. SAHARA
MOROCCO
ALGERIA
TUN.
LIBYA
EGYPT
Ammān
SAUDI ARABIA
IRAQ
IRAN
AFG.
PAKISTAN
NEPAL
BHU.
BNGL.
INDIA
OMAN
YEM.
DJI.
SOMALIA
ETHIOPIA
MAUR.
MALI
NIGER
CHAD
SUDAN
SEN.
GAM.
G.B.
GUINEA
S.L.
LIB.
I.C.
GHANA
TOGO
BENIN
B.F.
NIGERIA
CAM.
C.A.R.
E.G.
GABON
CONGO
ZAIRE
KENYA
RW.
BUR.
TANZ.
ANGOLA
ZAMBIA
MAL.
MOZ.
ZIM.
NAMIBIA
BOTS.
S. AFRICA
SWAZ.
LESOTHO
MADAGASCAR
Tropic of Capricorn
Equator
SRI LANKA
BURMA
LAOS
THAI.
VIETNAM
CAMB.
PHILIPPINES
BRUNEI
MALAYSIA
INDONESIA
Jakarta
PAPUA NEW GUINEA
AUSTRALIA
NEW ZEALAND

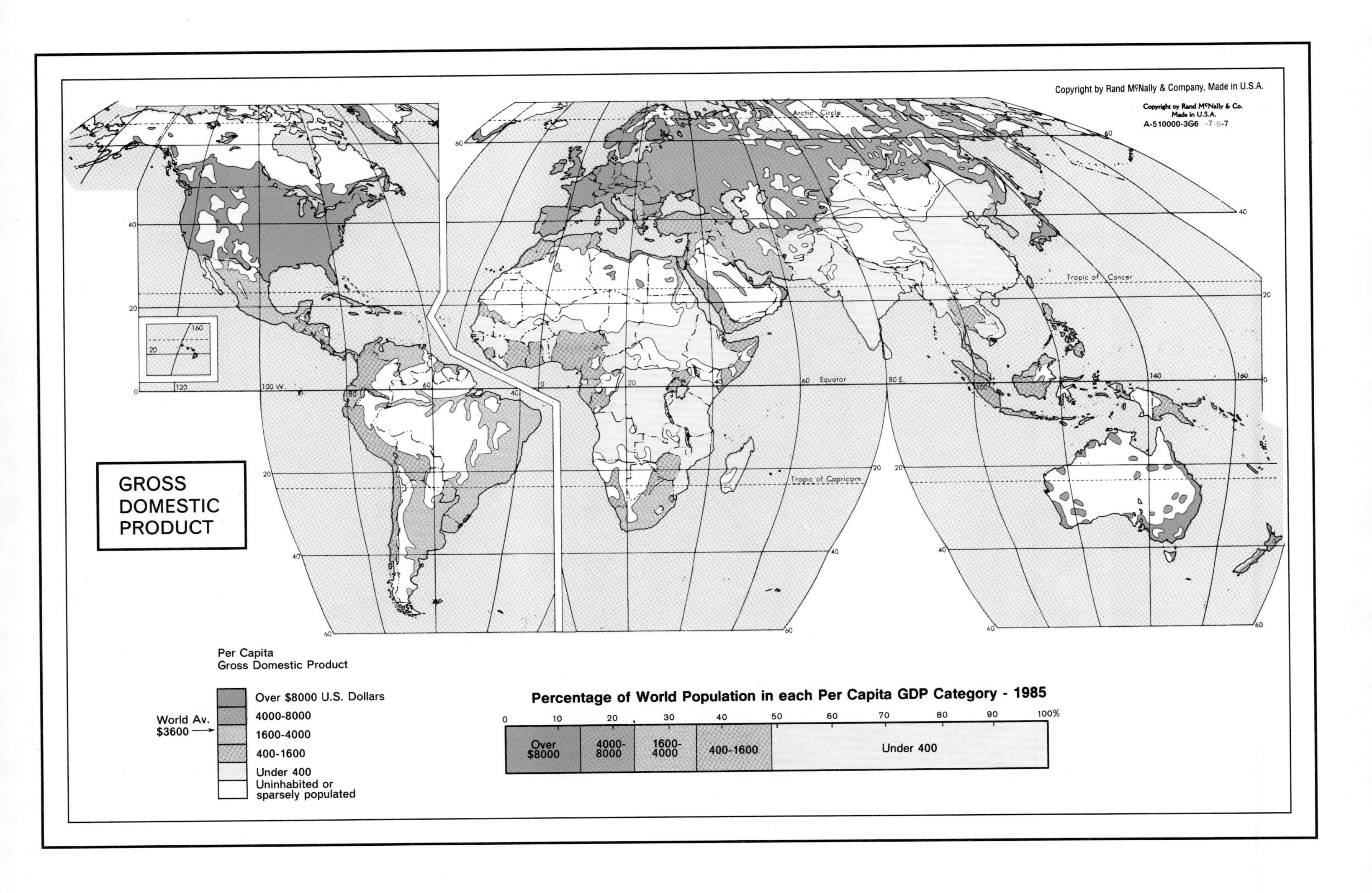
Copyright by Rand McNally & Company, Made in U.S.A.
Copyright by Rand McNally & Co.
Made in U.S.A.
A-510000-3G6 -7-6-7
GROSS
DOMESTIC
PRODUCT
Arctic Circle
Tropic of Cancer
Equator
Tropic of Capricorn
100 W.
80 E.
Per Capita
Gross Domestic Product
World Av.
$3600
Over $8000 U.S. Dollars
4000-8000
1600-4000
400-1600
Under 400
Uninhabited or
sparsely populated
Percentage of World Population in each Per Capita GDP Category - 1985
0
10
20
30
40
50
60
70
80
90
100%
Over $8000
4000-8000
1600-4000
400-1600
Under 400

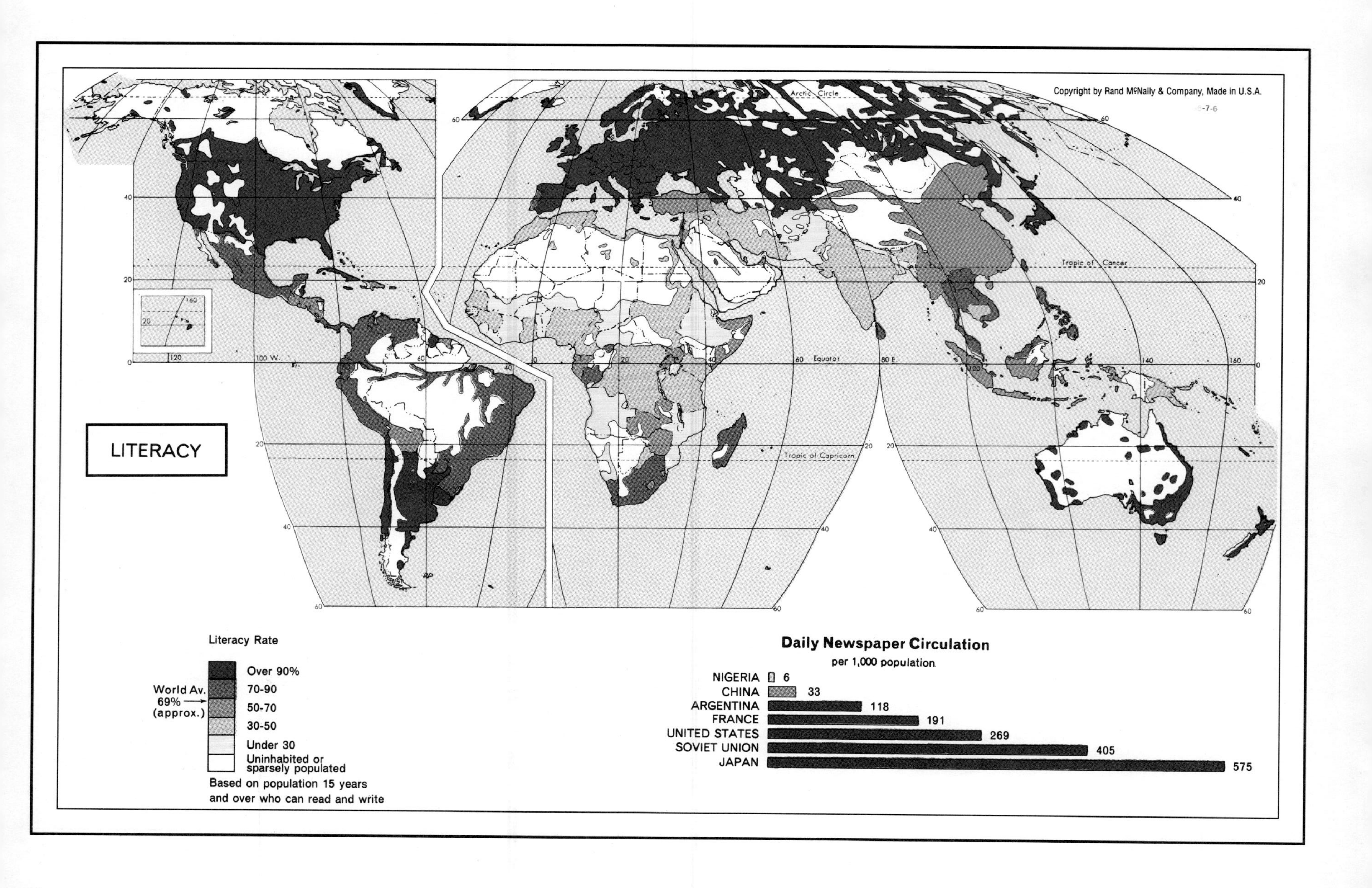

LITERACY
Copyright by Rand McNally & Company, Made in U.S.A.
Arctic Circle
Tropic of Cancer
Equator
Tropic of Capricorn
100 W.
80 E.
Literacy Rate
Over 90%
70-90
50-70
30-50
Under 30
Uninhabited or sparsely populated
World Av. 69% (approx.)
Based on population 15 years and over who can read and write
Daily Newspaper Circulation
per 1,000 population
NIGERIA 6
CHINA 33
ARGENTINA 118
FRANCE 191
UNITED STATES 269
SOVIET UNION 405
JAPAN 575

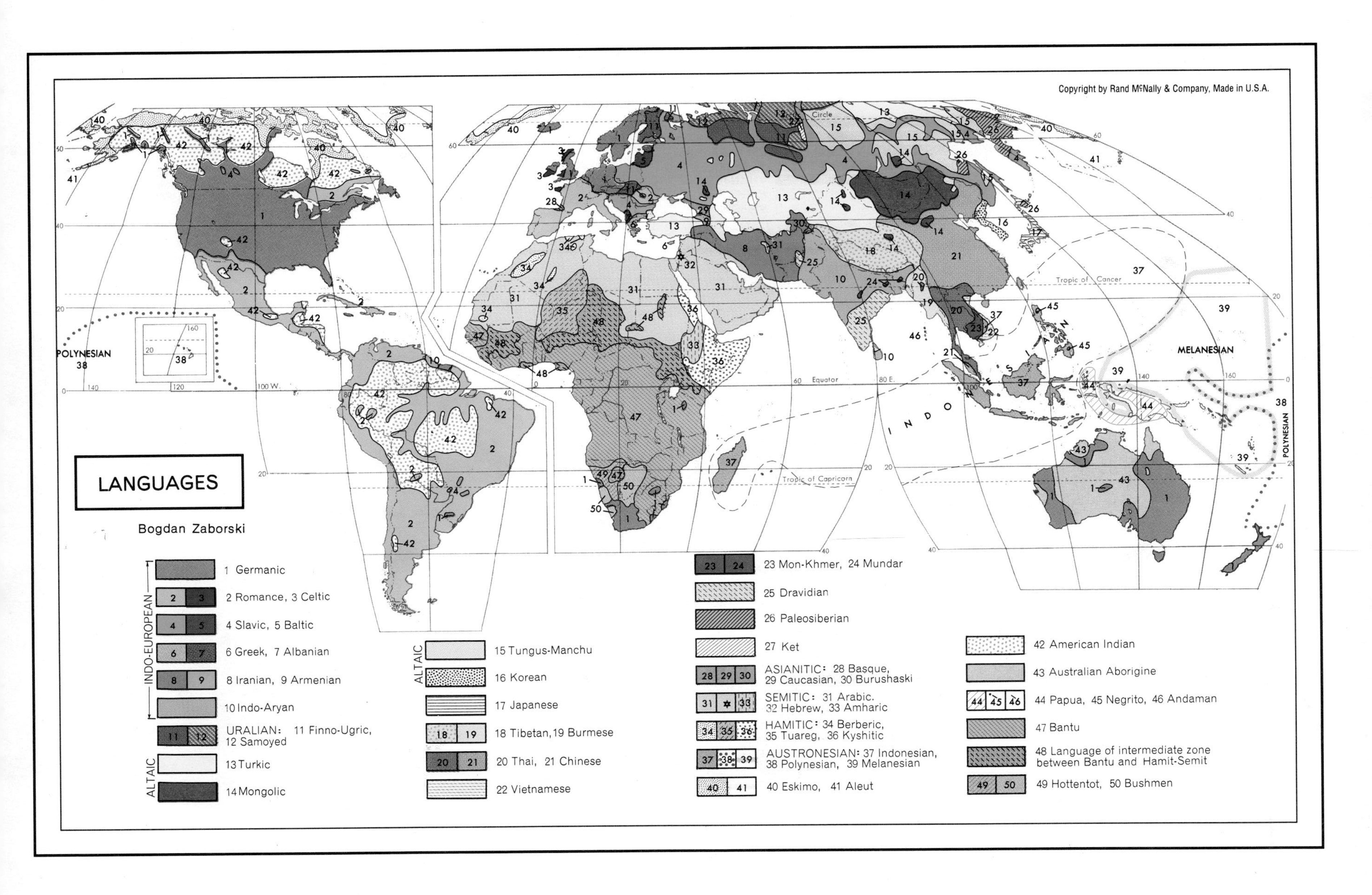

LANGUAGES
Bogdan Zaborski
INDO-EUROPEAN
1 Germanic
2 Romance, 3 Celtic
4 Slavic, 5 Baltic
6 Greek, 7 Albanian
8 Iranian, 9 Armenian
10 Indo-Aryan
URALIAN: 11 Finno-Ugric, 12 Samoyed
ALTAIC
13 Turkic
14 Mongolic
15 Tungus-Manchu
16 Korean
17 Japanese
18 Tibetan, 19 Burmese
20 Thai, 21 Chinese
22 Vietnamese
23 Mon-Khmer, 24 Mundar
25 Dravidian
26 Paleosiberian
27 Ket
ASIANITIC: 28 Basque, 29 Caucasian, 30 Burushaski
SEMITIC: 31 Arabic, 32 Hebrew, 33 Amharic
HAMITIC: 34 Berberic, 35 Tuareg, 36 Kyshitic
AUSTRONESIAN: 37 Indonesian, 38 Polynesian, 39 Melanesian
40 Eskimo, 41 Aleut
42 American Indian
43 Australian Aborigine
44 Papua, 45 Negrito, 46 Andaman
47 Bantu
48 Language of intermediate zone between Bantu and Hamit-Semit
49 Hottentot, 50 Bushmen
POLYNESIAN
MELANESIAN
INDONESIAN
INDO
Tropic of Cancer
Equator
Tropic of Capricorn
Circle
100 W.
80 E.
Copyright by Rand McNally & Company, Made in U.S.A.

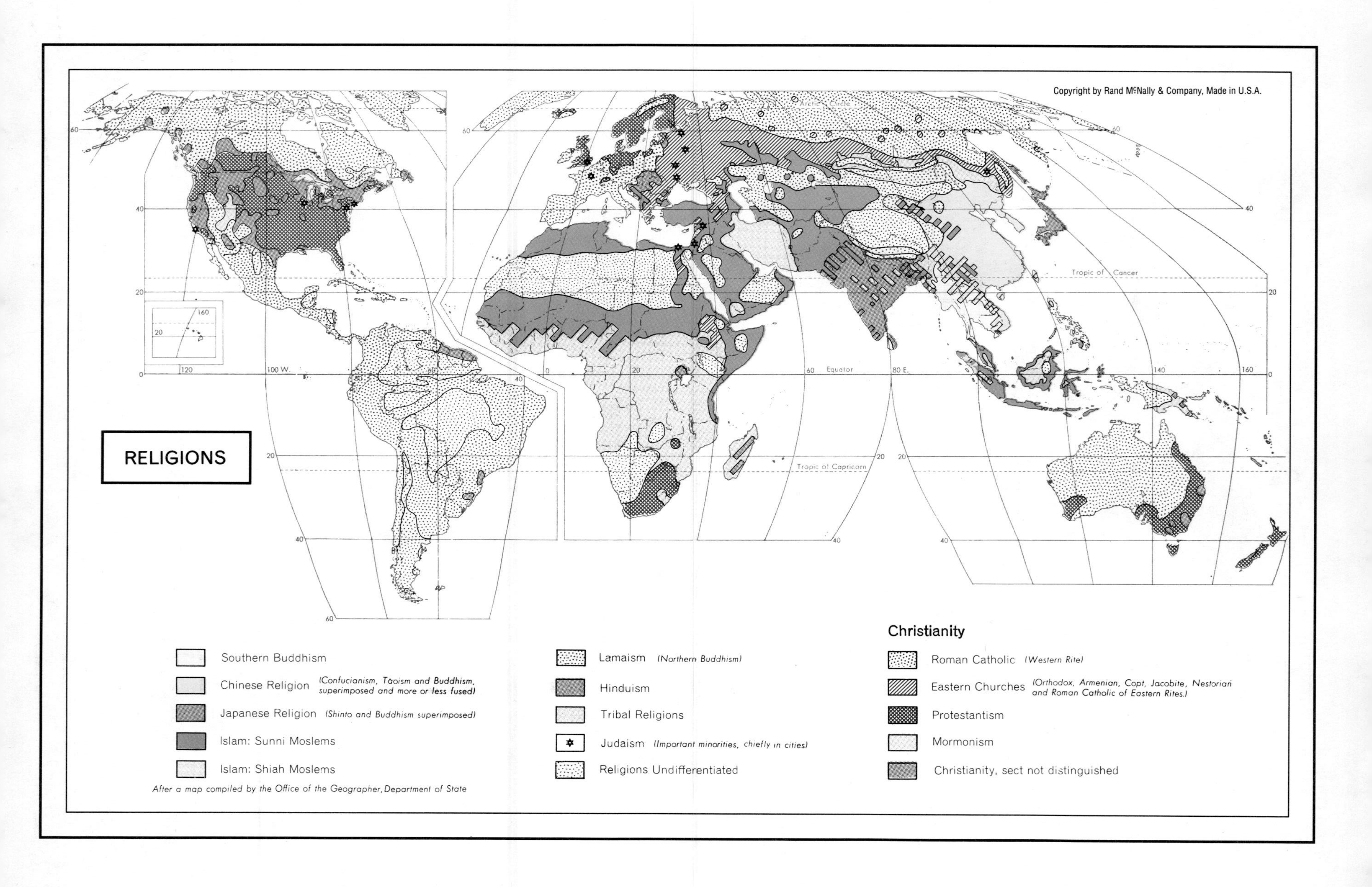
RELIGIONS
Copyright by Rand McNally & Company, Made in U.S.A.
Arctic Circle
Tropic of Cancer
Equator
Tropic of Capricorn
100 W.
80 E.
Southern Buddhism
Chinese Religion (Confucianism, Taoism and Buddhism, superimposed and more or less fused)
Japanese Religion (Shinto and Buddhism superimposed)
Islam: Sunni Moslems
Islam: Shiah Moslems
Lamaism (Northern Buddhism)
Hinduism
Tribal Religions
Judaism (Important minorities, chiefly in cities)
Religions Undifferentiated
Christianity
Roman Catholic (Western Rite)
Eastern Churches (Orthodox, Armenian, Copt, Jacobite, Nestorian and Roman Catholic of Eastern Rites.)
Protestantism
Mormonism
Christianity, sect not distinguished
After a map compiled by the Office of the Geographer, Department of State

ARCTIC OCEAN

Greenland
Baffin Island
Baffin Bay
Jan Mayen
Arctic Circle
Iceland
Faroe
Mt. McKinley △ 20,320 Ft. 6,194m
Yukon
Mackenzie
Canadian Shield
Hudson Bay
British Isles
London
Aleutian Islands
NORTH AMERICA
Rocky Mountains
Great Plains
Vancouver
Newfoundland
St. Lawrence
Appalachian Mts.
Washington D.C.
Cape Hatteras
Mississippi
Colorado
Los Angeles
Azores
Iberian Peninsula
Atlas
Midway Is.
Tropic of Cancer
Hawaiian Islands
Baja California
Gulf of Mexico
ATLANTIC
Canary Islands
Yucatan Peninsula
Cuba
Hispaniola
Puerto Rico
Jamaica
Caribbean Sea
Cape Verde Islands
Cape Verde
Niger
PACIFIC
Trinidad
Orinoco
OCEAN
Palmyra
N
W
E
S
Galapagos Islands
Amazon
Amazon Basin
SOUTH AMERICA
Kiribati
OCEAN
Cabo de São Roque
Andes
Marquesas Is.
Samoa Islands
Planalto do Mato Grosso
St. Helena
Tonga Is.
Cook Islands
Tahiti
Tropic of Capricorn
Rio de Janeiro
Easter Island
Paraná
Andes
△ Cerro Aconcagua 22,831 Ft. 6,959m
Buenos Aires
Archipiélago Juan Fernández
Chatham Is.
Patagonia
Falkland Is.
South Georgia
Tierra del Fuego
Cape Horn
South Sandwich Is.
South Orkney Is.
South Shetland Is.
Antarctic Circle
Antarctic Peninsula
Weddell Sea
Marie Byrd Land
△ Vinson Massif 16,066 Ft. 4,897m

World Physical

0 1000 2000 Miles

0 1000 2000 3000 Kilometers

• London Major City

International Boundary

Land Elevation

Meters	Feet
3,000 and over	9,840 and over
2,000 - 3,000	6,560 - 9,840
1,000 - 2,000	3,280 - 6,560
500 - 1,000	1,640 - 3,280
200 - 500	656 - 1,640
0 - 200	0 - 656

Water Depth

Meters	Feet
Less than 200	Less than 656
200 - 2,000	656 - 6,560
Over 2,000	Over 6,560

Land Elevations in Profile

OCEANIA — NEW ZEALAND: Mt. Cook 12 316; HAWAII: Mauna Kea (Vol.) 13 796; TAHITI 7 352

NORTH AMERICA — ALASKA RANGE: Mt. McKinley 20 320; CASCADE RANGE: Mt. Rainier 14 410; SIERRA NEVADA: Mt. Whitney 14 494; GREAT BASIN; ROCKY MTS.: Pikes Peak 14 110; Pico de Orizaba 18 406; Irazú (Vol.) 11 260; Mt. Mitchell 6 684; HISPANIOLA: Pico Duarte 10 417

SOUTH AMERICA — Chimborazo 20 702; LOS ANDES: Aconcagua (Vol.) 22 831; Nev. Illimani 20 741; PLATEAU OF BOLIVIA; Pico da Bandeira 9 482; IS. CANARIAS: Pico de Teide 12 188

AFRICA — ATLAS: Jebel Toubkal 13 665; Cameroon Mtn. 13 451; Ras Dashen Terara 15 158

Feet / Meters: 30000 9145; 25000 7620; 20000 6095; 15000 4570; 10000 3050; 5000 1525

Ocean Depths in Profile

PACIFIC OCEAN — INDOCHINA; HAINAN; PHILIPPINES BASIN 20 364; PHILIPPINES TRENCH 34 440; JAPAN TRENCH 34 036; MARIANA IS.; MARIANA TRENCH 35 810; Sea Level; ALEUTIAN TRENCH 25 574; HAWAII; MEXICO; A Section along 20°N. Lat.

ATLANTIC OCEAN — NOVA SCOTIA; GRAND BANK; PUERTO RICO TRENCH 28 374; ATLANTIC RIDGE; BRAZIL BASIN 20 076; A Section along 45°N Lat.

Feet / Meters: 5000 1525; 10000 3050; 15000 4570; 20000 6095; 25000 7620; 30000 9145; 35000 10670

Elevations and depressions

ARCTIC OCEAN
Franz Josef Land
Novaya Zemlya
North Cape
Scandinavian Peninsula
Yenisey
Lena
Siberia
Ob'
Ural Mts.
EUROPE
Volga
Moscow
Don
Alps
Balkan Peninsula
Caucasus
Mt. Elbrus 18,510 Ft. 5,642m
Black Sea
Caspian Sea
Sardinia
Sicily
Crete
Cyprus
Mediterranean Sea
Cairo
Zagros Mts.
ASIA
Altai Mts.
Pamirs
Plateau of Tibet
Himalayas
Mt. Everest 29,028 Ft. 8,848m
Ganges
Indus
Gobi Desert
Beijing
Huang
Yangtze
Amur
Sea of Okhotsk
Sakhalin
Kamchatka Peninsula
Bering Sea
Hokkaidō
Honshū
Kyūshū
Sea of Japan
East China Sea
Desert
AFRICA
Sahel
Nile
Red Sea
Arabian Peninsula
Mumbai (Bombay)
Deccan Plateau
Arabian Sea
Bay of Bengal
Socotra
Lakshadweep
Sri Lanka
Taiwan
Hainan Island
South China Sea
Mekong
Luzon
Mariana Islands
Guam
Wake Island
PACIFIC OCEAN
Tropic of Cancer
Ethiopian Plateau
Guinea
Congo
Congo Basin
Rift Valley
Kilimanjaro 19,340 Ft. 5,895m
Maldive Islands
Malay Peninsula
Mindanao
Palau Islands
Caroline Islands
Marshall Islands
Borneo
Celebes
Equator
Sumatra
New Guinea
Solomon Islands
Seychelles
INDIAN OCEAN
Cocos Island
Java
Zambezi
Madagascar
Mauritius
Reunion
Kalahari Desert
New Hebrides
Fiji Is.
Coral Sea
New Caledonia
Great Sandy Desert
Tropic of Capricorn
AUSTRALIA
Great Dividing Range
Darling
Sydney
Cape Town
Cape of Good Hope
Cape Leeuwin
North Island
Mt. Cook 12,316 Ft. 3,754m
Tasmania
South Island
Kerguelen Islands
Enderby Land
Wilkes Land
Queen Maud Land
ANTARCTICA
Victoria Land
Copyright by Rand McNally & Co. Made in U.S.A.
DM-510000-7A-CL1
EUROPE
ASIA
OCEANIA
MEDITERRANEAN SEA
INDIAN OCEAN
ARCTIC OCEAN
PACIFIC OCEAN
A Section along 10°S. Lat.
Meters Feet
given in feet

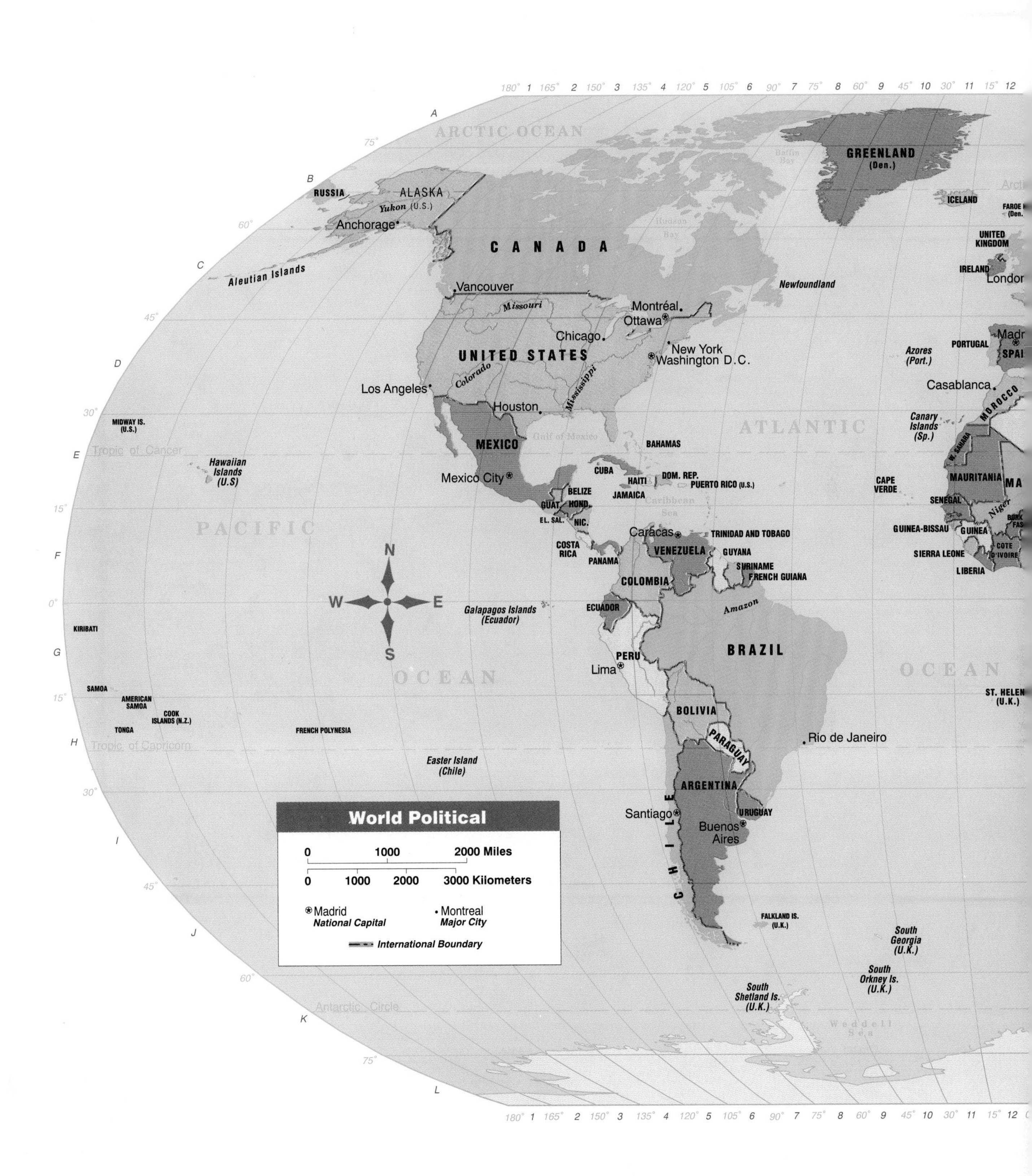
World Political
ARCTIC OCEAN
GREENLAND
(Den.)
RUSSIA
ALASKA
(U.S.)
Yukon
Anchorage
Aleutian Islands
CANADA
Vancouver
Missouri
Montréal
Ottawa
Chicago
New York
Washington D.C.
UNITED STATES
Colorado
Mississippi
Los Angeles
Houston
Newfoundland
ICELAND
UNITED KINGDOM
IRELAND
London
PORTUGAL
Azores
(Port.)
Casablanca
MOROCCO
Canary Islands
(Sp.)
ATLANTIC
MIDWAY IS.
(U.S.)
Tropic of Cancer
Hawaiian Islands
(U.S)
MEXICO
Gulf of Mexico
BAHAMAS
CUBA
HAITI
DOM. REP.
PUERTO RICO (U.S.)
JAMAICA
Caribbean Sea
Mexico City
BELIZE
GUAT.
HOND.
EL SAL.
NIC.
COSTA RICA
PANAMA
CAPE VERDE
MAURITANIA
SENEGAL
GUINEA-BISSAU
GUINEA
SIERRA LEONE
LIBERIA
PACIFIC
Caracas
TRINIDAD AND TOBAGO
VENEZUELA
GUYANA
SURINAME
FRENCH GUIANA
COLOMBIA
ECUADOR
Galapagos Islands
(Ecuador)
Amazon
N
W
E
S
KIRIBATI
PERU
Lima
BRAZIL
OCEAN
SAMOA
AMERICAN SAMOA
COOK ISLANDS (N.Z.)
TONGA
FRENCH POLYNESIA
Tropic of Capricorn
BOLIVIA
PARAGUAY
Rio de Janeiro
ST. HELENA
(U.K.)
Easter Island
(Chile)
ARGENTINA
URUGUAY
Santiago
Buenos Aires
CHILE
0 1000 2000 Miles
0 1000 2000 3000 Kilometers
Madrid
National Capital
Montreal
Major City
International Boundary
FALKLAND IS.
(U.K.)
South Georgia
(U.K.)
South Orkney Is.
(U.K.)
South Shetland Is.
(U.K.)
Antarctic Circle
Weddell Sea

ARCTIC OCEAN
Franz Josef Land
Novaya Zemlya
Yenisey
Lena
Ob'
RUSSIA
Volga
Moscow
Novosibirsk
NORWAY
FINLAND
SWEDEN
EST.
LAT.
LITH.
DEN.
BELARUS
POLAND
GERMANY
NETH.
BEL.
CZ.
SLVK.
AUS.
HUNG.
SWITZ.
CRO.
BOS.
YUGO.
UKRAINE
MOLD.
ROM.
BUL.
ITALY
ALB.
Rome
GREECE
TURKEY
Black Sea
GEO.
ARM.
AZER.
KAZAKHSTAN
UZBEKISTAN
TURKMENISTAN
KYRG.
TAJIK.
MONGOLIA
NORTH KOREA
SOUTH KOREA
Sea of Japan
JAPAN
Tōkyō
Beijing
CHINA
Yangtze
Shanghai
Sea of Okhotsk
Bering Sea
Crete
CYPRUS
LEB.
SYRIA
IRAQ
IRAN
ISRAEL
JORDAN
KUWAIT
AFGHANISTAN
PAKISTAN
NEPAL
BHU.
Ganges
TUNISIA
Mediterranean Sea
LGERIA
LIBYA
Cairo
EGYPT
SAUDI ARABIA
QATAR
U.A.E.
OMAN
Kolkata
(Calcutta)
BNGL.
Mumbai
(Bombay)
INDIA
Arabian Sea
Bay of Bengal
MYANMAR
LAOS
Guangzhou
TAIWAN
THAILAND
Bangkok
CAMBODIA
VIETNAM
South China Sea
PHILIPPINES
PACIFIC
OCEAN
Tropic of Cancer
NORTHERN MARIANA ISLANDS (U.S.)
WAKE ISLAND (U.S.)
GUAM (U.S.)
NIGER
CHAD
Nile
SUDAN
ERITREA
YEMEN
Red Sea
DJIBOUTI
Addis Ababa
ETHIOPIA
NIGERIA
Lagos
CENTRAL AFRICAN REPUBLIC
CAMEROON
UATORIAL GUINEA
GABON
CONGO
Congo
RWANDA
DEMOCRATIC REPUBLIC OF THE CONGO
UGANDA
KENYA
SOMALIA
BURUNDI
TANZANIA
SRI LANKA
MALDIVES
SEYCHELLES
COMOROS
PALAU
FED. STATES OF MICRONESIA
MARSHALL ISLANDS
BRUNEI
MALAYSIA
SINGAPORE
Borneo
Sumatra
Jakarta
INDONESIA
Java
New Guinea
PAPUA NEW GUINEA
SOLOMON ISLANDS
Equator
INDIAN
OCEAN
ANGOLA
ZAMBIA
MALAWI
MOZAMBIQUE
ZIMBABWE
NAMIBIA
BOTSWANA
MADAGASCAR
MAURITIUS
REUNION (Fr.)
SWAZILAND
SOUTH AFRICA
LESOTHO
Cape Town
Darwin
Coral Sea
VANUATU
FIJI
NEW CALEDONIA (Fr.)
Tropic of Capricorn
AUSTRALIA
Darling
Perth
Sydney
Melbourne
Tasmania
NEW ZEALAND
Wellington
Kerguelen Islands (Fr.)
ANTARCTICA
Copyright by Rand McNally & Co.
Made in U.S.A.
13 15° 14 30° 15 45° 16 60° 17 75° 18 90° 19 105° 20 120° 21 135° 22 150° 23 165° 24 180°
A B C D E F G H I J K L

Index

The following index lists important place names appearing on the maps in the *Historical Atlas of the World*. Countries and regions are indexed to the several maps which portray their areal and political development at successive periods. In general, each index entry includes a map reference key and the page number of the map. Alternate names and spellings are added in parentheses.